Biray Kolluoğlu is Associate Professor of Sociology at Boğaziçi University, Istanbul. She has published on late nineteenth-century and early twentieth-century Izmir. Her research interests include historical sociology, nationalism, sociology of space and memory.

Meltem Toksöz, Associate Professor of History at Boğaziçi University, Istanbul. She has published on the Eastern Mediterranean cotton agriculture and trade, Ottoman Mersin and the regional history of Cilicia. Her research interests include historiography, Ottoman intellectual history and the modernisation of state and society in late Ottoman history.

CITIES OF THE MEDITERRANEAN

FROM THE OTTOMANS TO THE PRESENT DAY

Edited by Biray Kolluoğlu and Meltem Toksöz

I.B. TAURIS

LONDON · NEW YORK

New paperback edition first published in 2014 by I.B.Tauris & Co. Ltd
6 Salem Road, London W2 4BU
175 Fifth Avenue, New York NY 10010

First published in hardback in 2010 by I.B.Tauris & Co. Ltd

ISBN: 978 1 78076 769 7

A full CIP record for this book is available from the British Library
A full CIP record is available from the Library of Congress

Library of Congress catalog card: available

www.bloomsbury.com

To the memory of Faruk Tabak

Contents

CONTENTS

Mapping Out the Eastern Mediterranean: Toward a Cartography of Cities of Commerce

Biray Kolluoğlu and Meltem Toksöz

Our mental mapping of the globe through continents rests on an imagery of large bodies of water constituting limits, boundaries and obstacles to the free flow of peoples, goods, information and knowledge while land masses connote integration and belonging. Perhaps the Mediterranean stands out as the only body of water representing historical connectedness and unity. Here the sea, at least until the nineteenth century, overshadowed the lands around it, thus rendering possible the question 'is it the sea surrounded by land or land by a sea?'[1] The Mediterranean seems to have lost this eminency in the last century. The unprecedented dynamism and dizzying speed of the modern world has so destroyed all former worlds, turning them into fading memories, that today our hegemonic geographic discourse is shaped by wests, middles, and easts of a continent. That is perhaps why the Mediterranean, after it surfaced from the whirlpool of capitalist social change, has mostly glittered on its northern and western shores. Indeed, when it is the dazzle of change that shapes our imaginary, it is not surprising that historical continuity is discarded as dreary. The centuries-old continuity of the Mediterranean, especially the role of its eastern shores, is buried under layers of rapturous social change.

This book is about the cities of commerce of the southern and eastern shores of the Mediterranean that have been the spaces of links, networks, and riches, also awash by conflicts, wars, and boundary contestations. These cities have occupied a central geo-political, commercial, and cultural place in the ever-expanding and ever-intensifying circuits of global exchange since the sixteenth century. We began to imagine this book in early 2004 in a city in the north, namely in Berlin at the Wissenschaftskolleg. We were invited to this Institute of Advanced Study as part of a working group on 'New Approaches to the History of Merchant Cities in the Ottoman Empire and Its Successor States'. Our working group was only one among many if one considers the large number of conferences and workshops, post-graduate research programs, and dissertations, articles and books on the Mediterranean cities of commerce of the nineteenth century, testifying to an explosion of interest in these spaces since the closing decade of the twentieth century.

'Ottoman port-cities' made their debut on the scholarly scene more than a decade ago via the world-system perspective, radiating out of the Fernand Braudel Center.[2] This group of scholars had set out with a specific agenda. They were not interested in port-cities *per se* but focused on the processes of peripheralization, not only of the Ottoman Empire, but also of India, and China. Eastern Mediterranean ports forced themselves onto their desks within the framework of the questions they asked as apparent nodes of commodity exchanges and other forms of capitalist encounters. In their research agenda, port-cities came to be treated as suitable means for the confirmation and further proliferation of the world-system analysis.

Today, the locales that this line of inquiry is taken up are multiple and varied. The above-mentioned conferences, workshops, post-graduate research programs, dissertations and books that are attempting to understand the dynamism of cities of commerce in history constitute a disconcerted effort. While the world-system perspective diffused an overly structured analysis, contemporary research is dispersed. The latter is being carried out not around a common perspective, but rather around a shared set of concerns meshed with those of urban history. Both the world-system perspective and the contemporary research have their pitfalls. The world-system perspective in its first attempt ended up drawing a picture in which the colors of the world-economy were exaggerated and colors of the local remained faint and shady. The shortcoming of the current research is its severely disparate character. While it is always incredibly important to gather detailed historical information about individual the Ottoman imperial center.[3] In other words, the specificity of such 'city histories' does not only render them separate from one another, but connected to a larger polity, the Ottoman state.[4] This ironically puts them in a structural position similar to the one in the world-system perspective. The world-system perspective ties the cities to an economic structure, whereas the current research places them at the mercy of the reforming Ottoman state's political power.[5]

As we were pondering the reasons behind this surge of research into Ottoman port-cities, we found ourselves rethinking the spatial, historical, and socio-political contours of the Mediterranean Sea. Although some of the new scholarship has reposited the Mediterranean not only as a viable unit of analysis but also as an economic, cultural, and socio-political *unity*, very little has been said on what made that unity last, from its inception *per se* in the sixteenth century to the first quarter of the last century.[6] The dominant tendency has been to construct micro-scale urban histories superimposed on a unity, without necessarily exploring the directions and venues of the connections. Hence, *our* pivotal concern crystallized as the quest for the venues, directions, and spaces of connections and flows that make and re-make the cartography of the Mediterranean. Rendering the wide spectrum of networks between cities visible has become our agenda here.

This book is a cartographic project that attempts to map out the roads on the sea that are constantly washed away by its waves. This cartographic project demanded the contributions of historians of art and architecture, sociologists, economists, ethnographers, urbanists, and social and cultural historians, and Beirut (which only recently regained its distinctive reputation as a node of different scales, levels and kinds of exchanges) presented itself as an idyllic space for a meeting of such a diverse group. The following collection is the outcome of a workshop held in Beirut in the last days of 2004, at a time when the city was still blissfully unaware of the awaiting catastrophe. As we are writing these words, the city once again has become the stage of a violent confrontation that makes us reconsider the historical possibility of the Mediterranean. We believe that this collection is timely and necessary, precisely because world societies and polities at the beginning of the twenty-first century are over-ridden with the opportunities and risks that come with increasing global interdependencies and connectedness.

In the following, we will elaborate on the processes that have triggered a new wave of interest in the Mediterranean cities of commerce, precisely because these, we argue, frame recent scholarship in specific ways. Today, social science discourses are marked by a fascination with the so-called unprecedented intensification and extension of networks of flows of capital, commodities, peoples, information and knowledge in contemporary capitalism, so much so that both academic and non-academic circles insist that this contemporary capitalism is qualitatively different from earlier versions and requires a new name that is, globalization. Cities have taken center stage in this literature, not only as focal points in these networks, but also as sites of valorization of global capitalism.[7] London, Tokyo, New York, Hong Kong, Istanbul and Bombay are all characterized by very heterogeneous populations and a relatively high autonomy from national structures. There are provocative, but little explored parallels between global cities of the contemporary world and port and merchant cities of the nineteenth century and earlier. Nineteenth-century cities of commerce can be seen in a similar light, in that they were sites where trade networks were concentrated, sites which enjoyed a considerable degree of autonomy from the empires in their hinterlands, and which housed heterogeneous populations. If capitalism has always been a global enterprise indeed, the current fascination with its globalization and global cities seems naïve in the face of historical patterns. Today, coming to terms with the so-called globalized condition appears more urgent than ever in the light not only of ever increasing flows, but also of the human costs as social and ecological danger, and violence escalate. Çağlar Keyder, who was among the pioneering group of researchers of the world-system analysis, re-visits the theme of the 'port-city' and opens this collection of articles, in the hope that this re-evaluation of the historical port-city can serve the relativization and bracketing of the nationalist experience. For him, politics always accompany the making of port-cities, facilitating their transformation as nineteenth-century global economy dictated restructuring in the Eastern Mediterranean. Eastern Mediterranean port-cities then became sites of all kinds of political projects, ranging from cosmopolitanism to nationalism. The twentieth century saw the dominance of nationalism, rendering cosmopolitanism a foolish chimera. That is why, for Keyder, the current wave of globalization is another chance to examine and theorize the history of port-cities anew.

This pressing need to theorize globalization implicitly forced many scholars to look at nineteenth-century urban change, not least because the ports acted as gateways and nodes of the workings of nineteenth-century globalization under British hegemony.[8] Furthermore, these cities of commerce presented themselves as terrains of multiplicity, both in terms of space and population. They attracted social scientists with their potential to mirror contemporary urban formations with increasingly heterogeneous and, in most cases, segregated populations. Put differently, with the rise of discussions on globalization of capitalism and culture in the last decade of the twentieth century, the cosmopolitanisms of these cities of commerce became a model that could both articulate and perhaps even present remedies to the new global condition. Yet, the contemporary debate on cosmopolitanism is very much engrossed in the discourse of the nation-state. Contemporary cosmopolitanism is articulated as 'an orientation and a willingness to engage with divergent cultural experiences', rooted in 'a detachment from the local'.[9] Since such cultural, social, political, or economic engagement rests on unequal power relations, contemporary cosmopolitanism is very much tied to a 'vision of "one world" which itself is a euphemism for "First World"'.[10] The problems embedded in the concept of cosmopolitanism can be seen in a different light if we sketch its geography and think through its history cartographically, as we hope to accomplish in this book. We are decolonizing the concept from the imaginary of the nation-state and European hegemony.

The collection opens with an essay tracking large-scale shifts in the economic structure and landscape of the Eastern Mediterranean in the longue durée, from the 1350s to the 1850s; this exactly provides such a conceptual decolonization. Faruk Tabak offers us an analysis that contextualizes nineteenth-century globalization, hence rendering it much less majestic and abrupt. He delineates two sets of longue durée transformation, economic and ecological, which spanned the centuries between the *Pax Neerlandica* and the *Pax Britannica* and gave the Eastern Mediterranean space constancy. Tabak first shows the resurgence of the Levantine trade in the 1350s to be part of the restoration of the trade circuit between the Indian Ocean and the Mediterranean, a trade circuit that made the southeastern part of the Eastern Mediterranean a viable unit in world trade networks. When the center of the world-economy shifted in the sixteenth century from the larger Mediterranean to Antwerp and Amsterdam, this resulted in the decline of the rich trades of the former; yet it 'did not simply undo the trading world of the Mediterranean but reshaped it'. Admittedly, the return of the Little Ice Age in the 1550s, which caused frequent flooding in the maritime and inland plains, prevented regular tilling, and resulted in a population decrease and the decline of Levantine trade and population decrease. These processes brought about a spatial shift in the center of gravity within the Eastern Mediterranean, from the southeastern Levant to the northern Aegean, with İzmir (Smyrna), Salonica (Thessaloniki) and Istanbul as its centers. Tabak also implies that this spatial shift from Aleppo and Cairo to the north, triggered by the rise of overland trade in the Anatolian and Balkan peninsulas, constituted a structural transformation that was to cause in the resurgence of the nineteenth-century Eastern Mediterranean. The end of the Little Ice Age in the 1870s sped up the process already underway and 'altered the region's landscape beyond recognition'. These radical changes were only an end point to the long-term processes of shifting interactions between the cities of commerce of the Eastern Mediterranean basin before the onset of nineteenth-century globalization.

The continuities and shared patterns in the historical trajectory of the making and unmaking of the Mediterranean in its entirety are taken up again by Edmund Burke III, in his epilogue to the volume. Despite the contemporary fractures that seemingly separate the northern/southern, and eastern/western shores of the Sea along religious and cultural differences, levels of economic development and state formation, Burke points towards a 'deep structural historical unity of the Mediterranean' at the political and cultural levels, by tracing the development of the modern state throughout the region and the patterns of incorporation of the Mediterranean in the world economy. Burke's structural reading of the Mediterranean as a unit offers a complementary analysis to the emphasis in this volume on mapping out the integrated nature and unity of the Sea through the prism of cities of commerce. His essay offers yet another framework rendering the constancy of space in the Mediterranean visible.

The strength and durability of the Mediterranean networks that remained viable despite major political upheavals and transformations including the devastation of the Great War can clearly be seen in İzmir's history. Özveren and Gürpınar argue that it was only the Great Depression that finally rung the death bell of world capitalism and intense competition, bringing an end to the way in which the Mediterranean networks had formed a particular historical unity by the nineteenth century. Put differently, not national economy, but rather its crisis ended the history of global port-cities, such as İzmir. Before the 1930s, no other crisis had been able to force the national government to steer the economy, and, hence the city, away from the Mediterranean and toward a new path of development. This argument emphasizes the particular Mediterranean continuum despite the interruption of political processes and invites us to think of İzmir as a site that experienced the transition from the imperial to the national, and of the Sea in a large array of possibilities.

Cities of Commerce

'Cities with ports differ from city-ports, the former building their piers out of necessity, the latter growing up around them by the nature of things. In the former they are a means and afterthought; in the latter, starting point and goal,' writes Matveyevic.[11] It is this feature that underlies our analysis of what we call cities of commerce. These terrains include particular spaces, groups, and socio-economic and political relations, with or without literal piers. But let us first explain our choice of the term 'city of commerce,' rather than 'port-city' or 'merchant city'. We believe that the term 'city of commerce' encompasses its fundamental activity and social relations that make and remake the city. The term 'port-city', while capturing the role of these terrains as gateways that connect different worlds, is imprisoned in the discourse of nineteenth-century British hegemony and the liberal world order that it maintained. On the other hand, the term 'merchant city', while making visible the group that lies at the heart of the social and economic life of these cities, tends to exclude all other relations and groups from workers at the piers to shipyard staffs, customs officers, storage and transportation workers, communication officers, to consulate personnel. We argue that the concept of the 'city of commerce' embraces the existence of different types of trade on a large scale and over an extensive area, as well as the multiplicity of relations and groups within the city or linked to it.

Cities of commerce of the nineteenth century are distinguished by certain spatial characteristics that produce and reproduce the specific social relations on these terrains. Spaces of commerce dominated the urban landscape. Entrepôt and storages safeguarded and ensured all commercial activities. Custom-houses regulated and taxed trade for both local and central treasuries. While shipping agencies, commercial houses and agencies regulated the flow of merchandise, insurance companies provided the security that this increased volume of trade called for. Inns (in the Ottoman context, *hans*) and hotels served as temporary lodging for traders and travelers.[12] Banks further commercialized the spaces of these cities, together with markets and, later on, department stores. The origin of the goods offered for sale provides a ready map of these cities' far-flung connections. In social clubs, which later turned into chambers of commerce, merchants played cards, read newspapers and periodicals from all over the Mediterranean, while conversing about politics, haggling over prices, finalizing transactions, and striking deals. All these activities called for spaces of connections: Railroads and tramlines carried people and goods inexpensively and speedily. Piers, and later on, ports accommodated the high volume of trade with steamships, also allowing entry and exit to 'illegal' goods. Telegram and, later on, post offices dispatched news and orders. The construction of rail and telecommunication lines as well as luxury residences created new commercial agenda including the need for timber, which then became a trade branch of its own. Printing houses produced reading material for the ever-increasing leisure and business needs of the inhabitants. These cities of commerce were also distinguished by spaces of leisure and public social relations: Theaters, beer gardens, dance halls, coffee houses and promenades reflected multiple levels of belonging.[13] Clock towers ornamented the cities and regulated a new life-style.[14] Sanitation facilities and hospitals dispensed health. Schools of different communities testified to the mixed populations.[15] French, British, German, Dutch, Italian, Greek, Portuguese, Spanish, Russian and American consuls and their families lived in the most luxurious quarters of these cities.[16] Unlike in other cities, monumental religious buildings did not dominate the cityscape; neither did the architectural signature of one particular confession prevail.

The spatial matrices of these architectural structures and infrastructures can be understood through the concept of cosmopolitanism. For cosmopolitanism is an intriguing concept that insinuates opposing spatial matrices, two opposite ends of a spectrum, with claims to universality on one, and parochialism on the other.[17] The immanent contradiction is unsolvable because the concept is bounded by and embedded in one locale.[18] Contrary to the common understanding of the term, a cosmopolitan is not a 'citizen of the world' or 'belonging to all parts of the world; not restricted to any one country or its inhabitants', but a 'citizen of a city', a city that embodies the former. This observation brings back the relation between autonomy and interdependence in cosmopolitan spaces. To put it differently, cosmopolitanism should not be conceptualized merely as an intellectual, aesthetic, or cultural stance but as a spatial phenomenon that mediates between the local and the global. Cosmopolitanism should be employed in this place-bound understanding, with cosmopolitan sites seen as sites that tie together flows of people, goods, and capital within the larger world in which they are embedded. Eastern Mediterranean cities of commerce are rendered cosmopolitan by their placement in the world economy and nexus of flows of peoples and goods. It is the different lingual, confessional, and ethnic communities' attachment and belonging to these cities which contribute to their connectedness. These terrains are conceptualized as cosmopolitan not simply because of their multiconfessional, multi-ethnic, and multilingual populations and dense and variegated cityscapes, but also because they occupied relatively autonomous spaces that mediated between different worlds.

This volume offers three articles that deal with representations of the Mediterranean as a spatial category and constructed spaces, by Carla Keyvanian, Christina Pallini, and Vilma Hastaoglou-Martinidis. Keyvanian uses sixteenth-century maps disseminated after the emergence of the printing press. Looking at the European reception of Italian and Dutch maps depicting Islamic cities, the author conceptualizes the Mediterranean as the unified locale of a particular intellectual visualization of the city. These widely circulated visions of the cultural, social, and economic characteristics of the city in the Islamic world reproduced the European worldview of the Eastern Mediterranean city as an intellectual construct much more nuanced than conventional east/west relations. This intellectual charting of the Mediterranean even surpassed the one following the discovery of the Atlantic, with three times as many maps of the Mediterranean as those of the New World produced in the sixteenth century. These maps turn modern perceptions of the New World, upside down, demonstrating the primacy of the Mediterranean in the early modern era.

The architectural layout of cities of commerce further emphasizes the solidity of the Eastern Mediterranean cartography. Christina Pallini uses architectural characteristics to read the Mediterranean cities through the location of their ports, tracing the structure of the port's hinterlands in relation to the city's residential layout. She focuses on the parallel histories of Alexandria, İzmir, and Salonica in the second half of the nineteenth and early twentieth century. Her essay invalidates the conventional representation of the Mediterranean as a great lake dotted with cities along its shores and represents it as scene encompassing vast, diverse, and interconnected lands. The architecture of these cities reveals the constant making of communities as institutionalized bodies separate from other bodies politic.

Some of these cities came to be institutionalized through yet another set of architectural and infrastructural projections and projects that prove more Mediterranean than European or national. Vilma Hastaoglou-Martinidis explores such nineteenth-century Mediterranean linkages through the activity of harbor-building. She takes issue with existing studies that explore the making of cities of commerce in the realm of Ottoman state modernization only and argues for a larger realm of port construction in which the Eastern Mediterranean became the site of a shared enterprise between 1860 and 1910. This was the common project of a network of international navigation companies, contractor firms, local municipal and port authorities as well as chambers and committees.[19] Hastaoglou-Martinidis argues that the technical aspects of the enterprise, the construction networks of harbor-building, entailed far-reaching architectural and urban innovations transforming the cities of the Eastern Mediterranean within a few decades from mere ports into a single modern entity.

The existence of multilingual and multiconfessional communities as well as the emergence of distinct class structures in cities of commerce accentuated the variety and levels of belonging in the particular spaces mentioned above. Population movements matted communities; migration rescaled the exchanges between the city and the hinterland and created two main groups, merchants and landholders who mediated between consumers and producers. This confrontation allowed for the creation of new kinds of terrains where multiple communities established conditions for their material relations, and attached themselves not only to communal, economic and political bodies, but also to the city itself.

On a range of scales, cosmopolitan groups remade the space of the city of commerce by enlarging it through the relations they established between the coasts and interiors while creating new practices of property.[20] From the beginning, urban and rural groups *penetrated into* one another thanks to this network, carrying new relations and practices with them and, hence remolding each other. Through this interaction, each group actually moved into each other's spaces and life while at the same time mobilizing and extending their own community. The motion involved two layers: One literally expanded the urban community through language, religion, ethnicity and family ties; the other created and preserved a new landholding class for whom communal and commercial ties with the urban community meant protection against risks and fluctuations. The city of commerce thus rendered the connections between urban and rural social relations much more visible, as its making enables us to view the groups involved as real people, communities and families. Members of closely-knit communities moved between rural and urban worlds, and marriages created new family branches beyond the city of commerce and its hinterland. Put differently, the migration, settlement and networking of individual families between the hinterland and the city of commerce reveal ties beyond those of cosmopolitanism. Communities extended beyond cosmopolitan sites through families, the group most mobile and best-equipped for establishing ties that gave stability to the networks between the worlds of the city, its hinterland, and the Mediterranean.[21] Either in the city, its hinterland or in an altogether different city of commerce, a family of a particular language and confessional community could marry into another community of a different language but maybe of the same faith, thereby extending community relations from those of religious to lingual. Children of such marriages continued to expand both levels and scales of relations. For instance, sons formed commercial and political ties by marrying into larger mercantile communities of another city of commerce more often than not, into Istanbul's communities who were already engaged in a variety of connections with trading houses, naval agencies, and consulates of countries across the Mediterranean. Sons could also become vice-consuls in their own city, working for various countries from Spain to the USA at different times. Daughters established further bridges with other families of the same community within the city or married into foreign families of investors, bankers, and merchants that settled and invested in the city and around. Some of the grandchildren married into the same confessional community in yet another city of commerce, while others married citizens of various northern countries of the Mediterranean. These familial networks between cities of commerce newly mapped the circuitry of production and exchange, which helped carve relatively autonomous niches with strong positions in the larger economic and spatial order of the Eastern Mediterranean.[22]

Through these niches, various communities established their own material conditions simultaneously, even if not always in an equally smooth fashion. In doing so, they favored their attachments to the city more than to any other entity, thus successfully avoiding social conflict, at least before the emergence of the nation-state.[23] Where did political authority materialize itself in the city of commerce of the Eastern Mediterranean, particularly in the Ottoman Empire before the era of nation-states? The

connections to political authority from municipal and provincial administration to central authority and rivaling foreign powers form yet another
level of relations encapsulated in the cities of commerce.

Attachment to the city did not outweigh political roles in its administration, which was for the most part in the hands of the cosmopolitan
groups congregating in the spaces described above. To the contrary,
political administration was in the hands of an aggregate of all groups, as
it was most visible at the municipal level, and in the representative and
advisory councils of provinces. They managed the city of commerce
relatively autonomously from imperial politics, and they did not hesitate
to interfere in these imperial politics when the need arose.[24] Situating the
city in such relative autonomy enables us to see cosmopolitan attachment
as including the state as part of social-material relations and not in opposition to the rule of the state.

Nineteenth-century modernity introduced its own peculiar set of experiences. One such experience had to do with educational migration
which facilitated the formation of yet another kind of network in the
Eastern Mediterranean: that of multiple belonging to cities of commerce
across the two shores of the Aegean. Migration and access to information
within the Eastern Mediterranean turned Athens and İzmir into exem-
plary sites of contestation for community members, spanning the very
space of the Eastern Mediterranean itself. In his essay, Vangelis Kechriotis illustrates the contribution of migration to cosmopolitanism as we
have outlined the term, for in his article the community fluctuations between Athens and İzmir made the respective communities more Mediterranean, rather than distancing them from each other.

Commercial activities of migrant and mobile communities in nineteenth-century port-cities are still one of the most obvious subjects of
study for both the world-system approach and the disparate trajectories of
case studies on single cities. In both, comprador relations played crucial
roles in linking the cities to the worlds beyond. Many of these have been
explored as part of communitarian networks, such as those of non-
Muslim merchants. Yet, the involvement of people who speak the same
tongue has not been used as point of departure. Isa Blumi studies the role
of Albanian-speaking actors in 'illegal' trade and provides another web of
relations beyond British, Italian and Ottoman trade regulations in the
Eastern Mediterranean. Circumventing the political and economic spaces
of the imperial custom regimes, these 'criminals' linked the Adriatic and
Balkan hinterland to various parts of the Eastern Mediterranean.

This kind of analysis of state–society relations in the cities of commerce
of the Ottoman Mediterranean is of historiographical significance as well.

Ottoman historiography is still determined by the centrality of the state, even if this state-centered approach has recently attempted to do away with explicit demarcations between society and state. In an effort to critically re-evaluate the world-system approach, urban historians –especially the ones studying the Arab provinces of the Ottoman Empire– have brought the 'state back in' and thus continued the historical tradition of placing the state's action at the heart of the vocabulary of nineteenth-century reform. It comes as no surprise that recent scholarship's attempt to avoid Orientalist and essentialist views by pointing to the weakness of the Ottoman Empire has inevitably and forcefully confirmed the central role of the state.[25] However, even the fact that urban administration is refashioned as a product of nineteenth-century central reform (*Tanzimat*) in the Ottoman Empire, does not automatically locate the city of commerce in the realm of imperial modernization, but rather proves that imperial orders do not readily delimit state and society. A cartographic analysis of cities of commerce with an eye to the permanence of the Eastern Mediterranean redefines all boundaries, including those of the state, in an aggregate and thus allows us to escape measuring the extent of state power. Constantin Iordachi's contribution to this volume points towards the larger boundaries of the Mediterranean, by establishing the Mediterranean's organic links with the Black Sea via the Danube. He concentrates on Sulina, Tulcea, and Constanţa in the second half of the nineteenth and early twentieth century. Iordachi argues that, while Tulcea (the administrative center of Dobrudja under Ottoman rule) was connected to the larger Mediterranean world via Istanbul, Constanta became the political center under Romanian rule after 1878. In the same period, Sulina was connected directly to Central European cities, serving as the main commercial gate between Central Europe and Anatolia. This essay illustrates our larger argument that the connections within the Mediterranean world are mediated through multiple scales of relations between political centers as well as economic and commercial networks.

The cartography of the Eastern Mediterranean permits us to re-imagine state and society in the same space without fixed boundaries. Cities of commerce do not surface as the locus of the power of an imposing state only, nor do they emerge only as entities able to reform. Instead, the city of commerce itself can be imagined as a cartographic entity. The spatial matrix of the city of commerce is not only an analytical tool: The city of commerce is defined not through, but *with*, its spatial matrix, thus rendering the cartography of the city a maze of multiple political happenings as they form variously scaled entities through rural/urban dynamics in provincial administration that simultaneously contact and contract with the dynamics of the imperial and global centers.

However, such contraction among the Eastern Mediterranean cities of commerce can even be delineated within an approach that includes the state. Johann Büssow draws our attention to the sharing of information and argues that in the early twentieth century knowledge traveled between the Mediterranean shores by steamboat, telegraph, and railways knowledge also traveled, and at a hitherto unknown speed. In his essay, Büssow takes the press as a case to evaluate the extent of the development of intellectual and cultural networks. His is a mental mapping out of the Mediterranean where the 'local' press connected Palestinian cities of commerce not only to their vicinity, but also to other Mediterranean centers.

'You take delight not in a city's seven or seventy wonders, but in the answer it gives to a question of yours.'[26]

The city of commerce can serve as a juncture of space, class, community and political authority. The city of commerce in the Eastern Mediterranean also provides many junctures in terms of methodology, between grand theory and micro history, in terms of the empirical between the *sui generis* and the all encompassing; in terms of discourse between the national and the global. The city forces us to find a new metaphor to address the many scopes and scales it constantly embodies: constancy of space. That is why this book insists on a cartography that looks at the terrains themselves, rather than at the forces contained in these terrains. The Eastern Mediterranean cities of commerce are stages, or rather sites, of the composition of happenings –mixture of events, actions and geography. The main medium was neither the early modern or modern state, nor the market, nor tradition. The Eastern Mediterranean composition has shown itself to be a maze of all these forces, with shifting positions in a hierarchy of influences; yet is not determined by any one of them even when historical change is analytically frozen. The composition of happenings that is the Eastern Mediterranean is larger, more tangible, durable, and visible than the matrix of sites on one level and the forces that shape them on another. This does not mean that the composition itself is immune to change. What reveals the durability of the unity of the Eastern Mediterranean despite changes is the space: The constancy is in the space, from the sixteenth to the twenty-first century. The city of commerce valorizes this space, cosmopolitanism generates the city, and the extended community is the city's fabric. Each written from a different vantage point the following articles deal with this process of valorization, making the Mediterranean visible through a cartographic analysis.

Port-cities in the Belle Epoque

Çağlar Keyder

I

Without port-cities, there would be no civilizational project associated with nineteenth-century liberalism. Port-cities evolved at the interface between the expanding dominion of European economies and the old lands of the East. They emerged as specific urban forms mediating the expansion of the world economy into weak agrarian empires. Port-cities emerged as an essential dimension of western expansion against the backdrop of free trade and the gold standard, the two pillars of British domination of the global system.[1] They were primarily populated by men pursuing commercial interests; but they quickly became cities approximating the nineteenth-century ideal form, accommodating rapidly modernizing urban populations. These new populations inhabiting new urban spaces, served as 'agents of change' in the terminology of modernization theory of a later vintage.[2] They played their part in expanding the boundaries of what once were enclaves. As new cultures flourished, these new populations shaped ever-expanding spaces into a new urban form: the peripheral version of the nineteenth-century city, carrying modernity.[3]

Port-cities flourished in liminal spaces where Europe could expand because the local state receded. They represented nodes in a world order based on the network model, where long distance flows provided the logic of existence.[4] The territory around them was weakly governed, and care was taken to guarantee that the states nominally in control agreed to liberalize economic activity along the networks, with minimal restriction. This liberalism following the British prescription spilled over into the political sphere as well, for instance in the Ottoman willingness to accept immigrants (from within and without the empire) into port cities and to grant them *quasi* expatriate status, with privileges such as special courts and consular protection.[5]

Thus, port-cities became locales for new populations, new forms of economic activity, social space, and material culture. They were also models of co-existence for the rapidly emerging multi-ethnic populations of empires who now had to live together, 'as congeries of racial, religious, and linguistic communities loosely joined in commercial endeavor'.[6] *Le doux commerce* would patch over ethnic suspicion and bring together imperial populations who were once a patchwork separated in communities. Now they lived in proximity and had to devise modes of multicultural tolerance in joint adherence to the global network of cosmopolitan traders. In their allegiance to a new model of development, transformed social conduct, and needs for different rules and guarantees, port-city populations thus became agents of a modernization-from-below, in a century when states in these empires were still too weak to embark on modernization-from-above.[7]

II

The typical port-city was the outlet for exports from its hinterland. Its economy depended on intermediation between producers inland and consumers across the sea; its primary population was merchants. A city like Istanbul did not qualify because the majority of its population lived on imperial revenues and by catering to those who received them; but in the Ottoman Empire İzmir and Salonica did, as well as Trabzon, Mersin, Beirut and Alexandria. The merchants of these cities could comfortably lead their environment: they were the wealthiest individuals, their business would determine the course of economic activity, their culture and taste dominated, their lifestyles and consumption patterns would be emulated. Their choices and habits of work, modes of dwelling and leisure would imprint the evolving urban space of rapidly growing cities. None of this was possible in a city like Istanbul where the imperial presence would easily outweigh, and could choose to hamper, the release of such potential implicit in the development of a merchant class. The commercial orientation of port-cities often had historical roots, pre-dating the nineteenth century. It was, however, the relationship with world markets that made port-cities and their merchant communities grow rapidly, eclipsing the (often inland) imperial administrative centers. As world trade increased by about fifty-fold over the nineteenth century, it was these cities that became the principal conduits of the increased flows of commodities, money, and people.[8] Most of the direct and indirect employment associated with trade was created in these ports.

But ports were located in cities, and while they provided the centers of gravity, port-cities became more than trading enclaves: The new networks also presaged new relations and a social structure, visible foremost in the formation of urban societies. Within these societies, the glamour of the western lifestyle, its freedom and glitter, as well as its consumption patterns became attractions. Port-cities came to exhibit an alternative universe to the rest of the realm, not only because of the economic opportunities and political privilege they offered, but as places of a different cultural practice and, through the new public spaces and buildings, a built environment which so glaringly expressed these differences. There were paved streets, department stores, European style hotels, and cafes. Street cars made real the idea of urban congestion and anonymous proximity and, most importantly, gas lighting made parts of the city accessible at night.[9] The second half of the century was remarkable for the invention of a technology of urban life in European and American cities; most of this technology was diffused to the port-cities, albeit at a reduced scale and with some delay. In fact, it was the novelty of the built environment which often struck those arriving from hinterlands.

The triumph of the nineteenth-century European bourgeoisie lay in imprinting the cities with their material and cultural needs; in doing so, they invented a new urban life. Port-cities carried this new lifestyle model to the peripheries. Their novelty immediately became attractive to the population around them. We would not be far off if we draw a parallel with the free cities of the late Middle Ages, which promised to the newcomer not only economic opportunities, but also freedom and a new élan.[10] The territory around nineteenth-century port-cities was also characterized by a peasant economy only superficially penetrated by commodity production. The cities by the sea exerted sufficient attraction to be able to pull their hinterland into their gravitation, not only through the development of trade and credit networks toward the interior, but also because they attracted immigrants. To their new populations, the Kordon in İzmir and the Corniche in Alexandria must have seemed as marvelous as did the town square and the great cathedrals in European cities half a millennium earlier.

III

The politics that accompanied the transformation of port-cities relied on the weakness and subservience of the states in which they were located. We can be more specific in the case of the Eastern Mediterranean and talk about the impositions of British hegemony on the Ottoman Empire, which allowed for the growth of trade, a merchant class, and the cities in which they were located. Crucial in this respect was the 1838 treaty liberalizing trade, which took away from the bureaucrats the major tool of control over both the content of trade and over traders.[11] Other legislation followed, regulating personal status and such irksome matters as jurisdiction in the event of conflict between locals and foreigners. Special courts were established in order to deal with novel situations. It is safe to say that the population of the interior was neither targeted nor particularly implicated in all this restructuring. In the port-cities, however, newly gained liberties and privileges created the foundations of a different life. Through the *Tanzimat* reforms, the empire was reconfiguring itself in the guise of a modern state, abolishing legal separation among the communities and *millet*s, and instead opting for a unitary citizenship.[12] Of course, for the vast majority of the population nothing much changed in the conduct of everyday life; for the denizens of port-cities, however, the new legal equality actually created a framework for a new mode of life within the bounds of these urban havens. Yet, unrestricted equality within a growing market economy, rendered increasingly autonomous from political control, carried risks of new levels of polarization due to differential success in the new economy. The new proximity of previously isolated communities could lead to new social realities, but was also pregnant with potential tension. Successful merchants got wealthier, and poor immigrants became urban proletariat. The division of labor which had always run parallel to ethnic lines now more lavishly rewarded the favored, and the relative deprivation experienced by the lower classes rankled more acutely.

Populations increased rapidly in port-cities, with growth rates similar to twentieth-century urban areas.[13] There were new working classes and lumpen groups, and eventually cultural and political intelligentsia, who found a more liberal environment in these outposts. The emergence of competing elites who were not all connected with trade indicated that the *échelles* would not remain the exclusive domain of the merchant princes. The new elites and middle classes who were not part of the commercial nexus did not all commit themselves to the liberal tenets of the world economy. In fact, more and more port-cities came to be known for their political fervor. Ethnic groups which had been contained in the separate legal regimes and traditional economies of former spaces of habitation were now thrown together into fast boiling cauldrons. Within this mixture, the more successful elements began to shift allegiance toward the true masters of the emerging world system, banking on continuing support and protection. Relatively freed from the need to curry imperial favors, they became more cosmopolitan. At the same time, the new stratification and intensifying inequalities lead others to imagine what a more principled embrace of the local could potentially offer. This potential divergence within the expanding urban population was one of the various rivulets feeding into the deluge that brought down the liberal construct.[14]

Yet, port-cities also attracted political activity which was not the product of real or perceived conflict on site. In the end-of-empire political frenzy, which seems to have engulfed the globe during the quarter century before the Great War, port-cities became privileged theaters where all kinds of political projects were launched: religious, ethnic, and secular-political. There were pan-Islamists, Zionists, Christian supremacists, revivalists; nationalists of every identifiable group in the vicinity; Marxists, socialists, and universalists. Whether in Salonica, Baku, Beirut, or Alexandria, one could find politics of all hues, ranging from cosmopolitanism to nationalism, from imperial atavism to urban separatism. Alongside merchants who were content with the smooth working of the gears of commerce and opposed any radical change, there were those in search of states that they could promote and perhaps influence. There were also imperial modernizers who naturally based their 'revolutionary' organizations in port-cities where an exposure to the reformist ideas wafting in from Europe was most likely. A center of Greek irredentism, Macedonian and Bulgarian nationalisms (and less importantly of Zionism), as well as the launching pad of the Young Turk revolution, Salonica is a good example.[15] Ottoman port-cities became crucibles of all shades of political activity during the pre-War period.

While most of the politics conducted in port-cities in the pre-War era was directed to nationalisms and imperial renaissance, the fate of the real captains of trade and finance was tied too closely to the fortunes of the hegemonic power. They ideally preferred to be guided by the lodestar of economic gain and, in the process, to devise a form of governance of their own choosing. In this alternative the port-cities would come under a relatively autonomous administration of the patriciate, reminiscent of the urban governments of autocephalous cities of the late medieval period. Merchants' associations, chambers of commerce, elite clubs, and masonic lodges dominated by expatriates and their local partners would survive under the benign umbrella of British protection. The *cercles* would be the privileged locales of negotiation and informal rule. From Trieste to İzmir, from Alexandria to Shanghai, port-cities had acquired stable hierarchies, capable of delivering efficient administration, testifying to the possibility of an accommodation with empires and to a form of governance under a market-dominated globalism. Against the background of absolute and undivided rule by imperial centers, municipalities that were formed in the 1860s and 1870s in Eastern Mediterranean port-cities were perhaps a rehearsal for the envisaged devolution.[16]

IV

These attempts at self-governance fit well into the network logic of the global economy, but ultimately remained frustrated in the face of the destruction unleashed by the War. Multi-ethnic empires were a tried and comfortable framework for containing diversity. After the Great War, the alternative of the nation-state became the rule, even the mandates under the authority of the League of Nations gained legitimacy as preparatory forms for autonomous statehood. A religious, ethnic or linguistic principle was employed in order to invest the population with a homogenizing zeal. This was necessarily based on the presumed traits of a majority and made life difficult for minority cultures. Of the successor states to the Ottoman Empire, the only country which, with dubious success, attempted to escape the process was Lebanon. Lebanon was, of course, shaped around Beirut, the erstwhile port-city, in order to maintain its intricate confessional balances in the new world of nation-states. The trope of Phoenician ancestors permitted Lebanon to define itself as a trading nation. The country was conceived as a sea-oriented merchant entity rather than a land-based territorial unit. In this sense, it was an exception to the dominant orientation of new nation-states. As to the rest of the Eastern Mediterranean, Ankara and Cairo represented territorial preferences against network logics. Their principal openings to the wider world, İzmir and Alexandria, did not stand any chance of embracing ethnic diversity against political prerogatives to effect homogenization. Neither of the two could remain a port-city in republican Turkey or post-monarchic Egypt.

In Turkey, the suspicion toward the denizens of port-cities served as the active principle in the formation of the national entity. The existence of the new population and the new geography was predicated on the active cleansing of the territory where the very minorities whose existence had defined the port-cities had to be chased out.[17] Port-cities became a collateral casualty of the immense human tragedy of ethnic cleansing, staged in the transition from empire to nation-state. The striking feature of port-cities had been ethnic co-existence. Population mixes in the littorals of the empires, whether China, India, or the Ottoman Empire, and especially in their port-cities, was substantially different from the interior's. The much expanded populations of the port-cities were much less homogeneous than any urban entity in history. Port-cities had evolved as geographies where the ethnic diversity of the empire, which elsewhere could be contained in more or less segregated territories, became concentrated within urban boundaries. In the case of Turkey, with the Armenian deportation and massacres in 1915 and the compulsory Exchange of Populations applying to Greeks in 1923/24, the cleansing was especially rapid and drastic.[18] More than two million Christians and a majority of the businessmen in the territory inherited by Turkey had thus been eliminated or driven out. If the conflagration in İzmir was a particularly extreme instance, the project of ethnic homogenization, which destroyed the social base for the operation of port-cities, was certainly the norm. Most foreigners left Republican Turkey, and non-Muslims were reduced from one-fifth of the population to less than 3 per cent. In Egypt the ousting of the 'foreign', global market-oriented population was more gradual, culminating in the decade after World War II. Despite this physical eradication, even after the virtual collapse of port-cities such as İzmir and Trabzon and many smaller ones, the nationalists continued to harbor a profoundly ambiguous relationship with the Ottoman legacy in confronting the previously cosmopolitan universe of the port-cities.

V

Structurally, the death knell of Eastern Mediterranean port-cities, *les échelles du Levant*, was the huge transformation of the world economy following the War.[19] The few years of recovery during the 1920s could not forestall the end of the globalization ushered in after the mid-nineteenth century under British auspices. World trade diminished to less than half of its pre-war level, and flows of long or short term capital virtually ceased. With the drawing of new borders after World War I and the dismantling of trade and credit networks following the crises of the late 1920s, standing economic structures were rudely disrupted; old links lost their usefulness, and the logic of economic activity changed. All of this occurred in tandem with the disintegration of the global economy, thus eroding the material basis for port-city viability. The politics of the new nation-states and the restructuring of the world economy conspired to shift the center of gravity away from commercial and cultural networks based on trading coastal cities. The new states legitimized themselves on the basis of an active suspicion of the geography of the old empires. Port-cities and their inhabitants were now regarded with deep distrust and accused of belonging to a different universe.

Port-city elites had done well under the weak umbrella of empires. They had been successful in negotiating with the imperial bureaucrats in order to sustain a style of economic, social and cultural practice different from the rest of the realm. Their attempts had yielded reforms at the level of market freedom, rule of law, and citizenship rights. Along with the empires themselves, however, port-cities were also added to the wreckage contemplated by the angel of history. Emerging nation-states sought to impose a substantive orientation to the economy which would necessarily threaten the formal logic of the autonomous market as expressed in the operations of port-cities. As a historical project, nationalism became the opposite of the nineteenth-century world order, when Europe pretended to modernize and assimilate the rest of the world through the agency of port-cities. Nationalism advocated the dismantling of the global geography of the world-economy; it promised a shift in the center of gravity from networks converging on London to territories within national boundaries, centered on capital cities; it preached full control over the fate of the nationals by the local states political as well as economic sovereignty. Networks of the previous global order had produced socially and culturally diversified populations; nationalists wanted to homogenize their populations through schools and through economic and social policy. Nationalists thought that cosmopolitanism was a chimera foolishly pursued by a suspect population and that their brand of national identity and belonging would provide the real thing. In this scheme the remaining inhabitants of the port-cities would have to be absorbed into new national societies and interact with the world only through the mediation of their governments located in capital cities: Ankara, Damascus, Cairo.

National, territorial economies created their own potential for the accumulation of wealth. New businessmen emerged, businessmen who were at first bound to political projects and necessarily subservient to politicians. Later in the century, however, in the new era of globalization, there was a sufficient development of self-standing bourgeoisies to press for policies similar to the market-embracing liberalism of the previous era. Of course, these policies would only make sense in the context of a new world economy once again organized around autonomous markets. States were forced again to accept legislating liberal rules of property and freedom from political intervention. In this new era of market-dominated liberalism and globalization in the final decades of the twentieth century, the history of port-cities, and especially of port-city autonomy, once again became relevant. It again seemed possible that a metropolitan order, a rule-based globalization, could connect with autonomous 'world-cities' contained within the weak and hopefully unobtrusive shells of nation-states, with the latter becoming less ethnic and more civic.[20] The collective memory of the late-nineteenth-century experience may have played a part here: A re-evaluation of the port-city past could serve many purposes, not least the relativization and bracketing of the nationalist experience. A look at what port-cities were and what their denizens intended to achieve could well illuminate the political and cultural spaces available to cities and urbanites within the current wave of globalization. On the other hand, the current experience has allowed us to regard the history of the port-cities with new eyes. We now understand the aspirations and dilemmas, the ties and constraints, and the tragedy of their demise with greater empathy and foreboding. We debate newly minted concepts such as 'urban citizenship' and 'right to the city', with the full knowledge that they would have been much cherished by port-city denizens a century ago.[21] And we indulge in an optimism that promises may yet be fulfilled the second time around.

Economic and Ecological Change in the Eastern Mediterranean, c. 1550–1850

Faruk Tabak

The Eastern Mediterranean that Ibn Battuta of Tangiers encountered in the mid-fourteenth century during his passage from Cairo to Jerusalem and Aleppo and, later, from Latakia to Alaiyye, was copiously dotted by port-cities, prominent and obscure, from Lajazzo to Tripoli in the north, and from Acre to Alexandria in the south. Despite the heavy toll inflicted on the region by successive waves of crusader attacks from the west and Mongol attacks from the east, and despite the appearance of malaria and, later, the Black Death on its shores, the Levant thrived nonetheless, thanks to the restoration of the Indian Ocean–Mediterranean trade circuit. The collapse of the Mongol Empire and the resulting breakdown in security along the land routes connecting the South China Sea with the Pontic Sea gave a new lease on life to the southern maritime route via Cairo; hence, the resurgence of trade in the Levant from the 1350s onwards.[1] The spread of sugar, cotton, and, to a lesser extent, silk cultivation along the banks of the Mediterranean basin in the fourteenth and fifteenth centuries contributed to the economic efflorescence of the Inner Sea as well. However, in the long run, the Levant lost its exclusive hold over sugarcane cultivation. In the sixteenth century, there were few Mediterranean coastal plains or valleys with adequate water supply that did not boast sugarcane cultivation.[2] Yet, the situation changed drastically at the turn of the seventeenth century. By then, the spice trade had shifted its route due to the emergence of Lisbon, Antwerp and, later, Amsterdam as its main points of redistribution. Sugar and cotton, too, had lost the pivotal role that they had played earlier in the region's economic vitality, largely because of the off-shore cultivation of these crops, first on the Venetian and Genoese-ruled islands that dotted the Greater Mediterranean, and later increasingly (and almost inexorably due to the greater availability of slave labor) on the Atlantic outposts of the Inner Sea. Already in the latter half of the sixteenth century, ships were carrying sugar from Madeira to Constantinople. Cotton ceased to be a plantation crop in the Mediterranean: it turned into a peasant-produced cash-crop in the Balkans, Anatolia, and the Levant as the increasing prominence of woolen textiles deprived the crop of the commercial *gravitas* it possessed during the high age of fustian cloth (a cloth of wool or linen combined with cotton) between the 1450s and the 1650s.[3] The Atlantic-bound journey of crops like sugar and cotton eventually deprived the basin of its precious rich trades, but their out-migration was compensated in part by the revival of typical Mediterranean crops, in particular tree-crops (and in part by the arrival of American food crops, such as corn and beans, a development which is outside of the scope of this chapter).[4] This double movement not only altered the vegetal make-up of the basin, but also altered its economic center of gravity. Unlike the exotic crops of the fourteenth and fifteen centuries, which thrived on the coastal plains and in the valleys of the Inner Sea, the new set of crops of the sixteenth century came to occupy its slopes and hillsides. Economic devolution thus altered the basic contours of the Mediterranean landscape.

Initially, the loss of economic activity that resulted from the departure of crops such as sugar and cotton from the eastern flanks of the basin was more than compensated by the growing significance of the spice trade, especially in the fifteenth century. Later, the decline in the share of sugar and, to a lesser extent, cotton exports was compensated by the growing share of grain exports from the Ottoman lands. Wheat was shipped primarily from the shores of the Aegean, but also from the Eastern Mediterranean, from Mecca to Jerusalem. The grain trade reached its zenith between the 1540s and 1560s. Ottoman grain went on to find its way into the Western Mediterranean until the 1620s, if not later, despite imperial restrictions.[5] However, by turning the region east of the Elbe into their breadbasket, northern merchants facilitated the provisioning of Italian city-states and Iberia with Baltic grain and reduced the demand for the already thinning supplies of the Inner Sea. The stranglehold that Dutch merchants established on the Baltic grain trade contributed to a revision of economic exchanges across the Mediterranean.

In the wake of the transfer of the trade in spices and luxury goods to the Atlantic, the easy and regular availability of Baltic grain on the shores of the North Sea and its advent in the Inner Sea delivered the *coup de grâce* to the Levant trade. Commercial opportunities available to producers and traders of the Inner Sea (notables, landholders, or governors in charge of marketing grain, whether legally or illegally) became scarcer as economic prospects weakened with each passing decade. Concomitant with the gradual relocation of the staples of the Levant trade outside the basin, the trajectories of the western and eastern halves of the Mediterranean, which had started to diverge from the mid-fifteenth century onwards following the colonization of the Atlantic islands, were securely sealed, to the detriment of the latter.

The establishment of Dutch hegemony did not simply undo the trading world of the Mediterranean, but reshaped it. The ongoing attraction of the rich markets of the Italian city-states played a crucial part in the economic vibrancy of the basin. So did the growing engagement of British and Dutch merchants in the Levant silk trade. All the same, in the eastern flanks of the basin, where economic fortunes were dimming, the sea changes of the seventeenth century brought about two closely related spatial rearrangements. First, the number of port-cities strung along the region's coastline declined significantly. Naturally, the exodus of the trade in spices and luxury goods and the decline in the grain trade signaled decreasing commerce in the region. As the Levant was relegated to a lesser economic position than it had commanded in its heyday, the port-cities that thrived on marketing local, regional, and transit goods suffered. The magnitude of economic contraction in the region was further compounded by the onset of the seventeenth-century crisis. Geographically speaking, the spatial impact of the economic devolution of the Levant was felt differentially, for the Aegean shores of the Ottoman Empire came to capture and house a larger share of the economic transactions conducted in the region, with İzmir and Salonica steadily gaining in prominence over Aleppo and Cairo. This northbound shift in the region's center of gravity thus constituted the second spatial transformation shaping the Eastern Mediterranean. In this shift, the growing significance of the overland trade which spanned the breadth of the Ottoman Empire and terminated in İzmir, its principal port of disembarkation, played a role to the detriment of the portcities in the Levant. Even when merchant caravans at times avoided the long land route crossing the Anatolian highlands for security reasons, the alternative routes they took were still northbound land routes, via Astrakhan, Brašov, Lwow, and Krakow.[6] Underlying this sea change was the transformation that the world-economy underwent from the 1560s onwards, with the gradual emergence of the Baltic and the North Sea as its new centers of gravity, or to be more precise, with the rise and consolidation of the *Pax Neerlandica*. The restructuring of global economic flows prompted a north-bound flow of goods and spices from the Levant, mostly via Istanbul and Lwow. The importance of this development was in that the new routes bypassed the territory controlled by the merchants of Venice. The proliferation in the number of regional fairs in north and east of the Alps, from Nuremberg to Leipzig, reflected and facilitated the growing significance of the land trade via the Ottoman Balkans. The rise of overland trade, both on the Anatolian and the Balkan Peninsula, manifested the above-mentioned northward shift of the center of economic activity in the Eastern Mediterranean. Within this new economic order, not only İzmir and, later, Salonica assumed the position of the Aegean's main ports of call, but also Istanbul, the capital that towered over the Aegean and the Black Sea, was transformed into an economic colossus; a position the city had largely lost following the collapse of the Central Asian trade emporium in the late fourteenth century.

Surely, the establishment of the *Pax Neerlandica* hastened the economic devolution of the Eastern Mediterranean. Yet this was not the only factor that reversed the fortunes of the Inner Sea. A contemporaneous transformation in the region's ecological make-up, brought about by the return of the Little Ice Age and the climatic variability associated with it, constituted the second major factor. Increased humidity and precipitation, soil erosion hastened by the wave of deforestation in the long sixteenth century (c. 1450–1650), and the advance of marshlands, and with it fever and malaria, transformed the exploitation of low-lying lands into a risky undertaking. Judging by the accounts of travelers who sojourned in the region, coastal plains that had previously boasted commercial cultivation or were put to use as cereal lands during the expansionary sixteenth century were largely abandoned in the following two centuries. The lowlands of Cilicia, home to the relatively long-lasting and economically viable Dulgadir principality as well as to the maritime Lesser Armenia, were mostly turned into grazing fields. The plain of Antioch was given over to rice cultivation. Throughout the Eastern Mediterranean sugar and, to a lesser extent, cotton fields were largely deserted. When Napoleon's armies besieged Acre, one of their staunchest enemies was the malaria-ridden marshland on the coast. Anatolia's Mediterranean coast was no exception: the ever-peripatetic Evliyâ Çelebi attributed the sparse population in the region to the presence of fever and malaria. Ecological changes in the plains and lowlands of the region accelerated the reversion of the formerly cultivated lands to untouched nature and thus magnified the impact of economic devolution brought about by the diversion of the Levant trade away from the Mediterranean. In broad terms, the drop in population permanently inhabiting the plains and low-lying lands and, in the final instance, the abandonment of these lands lasted until the latter half of the nineteenth century. The mid-Victorian economic boom, which boosted demand for cotton and wheat, and the end of the Little Ice in Age in the 1870s altered the region's landscape beyond recognition. That two-thirds of today's villages and nine-tenths of the cultivated parts of inner Anatolia date back only to the latter half of the nine-teenth century is a perfect testament to how scarcely-populated the peninsula had been previously. Between 1850 and 1950, in Syria an enormous amount of land only infrequently used in the past was brought under regular cultiva-tion and hundreds of settlements were transformed from hamlets to villages. Excluding the Jazirah, about 2.5 million hectares of new land were ploughed and about 2,000 villages established on this newly-won territory. The figures for Transjordan are 40,000 hectares and 300 villages.[7]

Two factors, then, one related to the world-economy, the other to the ecology of the region, transformed the lands around the Mediterranean. The shrinking of cultivated lands during the waning of the Mediterranean was exacerbated by the advance of marshlands and the abandonment of flood-prone low-lying lands during the Little Ice Age. These twin developments reshaped the Mediterranean landscape in the period between 1650 and 1850, roughly between the high ages of the *Pax Neerlandica* and the *Pax Britan-nica*. In order to trace this double transformation, this chapter will first offer a brief sketch of the economic changes precipitated by the commercial withering of the Inner Sea. How attendant changes in the basin's ecological setting compounded what the economic transformation of the Mediterranean had already set in motion will be dealt with later, with an eye on the chang-ing nature of, and interactions among, the port-cities that quartered it. The period spanning from 1650 to 1850 was not a period of devolution and economic regression, however. In the wake of the transfer of crops such as sugar and cotton to the West, the expansion of the region's traditional tree-crops (primarily mulberry and olive trees) which came to occupy its hillsides and, along with it, small livestock (sheep and goats in particular), which turned abandoned lowlands into winter grazing fields, fashioned a new economic landscape which was structurally different from the one that had characterized the region in its heyday.[8]

I

Charting the demise and afterglow of the Mediterranean demands a brief sketch of the erosion of the Venetian *stato do mar* and its results, especially after the 1560s, with the onset of the age of the Genoese. At its height, the emporium built by the Serenissima was marked by the *grand commerce* in spices and crops such as sugar and cotton. The rich trades may have formed the backbone of Venetian economic supremacy, but the provisioning of her far-flung maritime empire largely given over to cash-crops, demanded the inclusion of the prosaic grain trade into the commercial arsenal of its merchants, not to mention the imperial stratagems of the Signoria.[9] Interlinking the basin and centered in Venice were thus wide-spanning and dense economic networks that helped procure, market, and distribute on the one hand high-value goods (first and foremost, sugar and cotton) and on the other hand strategically sensitive bread crops. Not surprisingly, the prosperity of the Mediterranean in the fifteenth century was underwritten by the trade in spices and luxury goods, both of which went on to grow in volume until the turn of the sixteenth century. Furthermore, albeit lowly in stature for it fetched high profits only occasionally, the volatile grain trade was and remained the principal scaffolding of the Venetian *stato do maro*, as well as an indispensable component of the economic life of the Inner Sea, evidently for the provisioning of its numerous and populous coastal cities.

The erratic nature of the grain trade prevented it from falling into the hands of a small number of merchants; the attraction that this trade held for the many merchants involved was the easy availability of ready cash for payment. As a result, there were no serious disruptions in supply during the fifteenth century. It was in the sixteenth century that the steady availability of bread grains became a pressing issue, not only in the wealthy city-states, but also on the Iberian Peninsula where the infusion of American silver animated the lucrative wine and olive oil trades at the expense of cereals.[10] This transpired precisely at a time when crops such as sugar and cotton were gaining popularity in the Atlantic, hastening the contraction of arable lands. Concurrently, the diversion of the spice trade by the Portuguese merchants in the first half of the sixteenth century helped place greater emphasis on industrial production in Venice and elsewhere and, therefore, encouraged the flow of raw materials (wool, leather, skins) that served these industries. These raw materials were drained from the Ottoman dominions via the Balkans and the Adriatic, resulting in the rise of Ancona in the first half of the sixteenth century.[11] It was then that the tendency of supplanting rich trades with local goods gathered momentum; this tendency reached its height in the mid-sixteenth century with the explosion of the Ottoman wheat boom. Initially, then, the reconfiguration of trade routes around 1500 at the expense of the Mediterranean failed to deal a fatal blow to Ottoman trade.

Fortunate for the Levant, the drying-up of the spice trade following the circumnavigation of the Cape of Good Hope proved to be temporary at first. It was limited in duration to the first half of the sixteenth century.

However brief the hiatus in the spice trade was, the return of the rich trades did not signal a resumption of the trade patterns of the fifteenth century. Rather, the conduits through which spices traveled west multiplied in number, and the spice trade added new routes, mostly on land, to its westbound trajectory. A proliferation in the number of venues through which spices flowed reflected structural changes taking place in the heart of the world-economy. On the one hand, the growing prosperity of the North and the Baltic Sea, from Amsterdam to Bergen and Danzig, encouraged the merchants engaged in this rich trade to search for routes that would allow them to elbow out the merchants of Venice, so that they could market spices without Venetian intermediaries. On the other hand, the Portuguese merchants in the Indian Ocean opened up new avenues via Bandar Abbas during the revival of the time-honored Levantine route.[12]

In essence, what brought about this sea change in the patterns of merchandise flows was the shifting balance between the North Sea and the Mediterranean, to the injury of the latter. For one, the entrepôt trade handled by Venetian merchants gradually lost its pivotal role. The appearance of Hormuz as an important distribution center launched a process of dispersion in the westbound flow of spices. The port-city of Bandar Abbas was where the Portuguese eventually unloaded their spice cargo and re-loaded it onto camels to traverse the Syrian Desert and reach Aleppo, İzmir and Istanbul. Progressively, overland routes crossing the Fertile Crescent and Asia Minor and stretching into Central and Northern Europe via Bursa, Istanbul, İzmir, or Akkerman (by way of the Black Sea) gained salience. To be sure, when the spice trade revived after the 1550s, the Cairo–Alexandria and the Damascus–Beirut routes managed to recapture a significant share of the trade. Cairene spice merchants, for instance, were still transporting enormous sums of silver to Mecca to pay for their imports. But both of these routes were overshadowed by the rise of Aleppo and, later, an increase in the share of northbound land trade. The re-routing of some of the rich trades via Hormuz to Aleppo worked to the detriment of the port-cities south of Tripoli. From the second half of the sixteenth century to the 1620s, Aleppo and its port, Tripoli, held the place of pride, as they served as one of the spice trade's liveliest emporia where Venetian (and other) factors acquired their spices and drugs. Notwithstanding the centrality of the Aleppo–Tripoli route in the revival of the spice trade, the parallel growth in the share of overland trade through Ottoman Europe took away from Venice's North–South transit trade. It is not surprising that Amsterdam, as the most impressive clearing-house and warehouse of the world-economy, contributed immensely to the thriving of overland routes flowing into and out of it. The momentum was on the side of overland trade, partly because the golden age of the nobility in Poland, Hungary, Wallachia, and Moldavia (and the consumption that their newly-acquired wealth engendered) kept the routes passing through the Ottoman lands open and in continual use. Furthermore, over time local goods from silk and cotton to coffee and wool filled the void left behind by the egress of the rich trades. The withdrawal of the Sublime Porte from the task of overseeing the pilgrimage trade at the turn of the eighteenth century symbolically mirrored the diminished role of transit trade.

Equally crucial, the relocation of manufacturing activities across the Alps in rural (i.e. Southern) Germany and beyond supported a revision in trade patterns and routes, by solidifying the input and output flows of the reigning *Verlag* system and by increasing the disposable incomes of the inhabitants of these regions. Scores of fairs held in the Balkans after the turn of the seventeenth century for the resale of spices and other goods continued to prosper as demand from across the Danube remained strong. Fairs in Leipzig, Frankfurt and Nuremberg complemented those that mushroomed throughout the Balkans and provided an impressive infrastructure in the seventeenth and eighteenth centuries for the region's vibrant economy.[13] Part of the surplus of the Baltic trade percolated south through a series of linked exchanges between Eastern, Central and Western Europe, owing to overland trade through Poland and Germany. The western balance, in deficit with the northern ports, was partially compensated by a favorable balance in overland traffic, the payments being effected by way of the Leipzig fairs.[14]

Thus, as the Baltic and the North Sea started to set the tempo of the world-economy from the seventeenth century onwards, the economic geography of the Mediterranean was transformed accordingly. Venice and Florence expanded their field of operation across the Alps into southern Germany to keep up with the increasingly northbound flow of goods. Without a doubt, the port-cities that commanded a bigger share of the silver trade were located on or close to the coast of the Atlantic Ocean. And the politics with coastlines on the Mediterranean saw a shift in, and an eventual realignment of, their centers of economic gravity more in tune with the new order. Seville, the Spanish Empire's outlet into the Atlantic, lost all its sea trade to Cádiz which emerged as the port of disembarkation for New World silver and gold. Lyon, too, whose fortunes the French state had tried to bolster for most of the fifteenth and sixteenth centuries, had to bow to Paris. Livorno and İzmir emerged as the northern merchants' base of operations and favorite ports of call. In other words, in concert with the commercial rearrangements precipitated by the gradual withdrawal of Venice from her strongholds in the Levant, the Ottoman Empire's economic heart was no longer beating along the shores of the Mediterranean, but pumping toward a more northerly direction, along the coastlines of the Aegean and the Black Sea. The restructuring of economic networks north of the Alps to the benefit of overland trade placed Ottoman Europe at the heart of the empire's economic life, much to the disadvantage of the Levant. The new order favored port-cities located north of Aleppo, and Istanbul consequently replaced Cairo as the leading Ottoman port. In the meanwhile, İzmir took over the role played by Chios before 1566; it owed its prominence during the seventeenth and eighteenth centuries to its position as the terminus of overland trade. It was the Alexandria–İzmir–Istanbul axis that dominated the economic flows of the seventeenth and eighteenth centuries. Despite the fact that it was outside the boundaries of the Mediterranean climate and escaped the vagaries of the Little Ice Age, the Mediterranean leg of the axis, Alexandria, remained a pale shadow of its former self.

With the Aegean turning into one of the key sites of economic activity, Ragusa, which had previously made her living from a variety of different shipping trades, some local, others long-distance, was forced to abandon these activities and withdraw into the Adriatic. The city still attracted trade in hides and wool from the Balkans, but now these goods came from the great center at Novi-Bazar, by overland routes which had replaced sea routes. Likewise, Spoleto served as an outpost for Venice, because it had excellent access to the overland routes leading into the Balkan Peninsula. The demise of Ragusa was thus not solely due to the competition it encountered from the caravanner trade, but rather from the caravan trade, kept alive by a new network of indigenous Balkan traders and trade fairs which rose in the interior during the eighteenth century. The Thirty Years' War turned Southern Germany into a disaster zone, and the overland trade suffered as a result, only to resume its former vigor precipitously after 1648. The decades following the Habsburg capitulations of 1666 and the expansion of trade with the southern regions of the Ottoman Empire triggered the settlement of Serbian, Armenian, and Greek communities in commercial centers such as Buda, Vienna, and Leipzig.

Last but not least, the diversion of American silver away from the Mediterranean to finance the Habsburg dynasty's wars in the Netherlands may have been a signal for the waning of the Mediterranean; the northerly diversion of precious metals to pay for the purchase of Baltic grain strengthened this trend. In the coming two and a half centuries, it was mostly the northern latitudes of the world-economy (such as Poland, Sweden, England) and the English colonies of America which took turns to serve as breadbaskets of the seventeenth and eighteenth centuries.[15] The decline in the re-export trade of the Italian city-states, along with the growing reliance of these cities on home-grown grain from their *contadini* or Terraferma prompted a contraction in commercial agriculture in the Mediterranean. This dealt a blow to the livelihood of ports that provisioned these city-states in the fifteenth and sixteenth centuries. In short, the rise of the *Pax Neerlendica* altered the economic coordinates of the Mediterranean landscape until the turn of the nineteenth century. From an agricultural point of view, the reign of Baltic grain lasted well into the late eighteenth century, although its provenance changed several times. The widespread rural manufacturing throughout the continent also survived until the eighteenth century. Both of these trends, agrarian and industrial, went on to shape the course of Mediterranean history until the rise of the *Pax Britannica*. The British world order refashioned the world-economy by concentrating manufacturing (primarily in cotton) in urban centers, thereby undermining the rural wool and linen industries of the continent. Also, by generating demand for grain, first for the provisioning of the British navy during the Continental Blockade and later due to the passing of the Corn Laws, the *Pax Britannica* once again fueled commercial agrarian production in the Mediterranean. Together, these two developments boosted demand for cotton and wheat from Lower Egypt and Palestine to Hauran and Salonica. With the arrival of the steamship and the influx of Northern Europeans into the Mediterranean during the mid-Victorian boom, the caravanner and overland trade lost the prominence they had once commanded under the *Pax Neerlendica*. The new order gave the port-cities of the Eastern Mediterranean a chance to reclaim the function they had once performed so successfully.

II

The Little Ice Age stretched roughly from the 1300s to the 1870s, with a hiatus between 1450 and 1550, the Medieval Optimum.[16] Even though this climatic and ecological turn-around made its appearance at the beginning of the fourteenth century, the resulting environmental transformation started in earnest only in the second half of the sixteenth century, because of the fast pace of colonization and settlement of low-lying lands, on the one hand, and deforestation on the other. Timber, after all, was the key ingredient of construction, mining, and naval industries of the era.[17] Of the wide array of changes launched by the Little Ice Age beginning in the mid-sixteenth century, particularly the heightened climatic variability associated with it (droughts as well as floods, the characteristic of the age)[18] is of significance for the present analysis. The dawn of the Little Ice Age heralded the onset of cool summers and snowy winters in the North, while weather conditions in the Mediterranean were manifested in the form of increased precipitation, that is, torrential rain falls at lower, and increased snowfall at higher, altitudes. Both forms of precipitation led to increased fluvial activity and incidences of flooding. Given the rugged relief of the Mediterranean, the discharge from melting snow in late spring in particular inundated river beds and valleys with raging waters. Since deforestation prompted by the settlement efforts in the periods between 1100 and 1350 and between 1450 and 1550 had already diminished the absorptive capacity of soil on mountains and hillsides, valley bottoms and plains on the skirts of mountain ranges found themselves exposed to intermittent flooding. The central and provincial authorities repeatedly had to repair stone bridges destroyed by raging river waters in many regions of the Ottoman Empire during the seventeenth and eighteenth centuries. As a result of increased fluvial discharge and soil erosion, newly-forming marshlands extended at the expense of the region's lowlands which happened to be its crop lands.[19] This development affected the entire Mediterranean, as evidenced by river delta expansion from the Ebro valley to the Rhône, from the River Arno to the River Meander. Unfortunately, the fertile soil that was deposited along the banks of these rivers was, for the most part, not easy to bring under cultivation.

The calamitous consequences of the croplands' contraction were more pronounced in the lower regions and valley bottoms of the mountains enveloping the Mediterranean. Certainly, the intensity of fluvial activity waxed and waned over time, especially given the long span of the Little Ice Age. More often than not, periods of flooding were concentrated in time, maybe lasting five years in one single stretch.[20] Nonetheless, the persistent precipitation and recurrent flooding turned the cultivation of the basin's lowlands into a vexing and uncertain undertaking. Befitting the reach of the Little Ice Age, a similar scenario unfolded throughout the Mediterranean, in Malaga, the Roman Campagna, Sardinia, Corsica, Cilicia, and Palestine. Over time, settlements relocated from marshy settings to the surrounding hills and higher altitudes at a steadily accelerating pace. The growing exploitation of the basin's hilly regions, particularly when complemented by the overuse of forests and pasturelands higher up, oftentimes hastened aerial erosion. What is more, this was occurring at a time when grain prices stagnated from the 1620s onwards in most parts of Europe, and in the 1650s on the Italian Peninsula. Prices remained low until the mid-eighteenth century. The plummeting prices after the 1650s account for why agriculture did not necessarily become the domain of Grundherrschaft-like arrangements, even when lay and ecclesiastical nobility established much tighter control over the producers. Drainage, bonification, land improvement and colonization during the Little Ice Age, understandably costly for petty producers, seemed too expensive even to the landlords. Even in the rich Italian city-states, efforts by pontifical and urban governments and capitalists to reclaim land starting in the 1650s could not have been more ill-timed. They initiated investment in land at a time when in the valleys and coastal zones of the Mediterranean low-lying marshy landscapes were reappearing and, even worse, spreading.

Roughly from the 1550s onwards, a great number of coastal and inland plains dotting the Mediterranean basin started to turn into marshlands. The sown fields of Maremma in Tuscany were devastated by floods in 1590. The same happened on the western end of the basin, in Andalusia, where flooding turned into a perennial problem as the sixteenth century came to a close. This was also true of the eastern extremity of the Inner Sea, on the Pamphylian and Cilician plains. On the Pamphylian plain, it was primarily nomadic groups who, having built their villages in the surrounding higher areas brought the plains under temporary cultivation. On the Cilician plain, the population consisted of a few settlements containing less than 100 souls at the most, whereas villages on the surrounding hills housed at least 300. In both cases, vast swamps and malaria posed a serious threat to the nomads who tilled the plains on a temporary basis.[21] Napoleon, too, in his campaign to capture Acre, was forced to move his army on dangerous hilly terrain in a long single-file march rather than cross the marshy lands which cut through the Plain of Sharon.

The advance of swamplands was thus a region-wide phenomenon, and organized attempts to reverse it invariably occurred in the richer zones of the Mediterranean (such as the Italian Peninsula), and not in Andalusia or Cilicia. The task required large capital and infinite expenses which the financially strapped imperial bureaucracies and enterprising nobles could not afford. At the height of grain prices at the turn of the seventeenth century, the Roman countryside hence presented a landscape which stood apart from the rest of the region, with the possible exception of the Lower Languedoc, where marshy areas near Arles, Narbonne, and Fréjus were drained, albeit on a limited scale. As long as money was invested in agriculture, reclaiming lands from marshes and swamps remained a priority. By the same token, however, the fall in grain prices slowed down the return of money to land and with it the attempts to reclaim drained land. In fact, the draining of the Lower Languedoc was discontinued in the 1660s.[22] In the Eastern Mediterranean, even at the height of the mid-Victorian boom and with the contribution of British and French consuls, plans to drain the marshes near Alexandretta and to bring 600 hectares of prime land under cultivation never materialized. With the waning of attempts to drain swamplands in the Roman Campagna, the Mediterranean lowlands presented a much more uniform façade after the 1650s: its plains were invaded not only by marshlands, but also by vegetation that covered any open ground and slowly reclaimed even grazing land. Malaria-bearing mosquitoes swarmed the coasts and pushed back the limits of human habitation. The withdrawal of agriculture and rural life, in turn, helped extend the realm of the wild –the swamps, the reeds, and of course, the much-maligned sovereign of this natural milieu, the malaria-bearing mosquito.

When travelers visited the Mediterranean countryside in the seventeenth and eighteenth centuries, even in the relatively better attended Roman Campagna they were struck by a rolling landscape as far as the eye could see, sparsely populated by shepherds and flocks of sheep and occasional isolated farms and cornfields. They were struck by the fact that most villages were built on high ground, a long way from low-lying territories. To the west of the Agro Romano lay the great marsh, or *albufera*, of Valencia, fed by the rivers Turia and Júcar, and the Ebro river delta the draining of which started only in the 1850s. Likewise, only a tiny portion of the marshes of the Lower Provence was brought back under cultivation before the nineteenth century. To the east of the Agro Romano, the situation was not any different: vast tracts of brush and heather covered the countryside along the route between Gallipoli and Adrianople. The marshlands of the Cilician maritime plain made the air in Alexandretta (İskenderun) (its port-city and one of Aleppo's outposts on the Mediterranean) so unbearably humid that merchants and consuls who were stationed there believed themselves to be in imminent mortal danger. In this instance, the marshes tested the capabilities of beasts of burden (mostly horses and camels), for they were laden with merchandise and forced to cross this inhospitable territory on their way to and from the port. The local populace was able to evade the menace of malaria and fevers only by moving to the higher regions of the surrounding mountain range in the summer months, when the air was at its heaviest in the plains.[23]

For most of the two-and-a-half centuries from the 1600s to the 1850s, owing to the retreat of cultivation and permanent habitation, the inland as well as the coastal plains of the Mediterranean remained home to untouched nature. In the eyes of the settled populations, the lowlands were infested by serfs and outcasts, shepherds and wanderers, those with very limited agricultural production capabilities and those who made a living from the marshlands. The evacuation of the plains helped to populate the highlands, and most rural settlers chose a site halfway between the crops in the valley (or the plains) and the forests of the mountain-sides. Consequently, the plains of the Mediterranean remained thinly populated until the late nineteenth century.

III

This, of course, did not mean that the low-lying lands were completely deserted. Unlike the plague, malaria did not kill its victims but sapped their vitality. Also, one should not forget that however detrimental the advance of the marshlands was to winter crops and cereals, the spread of the fluvial environment of the seventeenth and eighteenth centuries cre-ated a setting which, if utilized to its fullest extent, could facilitate the cultivation of aquatic crops such as rice, or summer crops such as cotton, both of which depend on irrigation. The emporia of these crops, and of cotton in particular, extended along the shores of the Aegean, partly because in this region mountains and valleys run perpendicular to the coast, rendering it relatively easier to make use of bodies of water (unlike in the Mediterranean where mountains run parallel to the coast and where fluvial activity is difficult to control). The expansion of cotton cultivation and animal husbandry, an outcome of the new ecological setting, was reflected in the growing export of hides, wool and cotton from the region during the eighteenth century. It was not by chance that during the seven-teenth and eighteenth centuries the commercial center of gravity in the Eastern Mediterranean shifted northward to the Aegean and the Black Sea, as Bruce McGowan has eloquently demonstrated.[24] It was in these zones that *çiftlik*s (farms) mushroomed and landlords at times managed to force laborers to settle in these unhealthy environments to cultivate cot-ton, perhaps with plans to gradually drain these marshy lands. One could argue that the rise of *çiftlik*s and *latifundia* in the basin's low-lying lands was a response to the dire ecological conditions caused by the Little Ice Age. Similarly, reacting to the ecological condition of the lands under their control, the famous notables of the eighteenth century understanda-bly invested more in animal husbandry than cereal cultivation, from the Veneto to the Aegean. With the growing demand for cotton in the eight-eenth century, putting lowlands into effective use emerged as a viable strategy for those who could mobilize labor; yet, this development failed to gather further momentum until the latter half of the nineteenth century when demand for cotton and wheat skyrocketed. Now, the previous ad-vance of swamps turned the basin's hillsides, highlands, and mountain slopes into valuable sites of production: mulberry and olives trees populated the hillsides of the basin, as did vineyards.[25] During the seventeenth and eighteenth centuries, therefore, most port-cities served as point of collection for the products of their surroundings.

Overall, then, there was a double movement of retreat during the seventeenth and eighteenth centuries. The first movement, world-economic in nature, was away from the southern latitudes of the Mediterranean, to the advantage of the North, Ottoman Europe for one. The second movement, ecological in nature, was away from the basin's low-lying lands and plains toward its higher altitudes. The desertion of the low landscapes of the Mediterranean was all but final. Rather, the movement was cyclical. The next round of colonization in the basin's lowlands took place at the height of the *Pax Britannica*, when agricultural production gained momentum worldwide. Beginning in the mid-eighteenth century, new prospects included the extension of arable lands, first for planting the cotton that was in such great demand at the time and then, from the 1840s onwards, for cultivating wheat. These developments entailed turning the pastures and wastelands of the seventeenth and eighteenth centuries back into croplands, by draining low-lying regions. Under the *Pax Britannica*, world wheat production more than doubled, from 916 million bushel in 1831–40 to 2,120 billion in 1881–87.[26] Starting timidly in the nineteenth century, the process of agricultural expansion assumed greater force at the turn of the twentieth century, when the plains for example of Ebro, Cilicia, and Thessaly were opened up to permanent settlement. Other regions had to wait until after World War II. From this point of view, the Mediterranean landscape at the end of the nineteenth century had more in common with that of the late sixteenth than that of the early nineteenth century.

The end of the Little Ice Age in the 1870s and the singling out of the mosquito as the purveyor of malaria at the turn of the twentieth century altered this landscape drastically.[27] To a large extent, the success that drainage companies and central and local governments had in reclaiming low-lying maritime and inland plains between the 1850s and the 1950s was due to these two factors. Together with mounting demand for raw materials, these twin developments opened up plains to continual tillage, increased the arable land and, hence, cereal production. Port-cities that had served the rich trades in the fifteenth and sixteenth centuries and later turned into regional centers of collection and distribution for local goods found themselves rejuvenated by the onset of the boom in cereal and cotton production from the mid-nineteenth century onwards.

Maps and Wars:
Charting the Mediterranean in the Sixteenth Century

Carla Keyvanian

The number of studies about historical maps has sharply increased in the last two decades. Although recent literature has continued to examine technical aspects of cartography, such as the development of systems of measurement and projection, there has emerged a new emphasis on the interpretation of maps as symbolic objects whose messages are more complex than the identification of the coordinates of a place. The upsurge in these studies is in part linked to interest in the blurred boundary between art and science, a line that maps of the early modern period straddled, as geographical knowledge was conveyed through pictorial means. The same conjoined expression of artistic and scientific advances, which made maps so desirable to wealthy or erudite patrons, renders them now prime objects of inquiry for scholarship that favors an interdisciplinary approach.[1]

Another reason for the explosion in cartographic studies is the privileged access that maps grant to the worldview of the societies in which they emerged. Renaissance maps not only mixed scientific and artistic modes of representation, but also mingled geographical and historical observations, as well as information about flora and fauna or the habits of locals. These rich visual sources were examined through the lens of semiotic theories in the 1970s and 1980s and interpreted as meaningful systems of signs.[2] The traditional belief that maps were 'neutral' objects, indicating distances and locations as accurately as the knowledge and technology of their eras allowed, was largely abandoned and replaced by the realization that mapmakers interpreted and sometimes intentionally distorted the reality they portrayed in their charts. In turn, that portrayal shaped the vision of the world of those who looked at these images. Studies on cartography have thus increasingly regarded maps as objects that bear witness to the systems of representation (or ideologies) of both their makers and consumers.[3]

Particularly revealing in this respect is the proliferation of maps of the islands and cities of the Mediterranean in sixteenth-century Europe. Not heretofore studied as a group, these maps are the focus of this essay. The identification of the salient characteristics of these images generates some observations concerning contemporary cartographic production; but, more importantly, these charts can illuminate broader issues concerning East–West relations. A close look at these maps and their accompanying inscriptions reveals, I believe, a more nuanced view of that relationship. In my closing remarks, I draw some preliminary conclusions about Europeans' perception of their Eastern Mediterranean counterparts as evidenced by the images. To that end, I examine these maps within the context of cartographic production of the period, as well as in relation to the specific historical events they refer to.

The propagation of charts of the Mediterranean is part of a broader phenomenon of dissemination that, related to the technical advances of the period, characterizes Renaissance map production as a whole. The single most influential event in the development of early modern cartography was the rediscovery of Claudius Ptolemy's *Geographia*, a text produced in Alexandria in the second century CE. The text listed descriptions, locations, and distances related to more than 8,000 places known to contemporaries, as well as accounts on how to draw maps of the regions it described. Although the manuscript had survived in Greek versions, it was not until the fifteenth century, after a Tuscan scholar completed a Latin translation in 1406 and made it accessible to a larger literate public, that the ancient text revolutionized mapmaking. Medieval systems of representation based on Christian symbolism were abandoned in favor of a predetermined grid of latitude and longitude. The scientific developments of the Renaissance thus included the transformation of geographical knowledge. Henceforth, Italy, where the *Geographia* had been translated, dominated the field of cartographic production, which revolved around the hubs of Venice and Rome until the seventeenth century, when the Netherlands challenged that primacy.[4] Leonardo da Vinci's 1502 chart of Imola was the earliest monumental geometric or orthogonal map, i.e. the surveyed plan of a city devoid of three-dimensional renderings.[5] Many orthogonal maps were created in the following decades, as newly formed centralized states employed them for administrative and military purposes.[6]

The demand for maps also rose sharply among a public of art-lovers and armchair travelers who appreciated their aesthetic and educational properties. The pictorial advances of the Renaissance spilled over into cartography, enhancing the lifelikeness of maps and therefore their appeal among popular audiences. The genre that this public preferred was city views, images informed by the tradition of landscape painting.[7] Much favored was the bird's-eye view, an aerial vision that generally combined a measured profile of the city's boundaries with an artist's rendition of its urban fabric.[8] Unlike landscape paintings, bird's-eye views are maps that do not reproduce a vision that exists in nature, at least in principle. Even from the high vantage point from which they were supposedly viewed (before the advent of planes or hot-air balloons), cities would not have appeared as they are represented in these pictures, which are constructed images. Bird's-eye views, in other words, are graphic representations of an abstraction meant to convey geographical as well as other information and, as such, are akin to modern-day maps. The charts of Mediterranean cities that I will discuss all belong to this type of image, although geometric plans are sometimes included on the same sheet.

Traditionally, two main factors have been cited to explain the explosion of map production in sixteenth-century Europe. The first is the development of printing presses that could cheaply reproduce maps and made them accessible to a broad public. The revolutionary impact of printing presses through the dissemination of texts, the development of literacy, and the transformation of sixteenth-century European society has been analyzed extensively.[9] The spread of printed images played a crucial role as well. Before the advent of photography, making prints was the sole means of propagating visual information *en masse*.[10] In the case of maps, inexpensive printed images of distant cities and regions became available to large segments of the population, shaping their worldviews.

The presses, however, merely facilitated the production of objects for which there was an emerging taste and a demand. Indeed, side-by-side with the production of these popular images, a genre of expensive, individually produced maps was flourishing. These were largely portolans, nautical charts that mariners had used as navigational aids since the Middle Ages. These early portolans, centered on the great empty expanse of the Mediterranean whose coastal profile and convolutions were rendered with surpris-

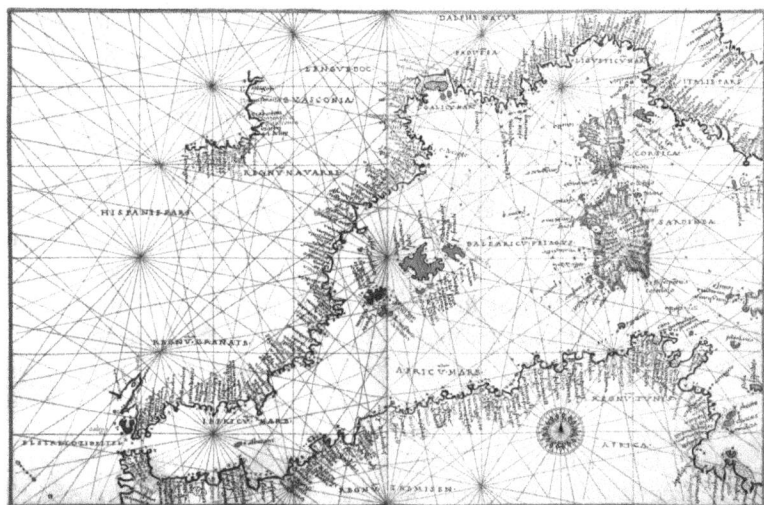

Fig. 1: Battista Agnese, Portolan Chart of the West Mediterranean
ca. 1544, Library of Congress

ing accuracy, emerged from the world of European seafarers. Unlike medieval land maps, which served eminently symbolic purposes until the end of the fifteenth century, medieval portolans were drawn using compasses and a rudimentary theodolite, so as to provide information crucial to sea travel. The names of ports and coastal settlements were carefully inscribed; dangerous ledges and rocks were identified; and a grid of lines covered the chart, representing compass points and wind directions.[11]

These practical tools of navigation rarely survived the wear and tear of use at sea. The bulk of surviving portolans are rather ornamental examples, commissioned by wealthy patrons who hung them in their studies to display their love for geographical knowledge. These lavish counterparts to the charts used on ships were embellished by pictorial details, among them elaborate compass roses, galleys and caravels, small sketches of cities, animals, and vegetation, as well as flags and symbols revealing the political or religious affiliations of the regions along the coast (Fig. 1).

Four times as many portolans have survived from the sixteenth and seventeenth centuries as have from the two preceding ones.[12] Even if allowances are made for the vagaries of survival rates, the numbers point to a burgeoning market. The laborious combination of accurate geographical information and skillful pictorial elements in these charts turned them into luxury objects. They were generally commissioned by the wealthiest patrons, often the nobility or royalty. Several suggestions can be put forward to explain the fascination with maps during the Renaissance. Benefiting from technical advances, maps had developed into more recognizable representations of physical reality and thus afforded greater intellectual pleasure to the viewer. One might also speculate that the recognition of familiar places depicted on the charts inspired confidence that curiosity about unknown lands could be satisfied by gazing at their cartographic reproduction. And in the wake of the discovery of the New World, which perhaps engendered a vertiginous sense of a world whose ancient boundaries had suddenly exploded, the visual and symbolic domination that maps provided countered such feelings of dislocation and uncertainty. These might all have been conjoining factors. Whatever their combination, however, the taste for spectacular portolans in the sixteenth century, a boom that paralleled that of cheap printed charts, makes it clear that the demand for maps was not merely the result of their inexpensive availability.[13]

The second main reason frequently cited to account for the diffusion of maps in the sixteenth century is the enthusiasm for the discovery of the lands across the Atlantic, which spurred the need to chart the newly found areas.[14] While the psychological impact of the explorations might have played a role, the easy equation between the Age of Geographical Discoveries and cartographic production has been called into question by the observation that for each map of the New World manufactured in the sixteenth century, about three were drafted of the countries around the Mediterranean. We only need to consider some of the major collections in Italy: The National Library in Florence, for example, boasts more than 300 specimens of printed maps, of which only a handful are associated with the New World. A similar proportion is found in the Vatican Library in Rome: The bulk of the 160 catalogued maps are of Europe and the Mediterranean, while only one charts America; three are maps of the world; three represent Asia and one Africa.[15]

A fact that has largely gone unnoticed is that many of the Mediterranean maps of the period are related to the confrontation with the Ottomans.[16] In many cases, the first map we have of a city or island in the Mediterranean was created to describe a phase of the hostilities. The clash with the Ottomans over the possession of strategic bases had immediate economic repercussions, and the vicissitudes of the war directly influenced not just those whose livelihood depended on trade and the safe arrival of ships and their cargoes at trading ports. Everyone became involved in one way or another, for the supply of everyday goods and their prices affected all. The need for updated information about the development of the conflict, most effectively

Fig. 2: Antonio Lafreri, Melita Insula *(Island of Malta), 1551,
Biblioteca Apostolica Vaticana, St.Geogr.I.73.*

presented in visual form, prompted the demand for charts of the affected areas. Immediate concern about the outcome of battles close to home, rather than curiosity about faraway lands, was the main reason behind the making of maps in this period. In the sixteenth century, the New World was still very distant, not just geographically, but also in terms of its commercial prospects and the cultural transformations it would eventually entail. Instead, the daily lives of the majority of the European population were influenced by the ancient and intricate web of commercial routes that crisscrossed the Mediterranean more thickly in this period than ever before. Take, for example, the vast number of views of Malta produced on the occasion of the Ottoman siege of 1565, known as the Grand Siege. Between May and September of that year, the military order of the Knights of Malta held the fort until the arrival of reinforcements forced the Ottoman army to retreat. Obtaining control of Malta, situated between Ottoman domains on the North African coast and Sicily, would have been a decisive victory for them. Europeans only had to glance at a map to comprehend the threat posed by an enemy base so close to the Italian islands.

The dissemination of maps and the demand they satisfied were tied to the spread of printed broadsheets, the progenitors of modern newspapers. These *avvisi*, as they were generally called (from the Italian for 'notification' or 'warnings'), were originally private reports that observers in the employ of princes and other rulers drafted to keep their patrons abreast of economic and political occurrences. In the sixteenth century, the *avvisi,* also called *gazzette* (from the name of the small coin needed to purchase them), evolved into printed publications sold to the public, reporting news about events near and far and especially about battles. Sold as single sheets or small pamphlets, the broadsheets often contained images.[17]

The maps of Malta, as well as other examples I will discuss, were engraved for such broadsheets and quickly disseminated because of a postal network that covered Europe, enabling the rapid transmission of news. News of the final Ottoman retreat from Malta took only six days to reach Rome, and eleven more to reach Brussels. The first graphically depicted news of the siege, including time for engraving and publication, appeared only one month after the beginning of the conflict.[18] Several more maps followed, making the confrontation probably the most frequently pictured event of the century. In the year of the siege, 65 maps of Malta were issued, more than fifty of them in Italy alone, documenting the various phases of the struggle.[19] Nor did the interest end with the fighting: Over the next eighty years more than seventy separate broadsheet impressions of the encounter were published.[20]

Several of the initial maps produced to document the Grand Siege of 1565 were based on an older chart of superior execution, compiled on the occasion of a previous clash with the Ottomans. This was a map of Malta issued in 1551 by Antonio Lafreri, one of the most prominent publishers in Rome, after whom such printed images were named (Fig. 2).[21] This finely incised copperplate is indebted to the seafaring culture that also instigated portolan charts and a related genre; the isolarii, books containing maps of islands, which found a market among would-be travelers.[22] Above the date and the name of the publisher, a scale surmounted by a compass is indicated in nautical miles –instruments of measurement that advertised the accuracy of what was portrayed. On the borders, on the left, the longitude and the latitude (39 and 35 degrees, respectively) are inscribed. The coastline is painstakingly rendered; the towns are thumbnail sketches but carefully labeled and connected by scrupulously drawn routes. The perspective contributes to the verisimilitude: Malta, seen from a high vantage point, appears as a large plank floating on waves, with a 'thickness' that is rendered in the border closest to the viewer. The island is fish –or whale– shaped, in accordance with a contemporary simile that compared Malta's form to that of a 'sea scorpion', a Mediterranean fish.[23]

Besides informing the viewer of Malta's geographical coordinates between Sicily and Africa, the cartouche identifying the island ('Melita, now called Malta...') announces that the Knights of Malta have success-

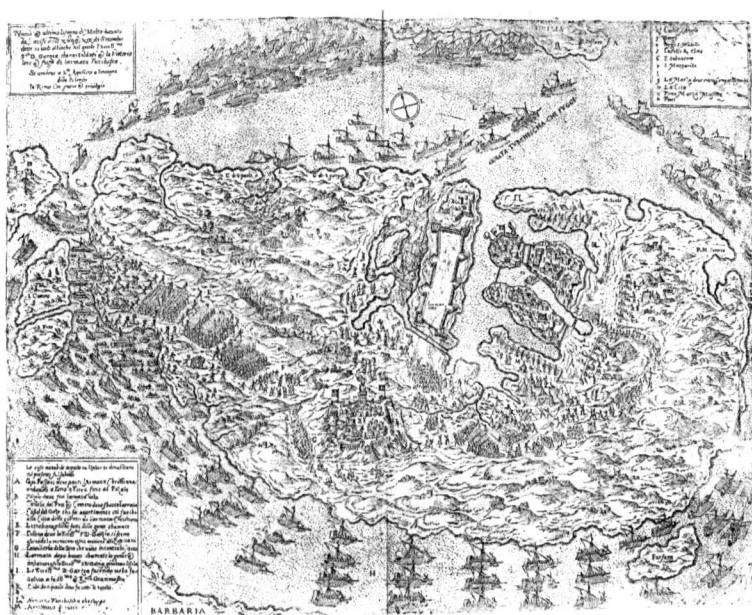

Fig. 3: Anonymous, Malta, *1565(?),*
Biblioteca Apostolica Vaticana, Barb.P.IX.47.

fully defended it against a Turkish attack. Nothing else in the map refers
to the conflict; the galleys and galleots that are pictured are placidly
sailing. This is not a snapshot-like depiction meant to convey the heat of
an event. The collision with the Ottomans in 1551 was short-lived and the
sophisticated print was engraved in Rome after things had calmed down.
The maps produced during the Grand Siege, in contrast, show specific
phases of the battle. To the rendering of the island were added the positions of the fleets, the encampments of attackers and defenders, and tacti-
cal movements; crucial details that called for the rapid revision of the
copperplates, as new states of the prints were created to document the
latest development in combat. Sometimes only a few hours passed between events shown in successive states of the prints.

In some cases, not only the island but also the lands closest to it were
shown. An undated and unsigned example sports an unshapely and de-
formed Malta, whose scale is grossly exaggerated, while the seas surrounding it have been reduced to little more than canals, barely separating
it from Sicily and the African mainland (Fig. 3).[24] The blatant distortion,
however, magnified Malta's strategic significance as a stepping-stone

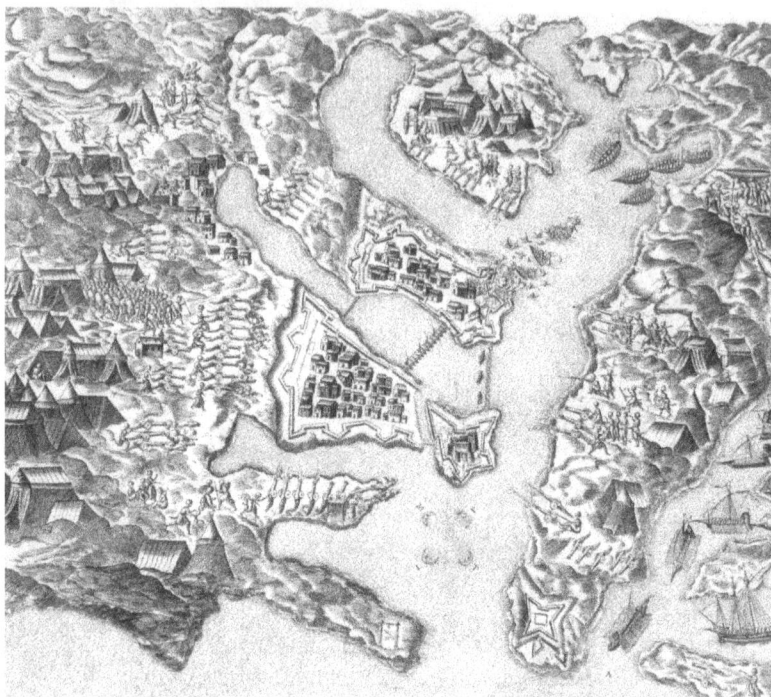

Fig. 4: Antonio Lafreri, Giovanni Orlandi, Harbor of Malta *(detail), 1565/1602, Gabinetto Nazionale delle Stampe, Rome.*

between Europe and Africa. The print depicts a series of linked episodes related to the arrival of the fleet from Sicily, carrying the long-awaited reinforcements for the Knights of Malta. The fleet is shown both disembarking troops in the west (on the left in the image), and then circumnavigating Malta before turning north, and bound for Italy, an action conveyed by continuous rings of ships surrounding the island. Discouraged by this show of force, the Ottomans make a half-hearted attempt to engage the fresh troops in skirmishes, shown in the upper part of the island, then sail off from the north coast, where a different fleet is labeled 'The Turkish army retreats'. The depiction of unfolding action is even more explicit in the numerous news-maps that, instead of portraying the entire island, show a close-up of the harbor area where most of the fighting took place. An example is another Lafreri map published in August 1565. The specimen reproduced here is a print reissued in 1602 by Giovanni Orlandi, an engraver, printer, and publisher who bought several Lafreri plates and dominated the Roman market in the first decades of the seventeenth century (Fig. 4).[25] However, the original was circulated while the fighting was raging. The image seems hastily pieced together, displaying various angles of vision. For example, the tents of the Ottoman encampment are shown almost in elevation, while the fortifications are portrayed in plan. The inscription apologizes for the map's lack of polish, citing the need to make fresh news from Malta rapidly available: 'If everything is not as polished as it should, the fault is of these turbulent times; those who sent this drawing from Malta made haste to provide news'. Information on the progress of the conflict was regularly transmitted from the island, to be engraved and printed on the mainland, but this is a rare legend that explicitly acknowledges the circumstances of production. In this case, the sketch on which the print was based can be identified as one produced by Girolamo Cassar, then the resident military engineer of the Knights of Malta.[26] In his manuscript map, the thin contours of the geometrical plan of the fortifications, which testifies to their author's familiarity with the survey systems used for military purposes, are emphasized in bold red ink. The rest of the sheet is an almost entirely empty expanse covered in bluish-green watercolor, which in the printed map is covered with tents and figures of Turks and Christians grappling or scurrying to fire cannons. Such colorful details, which could hardly be represented within the tight geometry of a plan, were necessary to entice popular audiences; albeit to the detriment of consistent draftsmanship. The publisher cleverly turned the discrepancies to his advantage in the inscription; the niceties of graphic conventions are eschewed in the interest of veracity and timeliness.

These maps are the trail left by a narrative unfolding in the Mediterranean in that period. One protagonist of that narrative was Jean de Valette, born in 1494 (or 1498, according to some sources) of small nobility in Rouergue, northwest of the Gulf of Lyon, not far from the Mediterranean. Around age 20, he entered the military Order of the Knights of St. John of Rhodes, as they were known before they settled in Malta, seeking his own fortune like so many cadet sons who could not hope for a part of their families' wealth. His fierce temperament assured him of a rapidly advancing career (he soon was commanding a galley) but also got him into trouble. He was imprisoned in Gozo, an island of the Maltese archipelago, and then exiled to Tripoli for almost beating to death a layman who had slighted him. After he was pardoned, he was captured by the Ottomans and rowed on one of their galleys for a year before being released as part of a prisoner exchange. His career flourished after his release, and in 1546 he returned to Tripoli, this time as its appointed governor. When the Ottomans attacked Tripoli in 1551, de

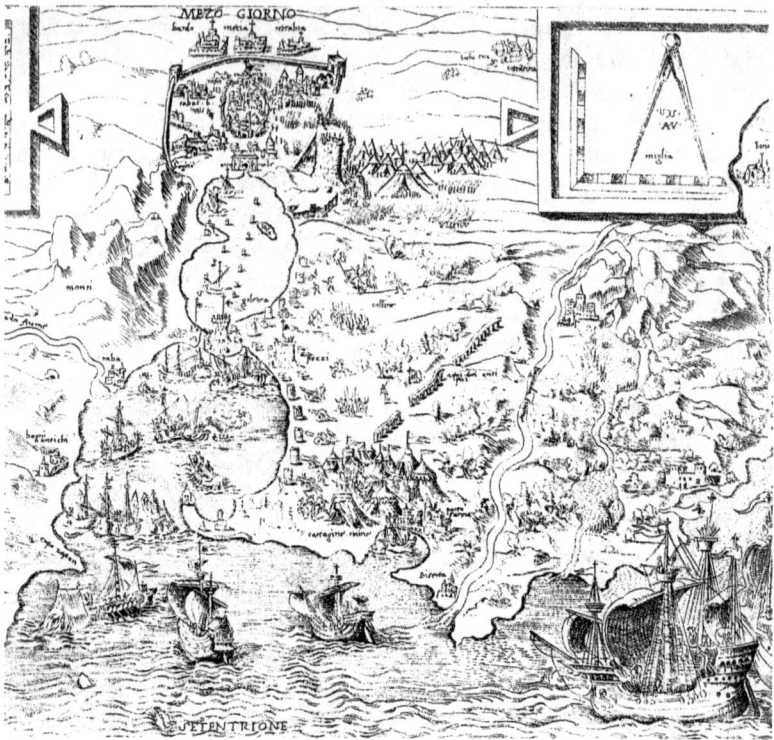

Fig. 5: Agostino Musi, Tunisia *(detail), 1535, Private Collection*

Valette was forced to abandon the city and retreated to Malta. He defended the island more successfully in the conflict commemorated in the whale-shaped Lafreri image of that year. For years he held on to a never-to-be-realized hope to-regain Tripoli and move there the headquarters of the order through the ranks of which he continued rising. In 1565, now Grand Master or commander-in-chief of the order and close to 70, he led the defense in the Grand Siege. His success received immediate acclaim: Public thanksgiving ceremonies were performed in his honor in Rome and as far away as in England, and he was offered a cardinal's hat. He refused and returned to Malta, finally reconciled to remaining on the island he had defended nail and tooth. Six months after the siege, he laid the foundation stone of the fortified citadel that would become the capital and bear his name.[27]

Jean de Valette's nemesis was Turgut Reis, known to Europeans as Dragut, or Dorgut. Born in Anatolia of peasant stock (according to some sources, of a Greek mother) he took to the seas and joined the corsairs, one of the few options for improving one's lot open to those of his social standing. He rose rapidly within their ranks, serving as lieutenant of the legendary Hayrettin Barbarossa. At Barbarossa's death in 1546, he became the undisputed head of the Barbary corsairs, at a time when privateering was a flourishing business. The sultan welcomed acclaimed corsairs recognized for their personal valor but lacking the privileges of high birth into the army. Under the banner of Süleyman the Magnificent, Turgut Reis led the victorious campaign against Tripoli and, as reward, was named governor of that city. By the time of the Grand Siege, he was an aging man (either seventy or eighty, according to different accounts), but nonetheless participated as a consultant, per order of the sultan, on all vital matters. Not shying from personal engagement in battle, he was mortally wounded in combat, and four warships escorted his body back to Tripoli.[28]

The siege of Malta was not only the final episode in Turgut Reis's personal epic, but also the climax of a series of clashes over strategic strongholds in the Mediterranean. The phase that culminated in the Grand Siege began when Barbarossa gained Tunisia for the Ottomans in 1534, seizing it from the local Hafsid dynasty. Emperor Charles V, concerned that Malta and Sicily were now within easy raiding distance of an Ottoman base, dispatched a fleet of Spanish, Italian, and German ships to Tunisia and conquered the twin fortresses of La Goletta that guarded its harbor, occupying the city on 14 July 1535.

To this event we owe the earliest map of Tunisia or, more precisely, of the area surrounding the harbor, issued the very same year. Agostino Musi (or Agostino Veneziano), a Venetian engraver who flourished in Rome around 1530, published a print commemorating the event (Fig. 5).[29] This early example of a news-map clearly announces a debt to the maritime tradition of portolans and *isolarii*. The coastline is again carefully rendered. The drawing takes great care to indicate names and courses of streams, the topography, and the locations and names of towns, although they are illustrated by little more than symbolic sketches. The long inscription in the cartouche on the left provides punctilious information about the fertility of the hills and the location of gardens; about the ruins of Carthage where the Christians had encamped; and about the navigability of the ports. The map's intimate knowledge of the land evidently came from detailed eyewitness reports and sketches as opposed to generic travelers' accounts that often resulted in imaginary reconstructions. The cartouche on the right reinforces the impression of accuracy by incorporating, in addition to the year of publication and the

Fig. 6: Antonio Salamanca, Algeri, 1541, Private Collection

author's initials, a compass and scale. The prominent depiction of the survey instruments, as in the whale-shaped Lafreri map of Malta, staked a claim for dimensional precision. In the case of a print that depicted a historical event, however, the implicit guarantee of truthfulness extended to the entire image, including the episode that was illustrated. The professed geographical reliability of a map enhanced its historical credibility as well as its allure for demanding consumers. Increasingly dissatisfied with the fantastic portrayals of faraway lands based on travelers' tales, consumers required reliable news that could faithfully be found in such an accurately delineated map.

Inflamed by the Tunisian success of 1535, Charles V turned his attention to Algiers, hoping to seize it from the Ottomans as well and break their chain of control across North Africa. In 1541, he attacked the city. This time, however, the fiery defense of Barbarossa and Turgut Reis, together with a gale that wreaked havoc on his ships, turned the emperor's campaign into a disaster. On board of one of the ships that made it back to Italy was an exceptional eyewitness: Cornelisz Anthonisz, a Dutchman who later became famous for a spectacular bird's-eye view of Amsterdam.[30] Anthonisz brought back from the expedition a drawing of Algiers that Antonio Salamanca, predecessor and eventual partner of Lafreri, adapted, engraved, printed, and circulated with a journalist's cagey timing (Fig. 6).[31]

There are several differences between the Algiers print and the Tunisia view made six years earlier. In the former, the city and its fortifications figure much more prominently. The buildings sport the pointy roofs and chimney tops that belong more to the urban environment familiar to its Dutch author than to a North African city. But the circuit of walls with its bastions and the fortified citadel, always the most distinguishing feature of a city, are meticulously recorded. On the other hand, the Algiers view contains neither scale nor compass in its iconography. It also lacks the conscientious labeling of localities and the detailed information of the Tunisia view about, for example, the fertility of the land or the usefulness of ports. The Algiers map was based on the sketch Anthonisz made on board a ship that, given the catastrophic outcome of the campaign, might not even have landed. There had been no opportunity to survey the land or gather local knowledge, and the print made no claim to such familiarity with the area shown.

The general treatment and composition of the Tunisia and Algiers views, however, are very similar. This is not altogether surprising, because Agostino Musi was the main engraver of the Salamanca shop, a meeting point for geographers. The Tunisia print probably emerged from the same shop that produced the Algiers view.[32] Both prints foreground the sea adorned with ships and show the formation and encampment of the Christian armies on the right; both place the main subject at the center of an expanse of land that frames and surrounds it; and both have prominently labeled cardinal points, written out in full at the center of each of the four sides of the map. Expressed more succinctly, both prints are oriented the same way, south being at the top of the sheet.[33]

Before the conventions of modern cartography that dictated the top of a chart as north, medieval maps placed east at the top of the sheet out of respect for the Holy Land (hence the term 'orientation'). By the sixteenth century, however, maps were oriented according to the mapmaker's convenience and generally with respect to his position *vis-à-vis* the region he charted. Thus, for example, a view of Rome produced in northern Europe would have south at the top of the sheet, the direction that the northern European would face if bound for the Eternal City. Locally produced charts of Rome usually had east at the top, not because of Christian symbolism but because the draughtsman faced east when customarily sketching the city from atop the Janiculum Hill, a high vantage point lying to the west of the city. Coastal cities of the Levant were also illustrated in maps with east at the top: The symbolic value was an added bonus, but the main reason for this orientation was because these cities were frequently portrayed as if seen from an approaching ship. For the same reason, views of North African cities, such as those of Tunisia and Algiers, often had south at the top of the chart.

Salamanca's engraved view of Algiers and its surroundings conflated two conventions. The city was depicted as if seen from aboard an approaching ship and Algiers was conveniently raised on an inclined plane for the draughtsman to see. The rest of the image was constructed as if seen from a cartographer standing somewhere between Italy and Spain. The print reproduces the imaginary vision of a mapmaker who looks down, that is, southwards, to see everything between him and Algiers on the North African coast. At the bottom of the print are the regions nearest his feet, southern Italy and Spain; the Mediterranean is at the center, and Algiers at the top. Italy and Spain were included at the expense of a heavy geographic distortion. Clearly both places were dear to heart of the publisher, as Salamanca was originally from Spain and worked in Italy. More to the point, the two countries had contributed a great number of ships and troops to the venture against Algiers. The exaggerated proximity of the North African city to Europe also heightened a sense of danger surrounding the Ottoman base, fueled by the inscription that invited viewers to 'note the location of Algiers with respect to Italy and Spain', while boldly assuring them that the image was 'truthful in its every part and proportion'.[34]

The maps of Tunisia and Algiers would enjoy lasting visibility by being included, three decades later, in a famous collection of city views, the *Civitates Orbis Terrarum*. Published in six volumes in Cologne between 1572 and 1617 by Georg Braun and Hans Hogenberg, the collection was highly successful and reprinted several times over the following two centuries.[35] The view of Tunisia in the collection was not the early specimen authored by Agostino Musi, but a map that modified Musi's composition to illustrate the city's recapture by the Ottomans in 1574. Titled 'True description of Tunisia and its fortresses, shown as they are being attacked by the Turks', this pictorially more enticing version was produced by Mario Cartaro, a leading Roman engraver who simplified the coastal profile but emphasized the star-shaped plans of the two fortresses by using a high angle of vision.[36] The view of Algiers in *Civitates Orbis Terrarum* was based on the Salamanca print, but Braun and Hogenberg altered it by making the city look less northern European and eliminating the depictions of Italy and Spain; distortions that perhaps could no longer pass muster. They added, however, gigantic flags emblazoned with the crescent waving from the fortifications, and preserved the sense of alarm in the Salamanca print by identifying the image as that of 'Algiers, a most powerful Ottoman city situated right in front of Spain'.[37] An ominous inscription running around the left edge of the bay informed viewers that here was the site where Charles V had been routed.

In the years following this debacle, the clashes intensified. In 1550, Turgut Reis transformed Jerba, a small island off the Tunisian coast, into his base. He meant to launch an attack on Tripoli from there, but had to postpone his plans. Jean de Valette, headquartered in Tripoli, spread the alarm further, and the Europeans launched a preemptive strike. In April 1551, Turgut found himself outnumbered and cornered in the sandbars between Jerba and the mainland by a fleet led by the Genoese naval commander Andrea Doria, who was seeking personal revenge: Years earlier he had been captured and enslaved on one of the corsairs' galleys before being ransomed by his compatriots. But the fight was personal for Turgut Reis as well: In 1540 he had fallen into an ambush led by Andrea Doria's father, Giannettino, and had ended up rowing on a Christian galley for three years before Barbarossa led his ships toward Genoa and threatened to bombard the city if his lieutenant was not handed back.

It must have been a desperate determination not to succumb again especially not to the young son of his first captor that spurred Turgut Reis to perform the remarkable feat of digging a canal out of the salt-flats and leading his ships to the safety of the high seas. He immediately headed for the court of Sultan Süleyman and, seeking swift vindication, persuaded the sultan to attack Tripoli and loot Malta, always a coveted prize. In August of 1551, Turgut Reis, together with Sinan Pasha, the sultan's general, furiously attacked Tripoli and ousted the Knights of Malta. Barely escaping capture, Jean de Valette fled to Malta, entrenching himself in what he could still defend. Next, the Ottomans headed for Malta but were less fortunate with the island. Perhaps the corsair's need for vengeance had been appeased with the conquest of Tripoli, of which he was made governor and later pasha. Or perhaps differences arose between him and Sinan Pasha, who was neither a mariner nor a man of war but the brother of the grand vizier. Whatever the reason, the Ottomans soon gave up their attempt to take Malta; the Europeans were relieved. Most probably, the elegant whale-shaped map of Malta produced by Lafreri in thanksgiving found many buyers.

In the meantime, Andrea Doria and his army settled in Jerba, built a fortress that surrounded the fort which the Hafsids had razed the century before, and issued a print to commemorate the feat (Fig. 7). The image shows a star-shaped fortress with four bastions, each dedicated to one of

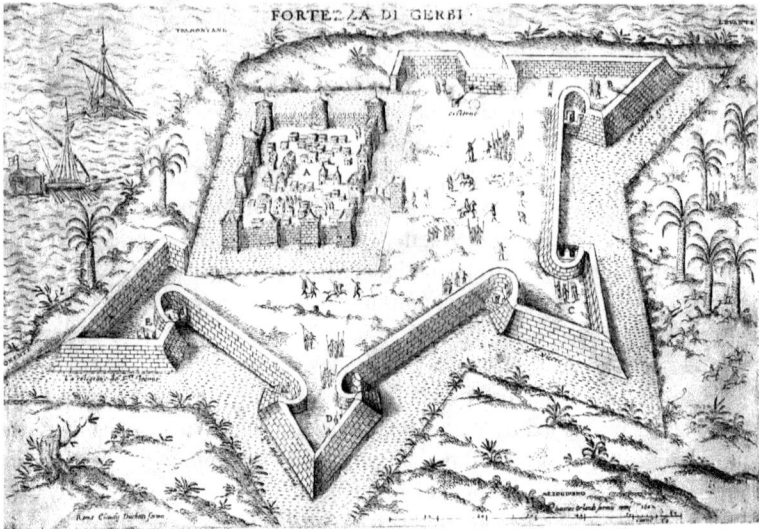

Fig. 7: Claudio Duchetti, Giovanni Orlandi, Fortezza di Gerbi *(Fortress of Jerba), early 1550s/1602, Biblioteca Apostolica Vaticana, St.Barb.X.I.80, Pl.20.*

the main participants in the campaign and with their names inscribed accordingly. The first two bastions on the bottom are dedicated to the Order of the Knights of Malta and to Andrea Doria.[38] Giovanni Orlandi signed the print reproduced here, reissuing a print by Claudio Duchetti (whose signature is on the left): Lafreri's nephew, who took over the print shop after his uncle's death in 1577, republished several of the existing plates with his imprint.[39] The numerous editions testify to the persistent interest in the image that originally must have been engraved in the early 1550s, shortly after the Europeans occupied Jerba, as suggested by the inclusion of the names of the military protagonists assigned to the bastions.

In 1553, around the time the original plate was produced, the Salamanca and Lafreri shops merged, following a period of exchanges and borrowings.[40] The partnership notwithstanding, the orientation of the view of Jerba is different from those of Tunisia and Algiers. The fortress is seen from the land beyond it, and the sea crowns the composition. The map is oriented with northeast at the top of the chart. If views were oriented as if seen by the mapmaker, the author of the sketch on which the map was based did not see the fortress from a warship, but through the eyes of

Fig. 8: Anonymous, Jerba, *1560(?),*
Gabinetto Nazionale delle Stampe, Rome.

someone who, at least temporarily, was on the island. He was probably part of the garrison left to man the fortress, a group represented in the image by the figures that mill about and take part in military exercises, or hunt outside the fort. The picture is one of respite from war, during which the anonymous sketch-artist had the leisure to produce a measured survey of the fortifications. The taut geometry of the fortress that dominates the image suggests that perhaps he was the resident military engineer. His interest in the infrastructure is evident in the two small polygons at the top, labeled 'cisterns', which must have been built together with the fort.[41]

It is not clear exactly how long the European occupation of Jerba lasted, but there was barely enough time to complete the fortress and send a picture back to make those at home proud. Turgut Reis soon re-conquered the island: A plaque of 1557 commemorates his restoration of the Burdj-al-Kabir, the old Hafsid fortress also portrayed in the map, reasserting the Muslim imprint on Jerba. But Jean de Valette did not resign himself to yet another loss. He pressured Philip II, son and successor of the deceased Charles V, to organize an expedition to repossess Jerba, as a prelude to an attack against Tripoli that would reclaim his old headquarters. By 1559, a large fleet had been assembled in Malta and in February of the following year it headed for Jerba, which was recaptured on 7 March 1560. An *avviso* on the 29th of that month made public the news dispatched to the Grand Master and embellished it with a print of the fortress, which was recycled to illustrate a more recent but in the eyes of Europeans equally felicitous event.[42]

Eventually, a new map was engraved of the otherwise unremarkable cluster of dunes, specifically related to the battle of 1560. This time, the entire island of Jerba was depicted with the fortress reduced to a small rough plan (Fig. 8). The new map shows the relationship of the island to the mainland and the sandbars surrounding it. Olive groves, the remnants of old fortifications and lookout towers, and the names of towns and quarters are provided. Like the print of the fortress, the map of Jerba is scaled and oriented with north at the top, viewed from a point on the island beyond the fort, and sketched by someone able to provide detailed local information. There is no date, but the caption identifies the image as 'Drawing of the island of *Gerbi,* with the sandbar that defends it from the flooding of the sea, and of the fortress built by the Christians. Five thousand brave soldiers have remained there to defend the island, with good provisions of food and ammunition that, with the help of God, will be sufficient to repel the attacks of the Turkish army'.[43]

In early May, Turgut Reis launched an attack that caught the Christians off guard and sunk most of their ships before they had time to recover. What was left of the once mighty fleet returned to the mainland, abandoning the besieged fort and its garrison to their fate. After Turgut Reis discovered and blocked the water sources that fed the cisterns of the fortress (perhaps those identified in the earlier print), the garrison surrendered, on 30 June. In the new map of Jerba, the two fleets (identified by the crosses and the crescents on their flags) confront each other, and several Christian ships are sinking. The siege was still underway and the inscription prayed for victory. The drawing must thus have been produced between early May and the end of June of 1560 and, given time for engraving, it was published about a month later.

Around the same time another print was published, this one in Venice: the earliest known map of Tripoli, shown surrounded by numerous European ships bombarding the city whose crescent-bearing flags flutter from its fortifications (Fig. 9).[44] Like the prints of Jerba, the city is viewed from the mainland, a characteristic that seems to distinguish maps produced by 'locals'. Although the map does not include a scale, it is clearly based on a survey, which must have been carried out before Turgut Reis conquered Tripoli in 1551. The walls are individually reproduced, with each tract accompanied by a precise indication of its length, and the

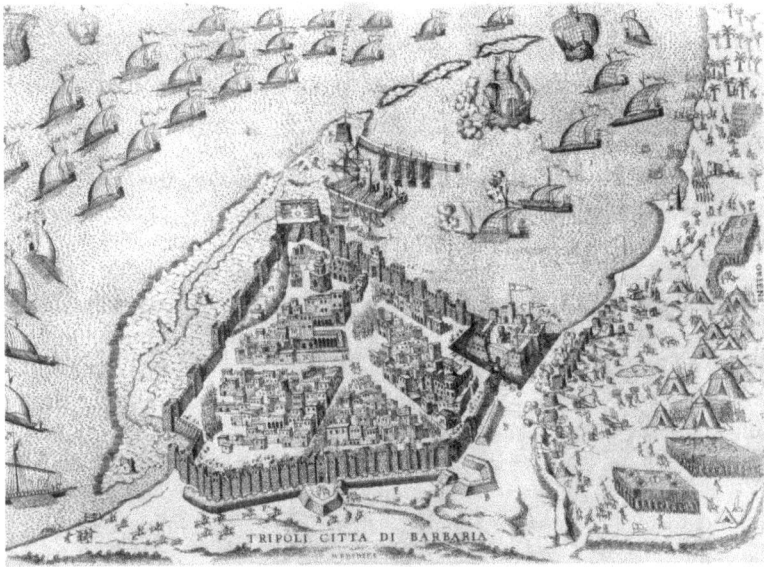

Fig. 9: Anonymous, Tripoli, *1560(?),*
Gabinetto Nazionale delle Stampe, Rome

sandbars and sea canals lying to the west of the city are diligently described.[45] Like the Jerba map of the same year, it conveys not only geographical knowledge but seeks to photograph, as it were, a historical
moment, unfolding in the thick of battle. Smoke from the ships and the
land armies billows up, horsemen ride frantically about, and the cannons
on the ramparts respond to enemy fire.

And yet the event is entirely imaginary. The Christian fleet, ravaged
by the Ottomans off the coast of Jerba, never made it to Tripoli. An
overly eager publisher produced the map to get ahead of his competition and have a print ready to sell as soon as the expected news of the
Christian victory should arrive. A well-informed inscription accompanied the chart, identifying the city as Tripoli of Barbaria and providing
a brief history of its possession by both Europeans and Ottomans,
which included the fact that it was restored and fortified by Dragut
Rays (Turgut Reis), 'the famous corsair'. It mentioned that the campaign had been organized on recommendation of the Grand Master of
the Knights of Malta and concluded with the remark that it even enjoyed the support of certain 'Arab lords' who had given their sons as
hostages to prove their good faith.

The attack not having occurred, the map became embarrassing and potentially incendiary. Contemporary accounts relate that the Venetian ambassador to the sultan's court, having obtained a print, showed it to the Florentine ambassadors and then burned it to do them a favor: Florence was technically at peace with the Porte but, unbeknownst to the Ottomans, had contributed to the expedition; it now feared repercussions if the print listing the Florentines as participants in the inscription and picturing the ships emblazoned not with generic crosses but with the easily recognizable coats of arms of each army should fall into the Sultan's hands.[46] The Venetians themselves had reason to worry about their diplomatic relations with the Ottomans, even if they were not represented in the print. For if the map was indeed published in Venice, the Venetians seemed remarkably knowledgeable about the enterprise. The great rarity of the original print containing the inscription might have been due, as has been suggested, to the Florentines and Venetians destroying as many copies as they could lay their hands on.[47] Most of the surviving prints come from what was now the Salamanca–Lafreri print-selling venture in Rome, who stripped it of the compromising inscription and reissued the map.[48]

The disasters of ineptitude represented in the prints of Jerba and Tripoli are testimony of a low period for the European military forces. The Ottomans seemed unstoppable, and the myth of their invincibility grew. When a few years later, in 1565, they headed for Malta once again, this time with a better-prepared fleet that had taken several months to assemble, the expedition threw Europe into panic and initiated the frenzied production of a rapid succession of news-maps. The caption 'The Turkish army retreats', appended to the Ottoman fleet in the map of Malta that shows the final phases of the Grand Siege, exploded the myth, and Europe exhaled a collective sigh of relief.

***

The circulation of prints that tracked the course of the war satisfied anxious curiosity and mitigated the Europeans' fears by providing a constant supply of visual information. But what these maps reveal for us, I suggest, is the possibility of tracing a more articulate outline of the web of exchanges linking the peoples of the eastern and western Mediterranean, more intricate than stale dichotomies currently allow. The analyses founded on a critique of Orientalism have raised a conceptual wall between polarized notions of 'East' and 'West' construed as opposite and mutually exclusive. In the ambit of cartography, this has encouraged the interpretation that the mapping impulse of Renaissance Europe expressed the effort to take intellectual and visual stock of the world as a prelude to a material domination of that world.[49] This assumption, however, projects backwards a discourse that evolved almost two centuries later. The notions of European primacy formulated to justify the colonial enterprise, starting at the beginning of the eighteenth century, did not belong to the Renaissance. When retroactively applied, these conceptions have raised an artificial barrier across the Mediterranean, a barrier that has had the paradoxical effect of blinding historians to the contribution of its eastern component to the formation of Renaissance society.[50] As a result, mainstream historiography of the fifteenth to seventeenth centuries has been greatly impoverished. There is recent evidence of change, as scholars investigate individual cases in specific fields. Two eminent examples are the study of art and architecture in Venice, traditionally a cultural as well as commercial go-between for the Eastern Mediterranean, and Islamic Spain. But if we are to achieve a fuller understanding of early modern society, it will be necessary to free ourselves from anachronistic perceptions that force onto that period a conceptual division between cultures of the Mediterranean, a division that emerged only at a later stage.

The great waterway had united peoples for millennia. In the sixteenth century, trade, if anything, intensified and cultural exchange ran parallel to commercial transactions. Books, prints, and ideas traveled on ships together with foodstuffs and luxury goods. A cultural convergence around fundamental texts, issues, and themes emerged on multiple shores. In this essay I have only considered European sources for a field and period that coincide with my specialty. Furthermore, I have focused on a handful of engravers and publishers that dominated the print market of the period. A sustained collaborative effort among scholars working on various localities will be needed to trace a history encompassing many more facets of Mediterranean exchange. Equally necessary are interpretations based on close examinations of objects, which would provide hard evidence of a reality more vivid than schematic interpretations would have us believe. A significant example that has recently been pointed out is linked to the rediscovery of Ptolemy's *Geographia* and the roots of modern cartography. Much has been made of how the ancient text's rational way of measuring and reporting contributed to the progress of a scientific and enlightened mentality in Europe. It is not widely acknowledged that elaborate copies of Ptolemy's text produced in Italy were dedicated to Sultan Mehmet II by a publisher who hoped to curry favor with a well-known patron of geographical studies, a ruler who already owned Latin copies of the *Geographia* and was sponsoring research into the Arabic versions.[51]

The maps examined here provide further evidence. They point to a relationship between Europeans and Ottomans that was certainly beset with conflict, but also marked by a realistic perception of the potential and might of the adversary. That is not to say that this awareness was not tainted by misrepresentations. It has been pointed out repeatedly that European maps intentionally display distortions, such as characterizing cities as Christian even when rule had long since passed to the Ottomans – Jerusalem being a central case in point. War propaganda and journalistic distortions made to fit specific agendas are not recent inventions. But diplomatic relations or temporary alliances advantageous to both parties, as exemplified by the episodes of the Florentine and Venetian ambassadors, and the 'Arab lords', accompanied the clashes that were motivated by economic reasons and sometimes colored by personal vendettas, but not perceived as the inevitable domination of a superior culture over another. Nor, by any stretch of the imagination, did Europeans think of their task as a civilizing mission, as they would in subsequent centuries to justify, in their minds, ruthless exploitation. Rather, these maps convey, together with the mixture of fear and fascination evoked by the opponent, the intellectual and cultural recognition that this very same opponent was readily accorded. Prints, as we saw, were engraved to document Ottoman victories as well as to commemorate European ones. The inscription recording the meritorious reconstruction of Tripoli by Turgut Reis paid homage to his achievements, even while praying for victory against him. One last image confirms the point. It is not a map in a strict geographical sense, but an image contained in the collections of these charts, pointing to the mental landscape of its makers. Compiled in Rome in 1557 by Lafreri and republished in numerous editions, the print illustrates the formation of the Ottoman military on the battlefield and is entitled, with unmistakable admiration that verges on awe, '*Il meraviglioso ordine del gran esercito Turchesco*', 'The wonderful array of the great Turkish army.'[52]

Geographic Theatres, Port Landscapes and Architecture in the Eastern Mediterranean: Salonica, Alexandria, İzmir

Cristina Pallini

An Architect's Viewpoint

The evolution of any single city brings to light the close links between its history and architecture, an evolution in which design often expresses more than merely a stereotyped conception of style, but rather responds to structural needs. A study of Salonica, Alexandria and İzmir during the nineteenth and early twentieth centuries clearly shows the relationship between architecture and a rapidly changing social order. After 1850, the adoption of the steam engine for sea and land transport redefined the geography of trade in the Eastern Mediterranean, requiring the reconstruction of port areas connected to overland routes.[1] Communities and colonies,[2] each to some extent engaged in this commercial revolution, experienced a phase of cultural transition, some of them consolidating the common ground of a shared ethnic origin or religious creed, to eventually build their own historical and political discourse.

Most public buildings of this period provide different interpretations of modernity and expression of cultural identity. Promoting the cohesion of the social fabric to which entrepreneurs were giving an economic drive schools, hospitals and buildings as well as theaters, boulevards, and public squares; all focal points of social life, can well be considered dominating themes that fulfill a fundamental urban role while at the same time allowing an eclectic architecture to showcase its collective meaning. The architecture produced in the 1920s and 1930s within the framework of a comprehensive town planning scheme often aimed at a strong evocative effect, treating single buildings or entire parts of the city as scenes and as a concentration of new symbols embodying a future collective projection. This required a new kind of architectural language that, whether inspired by the 'modern movement' or not, was in stark contrast to the pluralist eclecticism of the past, thus reflecting the profound crisis that afflicted cosmopolitan societies. Although each city showed this to a different extent, communities were rapidly degenerating into little more than groups of mutually hostile national, a turning-point which became dramatically clear in Salonica and İzmir, two cities that experienced major problems of reconstruction, of eradication, dispossession and the re-settlement of peoples.

This paper offers a contribution to mapping the Eastern Mediterranean from a project-oriented viewpoint, looking at Salonica, Alexandria and İzmir on various levels. Although important, a theoretical framework aimed at reconceptualizing history with the support of geography is not the overriding issue. While history and the geographic context can partly explain the problems posed by the evolution/revolution of cities so vulnerable to external events, cross-disciplinary research and a comparative approach bring to light important patterns in the complex settlement processes that have shaped Eastern Mediterranean ports.

Alexandrie entre deux mondes,[3] *Colonial Bridgehead*,[4] and *City of Memory*[5] are the titles of three important works on the legendary history of nineteenth and twentieth-century Alexandria, 'a transitory model of conviviality'.[6] Recent studies on Ottoman İzmir confirm the multicultural character of this 'forgotten city',[7] defined as a 'palimpsest of culture',[8] or as the 'metropolis of the Asia Minor Greeks',[9] recalling the expression 'infidel Smyrna', an indication of the marked presence of Christians of both local and foreign origin. Salonica, described by a Greek historian as a 'bazaarcity'[10] until 1944, was also known as the 'Jerusalem of the Balkans' for its predominantly Jewish population[11] and as the city fought over by Turks, Greeks, Bulgarians and Serbians during the Balkan Wars of 1912–13,[12] more recently described elsewhere as a 'city of ghosts'.[13] Are all these literary expressions merely aimed at reviving the memories of a vanished world? Can such anthropological conditions, resulting from centuries of cultural cohabitation and exchange, but also from a series of clashes, be explored through historical research alone? Over the past 20 years a number of substantial monographs have appeared on each of the three cities, while the political, social and economic life of Ottoman ports have provided a common source of interest for scholars from many disciplines. How socially or culturally definable groups moved from one port to another is a subject of growing interest at the present time. I posit that dominating themes, addressing as they did the collective purpose of architecture, may provide some useful insights into these complex societies; they may indicate how certain values (foreign/local, innovation/tradition, non-clerical/religious identity) were discarded or exalted within a framework of cultural competition, compromise, or even conflict. The location of these buildings, revealing the urban ethnic topography and its focal points of economic and social life, ensured visibility for each ethnic and social component of the port-city. Through this space-based form of pluralism, society manifested its nature, its mode of operation and its values much more openly than it did in Europe.[14]

Despite recent changes Salonica, Alexandria and İzmir are still characterized by buildings and districts that bear witness both to their celebrated cosmopolitanism and to its subsequent disappearance or eradication. We may therefore consider these architectural features forming 'books of stone'. In doing so, I have followed the example of E. M. Forster who, when writing a guidebook of Alexandria around 1915, lead the reader through eight urban sections, evoking step by step both topography and ancient life of the metropolis of the Ptolemies, to convey 'the magic and the antiquity and the complexity of the city'.[15] Similarly, I will make comparative surveys of Salonica and Alexandria, particularly of two urban areas where most of the former dominating themes are still concentrated. Pursuant to my project-oriented approach, I will then venture to look at the three cities in the longue durée, emphasizing the fact that they were all founded by Alexander the Great and his successors as isthmian ports of the Eastern Mediterranean.[16] Projects conceived on a grand scale in the first half of the nineteenth century identify Macedonia, the Egyptian Delta and the Aegean region of Asia Minor as geographic theaters whose ports form the keystones of a wider infrastructural context. I will then discuss some reconstruction projects by French planners, carried out in Salonica and İzmir in the 1920s, arguing that it was their overall approach and 'picturesque modernity' which laid the basis for the cities of today.

Salonica: From the Eastern Walls to Kalamaria[17]
The wedge-shaped area where the Sheikh Sou Forest approaches the sea today accommodates the International Fair, the Aristotle University, as well as several theaters and museums. Prior to the construction of the university and trade fair buildings, a large necropolis in use since Hellenistic and Roman times and

more recently taken over by Christians, Jews, Muslims and Dönmes,[18] had extended outside the eastern walls. It was perhaps the presence of this sacred space, furrowed by torrents, which led the Serbian geographer Jovan Cvijić to consider Kalamaria (the eastern suburbs) a city in itself.[19] Following what remains of Hospital Street, which once extended from the Kalamaria Gate[20] to Chalkidiki, we cross this wedge-shaped area in search of community institutions, public and military buildings established in quick succession in the 1890s and the early twentieth century. Clearly visible from various viewpoints, these western-inspired structures marked a clean break with the Ottoman city; combining principles of symmetry and regularity, their ornate façades gave a progressive western aura to each ethno-religious group, just as the state buildings expressed in stone the Ottoman government's major reforms.[21]

At the point outside the walls where Agiou Dimitriou crosses Ethnikis Amynis Street, there is a fine view of Salonica extending down a slope, overlooking the Thermaic Gulf with Mount Olympus in the distance. Farther along the walls is the wooded area of the Evangelistria cemeteries, opened in 1875 for the Greek, Bulgarian, Armenian and Protestant communities. Behind them stands the Municipal Hospital, designed around 1902 by the German-trained architect Xénophon Paionìdis, with its majestic lines and rational layout.[22] Continuing along Ethnikis Amynis Street, we come to the headquarters of the Ottoman mounted police, converted after 1922 into the Refugees' Hospital. Farther down on our left, the fake neoclassical façade of the old Faculty of Art stands out among the modern university departments. Originally designed along different lines by the Italian architect Vitaliano Poselli as a college for training officials for the Ottoman Civil Service (1887–88), it was first enlarged in 1908 and again altered before 1930 to house the newly founded Aristotle University. The busy Sintrivaniou Square brings us to the end of Egnatia Street which, despite its modern appearance, is the ancient artery linking the city to its extensive hinterland. After a short walk between the International Fair to the right and the Aristotle University to the left, having passed the Palais des Sport, we turn right off Nea Egnatia into Hospital Street.[23] At the first intersection we come to the little church of Agia Fotinì, named after the Greek Orthodox Cathedral of İzmir by refugees who, until the 1960s, lived in huts nearby. Opposite are large barracks built around 1903 close to the Military Hospital (*circa* 1890) and still functioning. Their linear layout, conceived by Vitaliano Poselli, included the Boulevard de l'Armée and a parade ground overlooking the sea, providing an ideal setting for drilling the reformed army while expressing the power and modernity of the state. Our walk continues to the Hospital for Infectious Diseases, formerly the Italian Regina Margherita Hospital (1894–1903), which consists of a series of pavilions set in a garden. Its late-neoclassical main building is the work of the Milan-trained architect Piero Arrigoni. The finest building on Hospital Street, however, is the Papafeio Orphanage, which is best reached by turning right into Serron Street. From there, a path crosses a luxuriant park to a monumental stairway leading up to an Ionic portico, the entrance to the 'palace of the orphans',[24] still a home for boys from Greece and from the Balkan countries who receive a sound technical and musical education. Endowed by a Greek merchant from Salonica who had made his fortune in Alexandria, İzmir and Malta, the orphanage was built to plans drawn up by Xénophon Paionìdis (1894–1903), who here expressed the political ambitions of the Greek community by adopting the same architectural language as that used by his colleagues for public and private buildings in Athens. From there, along Serron Street, we come to a former Bulgarian church (1907). At the intersection with Papanastasiou Street is the Theagenio Hospital designed in 1960 by the Greek 'pioneer of modern architecture', Patroclos Karantinos, to replace the old Greek Hospital by Ernst Ziller (1892). A massive Technical School (1950–52) occupies the adjacent block, taking the place of a model Jewish quarter built after the fire of 1890. On the same side of the street stands the Historical Archive of Macedonia, with its elegant façade of Corinthian columns, built in 1907 as a hospital for the Russian community. Finally, farther along Papanastasiou Street, we reach the Ippokrateio Hospital constructed for the Jewish community and funded by the Hirsch family, leading industrialists and financiers who undertook railway construction in the Balkans. Covering a wide area, this complex was designed by Piero Arrigoni and embodied the latest example of French hospital engineering (1904–08). Other Jewish institutions formerly lay along Fleming Street which leads away from the hospital's main entrance: the Matanoth Laevionim Soup Kitchen (1901), the Gattegno private school (1928), the Villa Ida (1886–90), and the Beth Saul Synagogue (1898), which in 1917 became the city's main synagogue. These last two buildings, designed by Vitaliano Poselli for a prominent Jewish family, no longer exist, having been replaced by the Umberto I School (1933) and by the building of the Italian state monopoly of the tobacco industry (early 1960s)

Alexandria: Chatby, Citadel of Education in the 'Region of the Dead' [25]

Situated between the historic center and the eastern quarters (Ramleh), Chatby is still marked by a large number of schools and hospitals. A terminus for routes arriving from Ramleh, Aboukir, Rosetta and Cairo, Chatby was formerly a vast suburban area of low hills and shallow depressions where the lazzaretto, slaughter house, municipal stores and stables stood side by side with indigenous dwellings, tanneries, garbage heaps and ancient ruins. In the 1920s, this was still a world in itself where every morning at dawn carts full of agricultural produce arrived from the Nile Delta.[26] But by the 1930s the picture had changed, and Chatby became the 'citadel of education' where the Italians chose a panoramic location for their grand Littorie School, close to the British and Greek schools, the college of the Frères, and the French Lycée.

Partly following E. M. Forster's path, our survey starts along the tramway line at Chatby Station. Opposite the station is the still-functioning Italian retirement home (1927). On one side of the tramway line stands Alexandria University (with its Faculties of Law, Philosophy, Economy and Commerce, Tourism and Hotel Management) and, on the other, the spacious complex of the Greek community, a number of schools and welfare institutions established between 1906 and 1909 by prominent notables to cater for a growing wave of immigrants. Their conversion to a Greek University has recently been under study.[27] All built to plans by the Greek engineer George Lezinas in collaboration with Ambrogio Cassese, the Salvago Professional School, the Benaki Girls' Orphanage and the Zervudachi Primary Schools are compact buildings facing one another, with courtyards and neoclassical façades combining to form a harmonious image of Greece as the motherland.[28] The adjacent Orwa el Woska School provides an example of Islamic revival: although of a modern type, its ornate shell includes architectural details such as recessed profiles and crenellations. On our way to Chatby-les-Baines Station lies 'the region of the dead',[29] a large rectangular site enclosing the separate graveyards of all ethno-religious groups that lived in Alexandria in the nineteenth and twentieth centuries. Near the station stands the College of the Frères, one of the better works of modern European architecture in Egypt.[30] Built between 1926 and 1928 to plans by the French art-deco masters Léon Azéma, Max Edrei and Jacques Hardy, the college is a huge brick building around a large courtyard; its monumental façade features a central dome and a two-storey portico overlooking the playing fields. Right opposite, across the tramway line, is a lycée in the French classical-revival style, sponsored by the French government in 1908 to promote non-clerical public education. The road alongside the Lycée Français is our third destination. On the right stands the boarding school of the Sisters of Charity, a geometric building designed by the Alexandrian architect Ferdinand Debbane (1930s). Further down the street come the Faculty of Science and the Faculty of Agriculture; the one built on a former sports ground of the Italian workmen's club, the other on the land formerly occupied by the Italian Littorie School buildings. Opposite is the El-Nasr Language School, once the English Girls' College, one of the cornerstones of the British-controlled educational system. These two latter complexes provide examples of the interplay between architecture and ideology in Alexandria of the 1930s. Designed by Clemente Busiri Vici for the Fasci Italiani all'Estero,[31] as an 'ivory castle in the midst of a park', the Italian Littorie School fulfilled several functions,[32] its plain symmetrical blocks shaping a monumental modern environment intended to symbolize Italy as a progressive country. In designing the English Girls' College, the London architect George Grey Wornum hovered between classical minimalism and vernacular references, evoking the spatial disposition of a Spanish-American house (where the patio furnishes a central focus for indoor and outdoor activities). Its comfortable atmosphere was intended to promote trust within the Anglo-Egyptian community at a time when the British hold on Egypt was becoming strained due to rising nationalist feelings. On Horreya Street we have the former Greek Hospital and the Faculty of Engineering, two imposing structures, each on its hilltop one facing the other. The Greek hospital built in the 1930s is perhaps the last attempt to stress the importance of Alexandria in the Greek world.[33] While its layout follows modern scientific criteria, details such as the stylized classical entrance and the neo-Byzantine arcade surrounding the main courtyard confer a Greek identity on the building. The Faculty of Engineering completed before the revolution of 1952 is a neo-pharaonic modern structure whose monumental entrance, designed by the Egyptian architect Kamal Ismail, recalls the pylons of Phylae and gateways of Karnak, a shared historical heritage expressing the strongest possible concept of national style as the basis for social cohesion.

The last stage in our itinerary brings us to the hospitals surrounding the El Manara Muslim cemetery. There, in addition to the Greek Hospital, we have the pompous Medical Research Institute, the German-designed Al Mouassat Hospital (1936), the neo-Romanesque Italian Hospital (Giacomo Alessandro Loria, 1921–23), the austere Anglo-Swiss Hospital (Aldo Marelli, 1908) and the Hospital for Infectious Diseases (1930–32) in a simplified art-deco style. The Italian Hospital is of special interest. Sponsored by the Italian Royal Family, the Ministry of Foreign Affairs, the Italian Charity Society as well as notable members of the community, it was intended to 'bear comparison with modern hospitals in Europe and Overseas'.[34] The design consisted of a series of blocks laid out in a straight line, to facilitate implementation at different stages and an efficient medical service in the wards; the hospital was fitted out with the most modern equipment. For the main building, which can be entered from the garden, two alternative styles were proposed: a neo-Renaissance or a neo-Romanesque façade, the former reflecting the preference of the municipality, the latter that of the Italian community.

Comprendre l'éclectisme[35]

As we have seen, Salonica is a city whose ancient cemeteries have been entirely erased, a city whose eastern periphery reveals a rich inventory of types clearly distinguishable from modern apartment blocks. While the buildings embody modern European engineering criteria, their prominence and monumental scale today still play an important part in the urban scene. These are public buildings whose eventful histories have proved their versatility, resisting any rigid functional classification. In Alexandria we have visited the 'region of the dead' where citizenship had been granted to various religious creeds, exemplified by the many schools and hospitals nearby, all exceptional in their size, their diversity of layout, styles and figurative identities. Some of the buildings express a tendency to drama- tize architecture by the creation of strong evocative effects, whether re- lated to the past or to fresh sources of formal inspiration. These parallel inventories of dominating themes illustrate the lines along which eclectic architecture developed from the last decades of the nineteenth century until 1950, making the most of artistic, technical and scientific know-how of architects, engineers, and contractors, all of varied provenances and training. Through its emphasis on this period of architectural culture, a recent book by Jean-Pierre Épron encourages the reader to appreciate eclecticism, as a method of experimental design and as addressing history of architecture as knowledge in evolution. One point is clear: eclectic architecture here has never been confined to relating an appropriate style to the function of a building; rather, it was loaded with symbolic values, particularly in those cases where structures proved essential for the life and visibility of each component of the wider composite society. A school, hospital or orphanage was seldom solely the result of an institutionalized building program. The combination of indoor and outdoor facilities, of functional and collective spaces, often created a sort of microcosm where individuals felt encouraged to strengthen their ties with the community, while appreciating the fact that their identity was also strongly rooted in the composite cultural environment of the city, a rich environment for becoming a citizen of the world. The monumental character of these build- ings was therefore never an end in itself. It is an intriguing exercise to discover, case-by-case, who promoted what building, how the architect in charge achieved balance between his client's demands and his own artistic personality, and why the building won the appreciation of its ultimate users. In considering how public buildings underwent continual change, architecture reveals the constant evolution of communities, as insti- tutionalized bodies, but also as transient groups of an ever-changing basis.

Geographic Theaters, Port Landscapes

A unifying point in considering Salonica, Alexandria and İzmir is the fact that Alexander the Great and his successors founded them all.[36] When marching against the Persian Empire in 334 BC, Alexander visited Mount Pagos where, in a dream, the Nemeses told him to found a city for the Smyrneans scattered among the neighboring villages. Ancient İzmir, destroyed by the Lydians in 589 BC, had occupied the rising ground at the head of a sheltered gulf. The new İzmir lay on the opposite side, partly on the slopes of Mount Pagos and partly on the coastal plain, built after Alexander's death by Antigonus and Lysimachus,[37] around a port accessible from the Anatolian plateau and from Central Asia. Alexandria ad Ægyptum, as the Romans said, marks the northwest corner of the Nile Delta, sufficiently near Egypt to benefit from its riches, sufficiently distant for independence. The port stands where the routes from the Nile and the Sahara oases meet the Maghrib–Syria route, crossing others from Europe to the Red Sea and on to Arabia, India and the Far East. It is well-known that Alexander himself chose this location in 332 BC, having observed the potential advantages of a small port sheltered by an island, halfway along a narrow stretch of coast between the Mediterranean and a huge coastal lake. Cassander who had assumed control of Macedonia after Alexander's death founded Salonica around 315 BC. To form the city, inhabitants of small towns and villages at the head of the Thermaic Gulf were relocated to a strategic site where the foothills of Mount Chortiatis reach the sea and the wide coastal plain, and where the southernmost route from the Adriatic Sea across the Balkan peninsula meets the north–south corridor from the great plains of the Danube basin down the Morava–Vardar valleys.

Isthmian ports located along routes connecting the Adriatic to the Black Sea, the Eastern Mediterranean to the Red Sea and the Persian Gulf, favored commercial prosperity and cultural advancement in the eyes of Alexander the Great and his successors. Salonica, Alexandria and İzmir well fitted such roles, each city being the focal point of Macedonia, the Egyptian Delta and the Aegean region of Asia Minor, each situated in a natural corridor extending far inland, followed again and again by migrant peoples, by armies and caravans of merchants on their way from Central Europe to India and the Far East. Laid out in a rectangular pattern, these three cities fully exploited the natural features of their sites, vital elements in their construction since the earliest days. In İzmir, the Golden Street encircled the north-west slopes of Mount Pagos, avoiding the swampy plain for greater safety of the routes from Ephesos and the Anatolian plateau towards the port. In Alexandria, the triumphal Canopic Street followed a depression in the strip of land between the sea and the lake, starting from the point where the Egyptian river system reached the seaports.[38] At Salonica a road, more or less following the course of modern Egnatia Street, ran parallel to the coast between the walled city and the port, channeling routes from all directions.[39] It is clear how these ports, that of Alexandria with the famous Heptastadium,[40] later to become the site of the Turkish town; or the inner harbor of İzmir, which also silted up and accommodated the Bazaar; or that of Salonica, with its elevated position commanding a view over the gulf as far as distant Mount Olympus provided each city with a basic structure on which settlements could develop time and again.

The Landscape as a Theatre is the title of a recent book by the Italian geographer Eugenio Turri.[41] Rather than visualizing landscape as the physical space transformed by man for the sole purpose of living and producing, he views the combination of natural and artificial features as scenery in its broader sense, where both the individual and society play their parts in daily life and in the longue durée. Suggesting that the landscape reflects, like in a mirror, the ultimate sense of a given culture, Turri's metaphor may be associated with Seldmayr's idea of dominating themes as a key to a project-oriented study of Salonica, Alexandria and İzmir.

At different times in the nineteenth century, Macedonia, the Egyptian Delta and the Aegean region of Asia Minor became the scenes of major change, forming an ideal terrain for financiers, geographers and naturalists, but also for engineers, architects and artists, who surveyed the crucially important natural sceneries for the construction of canals, railways and port works. This happened against an international background of the most vital stage in the development of a market economy. The Description of Egypt[42] by the scientists of Napoleon's army is an outstanding example of how the physical space and its many resources were subject to an overall approach, with a view to reviving broad natural highways leading from the Mediterranean towards India and transforming them into avenues of modern communication. The combination of favorable physical features, i.e. seas, rivers, confluences, plains, valleys was, in fact, of fundamental importance for the implementation of two schemes that would have redefined the geography of trade in the Eastern Mediterranean, namely the railway to the Persian Gulf and the overland passage through Egypt, two closely interconnected projects that aroused bitter international rivalry. An all-water route to India had been the object of French ambitions since Napoleon's landing at Alexandria on 2 July 1798, and a number of waterways across the Delta were proposed while the British were organizing the transit from Alexandria to Suez (1834), later on also building a railway (1854–58).[43] A British rival to the French Suez Canal

Canal (1869), the Euphrates Valley Railway, was first conceived in the 1830s[44] and revived again under the aegis of Germany when the occupation of Egypt in 1882 had put an end to British ambitions for alternative routes.[45] Opening the way for a wide range of scenarios, these two projects challenged the role of Alexandria, İzmir and Salonica in the Eastern Mediterranean. After an initial idea to reopen the ancient canals from the Nile to the Red Sea (circa 1799), much keen discussion followed as to whether or not these waterways should reach the port of Alexandria. Similarly, the future of İzmir largely depended on which scheme would be chosen for implementing the Euphrates Valley Railway project: the original idea of a southern connection from the Syrian coast to Basra, or the northern route via Istanbul and Ankara, or else a junction at İzmir using its efficient railway network.[46] What is certain is that both these great schemes entailed transit traffic through Macedonia, thus encouraging projects that led to the construction of the Vardar railway, linking Salonica with the European capitals in 1888.[47]

How far then did the geographic theaters, identified in antiquity, again play a part in the reconstruction of these three ports as epicenters of a wider infrastructural scheme? This question should be borne in mind when comparing the great nineteenth-century projects with their underlying strategic vision in attempting to discover how certain groups (ethno-religious communities, groups of interest, etc.) envisioned their futures based on the actual, and possible, resources of a given territory and geographic location.

In 1841 the French writer and politician Saint-Marc Girardin deemed that a number of ports, including Alexandria, was 'necessary and natural' in view of their positions on world routes. To him, these were intended by nature as 'havens' for trade and cultural exchange for many peoples from near and far, rather than the fortunes of any single people.[48] Whether by coincidence or not, his deterministic observations coincide with the re-founding of Alexandria at the time of Mehmet Ali, the first long-term plan for the Eastern Mediterranean implemented in the first decades of the nineteenth century.[49] The economic and political revival of Ottoman ports throughout the second half of the nineteenth century certainly opened up different perspectives for various groups. One such instance may be noted in the conflicting feelings that inspired the Greeks and Jews of Salonica when the city was at the height of its power at the beginning of the twentieth century: The Greeks anticipated the city's inclusion within the Hellenic Kingdom; the Jews counted on a future international status for the port, in line with the designs of Austria, Bulgaria and Serbia. In 1921, the British writer Henry Charles Woods, an expert on the so-called Eastern Question, believed that Greek control would turn out to be disadvantageous for Salonica and İzmir, as they would become politically separated from the territories of which they had formed an economic part.[50] His comments indicated the arrival of a new era, an era in which Salonica and İzmir would become part of Venizelos' Greece and Atatürk's Turkey respectively, consigning to the past any memories that might still remain of the 'Jerusalem of the Balkans' and of the 'metropolis of the Asia Minor Greeks'.

The 1920s: A Test for French Planners

In August of 1917, only five years after the annexation by Greece, a fire destroyed a large part of the Jewish, Greek and Muslim quarters of T; by 1915, the city had become the seat of a provisional government and a transit camp for the allied troops of the Entente. In September of 1922, a fire reduced the heart of İzmir with its Greek, Armenian and European quarters to ashes, marking the climax of a crisis begun with the allied naval bloc between 1914 and 1918 and continued by the Greco–Turkish war between 1919 and 1922. The compulsory exchange of population required by the Treaty of Lausanne forced 1.3 million Ottoman Christians to cross the Aegean Sea in exchange for half a million Muslims, crowding Salonica and its territory and causing İzmir's economy to decline dramatically.[51] Before the population exchange, proposals had been made to found two new Greek universities, one in Salonica and one in İzmir, to promote a cultural revival of these cities while upgrading the Greek educational system with new centers of scientific and technical learning. The Greek landing at İzmir in 1919 established priority for the Ionian University, which in 1922 was ready to open its doors under the direction of the mathematician Kostantinos Karatheodoris.[52] The Greek defeat in Asia Minor drew attention to the Salonica project, realized in 1924 as part of a wider program for the development of the newly acquired territories.

A well-informed traveler visiting the Eastern Mediterranean in the mid-1920s and landing at the once-thriving ports of Salonica and İzmir would have contemplated the extent of physical destruction, rendered even more desolate and socially unstable as a result of continual migratory movements. After all, this was the time of the end of World War I which had brought about the demise of the Ottoman Empire; and the Greco–Turkish war, culminating in the rise of republican Turkey, had led to the dispersal of some 1.8 million refugees.[53] Our traveler might well have considered these cities as complementary facets of a single tragedy, sharing the view of the French urban historian Pierre Lavedan, who thought that the war that caused so much cruel devastation had posed problems to a city, as a work of architecture, on a scale hitherto unknown.[54]

Harder even than founding a city, the reconstruction of Salonica and İzmir was to become a real challenge for the two French planners Ernest Hébrard (1875–1933) and René Danger (1872–1954). Almost the same age, these members of the *Musée Social* and the *Société Française des Urbanistes* were called upon by both sides of the geo-political scenario to 'recast, as in a melting pot, totally dissimilar elements and create among them some form of unity'.[55]

As a consequence of their new national roles, Salonica had become politically separate from areas for which it had long been the natural outlet, while İzmir had lost its ethnic groups that previously had fulfilled fundamental economic and cultural roles. In each case, Ernest Hébrard and René Danger had to face the immense task of reshaping century-old cities whose futures were literally at stake and, while doing so, decide which local conditions would best encourage their modernization. Both the Greek government and the young Turkish Republic, anxious to make a clean break with the past, regarded the rebuilding of Salonica and İzmir as an important task.[56] Reconstruction was not merely a technical problem: such a clean break and the achievement of such an idealized view of the future required an approach to town planning both 'scientific' and 'artistic'. This kind of town planning should restore the city's operational efficiency, while also envisaging an 'urban scene' that would express a collective national vision of the future. Furthermore, the idea of a new comprehensive layout for the built environment meant that the city and its natural context needed to be seen as a single whole.

Ernest Hébrard, trained at the *Ecole des Beaux-Arts* and at the *Académie de France* in Rome, was already in Salonica with the allied troops when the fire broke out and took a leading part in the reconstruction plan completed in 1918.[57] Six years later, in 1924, İzmir authorities appointed René Danger and his brother Raymond, then running the *Société des Plans Regulateurs* and well-known for their pragmatic approach to the subject, to draw up a reconstruction plan based on Henri Prost's advice.[58] Both Hébrard and Danger proposed a zoning scheme (industrial, business, and administrative districts, and residential areas of different types), designed to replace the old pattern of ethnic settlements with an orderly urban fabric made of blocks and aligned streets adaptable for future growth. Some isolated public buildings (the railway station, town hall, law courts, post offices, markets, schools and university structures) marked the cardinal points of the urban composition. Attributing great importance to accessibility, both plans proposed extensions to the port and envisioned it as an infrastructure in itself, backed by an industrial district and easily made accessible both by land (with improvements made to road and rail connections) and by sea (with new wharves, docks, and warehouses). It is worthwhile comparing the technical measures adopted by both plans in order to understand how they considered reconstruction as a work of architecture in itself. First and foremost, this meant grafting a new city center onto areas loaded with memories of the past. No longer focused on the port and the adjoining all-purpose markets, the modern city needed public spaces of a new kind, urban scenes for new functions and institutions, architectural and spatial patterns in anticipation of the future city. The fact that Hébrard proposed a large park as a focal point of social life and a city center more representative of public institutions while Danger imagined the new city center itself as a park, cannot be mere coincidence. As part of the wider natural scene, these parks provided an ideal ground on which to experiment with landscapes of modernization.

Ernest Hébrard in Salonica

To interpret and revive Salonica's urban structure based on the Hellenistic grid and Egnatia Street, which runs parallel to the seafront at a higher level, Hébrard fully benefited from his archaeological training in the French Beaux-Arts tradition, which he could apply on the spot while working with the Archaeological Service of the Armée d'Orient.[59] Having spent several months in the city before the fire, he would certainly have noticed many of its functional and representative features and appreciated the importance of streets leading from the sea front to the upper town, crossing the various ethnic quarters.[60] This thorough knowledge of the city was well reflected in the plan, anything but a formal exercise.[61] Hébrard treated the city as a work of architecture, adapting some principles of urban composition such as urban axes of symmetry as functional units, diagonal streets favoring circulation, and regular geometrical shapes for squares and open spaces to the original nature of the context, linking the city of the future with its natural landscape and with features of its ancient history. His new city center, the Civic Axis, was to follow the median line of the walled city, where supposedly the ancient Agora was located uphill of Egnatia,[62] with the sites of the oldest synagogues further down.[63] Along this line he envisaged a series of open spaces, each with its own function, rising from the seafront (the Grand-Place), across Egnatia street (the Civic Square with the Town Hall and the Law Courts), to the upper town (the square facing the Basilica of St. Demetrius and an open-air theater). Characterized by arcades and neo-Byzantine façades, the central Civic Axis opened unparalleled views towards the upper town and distant Mount Olympus. Hébrard suggested the addition of two urban axes to serve as key areas outside the eastern and western walls. On the site of the Jewish and Turkish cemeteries, he proposed a splendid park, a green wedge from the Sheikh Sou Forest towards the sea, with paths radiating towards university buildings, theaters, sports and recreational facilities. Close to Vardari Square, where overland routes converge approaching the port,[64] he envisaged a wide street connecting the docks, the wholesale market, and the merchandise and passenger railway stations.

René Danger in İzmir

In İzmir Danger pursued his firm belief that topography to which infrastructure is adapted to foster man's perpetual evolution could reveal the raison d'être of a city.[65] He therefore proposed a new transport scheme of fundamental importance for a full appreciation of his plan. This involved a single junction for the railway to Kasaba and Aydın and redesigned the street system by bringing overland routes into the city. His plan therefore amounted to a fresh interpretation of İzmir's urban structure: A city center, linked to the new Place des Caravanes where overland routes converged, was to lie between two wide boulevards along the former Kasaba and Aydın railway lines; and a new port served by railways and backed by the already existing industrial district was to develop beyond the Point (Punta).[66] The working class area was to concentrate beyond the railway junction, while the remaining quarters of the old town were equipped with three panoramic streets extending southwards of the residential areas. Danger's idea of harmonizing topography with infrastructure also influenced his composition on the urban level. To mark the center of the zone where fire had destroyed the European, Greek and Armenian quarters, Danger proposed a large park in the shape of a horse-shoe as the site of new cultural institutions such as university buildings, a museum, and several school complexes. Adjacent to the park, a lozenge-shaped built-up area stretched from the Grand-Place along the seafront to a square replacing the earlier Basmane Station at the edge of the old town, grouping several municipal buildings including the town hall, the police station, the fire brigade, and the post office and a large hotel. The compact park, which emphasized the new city center's presence on the alluvial plain in contrast to the old town crowned by the citadel on Mt. Pagos, may be considered Danger's contribution to reshaping İzmir as a work of architecture. In addition, most of his proposed roads were designed to combine the functional needs of circulation with an attempt to enhance the perception of the city as a vital part of a unique natural environment.

Port, Trade Fair and University

Although never carried out as originally designed, the plans by Ernest Hébrard and René Danger were destined to exert considerable influence on later decisions on Salonica and İzmir, perhaps even laying the basis for the cities as they are today. What, then, were the strategic visions underlying their subsequent modification and implementation? What were to be the roles of Salonica and İzmir: a regional metropolis or a haven for many peoples forced to migrate?

Answering such a question requires an account of events that accompanied the execution of Hébrard's and Danger's reconstruction plans, as well as of their extent and time-tables. For example, the port and railroads were not built until after World War II, and the railway junction in İzmir went no further than the design stage. However, the proposal for the city center and the park did take shape. It may therefore be said that rebuilding the city as a work of architecture was considered a basic step to promote a process of cultural, social and economic reconstruction.

Much may be learned from the debates, ideas, projects and architectural design competitions that eventually led to the construction of Aristotle University and the adjacent Salonica International Fair,[67] and to the implementation of the Culture Park in İzmir. It may even be said that, in partial compensation for a shrinking hinterland and for the loss of the cosmopolitan environment, both the trade fair and the university contributed to a partial revival of Salonica and İzmir as centers of economic and cultural exchange. A glance at these major reconstructed parts of the two cities may also reveal the lines along which modern Greek and Turkish architecture have developed, within the framework of the architectural program originally proposed with Hébrard's University Park and Danger's city center.

Hébrard himself was called in to propound his ideas after the establishment of Aristotle University in 1926, the year that the fair opened. Difficulties with the removal of the Jewish cemeteries delayed the construction of the initial university buildings until 1939. The complete destruction of the cemeteries came about during the period of Nazi occupation, which actually paved the way for further implementation of the project, including by then the fairground on the site of the Turkish cemeteries.

Opened in 1936, İzmir Culture Park occupied the horse-shoe-shaped park initially designed to accommodate the university;[68] the architect had adapted the original project to embody functional and landscaping features of the Moscow Gorki Park. At the 1923 Turkish Economy Congress, Atatürk himself announced the decision to found the İzmir Fair, a fact that sufficiently explains the urgency felt regarding a new role for the city. As Biray Kolluoğlu has expressed it, the Park of Culture was redesigned to create a scene in which new urban symbols represented the aspirations, images and future prospects of Republican Turkey; it was seen as a constellation of public spaces devoted to inscribing republican ambitions towards progress and modernization on the urban landscape.[69] Reading articles about the İzmir Fair and the Culture Park published in contemporary Turkish journals, one can still feel 'the spirit of celebration, youth, optimism, and progress embodied by the spaces of public gathering and recreation, a spirit that reached its zenith in the exhibition spaces of the republic'.[70]

Concluding Remarks

In presenting the idea of 'geographic theaters', my aim is to emphasize a project-oriented approach to Salonica in Macedonia, Alexandria *ad Ægyptum*, and İzmir in the Aegean region of Asia Minor, if the many exceptional advantages of their natural surroundings are to effectively become sceneries in the broader sense, where at different times throughout history both individual and society have played their parts. Physical, anthropological and cultural reconstructions have been frequent events, and the structural role of architecture has been revealed here more strikingly than elsewhere. Here, architecture has been able to express symbolic values in the urban scene and to interpret a *genius loci* in the most dramatic circumstances. How can these experiences help us envisage the cosmopolitan city of the past and its possible future? To what extent can these experiences challenge the modern idea of the city as a functional whole? How can they question the idea of architecture as a mere expression of individual talent, if not as a showcase of building technologies?

The amount of architectural work now undertaken in Salonica, Alexandria and İzmir expresses the far-reaching changes in progress and shows how the city of today is seeking a future role, not only within its own region but also in a much wider context. Architects like Hébrard and Danger identified new principles of urban and architectural construction and adapted their studies to the resources available for re-investment in a project for the future, taking the city's individual character as their basis. Whatever we can learn from these experiences may well be of real value when facing the challenges of today, not only in the contexts described here, but also wherever problems of industrial reorganization, migratory movements, and accessibility require a comprehensive, far-sighted approach.

The Cartography of Harbor Construction in Eastern Mediterranean Cities: Technical and Urban Modernization in the Late Nineteenth Century

Vilma Hastaoglou-Martinidis

The second half of the nineteenth century witnessed intense harbor building activity on the shores of the Eastern Mediterranean. The incorporation of this region into the Western economy resulted in a tremendous increase in trade. This, in turn, triggered various processes of modernization such as new financial institutions and associations, adequate transport infrastructures and advanced technical facilities, as well as new forms of urban space management. The arrival of steam ships in the region around 1830 exposed the inadequacy of the existing infrastructures; especially in the next twenty years it became increaseingly apparent that the Eastern Mediterranean port-cities were in dire need of more advanced transport facilities such as modern docks and wharves assuring easy and efficient loading and unloading, spacious custom houses and warehouses for the increasing shipping capacity, sanitation services, and the like. Thus, harbor construction was undertaken in all of the major cities of the region including Alexandria, Beirut, İzmir, Istanbul, Salonica, and Pireaus, as well as the lesser sea-trade centers of Patras, Scio, Syra, Dedeağaç (Alexandroupolis), Varna, Samsun, Trabzon, Alexandretta, and Haifa.

The construction of new harbors, accompanied by railways and other infrastructure facilities, acted as a catalyst for multiple changes in the cities of the Eastern Mediterranean and entailed their radical transformation within just a few decades. It re-oriented the economic activity of regions and cities towards the sea and the larger world. It enhanced the significance of certain towns and fostered an extended urban modernization, instituting new procedures for managing and making the city. It introduced an early form of zoning with specialized functions and rational organization of the site, which resulted in restructuring urban spaces.

Harbor construction, as it is presented here, clearly demonstrates how common this process was in the principal port-cities of Alexandria, Beirut, İzmir, Istanbul, Salonica and Pireaus. Their similarities in both geographic and topographic features and the uniformity in the technical models applied override the differences that stemmed from policies for technical and urban modernization in each political entity. Harbor construction fostered the modernization of the old physical and social structure of port-cities. Reformers instituted new professional and economic bodies, administrative councils and financing procedures, as they were related to the management of the construction and operation of modern facilities. These new institutions disregarded and overrode the existing structure of ethnic groups. Finally, they produced a singular urban landscape in which modernized districts intermingled with older quarters; this gave a new identity to Eastern Mediterranean cities.

This paper will produce a cartography of harbor construction in the Eastern Mediterranean region and bring to light the main facets of this process lasting from the 1860s to the 1910s. I will describe the traditional physical patterns of the port-cities and their lack of or the poor conditions in transit trade infrastructure; examine the preparation of this global harbor-building enterprise with a focus on the pressure exerted by foreign consuls, navigation companies, trading firms, and contractor firms; study the activities of foreign contractor firms and their engineers; analyze the technical and urban innovations that harbor construction instigated in the existing physical and social structure of port-cities; and, finally, I will highlight the broader modernizing impact on urban planning and architectural transformations that harbor construction entailed for Eastern Mediterranean cities within just a few decades.

The Traditional Urban Form: Port-Cities without Ports

The mid-nineteenth century not only saw the development of new maritime technology, but also the opening of the Suez Canal which significantly reordered ship traffic. In 1845, the first regular line of steamships from Marseilles to Malta, Alexandria and Beirut signaled the transformation of the Eastern Mediterranean basin into a potential market and the development of exchange between its eastern and western shores.

By the end of the eighteenth century, in the territories of the Levant where transportation was still based on caravans of pack animals and sailing ships, economic activity had already begun to gradually shift from the countryside to the port, mainly as a result of the changing conditions of agricultural production. This shift challenged the supremacy of inland cities and elevated coastal towns into all-important economic centers for their vast hinterlands.[1] Triggered by the growing demand of European industries for agricultural goods and raw materials, port-cities became the focus of trading activities.

However, the wooden piers and shabby warehouses on the waterfront of once-great port-cities and poorly kept land roads (if they existed at all) could not meet the increasing needs of trade. The old harbors were either working beyond capacity or neglected and derelict, if not completely deserted. Ships had to anchor at large, and passengers and goods reached land by lighters which were far too unsafe and expensive. Frequent accidents occurred due to tides or storms and destroyed the wooden piers and shabby warehouses (as it happened in İzmir in 1867), or caused steamers to run ashore (as it happened in Beirut in 1863).[2]

In the early nineteenth century, Alexandria was an introverted Arab settlement of 12,000 inhabitants, the last vestige of the famous ancient town in a unique natural setting. Located on the Nile, it occupied the small peninsula of Agami, the ancient Heptastadium, and was protected by a double enclosure of walls from the land side. Its port having no nearby competition since the ports of Rosetta and Damietta were situated 60 and 215 km to the east, respectively took the form of two crescents: one was the old harbor of Eunostos, and the other the great port of Antiquity, with the ancient island of Pharos forming a natural defense against winds from the sea. Yet, the shore was deserted and unapproachable, because of the sunk ancient docks, and served only as a refuge to a few boats.[3]

İzmir rose to prominence in the eighteenth century. Yet, even as late as in 1854, the city had no transit trade infrastructure. The city served more as a relay point in Europe's trade with Asia, and long strings of caravans arrived from all parts of Asia Minor, carrying the produce of the region.[4] The harbor of İzmir had replaced the ancient inner port of Roman times, its entry being protected by the Byzantine fort of Saint Peter. As a naval station and port of anchorage for the sultan's galleys in the seventeenth century, it had become filled in since the eighteenth century; its gradual occupation by the busy bazaar with its *bedestan*s, *han*s, and workshops turned it into the hub of city-life. The narratives of travelers to the Levant describe this port and its fort, which survived until the 1860s, and whose form is reflected in the circular tracks of the bazaar streets that Thomas Graves' plan shows as partly covered with buildings in 1836.[5] On the shore, an inextricable mass of warehouses and small piers met the needs of the intense commercial traffic starting from the mid-eighteenth century, when İzmir's economy really took off.[6] However, until the early 1870s the city did not have adequate facilities. The Italian engineer Luigi Storari, who visited İzmir in 1857 on the government's invitation to draw up a cadastral map of the city for the rebuilding of several districts damaged by fire, found it completely lacking: 'neither port, nor arsenal, neither headlight, neither bridges, nor motor-roads to communicate with the villages of the interior [...] nor municipality, neither communal fund, or road maintenance ...'[7]

The port of Istanbul, which had lead Mediterranean transit trade during the Byzantine era, retained its position as the trade hub for the Black Sea and Anatolia during the following Ottoman centuries. However, in the mid-nineteenth century the city was still confined within its walls; its natural harbor, the Golden Horn with a length of seven kilometers, width of 500 meters and depth of more than 70 meters, flanked by the dynamic European district of Galata and the traditional markets of Eminönü, was far from satisfying the needs of maritime trade. Old wooden quays and private small piers bordered the banks outside the walls, surrounded by warehouses, stores and hans, as well as the customhouses of Tophane and Sirkeci. The development of international trade and navigation starting from the *Tanzimat* era in the 1840s prompted the authorities to undertake minor rearrangements at the busiest spots and, after 1863, to allow the construction of private docks. A quay was built at Tophane after 1846, while in 1848 and 1849 repair and construction of smaller sections of quays took place at Karaköy.[8] The inauguration of coastal navigation after 1851 with the newly introduced steamboats of the *Şirket-i Hayriye* necessitated landing docks at various points on the Bosphorus. From 1848 onwards, between Sirkeci and Eminönü many attempts at laying out new docks were undertaken.

Enclosed by its walls, on the rocky shore of Saint George Bay, Beirut was an introverted town with narrow and tortuous streets, markets, and workshops. Although the city witnessed commercial growth and considerable naval traffic by the mid-nineteenth century, its minuscule port still consisted only of a lighthouse, a small pier and a shabby customhouse.[9] Originally built by the Crusaders in the twelfth century and very active throughout medieval times, it was filled in by Emir Fakr ed-Dîn (r. 1596–

1634) to protect the port from the Ottoman fleet. During the brief Egyptian occupation, in 1835 Ibrahim Pasha had it partly reconstructed in order to shelter caiques and lighters. Afterwards, the Ottomans filled in the passageway between the guard towers and opened a new entry at the north side. The bombardment by the Anglo-Austrian fleet in 1840 ruined the towers and the fort. Later, the Ottomans installed a headlight and built a landing point and sheds for customs officials on the ruins of the northern tower.[10]

Until 1869, Salonica, with its mixed Jewish, Christian and Muslim population, was enclosed within its medieval walls. When in the beginning of the nineteenth century the growth of trade in Macedonia turned the city into the *entrepôt* for the South Balkans,[11] maritime trade was still carried out on the small wooden pier outside the sea gate, near the traditional markets, the Frankish quarter and the populous Jewish neighborhoods that supplied the port with a cheap labor force. The harbor was located on the site of the Byzantine port, left to decay and gradually filled in during the Ottoman period, and constituted the only extramural installation. Surrounded by several stores and warehouses, it served the limited needs of the maritime trade of the time, still based on sail ships.

Until its designation as the new capital of the Kingdom of Greece in 1833, Athens was an insignificant fortress of 9,000 inhabitants and many monuments, which by the end of the Greek war of independence had been partially destroyed. Pireaus, with its ancient Emporium, the work of Hippodamus, had long disappeared and its 120-hectare basin had been reduced to a fishing port. When Chateaubriant visited the site in 1806, he found only the bay without ships; the ports of Phaleron, Munichia and Pireaus had been deserted, and on the shore a derelict monastery and a small warehouse with a customs officer often waited for months for a ship to arrive.[12]

Contracting Companies and Engineers

It was in these port-cities that we can observe the first development of harbor construction in the Levant. After 1845, steamers connected the cities of the Eastern Mediterranean at greater speed, shortening distances and requiring transport facilities that Levantine cities did not possess. Due to the expansion of European sea trade, major coastal cities saw increased economic activity. These cities also became heads of railway lines built from 1851 onwards[13] and assumed new functions which necessitated transit trade facilities. Hence, the construction of modern harbors became an absolute imperative for those cities with economic prospects dependent on the sea.

Several factors eventually led to such a dependency. Often, the railway companies ordered the construction of the harbors. According to a contract the Ottoman government signed in 1869, the Hirsch Company received the commission to build a railroad line in the empire's European provinces; the Ottoman government undertook the development of roads and harbor facilities in the ports of Salonica, Dedeağaç, and Varna, for the efficient operation of the Balkan railroad network and the improvement of agriculture and trade.[14]

Pressing the governments in Istanbul, Cairo or Athens for improvements, the consuls of European powers intervened on behalf of navigation companies, trading firms, banks, and contractors, for whom railroad and harbor construction represented a source of considerable profit. The concession for the building of İzmir's quay was hailed as the most significant improvement for the city by all diplomatic representatives,[15] as was the undertaking of the Golden Horn docks.[16] Local merchants also frequently played a decisive role, undertaking initiatives for the improvement of docks and roads for transit trade. In Beirut, the inadequacy of transit infrastructure led to the unanimous demand of its inhabitants for modern harbor facilities.[17] In 1869, the merchants of Alexandria agreed on paying a voluntary tax on export goods in order to provide the funds for paving the streets in the quarters where especially export articles were stored. They also built the nearby quays of the Mahmudiyya Canal.[18] Finally, the newly established municipal authorities in Alexandria, Salonica, Beirut, Pireaus and so forth in many cases tried to obtain the rights to manage the projects.

The construction of both land and sea transport infrastructure became an arena of antagonism between West European countries and their contracting firms. While British and German companies fiercely competed for railroad concessions, French contracting companies virtually monopolized harbor construction, which secured long-term concessions and special follow-up privileges, particularly in the Ottoman Empire. Many of them involved in the construction of the Suez Canal, harbor engineers crossed the Mediterranean, transporting know-how from place to place. Almost exclusively Frenchmen and primarily trained at the *Ecole des Ponts et Chaussées*, Europe's oldest and most prestigious engineering school,[19] they offered their services to governments or private contracting firms, planning modern docks or managing construction work: Auguste Stœklin worked in Alexandria and Beirut; Hilarion Pascal in Istanbul, Salonica, Varna, Patras, and other cities; Adolphe Guérard acted as engineering consultant for the harbors of Salonica and Istanbul and prepared plans for Varna, Bourgas, Constanţa, and Jaffa; Eduard Quellenec designed projects for the harbors in

Alexandria, Pireaus and many other Greek cities; and Louis Godard was commissioned to study the ports of Rodosto, Dedeağaç, Samsun, Trabzon, Rhodes, Mersin, Alexandretta, Tripoli and Jaffa. A graduate of the *Ecole Centrale* in Paris, Louis Barret drafted the first plans for the sea docks of Istanbul, Salonica and other Black Sea port-cities, while a Levantine engineer, Polycarpe Vitali, carried out projects for quays in İzmir and Salonica.[20] Marseilles was the main exporter of technical know-how, and the major harbors of the Levant were built following uniform patterns.

The building of modern harbor facilities which would consolidate the city's position on the new maritime routes was the constant concern of the Khedivial governors of Alexandria. Supported by the local elite, Mehmet Ali initiated the endeavor as early as in 1829, but it was the cotton boom of 1863 that mobilized viceroy Ismail to assign the project to Auguste Stœcklin, who at the time was engaged in the building of the Suez Canal. Yet, it was Linant de Bellefonds, a French pro-Saint-Simonist engineer who served the Egyptian government as Minister of Public Works in 1869, who drew the definitive plan after the city had been linked by railroad to Suez and Cairo.[21] The execution of the plan was granted to the London firm William Bruce Greenfield & Co, under the direction of William DuPort, an engineer from Liverpool. The project, which included a 750-hectar wharf, docks running a total length of 2,700 meters, and a 2.5-meter-high breakwater, as one of the few British harbor construction projects in the Levant, was completed in 1880.[22]

Major improvements of the port of İzmir began in 1867, after the railway to Aydın and Kasaba opened and three British merchants obtained from the Sublime Porte a concession to build a modern quay of 3.5 kilometers length along the old seafront. Soon after the contract was issued, the concessionaires contacted the Frenchmen Joseph and Elie Dussaud, who ran a most competent and reliable company (named Dussaud Frères) and had extensive experience in harbor construction in Marseilles, Cherbourg, Trieste and Port-Said.[23] The *Société des Quais de Smyrne* was established in 1868, and the Smyrniote engineer Polycarpe Vitali completed the project in 1875, including two well-protected wharves of 20 and 12 hectares each, with a customhouse and bonded warehouses on the jetties. Also, new railroad lines now linked the harbor to the railway station.[24]

As for Istanbul, minor improvements on the busiest spots along the Golden Horn started in 1840, necessitated by the growth of steam navigation. However, it was only after the operation of the Oriental railway, in 1872, that the railway company proposed the construction of modern docks, and its engineer, Louis Barret from Marseilles, designed a plan for docks in front of the rail terminal of Sirkeci. The following year Hilarion Pascal, a French engineer of the *Ecole des Ponts et Chaussées*, finalized the project. However, it took several more years and repeated diplomatic correspondence for the Porte to issue the concession to the Empire's General Administrator of Lighthouses, the Frenchman Marius Michel Pasha. The *Société des Quais, Docks et Entrepôts de Constantinople* was established in 1890. The project entailed the building of 3,000-meter-long docks on either side of the Golden Horn, from the bridge of Azapkapı to the Bosphorus. Work started in 1892, but was repeatedly delayed due to technical problems and the landowners' opposition to expropriation, as well as the objection of the lighter men to wharf duties. By 1900, only 1,128 meters of docks were finished on the banks of Galata and Sirkeci.

At Haydarpaşa, the Istanbul railhead of the Anatolian railways, a German subsidiary company named the *Société du Port de Haidar Pacha* had been charged with building modern harbor installations in 1900. Chief engineer Waldorp directed the project of a 600-meter-long breakwater and two docks of 150 and 300 meters until 1903. On the landfill beyond the railroad lines, cranes, large warehouses, and other facilities were installed, and the new railway station was built between 1905 and 1909.[25]

The increasing prosperity of Beirut after the astonishing commercial expansion of 1840 contrasted sharply with the lack of trade facilities. Local traders demanded a modern harbor in the 1860s; however, its construction was considerably delayed and started only after the building of the first carriageway to Damascus. Already in 1879, the governor, Midhat Pasha, seriously considered the development of the port and ordered the English engineer Austin to draft plans. Yet, the concession was granted only in 1887, to the Lebanese Joseph Moutran, and French shareholders of the construction company of the Beirut–Damascus road set up the *Société du Port, des Quais et Entrepôts de Beyrouth*.[26] The French engineer Henri Garreta undertook the implementation of the project according to the plan commissioned from Stoecklin by the navigation company Messageries Impériales back in 1863.[27] The work was completed in 1895, and modern docks were built on a landfill of five to six hectares.[28]

In Salonica, harbor construction started in 1869, when the city administration demolished a 1,650-meter-long stretch of the sea wall to make room for two vital transit trade facilities, namely the quays and the railway. However, this quay –built under the direction of Vitali, who had previously been involved in the construction of the İzmir quay– rapidly proved inadequate, for lighters were still being used for unloading. The question of building a proper harbor was raised once more immediately after the opening of the first railroad in 1872. The railway company commissioned the engineer of Marseilles, Louis Barret (who also had drafted the plan for the docks of Istanbul) to draw the plan for an artificial harbor along the quay. Two years later, this draft plan was finalized by Hilarion Pascal, chief-engineer of the Ponts et Chaussées, while a third version was produced by the French engineer Aslan at the same time. Yet, the construction of the harbor was granted some 22 years later to the *Société de Construction du Port de Salonique*, established by the Frenchman Edmond Bartissol, a public works contractor and former MP of the Department of Pyrenées. The task included the construction of a 800-meter-long and 130-meter-wide docking area, as well as the construction of two 200-meter-long moles, a 560-meter-long breakwater that encircled a 13-hectar wharf, the laying of 3,000 meters of railway lines; transit sheds, a new customhouse, the central railway station, and a grain storage.[29]

Pireaus was reborn in 1834 as the new seaport of Athens; its neoclassical plan matched that of the capital, but did not provide adequate harbor facilities. Migrants from the islands of Hydra and Scio soon populated the city. However, the spectacular development of its port, undertaken by the port fund and the municipality,[30] owed much to the opening of the Corinth Canal in 1893, which altered the route of ships and established the city as the first port and industrial center of the Greek Kingdom.[31] The development of the harbor through successive projects by French engineers (French Expedition Corps in 1840, and E. Quellenec in 1882) paralleled the expansion of the city. In 1907, it encompassed a wharf of 122 hectares, 4,000-meter-long docks on embankments of 17 hectares, moles and a navy yard, warehouses, sheds and a customhouse, totaling 14,000 square meters of surface area.[32] It was connected by rail to Athens in 1869 and to the rest of the country after 1880.

Minor cities soon followed in building harbors. According to the agreement between the Oriental railway company and the Sublime Porte, projects for the harbors of and Varna were put forward. From 1873 onwards, with Dedeağaç, a new town was created by the *Compagnie des Chemins de Fer de la Turquie d'Europe* as the seaport of the flourishing city of Edirne (Adrianople). In 1910, Conrad Schokke finally completed the harbor, which had seen the successive involvement of L. Dussaud, the contractor of the İzmir quay and Aslan in 1890.[33] For the port of Varna, the main outlet of the Principality of Bulgaria in the Black Sea region, six successive projects were suggested from 1873 onwards: first by Hilarion Pascal, the chief engineer of the port of Marseilles; by Sir Charles Hartley in 1890; and by Auguste Guérard, the chief engineer of the port of Marseilles, in 1894. Work started after 1895 under the direction of the port engineer P. d'Istria, a Frenchman who also worked on the harbor of Patras.[34]

After many years of effort, the concession for the harbor of Scio was granted to the *Société du Port et Quais de Chio*, established in 1896 by N. Pantelidis, a businessman from Scio, and K. Héliaskos, an Istanbulite Greek and one of the founders of the Athens Bank. Based on the plan previously drawn by the engineers E. Burreau and Anthony Matsas, the building project was prepared in 1896 by Theodore Koressios, an engineer from Scio who had trained in the *Ecole des Ponts et Chaussées* and the chief engineer of the company. The work that had begun in 1895 was completed in 1900.[35]

In 1873, the project for the harbor of Patras was assigned to Hilarion Pascal; the company of the French contractor Pierre Magnac started construction in 1881, and new docks were finished in 1894, after the laying down of the Peloponnese railroad network.[36] The concessions for the harbor projects of Samsun and Trabzon were granted between 1908 and 1909 to Sir Henry Babington Smith, director of the *Banque Nationale de Turquie*, while in Jaffa A. Guérard, E. Fancy, and Amat consecutively built the harbor.[37]

However, these initiatives did not always proceed smoothly. New docks eliminated traditional jobs and work sites and increased transportation cost. When trams were installed on the new quays of İzmir and Beirut, hundreds of porters lost their jobs. In Salonica, the rail link between the railway terminal and the quay saved transportation time but cost the porters their jobs, and after 1908 the lighter men's and porters' guilds repeatedly halted commerce.[38] The 'war of the tariffs' that lighter men, navigation companies and merchants launched in İzmir and Istanbul soon after the new docks were opened, frequently find mention in the records.[39] Often, landowners' opposition to expropriation caused significant delay in construction work and alterations to original plans, such as those of Istanbul and İzmir.[40] In İzmir, in 1868 the owners of land on the shore strongly opposed the expropriation rate for their plots and the tramway line along the quays, on operational, hygienic, and aesthetic grounds.[41] Nevertheless, soon commerce increased so much that at the beginning of the twentieth century new extensions of railway lines and harbor facilities became necessary.

In the meantime, urban political groups and merchants praised the new infrastructure. State officials, contractors, diplomats and members of the financial world attended the solemn ceremonies open to the public, on occasion of their inauguration. In Istanbul, the ceremony for the opening of the great passenger station on the docks of Sirkeci was celebrated with all due prestige on 22 October 1890, as a major social and economic event.[42] In Beirut, in March 1903 state officials and a host of local people attended the inaugural ceremony of the harbor station.[43] The opening of the new quay in Salonica on 4 June 1870 by the governor-general of the province was greatly celebrated in a ceremony by the sea, a ceremony which the consuls and other officials, as well as the prominent merchants of the city and many others attended.[44]

Construction of Harbors

Obviously, the adopted harbor types depended on the specific morphology of each city. But they nevertheless served the same end, either as outer ports, opening directly onto the sea (İzmir, Salonica and Beirut), or as inner ports, protected by their geographic situation (Istanbul, Alexandria and Pireaus). Their topological relation to the city followed a common pattern as well: the new harbors were built on the sites of ancient ports in immediate proximity to other parts of the city dependent on trade such as the European-style quarters and business districts, traditional bazaars, railroads stations, and the like.

In Alexandria the old port of Eunostos had been transformed into a modern harbor by the beginning of the twentieth century. The broad embankment of the interior docks (7.84 hectares) laid out in regular blocks, connected directly to the European quarter of the city-center, which had been rebuilt after the bombardment by the British fleet in 1882.[45] After 1896, sheds and massive storehouses, built of concrete, offered the necessary storage space. Among them were the cotton market and the two large storehouses of the Egyptian Bonded Store Company, rebuilt for enlargement and with electricity, administration offices, lighthouses, stations, telegraph, customs and quarantine offices, a passenger terminal, and offices for the navigation companies.[46] All of these additions refashioned the landscape of this highly functional zone, which cut the city off from the sea but opened it to the world.

The modern seafront of Alexandria was completed with the creation of the quay of Ramleh, the famous Corniche, running on a 3,947.5-meter-long curve. It was one of the most splendid projects undertaken during this period, comparable in scale with the project of the western port. The municipality undertook both design and implementation of the project. Here, a boulevard parallel to the shore occupied half of the 80-meter-wide embankment, while the rest was reserved for a new band of regular blocks along the boulevard. At the foot of the quay wall, parallel to the beach, the sewer collector was placed. The total surface area gained on the sea amounted to 52.6 hectares, with 21.6 hectares occupied by the boulevard and 31 hectares retained for the construction of private buildings. The municipal engineers Dietrich and Arcondaris prepared the project, and Gallois supervised the work. The cost approximately totaled FF nine million. The involvement of E. Quellenec, chief engineer of the Suez Canal Company, testifies to the importance of the task from the technical point of view. Construction started in 1901 and was completed in 1907 (of the quay wall and the boulevard), but the Italian company *Almagià* did not start building until 1920.[47] By the beginning of the twentieth century, the picturesque Arab settlement was enclosed between those two modernized façades, and, the harbor zone, which brought prosperity to the city and the Corniche of Ramleh where the eclectic residences of businessmen, merchants, and industrialists were established. Flourishing Alexandria reached a population of 370,000 inhabitants and became the third port of the Mediterranean in terms of its importance, after Marseilles and Genoa.

The quays of İzmir were built between 1869 and 1876. They encompassed a vast embankment of a 3.5-kilometer-long and 18.75-meter-wide quay that stretched from the infantry barracks to the Aydın railroad station. The area included a double track of rails on a parapet of six meters, connecting the station to the customhouse, a double wharf protected by a 240-meter-long jetty, and the sewers. For its part, the government granted the *Société des Quais de Smyrne* the use of all grounds gained from the sea (except for those privately owned), the exploitation of the railway lines, and the maintenance of wharf duties for a period of twenty years, in exchange for only two percent of the proceeds.[48] The port itself, located in front of the old customhouse, comprised an entirely protected wharf of a surface of 20 hectares for commercial operations including, between the moles, approximately 1,200 meters of docks. To its south, another wharf of 12 hectares was used as port for the coasters. The service buildings of the port were erected on the moles, to the north of which were the quarantine offices, the lighthouses, the office of the port captain, and the passport and the telegraph offices, while the customhouse (completed in March 1880) and the office of the Ottoman Public Debt Administration occupied the southern part. Many imposing stores bordered the quay in front of the harbor, providing necessary space to store large quantities of goods.[49]

The new quays of İzmir were celebrated as a triple achievement, technical, financial and urban.[50] The entire lower part of the city was cleaned up and thus radically refashioned on the large extension of some forty hectares gained on the sea. Straight and broad streets and a band of twenty regular blocks set the façade of the city, between the two longest and straightest roads of the city, the Kordon and the Parallel, replacing the inextricable mass of narrow plots with wooden piers, barracks, stores and cafes of the old shoreline. Repeated frictions emerged between the company and the owners of seawater plots concerning the right to compensation (*karşılık*): According to the concession, the owners of the seawater plots in front of their properties had to fill these plots at their own expenses; those who refused to or were unable to do so within the stipulated amount of time would forfeit ownership and receive the original price of their lots. However, the *Société des Quais* managed to lessen the tensions by making special arrangements with impoverished proprietors to fill their seawater plots over a longer period of time, and, according to the cadastral plan signed by the engineer Polycarpe Vitali, by 1889, almost all of the plots (192) were filled by their owners.[51] The allocation of new urban ground meant an impressive functional zoning. The 1,250-meter-long part of the quay between the barracks and the northeast jetty (where the principal entry to the harbor was located) was reserved for trade. Fronting the bazaar and the old business district of the city, this new area very quickly attracted offices and banks, trade agencies, insurance companies, stores, and the like. The other part of 2,075 meter length was used as a promenade, very dear to Smyrniotes as it became the cleanest, most comfortable and one of the most beautiful urban districts at the dawn of the twentieth century. The new urban blocks quickly filled up with the more elegant dwellings of the city, as well as embassies, luxurious hotels, cinemas, theaters and casinos, cafes, clubs; all tangible elements of economic growth. In less than thirty years, the picturesque aspect of the traditional façade was completely altered by the quay of İzmir, and all travel guides of the time recommended to visit the famous *Bella Vista*, the most distinctive feature and eminently modern European aspect of the city.[52]

In Istanbul harbor works started in April of 1892 with the dock of Galata. Laws concerning expropriation for public utility[53] settled the conflicts between the *Société des Quais* and the shore-owners.[54] In December 1895, 758 meters of docks in Galata were completed, built on concrete blocks in the example of the Marseilles quays.[55] Along the narrow embankment a street of 19 meters, wide by the standards of the time, was laid down, with a parapet of eight meters to allow loading and unloading. In addition to the criticism spawned by the high construction cost of FF 15,277,000, the company met the opposition of the lighter men and caique owners. Still, the European community of Galata and the commercial and financial elites of the city hailed the inauguration of the construction of the docks with great enthusiasm in March of 1896.[56] But the work on the bank was further delayed, with costs rising already to FF 11,840,000. On the Golden Horn and particularly on the historic bank which used to be the most important Neorion of the Byzantine era and had been filled in during the following centuries, successive collapses of the docks because of soft ground pushed back the completion of some 370 meter of docks between Sirkeci and Eminönü until 1900,[57] after extended repair work carried out by the French engineer Alphonse Cingria.[58] Although the execution of the second section of the initial plan was pushed back to a later date, the construction of buildings at the port started in 1900. New structures for the custom house, the port office, medical services, stores and multistorey warehouses were erected on both banks by 1910, according to plans approved by the government and with the help of the new concrete technology. The new customhouses in Galata and Istanbul with their imposing neoclassic form accentuated the modern façade of the city from the sea.[59]

The modern docks increased the capacity of the port whose traffic grew spectacularly despite unfavorable economic circumstances for the maritime trade of Istanbul at the time[60] and despite the shadow cast by the newly established port in Haydarpaşa, since 1900 terminus of the Anatolia railroad on the Asian coast of Üsküdar.[61] Of equal importance was the urban impact: Modern maritime façades were formed, containing specialized installations and rationally arranged buildings in front of the otherwise dense and irregular urban fabric. Soon the creation of the harbor attracted services necessary to its operation: navigation companies, stations, offices of commercial houses, banks and insurance agencies, hotels, department stores bordering on large and straight streets along the docks, in particular at Galata, all transforming radically the traditional face of the city from the sea.[62]

In Beirut, harbor construction started in January of 1890 and was completed in due course under the direction of Henri Garreta, engineer of the *Ecole des Ponts et Chaussées*, following the plan previously prepared by Stoeklin. The materials came from the quarries of Nahr el Maoud, located to the east of Alexandria, using a railway of 3.5 kilometers laid along the coast for this purpose.[63] In June of 1893, the completed section was ready, but the official reception took place in late 1895. The construction of the harbor included the creation of docks on a large embankment of five to six hectares: over 1,000 meters along the seafront between the point of Ech-Chamiyeh and the Moudaouar, with a dock of 100 to 150 meters in width and several moles. An 800-meter-long jetty provided shelter against the dominant winds from the northwest, while a 350-meter-long and two meter-high mole protected the port from the East. The wharf of 23 hectares provided a depth ranging from 14 meters in the center of the entry to 12 to eight meters along the jetty, the dock and the moles. On designated plots, the company of William Bruce Greenfield built the new customhouse and the police station, the utility of which was unanimously recognized by the merchants of the city. However, the more attractive improvement for the various navigation companies and the trade of the city was, after 1900, the extension of the Beirut–Damascus–Hauran railroad to within two kilometers from the port, and of the Lebanese Tramways.[64] Although the railway lines were laid down only much later and the merchants and the lighter men judged the tariffs excessive, port traffic increased considerably afterwards.

Here, engineers worked on a *tabula rasa*, laying out the only zone of the city of such a scale, and equipped it with specialized facilities such as a new business center where ships, trains, trams and other vehicles met. The emergence of this zone and the effect it had on the neighboring urban space were impressive; the docks were immediately animated by hotels, banks, offices for various agencies, private warehouses, residential buildings for private individuals, cafes and shops; all of these buildings accommodated new functions befitting the dynamism of the port.[65] The face of the city from the sea acquired a European appearance, when compared to the old quarters with the narrow and picturesque lanes where transportation still relied on pack animals. The modern façade of such a cosmopolitan Mediterranean city replaced the traditional shore of Beirut, as the ruins of the medieval port with the rare old monuments of the city so often depicted by the artists of the time (such as the watercolor of Amadeo Preziosi in 1862) disappeared forever.

The harbor of Salonica, needed since the early 1860s when the city had approximately 80,000 inhabitants, was initiated in 1869, when on the proposition of the Governor-General of the province, the Sublime Porte consented to the demolition of the sea walls for the construction of a quay of 1,650 meters length on an embankment of approximately seven hectares; there, a line of building blocks and a 12-meter-wide traffic artery were laid down.[66] The plan provided for a strip of 16 large building blocks: six in front of the old harbor site, assigned to port usage, and another ten in front of the housing districts, qualified for urban usage.[67] A number of plots were set aside for the first square of the city and for public facilities such as the residence of the governor, a naval hospital, the custom house, and the municipal market.[68] For the implementation of the project a state enterprise was set up, the *Société des Quais de Salonique*, with a loan from the provincial fund. The works started in early 1870 under the direction of Polycarpe Vitali, the civil engineer who was previously involved in building İzmir's quays. Facing serious financial difficulties due to the alleged abuse of a considerable sum of the return from the sale of new land and an unwarranted increase in the scheduled budget, construction was delayed, while the public building program was abandoned and the number of building blocks raised from 16 to 30 in order to accommodate smaller plots for sale to private owners.[69] The construction was completed only in 1882, and with supplementary public financing. The Europeanized part of the city also became its busiest part, attracting a wide range of uses: manufacturing premises, workshops and warehouses, offices and shops, coffee houses and hotels, municipal market, recreation spaces, and private residences.

However, the quay rapidly proved inadequate, for lighters still had to be used for unloading and disembarkation. In 1872, the *Compagnie Générale d'Exploitation des Chemins de Fer de la Turquie d'Europe* ordered the engineer Louis Barret to produce the draft project for the development of the harbor along the city front, with four moles arranged at right angles to the quay and a breakwater parallel to the shore.[70] In 1874, Hiralion Pascal himself was involved in the project, which limited the harbor zone at the west end of the quay, with two moles in front of the ancient port and in the immediate vicinity of the railway installations.[71] Yet, construction was suspended until 1896 when the city had more than 120,000 inhabitants and became a hive of economic activity. The Minister of the Civil List and Edmond Bartissol, former MP and public works contractor from Paris, signed the relevant contract. Work began in 1897 following the project drawn up in 1874 by Hilarion Pascal and was put in the hands of Jules Robert, engineer of the *Ecole des arts et des manufactures* of Paris. The task included the construction of a 800 meter-long and 130-meter-wide docking area on a ten-hectare landfill in front of the quay at its west end; the construction of two 200-meter-long moles at right angles to the quay; the construction of a 560-meter-long breakwater parallel to the quay, sheltering a warf of 13.2 hectares. Railway lines, five cranes, transit sheds, a new customhouse, a central railway station, and a grain silo followed suit. In 1904, the construction of the buildings necessary for port operation began on the quays and in the open spaces. The Ottoman Public Debt Administration building and the adjacent warehouses of the Salt Monopoly were designed by a French architect in 1905. The warehouse of the Ottoman Bank was erected in 1909, while the silo constructed by the local engineer Eli Modiano and the new customhouse were ready by the end of 1912, based on the plan of the Levantine architect Alexandre Vallaury, the architect of many public buildings in Istanbul, such as the Ottoman Bank Headquarters, and the Archeological Museum, among others.[72]

Until 1912, when the city was incorporated into the Greek state at the end of the First Balkan War, the landscape of the harbor was completed with the addition of large banking premises of the Ottoman Bank, the Bank of Athens, and the Orient Bank, large commercial houses, additional customs offices, and the sanitation department. The offices of navigation companies, banks, and insurance agents, the postal services, shops large and small, hotels, and cafes soon occupied the surrounding area.

For the harbor of Pireaus, the period of great construction activity started after 1880, when the opening of the Corinth Canal in 1893 reduced the trip from Marseilles to Pireaus (and to İzmir and Istanbul) by 90 miles and its port traffic outgrew that of other Greek ports. In 1882, the French Mission of Public Works arrived in Greece with E. Quellenec as chief-engineer, to whom the government entrusted the project for the overall arrangement of the port of Pireaus. Quellenec's plan located the port on the grounds surrounding the city, in the form of a canal encircling urban space, on the docks of which warehouses would be erected, a design which evoked Cordier's plan for the harbor of Alexandria in 1864. Considered impractical, this plan did not find application, and the engineers of the French Mission produced another project, less original but more realistic.[73] Its implementation progressed without problems after 1898, and in 1907 the port took its definite form. It included a basin of 122 hectares with a depth varying from five to 27 meters, two jetties, an embankment of 17 hectares, 4,000-meter-long docks, moles, and the railway station. Customhouse and stores occupied 14,000 square meters.[74]

By the beginning of the twentieth century, Pireaus was the only industrial Greek city with modern harbor installations, with a population growing from 43,000 in 1896 to 70,000 in 1907. The impact on the urban landscape was impressive: The urban fabric around the port accommodated the movement of the ships, stores and workshops, banks and navigations companies, and insurance services, forcing the civil center to move even further. Indeed, a spectacular transformation took place as the neoclassical quay that bordered the urban bank was transformed into a zone filled with cranes and chimneys, massive structures of warehouses and the railway station, becoming both border and gate between the city and sea.

Harbor Works: Projects, Engineers, Contracting Companies and Urban Transformations

City	Harbor Project, Date	Contracting Company, Construction Date	Landfill (ha)
Alexandria	West Port: Linant de Bellefonds, 1869 William Janvrin du Port, 1870	*William Bruce Greenfield and Co*, London, 1870–80	15
	East Port and Corniche: Leopold Dietrich and Archondaris	Municipality, *Eduardo Almagià*, 1901–7	52.6 (4 km long)
İzmir	Polycarpe Vitali, 1868	*Société des Quais de Smyrne*, Dussaud Frères, 1868–75	40 (3.5 km long)
Istanbul	Sirkeci and Galata: Louis Barret, 1872; Hilarion Pascal, 1873; Alphonse Cingria. 1898	*Société des Quais, Docks et Entrepôts de Constantinople*, Marius Michel, 1890–1900	3
	Üsküdar, Haydarpaşa: Waldorp, 1900	*Société du Port de Haydar-pacha* (subsidiary of the Baghdad Railway Company), 1900–3	13
Beirut	Austin, 1879; Auguste Stoecklin, 1863; implemented by Henri Garetta, 1889	*Compagnie impériale ottomane du port, des quais et des entrepôts de Beyrouth*, 1887–95	5–6
Salonica	Quay: Polycarpe Vitali, 1870	*Société des Quais de Salonique*, 1870–82	6.2 (1.6 km long)
	Harbor: Louis Barret, 1872; Hilarion Pascal, 1874; Jules Robert, 1897	*Société Anonyme Ottomane du Port de Salonique*, Edmond Bartissol, 1897–1904	10
Pireaus	Edmond Quellenec, 1882; French Mission of Public Works, 1888; Edmond Quellenec, 1891–93	Port Fund, 1882–1907	17

The Modernizing City

Harbors together with railroad construction reshaped the commercial map of the Levant and channeled all import and export trade as well as passenger traffic to major port-cities. The shift from the interior to the coastline resulted in the increasing population concentration and activities in the littoral, which in turn had great impact on the economic and demographic growth of coastal cities, attracting people of various ethnic, religious and regional origins.

By the end of the nineteenth century, coastal cities became the center of economic activity in their provinces. With the changes in transport, the center of gravity soon shifted from the port function to the city itself and demanded modern amenities, civic squares, new residential areas for their expanding population, and more fashionable quarters for the emerging bourgeoisie. The renewal of the urban space gradually became a driving force of economic development. The cities witnessed a systematic implementation of urban management, including the enforcement of laws and regulations, and the establishment of municipal, commercial and health councils. For instance, in 1856 the Ottoman government enacted the law of expropriation for public utility, to allow railroad developers and harbor contractors to acquire strips of land and to facilitate urban embellishment and revitalization projects. Furthermore, new building and planning regulations were introduced in 1864 for the first time and amended in 1882 and 1891. The municipal institution was officially initiated in Istanbul, in the district of Pera, in 1855.[75] The emerging awareness and the will to modernize the parochial city manifested itself in the initiatives and projects undertaken by local authorities in the following years.

The positioning of modern transportation infrastructures in the traditional fabric of the Levantine cities clearly depended on the sites' specific conditions. But they still followed more or less uniform patterns. New harbor facilities drastically reordered the traditional sea front, and railway terminals were all situated on the old sites of access points of land roads in the vicinity of the port, usually on the perimeter of the old nucleus, where land was available for the purpose, or within the new urban fabric, in direct contact with the business center, the market and the burgeoning industrial quarters.

In order to accommodate modern harbor installations and to facilitate communication, the demolition of medieval walls became imperative. In Salonica, the construction of the new quay and the installation of railways in the western part of the city required the demolition of the sea wall in 1869, and large sections of the lateral walls by 1890. The Genoese walls of Galata were pulled down in 1863 to facilitate communication with the Europeanized district of Pera,[76] while in Istanbul the Byzantine walls were pierced in many spots to allow railroad passages in the early 1870s. In Beirut, the demolition of the walls began in the 1850s, when the Ottoman barracks and military hospital were erected, while the old castle and seaside fortification gave way to the demands of the new harbor. Consequently, the city walls no longer existed by the 1880s.[77] In Alexandria, the demolition of the Arab enclosure began in 1855 on its northern side and continued with the pulling down of the west side by 1868, to ensure the connection with the port and the Gabari district. In 1876, for the installation of the new passenger terminal, the south wall was pierced near Muharram Bey Gate and totally demolished by 1902.[78]

Thus, after long centuries of enclosure, the Levantine cities ripped open the limits prescribed by their walls and spread beyond their traditional nuclei. Harbors acted as focal points defining the guidelines for the expansion of the city, restructured the traditional urban patterns radically and swiftly, and reordered urban functions by introducing an early form of zoning with residential districts, civic and business centers, commercial and manufacturing areas. Manufacturing workshops and factories began to appear in the vicinity of new docks and railway terminals: in Alexandria, the new docks and the railway terminal transformed the area of Gabari into an industrial quarter, occupied by warehouses and workers' housing; in Salonica, the western extension near the harbor and the railway station developed into an industrial zone; in Pireaus, the area north of the railway station turned into a workers' residential district. The areas gained from the demolition of walls were used for widening roads and providing space for modern buildings, housing projects, or parks. This was the case with the new residential zone, arranged after 1890 in the eastern part of Salonica for wealthy families from all ethnic communities of the city, or with the parks and gardens (for example, the Nouzha Park) fashioned on the grounds of the south walls, which made Alexandria's reputation as one of the 'greenest' Mediterranean cities.

The urban landscape was radically transformed; while traditional trades persisted in the souks and bazaars in the old nuclei, now serving as the residence of the poorer classes. The center of gravity shifted irrevocably to the renewed areas of the city, the new quays, civic and business places and residential quarters that had little or nothing of the so-called 'oriental' in their composition. Old quarters were at least rearranged in regular street patterns, and new streets connected them with major communication points of the city. Housing developments were in demand, meeting the needs of the new inhabitants attracted by the railway, the harbor and the growth of trade in general. New civic places were created: In Alexandria, the famous Consuls' Square was refashioned by the Frenchman Joseph Cordier in 1860, and gradually the center moved to the square as well as to the 4,000-

meter-long corniche, built along the east port by the municipality between 1901 and 1907 on a large landfill of 52.6 hectares, 31 hectares of which were reserved for private construction.[79] In İzmir, the new land of more than 40 hectares gained along the waterfront was arranged in regular plots, and its north section, which was excluded from harbor use, soon attracted fashionable residences, theaters, and hotels, becoming the hub of social and civic life.[80]

All those changes propelled an unprecedented expansion of urban space. The surface area of Alexandria almost quintupled between 1850 and 1880, from 120 to 500 hectares, and its population of a unique cosmopolitan mix from every Mediterranean region rose to 230,000 inhabitants.[81] In Salonica, the extramural extension of urban space had added an area of 150 hectares to the old nucleus of 320 hectares by the 1890s. In late-nineteenth-century Beirut, the new town grew within a radius of a mile and a half around the medieval nucleus, with modern houses, carriage roads, gardens, colleges, schools and hotels.[82] In İzmir, the empty areas between the railway lines and the mid-nineteenth century urban perimeter were completely covered by modern residential extensions by the 1910s, and the surface area of the city grew from 190 to almost 400 hectares.

Other initiatives for the improvement of urban living, such as street paving and lighting, sewage and water lines, all undertaken by municipal services followed these spectacular transformations. For instance, amelioration and paving of the roads in Alexandria had already begun in 1869, and by 1878 a total of 541,752 square meters of pavement covered the streets of the city.[83] The building of modern railway stations, custom houses, and warehouses added to the prestige of the reordering in the old shores and renewed the architectural vocabulary of the city; they were designed by well-known architects, local or foreign: the Sirkeci Train Station in Istanbul was designed by the German architect Jachmund in 1890, and that of Haydarpaşa by the German architects Helmut Cuno and Otto Ritter in 1910; the Gabari Station in Alexandria was the work of the British architect Edward Baines, constructed in 1856; in Salonica, the new custom house was designed by Alexandre Vallaury in 1910, and the railway station in 1894 by the Italian architect Pietro Arrigoni. These new types of buildings introduced novel construction technologies and disseminated the use of concrete and iron structures. A fact worth noting is that, by 1910, the Bureau Technique of François Hennebique, the Parisian patent holder for concrete, had established regional agencies with associate concessionaires in Istanbul, İzmir, Salonica, Athens, and Cairo. Between 1892 and 1902, his agencies worked on 7,205 building sites, for a total amount of FF 120 million.[84] The concept was soon taken over in the subsequent construction of new bank and office buildings, manufacturing premises, department stores, apartment buildings, renovated hotels, restaurants, and the like, which produced a new urban environment.

Concluding Remarks

The building of modern transportation infrastructures acted as a major catalyst in nineteenth-century Eastern Mediterranean cities, transforming them radically within just a few decades. The ancient quays and roads of introvert cities that used to center on their vital market slipped into decay, before finally disappearing. Their urban spaces had evolved gradually over time, almost sluggishly assimilating to economic demands and disasters caused by both nature and war.

The building of new harbors reversed this situation. It opened up cities both to the world and to a new era and endowed them with spaces for all types of exchange. Far from being a sole venture of European capital, technology transfer and an emblem of modernization, the modern quays with railroad facilities became symbols of the integration of these cities with the world of international trade and the principal locus for the intermingling of ethnic groups and the creation of new, economically determined hierarchies.

Harbor construction constituted by far the most significant urban innovation undertaken until the beginning of the twentieth century, fostering various transformations in the inherited physical and social structure of Levantines cities. They introduced a new form of management and planning of the city, while the contracting companies became part of city governance, in comparison to other, less effective, bodies involved in the making of the city such as the recently established municipalities. It was the first time in their recent history that the cities of the Eastern Mediterranean expanded their space to such a great extent, through a construction process that emphasized public utility and surpassed the individual initiatives of ethnic communities.

As instruments of change that brought to the fore new protagonists, harbors became nodal points for the remaking of urban space. Their operation created new points of concentration for industry, services and markets. As a singular urban creation as well as an instrument of development, the harbor introduced novel planning and architectural models; an early form of zoning with specialized functions and judicious organization of the site that increasingly reduced the surrounding traditional fabric; as well as a new architectural aesthetic and modern construction technology, both of which influenced the conception of the city beyond the harbor. At the beginning of the twentieth century, the modern identity of the Eastern Mediterranean city was solidly established.

Mental Maps: The Mediterranean Worlds of Two Palestinian Newspapers in the Late Ottoman Period

Johann Büssow

Since the late nineteenth century, Ottoman reform policies and the expansion of trade connected the Eastern Mediterranean port-cities more firmly to Istanbul and to the various economic centers of Europe. At the same time, they created new links between these cities themselves. Through the steamboat, the telegraph, and the newly-built railways, not only people and goods, but also information traveled at a hitherto unknown speed. Inspired by a shared enthusiasm for contemporary liberal ideas, intellectuals, artists, and political activists around the Eastern Mediterranean made use of these new possibilities in order to acquire first-hand information on trends and developments in other regions, as well as to establish new links with like-minded individuals and groups. Such relations could be upheld even more easily in port-cities where steamships called at regular intervals, bringing with them goods, officials and soldiers dispatched from Istanbul, foreign travelers, and the latest news. Thus, intellectual and cultural networks paralleled administrative and economic integration.

In the Ottoman Empire, however, intellectual exchange and public discussion were severely hampered by the oppressive censorship regulations under Sultan Abdülhamid (1876–1909). Especially journalists faced severe restrictions. Their time came with the *Young Turk Revolution* of 1908, when the censorship laws were lifted and the so far curbed energies of many intellectuals and political activists burst free in an unprecedented wave of new newspapers appearing on the market.

After the first enthusiasm had ebbed away, it became often painfully clear to the pioneers of the press that the political change in the empire could not solve all problems of society at once. In an editorial of 1911, marking the first six months of their paper's existence, two Palestinian journalists, 'Isa and Yusuf al-'Isa, gave a vivid impression of both the obstacles they confronted and the high expectations they had toward their own work:

> From time to time we have provoked the public opinion in order to see how strong it would react.177 It is sad to state, but we could not find any proof for its existence in this district. [...] From this, two things have become clear to us: First, the profession of the journalist in our country is more difficult than in foreign countries, because there the journalist [only] has to transport news, whereas here he has to create a public opinion and to cause a revolution of morals and traditions. Secondly, the educated strata accept the things presented to them as they are, without bothering themselves with the trouble of independent thought or criticism. The ignorance of the uneducated strata, however, extends to all walks of life. This is the state of a nation in which the educated account for two percent of the total population![1]

However difficult the journalist's craft may have been, it is quite clear that the newspapers had an enormous impact in late Ottoman Palestine. From now on, a wide range of critical social and political issues was openly discussed in the forum of the press, and quite a few state officials came to discover how useful it was to have the public opinion on their side.[2]

This chapter argues that after 1908 the press became not only a political actor, but also a major agent in establishing and sustaining linkages between Palestinian cities and other Mediterranean centers, and that these linkages in turn rested very much on the personal networks of local journalists.[3] It explores the ways in which these networks were established, which forces shaped them, and how they contributed to the creation of specific mental maps of the region. My main sources are several volumes of two Palestinian newspapers of the late Ottoman period: the Arabic *Filastin* (Palestine, published in Jaffa) and the Hebrew *ha-Herut* (Freedom, published in Jerusalem). Reconstructing mental maps entails a number of more specific questions: Which images of their surroundings, their region, and of the wider world did the two Palestinian readers' communities receive by reading their newspapers? Where did the resulting mental maps overlap and where did they differ from each other? Before turning to these questions, however, we first need to set the scene by briefly introducing the cities of Jerusalem and Jaffa and the two newspapers.

The Jaffa–Jerusalem Region in the Late Ottoman Period

Since the late nineteenth century Jaffa and Jerusalem had grown ever closer. The impact of new infrastructure and communication networks, on the one hand, deepened the traditional symbiosis of a religious and administrative center in the interior with its port; on the other hand, it also established a hierarchy between the two types of cities.

Jaffa, at the dusk of the Ottoman Empire, was still one of the smaller commercial and cultural centers of the Levant. Politically a part of the district of Jerusalem, the city of roughly 40,000 inhabitants[4] drew most of its importance from three sources: the quickly growing export of local agricultural products to the European market (the famous Jaffa oranges, as well as grain and olive oil soap), the import of foreign goods for local consumption (most prominently rice, cloth, petroleum, building materials, and luxury articles), and the stream of visitors and pilgrims that traveled from its harbor to Jerusalem.[5] Beginning in 1892, both cities were closely connected by a narrow-gauge railway, with two daily trains running in each direction and a nightly cargo train. The railway was not only an important factor in the development of commercial life in both cities and their hinterland; it also facilitated the communication between the inhabitants of both cities. Reports in the local press as well as memoirs show how at least the wealthier made frequent use of the train to visit business partners, friends and family.[6]

Jerusalem in that period still had slightly more inhabitants than Jaffa with approximately 50,000, but it grew at a much slower rate.[7] Its importance rested mainly on two assets. One was its traditional status as a holy city, greatly enhanced during the second half of the nineteenth century due to various initiatives of Christian missionaries, the European powers, and the Ottoman government. The other was its status as the administrative center of the independent district of Jerusalem, which gave it the same status as the capitals of one of the empire's provinces established through the 1864 Provincial Code.[8] Jerusalem's economic and cultural situation, however, was characterized by its growing dependence on Jaffa. Not only did almost all of the tourists and pilgrims come through this Mediterranean gateway, but also did the city's economic elite try to take part in the profitable export of oranges, by acquiring and developing lands on the coastal plain. Culturally, Jaffa was a source of fascination by virtue of its rapid urban development and more liberal and Europeanized lifestyle. This led to a new self-image of many of Jaffa's inhabitants as being more modern and progressive in comparison to Jerusalem.[9]

Finally, the term 'Palestine' needs some explanation, as it was somewhat ambiguous. Palestine was equated with the idea of the Holy Land, which existed in the traditions of all three monotheistic religions but had only loosely defined borders. Following the Biblical formula 'from Dan to Beersheba', the Holy Land included not only the province of Jerusalem, but also the Ottoman districts of Nablus and Acre, although these were administered from Beirut.[10] However, in daily usage, and especially with regard to political developments, Palestine was often equated with the district of Jerusalem.[11]

The Journalists and Their Readership

The first private newspapers began to appear in Anatolia, Egypt and the Levant already in the 1870s, but in the Arab regions of the Ottoman Empire one can talk of the press as an important factor in political and cultural life only after 1908. The main centers of Arabic journalistic activity in the Eastern Mediterranean were Beirut, Damascus and Cairo. Palestine with its comparatively small urban population and its few institutions of higher education was in this respect only a place of secondary importance. Until 1908, Palestinian Arab readers had to rely on imported newspapers from Syria and Egypt, if they were not satisfied with the official paper *al-Quds al-Sharif/Kudüs-i Şerif*. The only other periodicals available were about ten Hebrew newspapers that catered to an almost exclusively Jewish reading public. It must have felt like a dramatic outburst of creative energy when in the period between 1908 and 1914 thirty-four Arabic and at least five additional Hebrew periodicals appeared in the territory that later was to become Mandatory Palestine.[12] For the historian, this phenomenon provides a type of source lacking for the preceding period. As Rashid Khalidi puts it, 'a society which until that point seemed almost opaque in many respects is suddenly illuminated to the historical observer'.[13] The two newspapers which I have selected for comparison, *Filastin* and *ha-Herut*, originated from different ethno-linguistic sectors of Ottoman-Palestinian society. Yet they shared two characteristics: They both relied on specific networks, and they were characterized by a clear political profile.

Filastin *(1911–14)*

The Arabic newspaper *Filastin* was published in Jaffa between 1911 and 1914 and appeared three times a week, published and edited by two cousins, 'Isa al-'Isa (1878–1950) and Yusuf al-'Isa (d. 1948). They came from one of the most prominent Arab Greek-Orthodox families in Jaffa who had acquired considerable wealth by trading in olive oil and soap and by renting out residential buildings in the commercial center of Jaffa.[14] By the beginning of the twentieth century they seem to have been well established in the town's business community as well as in the Greek-Orthodox community.[15] Before entering the field of printing and journalism, the two cousins had pursued independent careers. After studying in Beirut and Cairo 'Isa al-'Isa had worked for an Egyptian company.[16] Meanwhile, Yusuf had become a member of various Greek-Orthodox church institutions and worked as an employee of the Jaffa–Jerusalem train company.[17] Although the quote above suggests that they still felt as pioneers when they started to publish *Filastin*, the two cousins had already had some experience in the field of journalism. In 1908, Yusuf's older brother 'Abdallah al-'Isa had published the literary-political monthly *al-Asma'i*.[18] The ambitious journal ceased publication after only five months, but when 'Isa and Yusuf al-'Isa three years later started *Filastin* they could rely on a network of contacts with eminent authors who had already contributed to *al-Asma'i*. Among them were many intellectuals of the younger generation, such as the Muslim writers Is'af al-Nashashibi and 'Ali al-Rimawi and the Arab Orthodox intellectual and educator Khalil al-Sakakini. All of them shared an emphatic commitment to the Arabic cultural reform movement (*nahda*), as well as a positive attitude towards the Ottoman state and the Young Turk revolution. With Khalil al-Sakakini the 'Isas shared even more. All three of them were involved in another reform movement, termed *al-nahda al-urthuduksiyya*, a movement that attempted to give the local Arabic-speaking Christians equal rights in the church institutions hitherto dominated by Greek clergy.[19] In *Filastin* a special column was reserved for 'Orthodox matters' (*shu'un urthuduksiyya*). A clear advantage of the newspaper was the two cousin's close association with the Committee for Union and Progress (CUP), the ruling party after the revolution and an increasingly independent force in Ottoman politics. The editorial office of *Filastin* even functioned as the headquarters of Jaffa's CUP branch.[20] The paper's title, together with the publishers' and editors' political affiliation, characterizes the profile of the newspaper as adhering to Arabism in a cultural sense and to Ottomanism with regard to politics.

ha-Herut *(1909–17)*

In contrast to *Filastin* with its mixed Christian-Muslim body of authors, the Hebrew newspaper *ha-Herut*, published in Jerusalem between 1909 and 1917, was firmly tied to one particular community –the Sephardic Jews of Jerusalem who spoke Judeo-Spanish (Ladino). First a weekly and then from 1912 onwards a daily paper, it was published by Moshe Azriel (1881–1916), a Sephardic Jew who since 1900 had been the owner of a Hebrew publishing house in Jerusalem.[21] Haim Ben 'Atar (born in 1886 in Azemmour, Morocco), its first editor, had been working for Azriel's publishing house from a very young age.[22] Similar to *Filastin*, another project by the same publishing house, the Ladino *El Liberal* (*The Liberal*), preceded *ha-Herut*. After only three months and internal disputes over Sephardic community matters, the paper not only changed its editor-in-chief but also its language. Avraham Elmaliah (born 1885) replaced Haim Ben 'Atar, and the Ladino *El Liberal* turned into the Hebrew *ha-Herut*. The paper now had a much wider potential readership, as it became accessible to Jews from a non-Sephardic background. Thus, while *Filastin* was trying to bring Arab Orthodox Christians and Muslims together, *ha-Herut* was devoted to bridging the divide between the Ashkenazi and Sephardic communities.[23] Another similarity between *Filastin* and *ha-Herut* was the cultural and political orientation of their editorial boards. Parallel to *Filastin*'s commitment to the revival of the Arabic language, *ha-Herut* advocated the use of Hebrew as the 'national' language of the Jews in Palestine and at the same time avowedly followed a pro-Ottoman political line.

ha-Herut relied very much on Sephardic communal networks extending across the entire Eastern Mediterranean. The owner's publishing house had close contacts to the major centers of intellectual and literary activity among the Sephardic communities, since a great deal of the literature printed by Azriel came from other towns and cities throughout the Ottoman Empire, especially from Istanbul, Salonica and İzmir. Azriel exported books to all these cities, as well as to Ladino-speaking communities outside the Ottoman Empire.[24] Cairo, for instance, was an important community center outside the empire. As the opening article of *El Liberal* proudly reveals, the paper had its own 'consultant on Ottoman affairs' there, Avraham Galanti, a well-known Sephardic journalist. That Galanti was well acquainted with Ottoman culture and politics is indicated by the fact that only a short period later he was to become a professor at Istanbul University.[25]

The social milieu from which *ha-Herut*'s editorial staff originated was even more marked by religious networks than that of *Filastin*'s. Its editorial office was in the Jewish neighborhood of the old city, in the upper story of the Sephardic community house (*kolel ha-Sefaradim*).[26] Moshe Azriel and his editors came from families with a long tradition of rabbinic learning, and they all received their higher education in a traditional Talmud-Torah school. Azriel further strengthened his ties with the rabbinical elite by marrying the daughter of a famous Sephardic Rabbi in Jerusalem, Haim David Surnagana. The second issue of *ha-Herut* published a congratulatory note to the editors by Rabbi Abraham Danon (1857–1912); one of the most prominent exponents of the Jewish reform movement (*haskala*) in the Ottoman Empire, in many respects the counterpart of the Arabic *nahda*. However, in comparison to the conflicts of the 'Isa brothers with the Greek-Orthodox religious establishment, the relations between the young Sephardic intellectuals and their community leaders were more harmonious.[27]

Sources of Information

The most important source upon which both newspapers based their reports and articles was first-hand information through correspondents in Palestine and abroad. Since probably very few contemporary newspaper publishers had the financial resources to pay full-time employees other than the workers in the printing house, the availability of correspondents was to a great extent dependent on the publishers' and editors' personal networks.[28] *ha-Herut* seems to have had a greater number of more formalized relations with its contributors, as a considerable number of the articles were introduced with the line 'from our special correspondent' (*mi-sofrenu ha-me'uhad*).

At the turn of the century, news agencies were already an essential source for local journalists. The most important among them was Reuters of London. Next to it, a number of other agencies tried to enter the news market, some of them sponsored by European governments trying to influence local public opinion.[29] The bulk of world news was based on news agency reports. Thanks to the wire services, Palestinians could follow events in the Ottoman Empire and the rest of the world almost in real time. These services also created new relations between time and space: Reports from other Mediterranean centers or 'the greater world' (*ba-'olam ha-gadol*), as a regular column in *ha-Herut* was entitled, often reached the readers in Jerusalem and Jaffa quicker than news from the villages and towns in their vicinity. An additional source was other newspapers, especially those from places that were not regularly covered by news agencies. Frequent quotations in both papers suggest that almost all the major Arabic newspapers from the Eastern Mediterranean region were available in Jaffa and Jerusalem, in addition to a number of Greek, Italian, French and German papers.

The Readers

It can be assumed that after 1908 the composition of the newspaper readership in Palestine changed quite dramatically, especially as Arab readers suddenly had access to a wide range of locally produced papers in their own language. Unfortunately, it is impossible to determine exact numbers concerning the two newspapers' circulations, so that one has to rely on scattered information, mostly found in the newspapers themselves. According to an article in *Filastin*, 1,121 persons were registered as subscribers at the end of the year 1912. The total number of printed issues was probably higher, considering that *Filastin*, like many other local newspapers, was also sold on the streets.[30] Thus, it was probably the largest Palestinian-Arabic newspaper at the time.[31] *ha-Herut*'s circulation seems to have been of similar proportions. In the opening article of the second issue in May 1909, the editors proudly state that 'within three or four hours' all 1,200 exemplars of the paper's first issue had been sold out.[32] Although citing a lower number, the German consulate in Jerusalem still rated *ha-Herut* as the third-largest Hebrew newspaper in Palestine.[33]

With regard to the readers' class affiliation, it has to be noted that newspapers at this time were comparatively expensive.[34] This had a dual effect: On one hand, it probably led to a fairly homogenous social structure of the subscribers as urban and rather affluent. On the other hand, Palestinians adopted specific strategies to overcome the hurdles of poverty and illiteracy,[35] the most important being the practice of public reading. Therefore, the total number of consumers of both newspapers greatly exceeded the circulation numbers cited above. The class gap was also very much linked to a gap between urban and rural areas, which *Filastin*, driven by a democratic and populist impetus, tried to bridge with a remarkable initiative: The headmen (*mukhtars*) of all villages in the subdistrict of Jaffa with more than 100 inhabitants were rated as 'natural subscribers' (*mushtarikun tabi'un*), receiving the newspaper with the daily patrol of the gendarmerie.[36] It seems likely that this unusual cooperation between a private newspaper and the security forces was facilitated by 'Isa and Yusuf al-'Isa's good connections to the local authorities via the CUP.[37]

Concerning the religious affiliation of both newspapers' readers, we have only a few reliable indications. The editors of *Filastin* were, as they wrote, 'proud' to have Muslim authors writing for their paper, and it is quite likely that it was also read by Muslims.[38] In contrast, *ha-Herut* had very few Muslim or Christian authors. The only articles by non-Jews were occasional contributions by native speakers of Arabic who had learned Hebrew in one of the Jewish schools in the country.[39] By the same token, there were also very few potential readers from the Arab-speaking Muslim and Christian communities. In 1912, when open conflict broke out between the two newspapers and *ha-Herut* called for a boycott of *Filastin*, Yusuf al-'Isa wrote in a rather belligerent editorial that such a boycott would not be too harmful, since his newspaper had only twenty Jewish subscribers.[40] Thus we have to imagine the overlap between the readerships of the two papers as quite marginal.

The two newspapers were not only read in Palestine. A survey conducted by the German Consulate states that far more than half of the total circulation of both newspapers were sold outside Jaffa and Jerusalem. The subscription of *ha-Herut* is listed as '300 in the country and 500 in Turkey' [sic], that of *Filastin* as '465 in Jaffa and 1,200 in Turkey' (meaning the rest of the Ottoman Empire).[41] Even though the reliability of these reports is not beyond doubt, they give at least a sense of proportion and underline the fact that both *Filastin* and *ha-Herut* were far more than merely local newspapers. In this they maintained the trans-national nature of the religious communities to which they belonged.

The Newspapers' Cartographies

What kind of picture of their region and the wider world did the two Palestinian readers' communities receive by reading their newspapers? And to which extent did these mental maps overlap? In order to answer these questions, I will distinguish between five concentric circles of coverage: The cities and their immediate hinterlands, the region of the Levant, the political capital Istanbul, the Mediterranean as a whole, and, finally, the wider world.

Filastin

Filastin covered Jaffa's immediate hinterland in a rather selective manner. Due to the lack of adequate roads, the city was practically cut off from much of its surrounding countryside. News from towns such as Hebron or Jericho sometimes needed days to reach the markets, coffee-houses and other public places of Jaffa, and then still had to be confirmed by journalists. Travelling was so difficult and time-consuming that the editors themselves did not know all the towns from first-hand experience. For example, a report from Gaza (about 60 kilometers from Jaffa) almost reads like a travelogue from a foreign country.[42] Yet, the paper's readers were well informed about the events in their district capital Jerusalem as well as in the smaller towns of Ramla and Lydda, which were well connected by the Jaffa–Jerusalem railway. In Jerusalem, the newspaper had a regular correspondent who reported in almost every issue on the actions of the governor or the discussions in the local councils.[43] Furthermore, one finds reports written by the editors themselves who visited Jerusalem on a regular basis in their capacity as journalists as well as to take part in meetings of the Greek-Orthodox institutions. A clear advantage of *Filastin* was its proximity to the port of Jaffa. This gave the journalists the opportunity to get acquainted with all the high-ranking Ottoman officials sent to the district right after their disembarkation in Jaffa. Only occasionally did reports come from Hebron, Beersheba, Jericho and other smaller towns and villages, among them the Jewish colonies in the Jaffa region.

From Northern Palestine, which was not part of the district of Jerusalem, *Filastin*'s readers received only very scarce and unsystematic information. The most frequently mentioned place to the north of Jaffa was Haifa, a city of growing economic importance due to its modern port that had been connected to the Hijaz railway in 1905. In *Filastin*'s monitoring of Haifa there was also an obvious element of competition, since the city of Jaffa was in danger of lagging behind.[44] It should be added that 'Isa and Yusuf al-'Isa apparently were on close terms with Najib Nassar, the Arab Orthodox editor of Haifa's leading newspaper, *al-Karmil*, and frequently quoted from his articles, especially on matters of Jewish settlement. At the same time it is obvious that northern Palestine was only of minor interest to *Filastin* and its readers. Here, Ottoman realities clearly influenced the regional orientation. This is further underlined by the fact that the authors writing in *Filastin* often equated Palestine with the district of Jerusalem.[45]

The cities of the Levant (such as Damascus, Tripoli or Karak) were the subject of frequent reports in *Filastin*, many of which originally stemmed from other local Arabic newspapers. Not surprisingly, Cairo and Beirut figured most prominently as the main economic and cultural centers of the region. It is possible that the paper still benefited from 'Isa al-'Isa's personal knowledge of both cities, for he had studied in both places. Several issues of *Filastin* were sent to subscribers in Cairo, many of them possibly personal friends of the editor.[46] As an inhabitant of Jaffa, one could sustain such links much easier than from elsewhere, because the steamship lines that ran between Alexandria, Beirut and Istanbul regularly called at the city's port. Therefore, the trends of the Arab cultural centers reached Jaffa earlier than other areas of Palestine. For instance, Egyptian theater troupes visited Jaffa, and film screenings started to become a regular event as early as 1911.[47] Not only artists but also novel ideas made their way along the Mediterranean coast: texts of Egyptian and Lebanese authors were reprinted in or exclusively written for *Filastin*. Among the most prominent cases were articles by the Egyptian feminist Sara al-Maihiyya; by the Druze politician, intellectual and pan-Islamist activist Shakib Arslan; and by the writer Jurji Zaydan, one of the most prominent exponents of the Arab literary *nahda*. Arslan and Zaydan both visited Jaffa, an event that gave the 'Isas the possibility to share in their prestige.[48]

Beirut was frequently mentioned as the capital of the growing Arab nationalism. In *Filastin*, this movement was portrayed in a rather ambivalent manner, since its editors shared many of the cultural ideas of the nationalists, but not their political initiatives that undermined the Ottoman state they were trying to defend.[49] Nevertheless, next to Alexandria, Beirut, 'the city of science, commerce, and ceaseless activity' was depicted as a model for urban modernity.[50] In a leading article, Yusuf al-'Isa proposed a reform agenda to the regional council (*majlis 'umumi/meclis-i umumi*) in the district, which included the opening of the local councils to foreigners. Yusuf al-'Isa cited Alexandria as a positive example, where the municipal council included Syrians, Italians, French and Greek among its members. In his opinion, this inclusion of foreigners had contributed to making the council a highly efficient institution. According to the same article, the governor of Beirut also planned to convene a mixed local-foreign commission to discuss the reform of municipal affairs, and 'Isa proposed that the provincial council of Jerusalem (*al-majlis al-'umumi/meclis-i umumi*) should emulate this example.[51] In this passage, Yusuf al-'Isa seems to evoke a common identity of progressive and international Mediterranean port-cities which included Beirut as well as Alexandria in British-occupied Egypt.

News from the imperial capital Istanbul reached *Filastin*'s readers almost exclusively through the reports of news agencies and translated excerpts from Ottoman Turkish newspapers; very few of these news pieces concerned life in the city itself. The fact that *Filastin* was very much a part of the struggle of Arab Orthodox laymen against the Greek clergy may explain the conspicuous absence of reports on the Greek-Orthodox patriarchate or community matters in Istanbul. The city was mostly mentioned as the seat of high politics and without drawing direct links to the government's policies in Palestine. The only political links frequently mentioned are the governor and the three local members of parliament, who are mentioned and portrayed on various occasions. Nevertheless, through extensive quotes and summaries from the Ottoman press and the parliamentary debates, *Filastin*'s readers were well informed about the major trends in the imperial government. It seems that Yusuf and 'Isa al-'Isa's involvement in the CUP was mainly a political matter and did not entail a particular affinity for Turkish culture. To them, Istanbul as a cultural center was of much less importance than the Arab cities.

The core region of interest for *Filastin*'s journalists and readers seems to be congruent with the region where Levantine colloquial Arabic is spoken, roughly from Tripoli to Gaza.[52] Other Mediterranean centers did not figure very prominently, except for the arenas of major political and military crises –such as Albania or the province of Tripoli (Libya). To its readership, these were neither of particular economic nor cultural interest. The coverage of Europe was dominated by England and France, due to 'Isa and Yusuf al-'Isa's economic and cultural priorities. Liverpool was the port to where the bulk of Jaffa's oranges were shipped,[53] while French was the main foreign language in the 'Isas' social milieu and, apart from the Arabic classics, French literature was clearly their cultural model.[54] But there were other places that figured even more prominently on the mental map of many of the Arab Orthodox readers of *Filastin*: As the newspaper was read by a number of the mainly Arab Orthodox Palestinian emigrants in the diaspora communities of the Americas, news from there and about the community life in the new home appeared regularly on *Filastin*'s pages. One finds letters from Cleveland, Ohio, as well as from Chicago and several cities in Brazil, Mexico and Chile.[55]

ha-Herut

Not surprisingly, *ha-Herut*'s map was very much determined by the trans-national character of the Sephardic community. We find the same close connection between Jerusalem and Jaffa as in *Filastin*. As in the Arabic newspaper, other Palestinian cities were also covered by a wealth of reports from local correspondents or letters from individuals. The Ottoman unit of the district of Jerusalem seems to have mattered less to the Jewish authors than it did to the authors of *Filastin*. Although politically belonging to the province of Beirut, the towns of Haifa, Safed, and Tiberias with their large Jewish populations were covered as extensively as Hebron and Gaza in the south. As in *Filastin*, among the northern cities Haifa received most coverage. Many of the reports from there dealt with the worsening relations between Haifa's Jews and their Muslim and Christian neighbors, and very often the articles of the Arab Orthodox *al-Karmil* were blamed for this situation.[56]

Among the Arab cities of the Eastern Mediterranean, Beirut, Cairo, and Alexandria received most coverage in *ha-Herut*. All three places were frequent stations in the educational and professional careers of the younger generation of Palestine's Sephardic elite.[57] Trends and events in Egypt were regularly covered through the articles of the paper's correspondents who reported from the country, usually in a weekly rhythm under the heading 'From the Land of Egypt' (mi-erets Mitsrayim). Here, provincial towns such as Tanta are also frequently mentioned. This column most commonly treated topics such as the cotton trade, the security situation, Jewish community matters, and Egyptian politics.

In marked contrast to Filastin, but in accordance with the structure of the Ottoman Sephardic community, ha-Herut displayed close ties to the cities of İzmir and Salonica, the strongholds of Sephardic life in the Eastern Mediterranean. On an almost weekly basis a correspondent reported from each city. The amount of news ha-Herut's readers received from these places almost equaled that from Jaffa and Haifa. Most of it concerned internal Sephardic community matters such as the situation of the community's schools and the financing of social services. Many of the contributions from the two major Sephardic centers might have been acquired through the contacts of Azriel's publishing house. Central and Eastern Anatolia, however, are absent from ha-Herut's cartography, as they are from Filastin's.

The coverage of Istanbul equally differs from that of Filastin. Since many Sephardic Jews from the district of Jerusalem maintained close ties with their co-religionists in the capital (which the Arab Orthodox lacked), they held a greater interest in the city's local politics than Filastin's readers.[58] With frequent reports on Istanbul's municipal and Jewish communal matters alike, the capital must have looked less foreign to the eyes of Jerusalem's Sephardic Jews than to its Arab Christians.

With regard to the Mediterranean basin as a whole, the mental map of ha-Herut's readers must have looked quite different from that of Filastin's. Although the accent clearly lay on the Ottoman domains and Egypt, the editor's selection of telegrams from the Reuters news agency contains many reports on cities such as Athens, Belgrade, Naples, Rome, and Lisbon. Apart from their political relevance, the reason might have been family, business and community ties which connected some of ha-Herut's readers to these places. In Athens, the paper even had a regular correspondent.[59] An additional focus within ha-Herut's coverage of world news was the centers of Jewish life all over the world. Of special concern among these were the Jewish communities in Russia and Yemen, who both suffered from discrimination and persecution. Very much in tune with the editors' cultural-nationalist convictions, a series of letters, often printed on the front page, served to enlighten the readers about the situation of different Jewish communities. In addition, Berlin and London were often mentioned as the centers of Zionist activities in Europe. There are no similar articles in *Filastin*. 'Isa and Yusuf al-'Isa's main concerns were the rights of non-Muslims in Palestine. They did not identify with the structures and institutions of the Greek-Orthodox *millet* beyond the Arab-speaking Orthodox communities of Palestine and Bilad al-Sham.

Conclusion

The way in which the two Palestinian papers mapped the Eastern Mediterranean and the world at large shows commonalities as well as differences. First of all, the mental maps of both reading communities were shaped by the framework of the Ottoman Empire. Thus, while the readers of *Filastin* and *ha-Herut* were well acquainted with politics in the Ottoman capital, Europe seemed far away. In both cases, the coverage of other parts of the world correlated to a great extent with the concentrations of the respective diaspora communities.

Yet we find different accents in how the Eastern Mediterranean was mapped by the journalists: *ha-Herut* showed a close association to the Sephardic centers in Istanbul, Salonica, İzmir, Cairo, and Alexandria. As a rule, the paper exclusively covered places with a considerable Jewish, preferably Sephardic, community. Apart from that, we see a palpable interest in the events and developments in the wider Mediterranean world. In contrast, the rest of the Arab World or the Middle East is much less present. As a whole, *ha-Herut*'s outlook can be characterized as more Ottoman and international, but at the same time less political and more community-oriented than that of *Filastin*. *Filastin*'s outlook, on the other hand, appears to be more Arabo-centric. According to the paper's ambition to serve both a Christian as well as a Muslim readership, the places covered were almost invariably Arab cities of the Levant. The Anatolian lands, it seems, were of only minor interest to its reading public. The Greek-Orthodox community in Istanbul was not a focus of solidarity because of the language divide, and because many of *Filastin*'s authors were at odds with the Greek clergy. All the more prominent were Beirut and Cairo with their rapid urban development, their institutions of higher learning and their artistic and intellectual scene of the Arabic *nahda*.

Both newspapers and the communities they represented appear to have been well integrated into the structures of the Ottoman Empire, although with different accents. The Arab Orthodox Christians represented by 'Isa and Yusuf al-'Isa did not trust the framework of their representation through their community's ecclesiastic institutions in Istanbul and were actively using the institutions and the vocabulary of the constitutional period to promote an alliance with the Sunni Muslim majority. The most obvious platforms for such an alliance were the Arabic language and the political structures of the Ottoman Empire. Thus it comes as no surprise that these two areas were privileged in their coverage of the current events. In contrast, for the Sephardic community represented by *ha-Herut*, the institutions of their *millet* seemed to work well. The Sephardic Jews who supported *ha-Herut* might have been one of the most Ottoman-ized social groups in Palestine.

Yet, the visions of the Eastern Mediterranean contained in these two Palestinian newspapers of the early twentieth century also share many commonalities. Their image was dominated by urban centers dotting the line of the Mediterranean coast; the countryside was to a large extent a blank space between these urban nodes. The underlying cause of this picture seems to have been the unequal pace with which infrastructure and communication networks had developed in the Eastern Mediter-ranean, a process which confirmed as well as upset the traditional hierar-chies between and among urban and rural settlements.[60]

Port-cities like Jaffa had a large advantage by dint of their location, as they had access to the network of steamers, then the main medium of exchange throughout the Mediterranean and the wider world. The port-cities were followed in rank by the provincial capitals in the interior, such as Jerusalem, which were increasingly well connected to the larger world through improved streets as well as telegraph and railway lines. Next was a group of secondary towns that happened to be situated on the commu-nication lines between the regional centers or profited from their prox-imity. In the *sancak* (district) of Jerusalem, places such as Ramla, Lydda, and Bethlehem fell into this category, followed by Hebron and Gaza. In the case of Gaza, this third-degree rank signified a severe loss of status, considering that it once held a commanding position, before the caravan routes between Bilad al-Sham, Palestine, and Egypt were overtaken in importance by the sea trade.[61] Finally, the villages and small towns of the hinterland were largely left behind. Not only were they not connected by paved roads and telegraph lines, but the rural elites in general lost much of their former influence when the Ottoman state asserted its monopoly of power even in the most remote corners of Palestine.[62] In short, whereas the cities were more or less well connected to the larger world, not all the hinterland was connected to the cities. This in turn led to a change in the relations between time and space, so that for many newspaper readers in

Jerusalem and Jaffa Beirut or Alexandria could seem much closer than the immediate surroundings of their cities.

Despite a high degree of spatial mobility within late Ottoman Palestinian society, the mental maps of Palestinian journalists and their readers were clearly circumscribed. The geographic scope of the bulk of the newspapers' coverage was limited by the borders of 'a regional core world' constituted by the Levant.[63] This was supplemented by coverage of Istanbul and Egypt and the diaspora communities of the respective *millets* abroad. The picture conveyed by the Arabic *Filastin* and the Hebrew *ha-Herut* is an urban-centered vision of space shaped by the Ottoman political order, the structures of *millet* communities, and the personal networks of a new group of mobile middle-class actors. In the period under survey, local patriotism and the trans-national outlook of the *millet* communities were no contradiction, since both could be combined in the framework of the Ottoman state. This changed dramatically with the collapse of the empire and the sudden emergence of a world of nation-states. The stories of the two editorial teams after World War I show to what extent their visions were compatible or incompatible with the age of nationalism. *Filastin*, now managed by 'Isa al-'Isa alone, continued to advocate a Christian-Muslim rapprochement, and became one of the leading Arabic newspapers of Mandatory Palestine. *ha-Herut*, however, ceased publication, because there was no longer any room for its trans-national, community-oriented perspective. Thus, with the sudden demise of the age-old Ottoman hegemony, the advent of nationalisms, and the subsequent end of the age of multi-cultural port-cities, the mental maps of the Eastern Mediterranean underwent a radical change.

Adding New Scales of History to the Eastern Mediterranean: Illicit Trade and the Albanian

Isa Blumi

Seeing the Eastern Mediterranean as a series of interconnected zones of commercial, political and cultural exchange offers the scholar a crucial perspective to the emergence of the modern state in the nineteenth century. Most important in this context are the continued socio-economic interactions in the Eastern Mediterranean that instigated a full range of state reforms that informed European imperial relations at the time. Scratching the surface of these reforms reveals the local at the heart of most events.

I argue throughout this paper that local activities intensified the tensions between state attempts to regulate (and harness) regional trade and the seemingly parochial interests of coastal trading families, highland smugglers, and regional governors. Often, the tension between the state's ambitions and local needs translated into the legal marginalization and open persecution of local commercial activity. Local trade routes, for example, were suddenly blocked by tax collectors who condemned traditional patterns of trade as impermissible acts of smuggling. In this chapter I suggest adopting a less rigid way of characterizing these kinds of transactions in the Balkans during a crucial time of transition in the late nineteenth century. In order to begin to add new layers to our understanding of the region's modern history, I wish to remain

open to the idea that other factors may be behind certain policy decisions during such a transformative period. An openness to contributing
factors to history other than the state helps attribute new forces of
change to events otherwise trapped in the unhelpful jargon of ethno-
nationalism, sectarianism or banditry.

I study here informal trade patterns in the context of reconfigurations
of state power in the Balkans in order to suggest a general reorientation
of how history in the larger Mediterranean world can be written. As is
perfectly clear in our world today, too often interpretations of moments
of violence fall under the crude rubric of 'terrorism' (or in the context of
the nineteenth century, 'banditry'); this approach effectively precludes
new ways of interpreting the foundation of events. A more careful reading of past events that is sensitive to both the subject and the object of
imperial *and* indigenous interests may ultimately translate into a new
and more flexible methodological *scale* to interpret events in the contemporary Eastern Mediterranean world.

Rather than limit our understanding of so-called illegal forms of
commercial activity by using terms set by the imperial state, it may
prove worthwhile to revisit such interactions as part of a dynamism that
cut the across regional, topographical, racial, ethnic and sectarian divisions so frequently encountered in studies on the Eastern Mediterranean
world. By recasting 'piracy', 'smuggling', and other illicit forms of trade
that often resulted in direct state persecution, we may allow for the pro-
ductive component of local economies to contribute to a new story of the
Eastern Mediterranean. At the heart of this new analysis of the Eastern
Mediterranean are the interactions between state regulators and local
populations. The most common evidence of such exchanges is the violent moments of engagement when state authorities attempted to control
local economic activity. Among the many tools of state regulation were
the selective use of military force, the imposition of laws regulating land
use, the manipulation of com-mercial alliances, and the settlement of
outside people at the expense of rebellious indigenous communities.
This is certainly the case on the Ottoman Balkans between 1872 and
1908, when changing fortunes for Orthodox Christian Slavs resulted in
the creation of ethno-national states that incorporated large tracts of –as
in our case here– Albanian Muslim and Catholic lands. The resulting
adjustments and reactions most readily evident in Balkan national historiographies in terms of sectarian and ethnic tensions may in fact indicate
a far more complex set of considerations that ultimately account for
change in the modern world.

The Albanian Context

While regional histories have dealt with rebellion and even occasionally 'illegal' trade, they have rarely considered an important interconnecting factor in this period. We may begin to appreciate the entire Eastern Mediterranean in new terms, for example, if we effectively identify the contributions of Albanian-speakers to certain kinds of transformations fundamental to the emerging modern world. More important than simply identifying a new group of participants in the dynamics of Eastern Mediterranean commerce and modern state building, however, is to explore how certain forms of informal trade and patterns of settlement changed the nature of imperial rule. Illicit commercial transactions within the larger context of Albanian social, political and economic history may, therefore, provide examples of how Ottoman administrative reforms throughout the *Tanzimat* and post-*Tanzimat* era can provide an alternative *scale* of analyzing relations in the modern world.

Albanian commercial networks, either established by century-old merchant houses or, as it will be suggested here, as reconfigurations within refugee settlements, proved capable of circumventing the formal political and economic spaces that reforming imperial regimes imposed. This autonomy from the imperial state was so extensive that over a crucial period of transition, from the middle of the nineteenth century to World War I, the modernizing institutions of imperial powers operating in the Eastern Mediterranean saw themselves actually compelled to adopt new forms of fiscal, political and economic organization. In other words, local trade that official documentation identified as illicit played a central role in the institutional, social and political transformations of the period.

The 'illegal' trade that one could observe in refugee communities and established Albanian merchant houses alike extended from the Adriatic coast and its hinterland to various parts of the Eastern Mediterranean (especially Cyprus, Egypt, and Lebanon) throughout the nineteenth century. These networks proved so lucrative that the patriarchs of these merchant houses gained considerable political influence in the region. At key moments of the nineteenth century, the imperial state had to concede considerable power to these men. In the process of forcing state officials to negotiate with them on terms often determined by the extent of their influence in the Mediterranean, local traders thus managed to transform the stigma of pirate, smuggler, bandit or rebel into the officially documented role of community leader, revolutionary, or legitimate merchant. This fluid pattern of interaction between state and subject is crucial to reconsidering the region's history. In time, many forms of trade in the Eastern Mediterranean became formally recognized engines of change, and previously persecuted commercial trans-actions became objects of state institutionalization and, ultimately, normali-zation under the guise of imperial reforms.

The primary context for appreciating these types of transformation re-quires revisiting the entire nineteenth century, a period during which well-placed commercial families enjoyed considerable autonomy in their areas of influence. In time, these areas, which included much of the Albanian-speaking regions of the Balkans as well as North Africa and the Mashriq, proved vital to the reconfiguration of commercial networks linking much of the Arabic-speaking Mediterranean with the Ottoman Balkans and Anato-lia. Especially vital to this regional dynamism were the Albanian merchant enclaves established in Algiers, Malta, Tunisia and Sicily from the six-teenth to the end of the eighteenth century. Throughout this period, Alba-nian diaspora communities maintained commercial ties with each other, allowing the Ottoman state to influence in informal ways the affairs of most of the Mediterranean. It was Northern Albanian families such as the Busha-ti, Sarachi, and Çoba, along with more widely known figures such as Mehmet Ali Pasha of Kavala and Ali Pasha of Tepelen from Southern Albanian who inherited these patterns of commerce at the beginning of the nineteenth century. Much like their predecessors, this new generation of patriarchs maintained long-distance trade links that connected the Albanian ports of Shkodër/Scutari and Ulqin/Dulcino (today in Montenegro), Draç/Durrës, and Preveza with Egypt, Malta, Syria, Tunisia, and the Ae-gean islands.[1] As in the past, such commercial links translated into consid-erable political power for connected families, power that directly clashed with Ottoman, French or British efforts to control regional trade. The strug-gle over the control over these trade routes precipitated a dramatic period of transformation in the Eastern Mediterranean.

These confrontations may be particularly helpful for studying the larger context of the Tanzimat reforms as well as contemporary reforms in Europe. As argued elsewhere, many of the institutional adaptations which accompanied modern state-building reforms throughout the Mediterranean world (not only in the Ottoman Empire, but also in Italy, France and Egypt) suggests that the development of the modern state and local capacities to thwart state centralization go hand-in-hand.[2] While there is still consider-able room for improvement in our understanding of the first half of the nineteenth century in regard to such confrontations, for our purposes here the reforms most readily associated with Sultan Abdülhamid II (1876–1909) may suffice in making a larger methodological point. As a by-product of the interactions between the Ottoman and European imperial states and local Albanian subjects, the reforms imposed by the Hamidian state should not simply be treated as a gesture of governmental power. This distinction is crucial for allowing locals political agency, as well as for avoiding the mistake of ignoring the numerous factors behind decisions made at the highest levels of government.

The Grandee Families of the Albanian Mediterranean

Based in the Adriatic trading port of Shkodër/Scutari (İşkodra in Ottoman Turkish) of the late eighteenth century, the local Albanian Bushati family proved especially adept at securing political and economic independence from Istanbul, while linking the Adriatic port-towns under their control with both the Balkan hinterland and the larger Mediterranean world.[3] Mehmet Bushati in particular became a significant player in the larger Mediterranean by 1757, when as a concession to stop local revolts Istanbul appointed him governor of the district (*sancak*) of Shkodër. Bushati's appointment merely intensified the family's power in the region, a development which forced the Ottoman authorities to redraw the *sancak*'s frontiers to include the hinterland town of Peja/Ipek; a cartographic concession to the new governor who wanted to formally link Kosova with Shkodër and thus the larger Adriatic commercial zone. This early institutionalization of a series of internal dynamics far from Istanbul's direct control led to successive governorships held by the Bushati clan until the early nineteenth century. In 1785, for example, Mehmet's son Mahmut used the resources allocated to him as governor (*vali*) in order to proceed with the military subjugation of much of Central Albania and Kosova, so as to expand his family's commercial interests. By the time he died in 1796, Mahmut Bushati had extended the commercial ties of the port-city of Shkodër's to the Albanian hinterland, especially Kosova, to the point that some contemporary observers could discern a long-term agenda to politically unify all Albanian-speaking territories.

While Albanian historians have often erroneously conflated Bushati maneuvering with proto-nationalist ambitions, it would also be a mistake to remove the Bushati family from the larger Mediterranean context. Apart from the many activities that the members of this grandee family pursued in the immediate Albanian homeland, Mahmut Bushati realized that the family's interests lay well beyond the confines of the Adriatic Sea and its hinterland. Bushati may have hoped to establish an independent confederation based in present-day Montenegro, but these gestures also came from a family that saw the larger Balkans and Mediterranean as a source of wealth and power, and not necessarily in strictly ethno-national terms. For example, the Bushati family openly supported the French revolutionary army as it advanced into the neighboring Italian peninsula. The removal of entrenched rival North Italian families was most likely the goal behind such support, but it is not out of the question that republican idealism may also have contributed to such decisions. This combination of liberal values and commercial interests probably explains the family's assistance in the local rebellions scattered throughout the Balkan Peninsula at the time.

The Bushati's financial and logistical support included direct assistance to the rebellions in Serbia and Greece that undermined Ottoman rule in much of the Balkans and ultimately resulted in the creation of independent states.[4] Importantly, the rebellions in Serbia and Greece were at least initially based on the principles of a multi-ethnic cadre of merchant-*cum*-revolutionaries who did not envision a world in which ethnicity and sectarianism would interfere with the interaction of people. Perhaps the most important example of this is the creation of independent Greece, which for much of the first fifty years of its history was a bilingual state, with Albanian Christians (such as Greece's first governor, Jani Kapodistria from the Cham region) playing central roles both in the military, especially the navy, and in government.[5]

While the long-term impact of such patronage requires deeper investigation, for our purposes here the Bushati dynasty's history is emblematic of the larger process of interaction and state reaction to local/trans-regional change. Ostensibly, the exploits of the Bushati family created for other local Albanians with firm commercial links in the larger Mediterranean region a model for how to resist Istanbul's (or other European powers') direct rule. As much as Bushati's economic independence was assured by the lucrative trade that the family had secured over generations, so too did the family's contemporaries further to the South exploit opportunities to achieve political and economic autonomy from Istanbul. By openly challenging the Ottoman state to effectively monitor commerce in the Adriatic and the larger Eastern Mediterranean, Albanians such as Ali Pasha of Tepelen (Ali Pasha of Janina/Ioannina/ Yanya) and Mehmet Ali of Kavala played an important role in great power politics, a role that had an even greater impact on the region's history.

The ability of these Albanian notables (*ayan*) to forge independent political entities in Yanya and Egypt respectively was largely predicated on their ability to secure commercial alliances that seem to have required common cultural/linguistic associations. A much-studied case, Ali Pasha Tepelen, based in Janina in Southern Albania, gained long-term political influence by maintaining trade links with Albanian families scattered throughout the Arabic-speaking world.[6] Similarly, Mehmet Ali of Kavala, with his own links to the Albanian merchant and military elites spread throughout the Eastern Mediterranean, secured in Egypt virtual political and economic independence from Istanbul by 1816. Indeed, even more so than his fellow Albanian *ayan*, Mehmet Ali and his sons expanded the commercial and political influence of his Egyptian state to incorporate the entire Eastern Mediterranean world and linked it to the larger Red Sea/African context by the 1840s.[7]

Along with measures to counter similar examples of local autonomy won elsewhere over the century such as in Tunisia, Libya, Greece, Cyprus and Sicily, these actions introduced a new order in imperial relations, a new order which modern historians have described in terms of modernity. In the case of Egypt, imperial powers feared that a weakened Ottoman state incapable of maintaining economic and political order in the Eastern Mediterranean would encourage rival empires of Russia, Austria, France and Britain to take advantage of the situation. As a result, the British and the French directly intervened to eradicate Mehmet Ali. Such measures ultimately introduced the types of reform meant both to empower the Ottoman Empire to effectively manage its diverse lands and to render it a subordinate but invaluable extension of British and French hegemony in the region.[8]

Ironically, it was the Balkans inhabitants' response to the increasing efficiency of the Ottoman state in their region that ultimately led to the Russo–Ottoman War of 1876–77 and to the establishment of independent states in the Balkans. It is at the point of the Berlin Congress of 1878 and the treaty under which the Ottoman state was to concede a new political order in the Balkans that we can study in greater detail how Albanians contributed to the following set of transformations in the Eastern Mediterranean. This process exposes the impact of an important new generation of diplomatic and commercial regulations implemented by the new sultan, Abdülhamid II, in 1878. Paradoxically, these measures intended to strengthen a weak Ottoman state actually spurred local communities (such as those along the Albanian coast and in its hinterland) to intensify their resistance to the intrusive state centralization schemes that outside powers considered so crucial to the long-term success of the Ottoman state. The clashing agendas of Albanian locals and the imperial states contributed to a new world order.

Establishing a New World Order

It is interesting to note that the key obstacle to enforcing the treaties that the Berlin Congress imposed on the Ottoman state was local insubordination. Particularly in the Albanian highlands, an area linked by old trading routes established by Shkodër- and Ulqin-based families, local communities openly resisted attempts to draw territorial boundaries through their lands. As demonstrated in previous work, despite being declared 'just and fair' twice, the contested boundaries meant to separate a newly established Serbia and Montenegro from Ottoman Albanian had to be modified to placate local objections.[9] Here we find the first of many important lessons to draw from the Berlin Congress and the modern order it supposedly introduced. Ultimately, the extent of local Albanian resistance to new forms of governmental control and the Ottoman state's inability to enforce them compelled European powers to change their own practice of administrating territorial frontiers throughout the world.

Local resistance ultimately forced the Great Powers to modify their diplomatic decrees as well as expectations about how states were to administer their territories. In response to local Malësore's resistance, the Great Powers introduced a dangerous series of measures that would ultimately sanction the use of force in order to permit regional states (such as the newly independent Montenegro and Serbia) to assert further claims on Ottoman Albanian territories. Montenegro, for instance, was awarded the Albanian-inhabited port of Ulqin, thereby creating conditions leading to the confrontation between local Albanians and the outside world that would have long-term consequences for commerce in the Adriatic. Tellingly, the manner in which Montenegro and Serbia, both self-declared Christian Orthodox kingdoms, attempted to administer their newly awarded territories by forcefully expelling large numbers of Albanians unintentionally became one of those cumulatively disruptive forces of change that transformed the region. The Montenegrin and Serbian states' policy of selective ethnic homogenization created new opportunities for a new cast of characters who strategically mobilized Albanian commercial networks for the next forty years.

Montenegro's policy towards the Albanian-speaking communities straddling the newly established border is especially valuable as a case study to appreciate this new regional dynamism. While the ultimate goal was to homogenize the territories along religious and ethnic lines (Montenegro did encourage settlers from Herzegovina and Serbia to set up communities along its frontiers) the new kingdom at the same time opted for a policy of selective expulsion. As noted by British officials, this policy had its long-term economic rationale.[10] The central concern in Montenegro's newly formed government was to extract as much wealth from the indigenous population and then to expand trade in the region in order to give Montenegro leverage over its Ottoman rival. This required keeping a well-oiled economic machine running. This economy could only be maintained, however, by the Albanian merchant families who created it. This realization compelled the Montenegrin state to allow fragments of these vital commercial families to remain in the country while the vast majority was expelled to Ottoman territories.[11]

For the most part, Montenegro's strategy balanced the use of violence and the economic, cultural and political isolation of targeted populations with financial inducements for those Albanians deemed essential for keeping the state's economy connected to the outside world. Thus, Prince Nicholas' entire campaign of repopulating his newly created state with Slavs from Herzegovina required a nuanced approach to his inherited multi-ethnic population. Nicholas recognized that it would have been economic suicide to force embedded populations to migrate *en masse* all at once. This was especially true in larger centers of trade where Albanian merchants were entrenched in the region's commercial networks and therefore commanded a central role in the future stability of Montenegro's economy. Recognizing that Montenegro practiced a policy of selective violence is especially important in the context of recent events in the region. Despite the appeal of the idea of ethnically cleansing the region of non-Slav peoples, a new political order in the region did not necessarily mean that it was either possible or responsible to destroy a country's economic foundation. The century-old activities of Albanian grandee merchant families ultimately secured a permanent role for many Albanians in Montenegro after 1878.[12]

In order to successfully pressure most non-essential Albanians to leave Montenegro without destroying the economic vitality of the newly created country, Nicholas' government adopted a strategy of applying economic pressure on selected Albanians through state mechanisms. The need to forcefully remove most Albanian inhabitants required new bureaucracies and enforcement mechanisms, some of which creatively legitimized the practice of arbitrarily confiscating property. The principle of 'imminent domain', a policy that resulted in the impoverishment of many of the historically wealthy families, would prove for the state an invaluable tool, not only in Montenegro, but on the Ottoman side of the border as well.[13]

It is important to recall that, while Montenegro used new state regulations to antagonize, intimidate and often forcefully expel Albanians, many of the most important trading families were still encouraged to leave a small representative core behind in order to continue the family business. Even the most prominent Ulqin families did fall victim to this strategy. By all accounts, large numbers of members of the Bianki and

Çoba families of were expelled from Montenegro. At the same time, however, a small portion of these same families were allowed to stay behind and, more importantly, most of the shops and property owned by these families were allowed to remain in their hands.[14] This selective use of ethnic cleansing clearly undermines the sometimes sloppy reading of the region's past and ultimately questions the value of seeing today's events in strictly ethno-nationalist terms. Clearly, Montenegrin officials adopted a far more creative understanding of state interests, including the preservation of the region's the economic vitality.

Paradoxically, this selective dispersion of Albanian merchants and craftsmen proved to be an invaluable asset for the Ottoman state. Officials in the Ottoman territories recognized the opportunity that the massive influx of expelled Albanians presented and set up a commission that supervised the resettlement process. In addition to securing homes for them, the commission actively lobbied for financial compensation as well. The call for restoring the financial vitality of many of the region's old merchant families reflects an underlying hope that these Albanians would maintain their old commercial connections with the outside world.[15]

This process of selective expulsion by the Montenegrin state and their state-funded resettlement by the Ottoman administration along the newly drawn frontier clearly demonstrates both governments' appreciation of the strategic value of Albanian merchant communities. At the same time, as a result of government efforts, these settlement patterns may prove useful for understanding how periods of transition (such as those after 1878) contributed to shaping the entire Eastern Mediterranean during the following four decades. It is clear that the nature of the exchanges between members of the Albanian commercial elite and Ottoman officials during this crucial transitional period between 1878 and 1912 almost immediately transformed the way business was conducted in the larger Mediterranean context. One way of observing this transformation is to look more closely at how the Ottoman local government resettled the massive influx of expelled Albanians from newly created Serbia and Montenegro.

The Politics of Resettlement

The first area in which Ottoman officials settled Albanians from the commercial towns of Ulqin, Antivari (Bar) and Podgoritza (all ceded to Montenegro) was Tuz, a new boomtown located on the recently drawn frontier in the Albanian highlands. As would become clear later, this resettlement did not cut the Albanians' commercial ties to Montenegro by any stretch of the imagination. Both the Ottoman state and Montenegro saw an opportunity in this new border community and did their best to encourage trade within the region. Some ten years after this policy was initiated, Ottoman officials observed that many of the expelled Albanians based in Tuz were not only doing well, but were also able to maintain their businesses in Montenegro. Many of those profiting from the trade that linked the coast with this highland boomtown retained a family member in one of the port-towns or, an increasingly viable option, paid newly settled Slavs to manage their affairs on Montenegrin territory.[16]

In addition to the both states' shrewd assurance that individual interests were not completely cut by the new frontiers, a new logistical consideration was integrated into local policies as a direct result of the transforming regional economy. The reconfiguration of the regional economy and its infrastructure reflects a desire to fully exploit opportunities that were ironically created by a policy of selectively expelling Albanians from their homes. The Montenegrin state, for example, started to build a road connecting the two port-towns still populated by Albanians (Ulqin and Antivari), and the Ottoman frontier. In time, this road actually facilitated the illegal export of goods from Montenegro to Ottoman markets just across the border. Such an investment demonstrates a state interest in facilitating communication between the now displaced communities living in a rival state and its own market towns.[17]

One of the more remarkable examples of Ottoman bureaucratic maturation in the Hamidian era was the speed with which the administration built the infrastructure to handle, feed and settle large numbers of people. The emerging institutions not only secured homes, but also created opportunities to raise the revenue needed to fund these measures. One means of securing the additional funds needed to assimilate nearly a million of expelled Albanians was to tax all commerce passing through the newly created frontiers. However, the anticipated windfall of revenue did not materialize overnight.

Among the more interesting consequences of this attempt to tax trade crossing the newly created Ottoman frontier was the expanding influence of Shkodër-based families within both the Montenegrin and Ottoman administrations. Such influence did not arise, however, from the immediate cooperation of these families with the new political and economic order. On the contrary, they proved to be preeminent smugglers. It was these families, and especially the Sarachi, who extended commercial links with Montenegro in order to profit from the demand for smuggled goods that skirted Ottoman customs agents. Realizing that Montenegro's newly built roads and bridges connecting ports with key trade routes on Ottoman territory offered a lucrative opportunity, the Sarachi and others quickly challenged the ability of local Ottoman governors to maintain control of the region's economy. Much of the trade between Montenegro and the Sarachi family was conducted beyond Ottoman state control. As much as these activities had an economic consequence, they were also important for creating political opportunities, as the growing Ottoman concern with 'illegal' trade forced officials to adopt new methods of governance. The trade passing from Montenegrin-based Albanian families to those who processed the distribution of smuggled goods on Ottoman territory helped create new concentrations of political and economic power throughout the region that compelled the Ottoman state to make generous concessions to these families.

At the same time, rapidly changing patterns of commerce also created new trade zones along the frontiers, empowering and enriching (but also marginalizing) a wide range of actors formerly excluded from the region's trade networks. As a result, the business of smuggling everything from weapons to cloth ultimately changed the region, resulting in a transformation of the way the Ottoman state perceived its interests in the region as well as local political fortunes. For instance, efforts to stop the smuggling of certain goods led to new policies in the Ottoman administration, one of the most dramatic being the settlement of large numbers of Albanians expelled from Montenegro specifically in the border regions. Not surprisingly, while securing the frontiers by settling refugees proved effective at times, such a policy also openly threatened communities that thrived on the new lucrative economic relationships established along the border.

The problem not only affected Ottoman territories. Albanian communities who smuggled goods from Ottoman territory into Montenegro were equally threatening to the Montenegrin state. According to the Italian consul based in Shkodër, the inhabitants of the Albanian region of Selza (Kelmendi) often were in open conflict with Montenegrin officials, as they too started to collect taxes on trade from the region.[18] This confrontation between Montenegrin officials and locals clearly points to a change in policy by 1890. The profits that smuggling produced for the local economy over time translated into either costly measures to suppress it or lucrative opportunities for individual agents of the state to be corrupted. The range of possible ways to engage in local trade ultimately transformed the nature of governance in the region. In time, it became less and less clear that Montenegro (or, for that matter, the Ottoman state) would be able to fully control this lucrative business. As trade grew in the region, Montenegrin officials, and especially those newly appointed to 'protect' national borders, saw the commercial activity as a source of personal income instead of as an important concession to locals. When transactions took place without paying the officials their 'cut' while smuggling goods into Ottoman territory, cases like the arrest of four local Kelmendi traders found in the archives provide an example of the transforming nature of relations between locals and state.

The controversial arrest of four small-time Albanian smugglers for 'illegally entering' Montenegro was ultimately a reaction to a source of revenue that escaped the control of border officials. The dramatic escalation of a local dispute suggests that an unspoken rule regulating the interaction between local traders and state officials had been broken. Almost immediately after the arrest of the four shepherds, relatives attacked the representatives of the Montenegrin state. Local patterns of trade temporarily shifted, as Montenegrin officials responded with greater efforts to police the commercial activity passing through their jurisdiction.

When analyzing these events, it is important to consider who benefited. The subsequent battle between locals and Montenegro served not only the interests of the Ottoman state, but also those of the regional cluster of merchants who exploited newly created opportunities. Among the more intriguing consequences of local confrontations such as those in Kelmendi was the new importance given to good relations between the Ottoman administration and their local allies. The significance of seemingly local problems such as these for the Eastern Mediterranean's modern history can best be appreciated if we further explore the phenomenon of the settlement and adjustment of Albanian merchant families after the Berlin Congress through the prism of Ottoman state adjustments to local resistance to trade regulations.

Exile in the Ottoman State

As noted earlier, Istanbul decided from the very beginning of this transition period to incorporate expelled Albanian into communities living along the empire's frontiers. Perhaps the most important motivation was to secure the new frontier region. The underlying logic was that a significant population along the borders would make it far more difficult for the relatively small armies of Serbia and Greece to invade. Such calculations were clearly at play in the manner in which refugees from the recently ceded port-city of Ulqin were immediately resettled along the frontier in Tuz and in the mountains surrounding Shkodër. More than simply using the population as a buffer to possible future invasions, however, Ottoman officials also used these refugees as willing trouble-makers by allowing them for long periods of time to conduct raids against the Slav settlers who moved into their former lands on the other side of the newly imposed Montenegrin borders.[19]

This policy of resettlement also had its problems. In an important way, the exodus from Montenegro and Serbia had a great social impact on the local communities on whose lands the expelled Albanians were settled. Host communities in the *vilayet*s (provinces) of Shkodër and Kosova were regularly compelled to bear a great economic and political burden in order to accommodate the newcomers. This burden became a force of change in its own right and would have long-term consequences for the Ottoman Empire and the larger Mediterranean context.

A particularly valuable case emerges with the Catholic region of Mirdita, an area that traditionally resisted Ottoman efforts to directly control it. It is in Mirdita that Vasa Pasha (the well-known governor (*mutassarrıf*) of Mount Lebanon) led the disruptive rebellion that resulted in his exile to Lebanon. Tellingly, many Albanian refugees from Montenegro and Serbia were sent to this traditionally rebellious region from 1880 onwards. Obviously, there is a clear institutional rationale behind this settlement of refugees to this region. As already noted, Ottoman officials were keen on helping wealthy Albanian merchants find suitable homes in their newly established frontier areas. In addition, however, the administration without a doubt calculated that settling these wealthy and well-connected families in this traditionally rebellious region could effectively dilute the power of Mirdita's historically resistant leaders.

The blatant attempt to use thousands of expelled Albanians to stamp out the power of Mirdita's elite, among whom counted Prenk bib Doda Pasha, would create a new series of reactions and counter-actions that intensified local power struggles and opened disputes over land for the rest of the century. Recognizing that tensions do arise during population transfers such as those of 1878, even if they involve Albanians moving into Albanian population areas, sheds new light on the dynamics of regional politics. Most importantly, the case of Mirdita forces us to abandon the idea that ethnicity is the quintessential historical factor at play.[20] Rather, it is imperative that we consider other factors informing the actions of individuals and communities in the face of new challenges.

For one, Ottoman distribution of local land to placate refugees became a policy that changed the way locals conducted trade in the area. In one sense, it encouraged smuggling, as well as the creation of new commercial alliances that had long-term political consequences for Montenegro and the Ottoman Empire. This appears to have been especially problematic where the boundaries of administrative districts changed to accommodate new communities. For example, the consolidation of the districts of Mat, Mirdita, Akçahisar into Shkodër led to a change in how authorities administered the region. In the second half of the 1880s, for example, the responsibility of administering this newly consolidated border region, filled with tension as refugees settled amid locals, was given to Derviş Pasha. The new administration did not any waste time and completely restructured the way local economies were organized and local resources exploited. In each one of the sub-districts created by the reforms, Derviş Pasha initiated the process of negotiating and then implementing a distribution of land to refugees from Montenegro, as well as to Italian and Austrian prospectors interested in exploiting the region's forests.[21] Such dramatic changes caused long-term problems for locals like Prenk bib Doda Pasha, who lost considerable portions of his family's land to newly settled neighbors and European investors who had been granted concessions.

A key component of this process was the action that the refugees themselves took. Representatives of the Albanian refugees from Podgoritza – such as Hasan Bey, Mustafa Ağa, and Ibrahim Ağa– aggressively lobbied Derviş Pasha to put pressure on the central Ottoman government to compensate their financial losses.[22] The activism of the expelled Albanians highlights how certain personal tragedies can inspire the creation of a new political force. It also suggests that there were dramatic consequences to the solutions sought by Ottoman state officials, leading to a new drama emerging between the expelled families and their host communities. While the trauma of being expelled from their homeland was supposedly addressed by the Ottoman state, it was done so largely in confrontational ways. Large numbers of refugees were simply given land in regions like Mirdita.

The first cause of conflict was the way in which Ottoman authorities confiscated communal lands and forests from the native inhabitants of frontier regions such as Tuz and Mirdita.[23] The government's justifications for such confiscation in the face of local opposition further reveals how imperial frontiers both imposed new kinds of socio-economic realities and helped transform the nature of the co-existence of local communities with the Ottoman and Montenegrin states and each other. Resistance to such policies rested on indigenous notions of property ownership and local rights. To most inhabitants of the regions affected, the idea of denying another's territorial claims and ceding land to an outsider was the gravest sin.[24] In order to confront local objection to the manner in which land was handed over to outsiders, officials sought to weaken individual claims to what all of a sudden was legally deemed *miri* (state-owned) lands. Over time, the government adopted the concept of state ownership (*rakabe*), so that state officials could legally confiscate any land they deemed 'underutilized' (*mevat*) and redistribute it to political allies who, in theory, would convert such land into revenue-producing farms or properly exploit its forests. This doctrine, initially outlined in the famous

Land Code of 1858 (*Arazi Kanunnamesi*), helped create in places like Kosova and Shkodër the kinds of tension that characterize property disputes in the modern era and actually provided opportunities for individuals to become central to the development of the Eastern Mediterranean.

There is a long list of examples of the state being forced to modify its policy as it faced local opposition led by 'notables' such as Prenk bib Doda Pasha for much of the 1880s. Interestingly, as much as Prenk bib Doda resisted, the efforts by the state to counter his resistance led to the empowerment of new clusters of local actors willing to cooperate. In order to improve the management of land resources, the Ottoman government ultimately handed over certain administrative responsibilities to what it initially hoped were local allies, while at the same time granting significant transfers of land that belonged to those less cooperative, especially Prenk bib Doda. So-called imperial allies identified opportunities to exploit the state's policy of rewarding loyalty while at the same time punishing dissenters. Such approaches to government unintentionally gave long-term power to locals who strategically tuned their resistance in order to maximize the concessions offered by state officials.

This was especially evident in frontier zones where certain individuals were able to secure significant control over smuggling networks. In order to placate and ultimately harness the accumulated power of rebels/smugglers, the Ottoman authorities resorted to remarkable gestures of cooptation through land grants. At times, judges were instructed to grant part-time rebels such as Ali Pasha of Gosine land concessions, so as to convince him to remain loyal to the sultan. In this case, the state authorities' desire to reward loyalty with land extended even beyond Ali Pasha's own life. By order of a judge (*naib*) of Üsküp (Skopje), Ali Pasha's widow, Altun Hanım, received a generous amount of land recently taken from villages guilty of rebellion. While the land grant was cloaked in the language of legal compensation, in reality Ali Pasha's smuggling network –now under the influence of his widow and his former close associates– compelled the Ottoman state to reaffirm a lucrative relationship even after his death.[25]

The policy of granting land to placate local allies, often those who had previously led successful smuggling operations at the Ottoman state's expense, frequently appears in Ottoman archival records. The almost inevitable result of this policy, however, was to antagonize those communities whose lands were confiscated. In this case, Ottoman authorities applied an evolving notion of *terra nullius* (no-man's land) in order to rationalize an otherwise unprecedented number of state interventions to the benefit of some while hurting others. On the Balkans, the principle of *terra nullius* also reflected a tenuous relationship between international law and inhabitants labeled external to 'civilization'.

The use of pejoratives frequently noted in Ottoman documents is especially important here. The purpose of denigrating rural communities living in areas intended for state confiscation was to assert that they somehow were not lawful occupants of the land in question. This was done by claiming that the current inhabitants used the land in an irrational way. Accordingly, in order to realize its real market value the land needed proper state management, thus justifying uncompensated confiscation. In many cases, justification for the appropriation of land took the tone that such dispossessions were necessary to properly settle 'savage' (*vahşi*) peoples pursuing 'primitive' (*bedavet*) modes of production, such as seasonal sheep herding.

This method of land management has unanticipated connections with the emerging realities of Ottoman military defeat and the presumption of European (Christian) military and moral superiority after the 1880s. Ottoman circles of power increasingly perceived imperial decline as directly linked to a combination of moral degeneration and illiberal economic practices, such as the misuse of natural resources evident on the Albanian highlands. Especially after the Young Turk coup of 1908, many felt that the only way to secure Ottoman imperial power was to transform the way Ottoman subjects interacted with the larger world. This meant adopting prototypical liberal economic and social values that so happened to correspond to policies of land confiscation that made some authorities and their local allies extremely rich.[26] In the context of land redistribution, by the 1890s those who fitted the criteria for civilization would participate in the development of Albanian lands, while those who did not (rural Albanians, some refugees and some Ottoman officials) were expected to remain on the margins of the modern world.[27] This was the case with the highland community of Mirdita.

Management of Land Resources: The Mirdita Forest

Ottoman redistribution policies especially targeted under-used forests and pastures in Mirdita. Labeled as uninhabited and thus categorized as *terra nullius*, local state authorities who were eyeing valuable forest land historically under the protection of Prenk bib Doda Pasha, a long-time thorn in the side of the sultan, were able to place legally binding claims to common land and redistribute it as they saw fit.[28] That the concept of *terra nullius* (*mevat* in Ottoman) did not really work on the Balkans becomes clear with the European powers' subsequent attempt to rationalize their expansion into Mirdita at the expense of the Ottoman Empire in the 1890s. Local resistance to the efforts of the Ottoman state (and at times outside powers) to consolidate influence over local affairs resulted in the modified application of imperial institutions. This adjustment included the expulsion of Prenk bib Doda Pasha to Lebanon. It is important to note here that no single policy of the Sublime Porte could actually be sustained in these regions without the help of the local elites. This left locally based officials to deal with the fact that no policy was sustainable in their area of responsibility without the cooperation of Prenk bib Doda Pasha, who ironically was now located in Lebanon. In the end, it was the local subject who even in exile was the focus of imperial power, creating a new set of opportunities for a growing number of players in regional events and strengthening the influence of many who in the past had been targeted for marginalization.

The forested hinterland that served as a vital zone of confrontation between Ottoman and local aspirations also played a central role in the wider Mediterranean economy. Now linked by better roads and connected by bridges that spanned the many rivers and streams of the Albanian highlands, the domain of Prenk bib Doda Pasha started to draw the attention of European investors. What began to happen on the frontiers of Ottoman Albania was a transformation by integration, one in which European interests in the land's natural resources once again introduced a force of change, much in the same way as the influx of expelled Albanians transformed the period between 1878 and 1880. The interplay between various commercial interests and those who had access to much of the region's resources, and especially its forests, became a complex story essential to appreciating the underlying socio-economic dynamics of empire in the modern era. Tensions over land use, claims of ownership and state favoritism produced a hostile mix of expropriation, animosity towards non-locals, clashes over limited resources, and conflicting notions of the land's value.

The forest, much like the pastures and water sources, represented to locals a fragile commodity that required protection from foreign intrusions, not only for the sake of preserving territorial integrity, but also as part of a long tradition of safeguarding the community's power. In the period under study, the excess cutting of trees by resettled refugees was often resisted because of the well-understood impact that unmanaged deforestation has on the topsoil. Similar concerns were tied to overgrazing, against which Malësore Albanians were particularly apt to defend their land. In the contested frontier region of Tuz in the province of Shkodër, both pasture land (*mer'asi*) and the adjoining forests were aggressively protected against the Slav migrants' and recently settled refugees' attempts to graze their flocks. The fear of land misuse so evident in the regional folklore was part of a language that the Ottoman and its neighboring states were incapable of appreciating, as a long list of 'outsiders' began to exploit the region's resources for political and economic reasons.[29] In this light, the state's efforts to forcefully impose certain kinds of economic activities in regions with well-established traditions of land management were to have dire, long-term consequences.

In the meantime, many of the refugees expelled from newly created Montenegro developed in their adopted region patterns of assimilation that had an important impact on how Ottoman authorities and local allies alike could exploit local natural resources. In particular, the case of Hafız Ali Şükrü Efendi suggests that the experience of resettlement often strengthened an individual's sense of being part of a larger community. In the case of those expelled from Montenegro and Serbia, the impact of displacement helped in forging a sense of belonging among those resettled in key areas. This bonding among refugees proves essential to understanding the subsequent struggle for local power.

Hafız Ali, originally from the port-town of Ulqin, over time articulated communal demands that frequently contradicted state efforts to harness the frustrations of expelled Albanians against Ottoman enemies. For instance, Hafız Ali played an active role in advocating the development of the Albanian language in direct opposition to the Ottoman state. He openly opposed the domination that the Ottoman language had over the lives of his fellow Albanians and started a campaign of translating important religious texts. Considering the fact that Hafız Ali had been resettled in Northern Albania and awarded land by the Ottoman state, the actions demonstrating his strong sense of Albanian heritage highlight that the state's measures did not necessarily guarantee the loyalty of state aid recipients.[30]

More interesting still is the conflict that arose between the newly resettled Hafız Ali and the local grandee, who in the past had at times left him in direct confrontation with the Ottoman state. Hafız Ali's primary goals of unifying newly resettled Albanians led to conflicts with locals like Prenk bib Doda Pasha. At this crucial juncture, local tensions were very much a reflection of the fear that outside leaders, such as Hafız Ali, were developing loyal constituencies that had once professed loyalty to Prenk bib Doda. The result of this situation was a conflation of interests: the Ottoman state, concerned about Hafız Ali's activism, found a willing ally among those close to the exiled Prenk bib Doda, who also feared that the outsider's activism would grow popular among local peasants. The conflict over land use and trade links with the outside world ultimately changed in Mirdita, as Ottoman and local elite interests fused at a crucial point in time.

Despite the long history of clashing agendas, this new alliance was made possible by the lucrative business opportunities that the exploitation of Mirdita's raw materials offered. One key element of this exploitation requiring cooperation between the Ottoman state and the local patriarch, Prenk bib Doda, was the construction of expensive transport systems in Northern Albania to facilitate the export of wood and minerals. In this regard, the Catholic enclave of Mirdita started to attract the attention of a group of French, Austrian, and Italian investors.[31] The drive to 'develop' these areas blessed with vast forests began as lobbyists linked to Italian and Austrian timber and engineering companies initiated direct contact with Prenk bib Doda while he was in exile in Lebanon.[32] Realizing that they needed to go directly to the exiled patriarch, Austrians and the Italians successfully recruited him through local Beiruti channels, thereby opening up new opportunities for cooperation between a number of actors involved in the exploitation of Ottoman territorial wealth both in Albania and in far-off Lebanon.

The sale of vast expanses of communal forests along these frontier regions to Italian and Austrian interests began through such alliances with locals and key figures within the Ottoman ruling class. It is clear that without the support and assistance of local players, most of the lucrative deals signed during the first fifteen years of the twentieth century would not have been realized. The concession granted to an Italian firm owned by Giacinto Simini is a particularly interesting case. Simini's company received permission to extract and produce charcoal from the forests around the village of Skurai. A local lawyer named Antonio Dagna had established close links to Prenk Bib Doda Pasha, which allowed Simini to obtain the signatures of community leaders to sanction the concession.[33]

Simini proved to be the key component to the exploitation of local natural resources, by linking corrupt officials with outside investors.[34] It was the local leader, eventually freed from exile thanks to Austrian lobbying who sanctioned the exploitation of local forests that, seen through a different lens, proved harmful to an entire region's population and constituted an affront to the local traditions that punished the unnecessary felling of trees.[35] Suggestively, Prenk Bib Doda's career both as local power-holder and future partner in the timber industry began with an unlikely relationship that he established while in exile. Earlier in his life, Prenk bib Doda had thrived in his native Mirdita as the recognized patriarch who, much like his ancestors, refused to accept the absolute authority of the Ottoman sultan. Unlike his counterparts in other Northern Albanian regions, Prenk bib Doda was sent to internal exile in Lebanon resulting in new opportunities for the Mirdita patriarch that went beyond his continued influence over events in Mirdita.

Austrian representatives' reports from Lebanon during this period of exile suggest that a local Beiruti grandee family, the Malhames, openly petitioned Istanbul to make Prenk bib Doda the *mutassarrıf* of Mount Lebanon.[36] This intervention on the part of the Malhame family is indeed very intriguing, considering that the sultan awarded the post of Minister of Mines and Forests to a member of the Beirut family, as a means to formally incorporate him into the fold of government. As noted above, through appointment to government offices, the Ottoman state formally entangled influential, and potentially dangerous, merchant families whose commercial interests spanned much of the Eastern Mediterranean. The fact that the Malhame family became keenly interested in the fortunes of the exiled Albanian Catholic from the resource-rich region of Mirdita and would spend considerable time working with European investors to develop this very region for exploitation provides further evidence of deep commercial links between the Balkans and the Middle East.

Another essential aspect of exploiting the forests of Mirdita and elsewhere was the building of a transportation network that would link the forests with the ports. As noted above, outside interests, corrupt officials based in Albania, and influential locals worked together to develop the regional infrastructure. At times, this consortium of speculators was able to pressure the Porte to float loans in order to help finance the expensive construction projects. Of these projects, a train line from the port-towns of Medua and Draç to Mirdita and Tirana, respectively, became the centerpiece of competing Austrian and Italian economic interests in the region.[37] For example, the Roshfol Company based in Trieste hoped to extract Central Albania's timber by constructing a rail line that connected the port of Draç with the hinterland. Roshfol eventually won the concession to build the line after intensive lobbying facilitated by local officials.[38]

A parallel contract awarded Italians access to harvest other inland forests. Large tracts of the Cadralicci forests, to be made accessible by the Roshfol rail line, were conceded to Giuseppe Carbonne who enjoyed direct links with the Ottoman Minister of Forests and Mines.[39] A local administrative change during the ongoing railroad construction created a scandal of sorts when local interests successfully challenged the concession granted to Carbonne. Recognizing that their resources were under threat, Ziya and Celal Bey, two key landholders in the region, confronted the state in an embarrassing exchange between loyal subjects with strong influence over the regional government official and a corrupt central administration that favored Carbonne. At the heart of the conflict was a clear change in practice of the empire, whose Ministry of Forests apparently sold to Carbonne land claimed by locals.[40] The case dragged on for years, as Carbonne petitioned the Italian state to intervene and rescue his lucrative concession, while locals grew increasingly frustrated with Istanbul's corruption.

The railroad became a point of controversy as locals feared being usurped by foreign investors. These conflicts ultimately exposed the real interests of the state and its willingness to sacrifice local interests for foreign profit. An Ottoman army commission sent to report on the feasibility of Austrian projects approved a plan to develop the region by building the rail line. Army engineers asserted that locals were amenable to the building of such a line and would assist in the general reform measures implemented throughout the region. In the end, the railroad was built, over the objection of the locals, because it satisfied a set of criteria deemed important by the state. Clearly, there was no distinction being made between the state's ambitions to develop a region (and to secure better military mobility in the mountainous terrain) and foreign plans to exploit resources belonging to local inhabitants.[41] Istanbul's position ultimately compelled locals to conclude that their interests were not being served by the Ottoman state, opening the door for a new period of conflict. It is this moment of conflicting interests that translated into a new wave of revolts in Albania, revolts that ultimately created the conditions for new wars in the Balkans and ultimately World War I, attracting the major imperial powers to finally devour the Ottoman Empire.

Conclusion

The functioning of empire itself often went beyond the artifacts of confrontation. Local reactions to imperial policies often forced Great Powers to modify territorial and political ambitions. In the end, the frontiers created in the Balkans in 1878 and then again in 1919 were as much legacies of local actions as they were of imperial power. This aspect of the evolution of the modern imperial state helps us recalibrate the impact historic empires have on our world today. The native did have a role in history by participating on the margins of the state's formal economic policy.

What happened in the provinces of Kosova and Shkodër between 1878 and 1908 reflected an increasingly counter-productive relationship between the Ottoman state and its subjects. The initial process of enforcing frontiers created over a short period of time a disastrous set of conditions for communities found on the 'wrong' side of the border. In addition, the creation of ethno-national spaces constituted a new form of bureaucratic abstraction that further complicated the Ottoman Empire's territorial administration. Furthermore, the administrative act of setting up villages full of expelled Albanians to affect a more 'rational' system of taxation and administration created clusters of interests that offered new possibilities of alliance as much as it created serious confusion. This paradoxical chain of transformations ultimately changed the dynamics of power in the communities found within, along and beyond the various borders created in this period.

Responding to the need to identify, catalogue and distinguish people in the context of drawing international frontiers, Ottoman reforms, internal boundary modifications and the objectification of people resulted in the introduction of demands that ultimately were exploited by a new group of local actors. Sometimes, the measures adopted as a rapid response to events taking place in the Balkans bear testament to the types of changes that the Ottoman state could bring to the entire empire. For example, in an attempt to control the potentially chaotic resettlement process caused by war, Istanbul introduced new bureaucracies in Kosova and Shkodër; the subsequent system induced some of the following four decades' social, economic and political transformations discussed throughout this chapter. One of the major consequences of these measures was the creation of a zone of commercial activity that unexpectedly offered Ottoman officials the opportunity to raise revenues, by taxing the trade that crossed the newly created international frontier. These new bureaucracies also helped to create new channels for local elites to exert considerable influence on the local economy and often well beyond. Moreover, as the local economy, always linked to the larger Mediterranean, developed new significance in a regional struggle for power between rival states, a new set of cross-regional ties emerged, ties that rivaled those established in the first half of nineteenth century. As a result of the formal linking of the Adriatic coast with highland Albania and Beiruti merchant families, for instance, the further integration of the Eastern Mediterranean into a new world order would take place.

Educating the Nation: Migration and Acculturation on the Two Shores of the Aegean at the Turn of the Twentieth Century

Vangelis Kechriotis

The Mediterranean port-cities under Ottoman sovereignty have recently become the focus of much systematic research and intensive debate. They have either drawn attention thanks to their privileged position in a region's economy, or for being the cornerstone for the integration of the Eastern Mediterranean into the world economy. This research has also raised new questions about social issues, investigating the port-cities' inhabitants' position between international trade and local society and thus challenging the earlier description of local elites as 'compradore bourgeoisie'.[1] One new approach has focused on the role of individuals in local institutions,[2] or in everyday life.[3] What is crucial in such studies is that they emphasize distinct cases, rather than the role of the state, in order to shed light on the differences and peculiarities among communities and individuals, as well as on their various interactions with each other. Despite their clearly innovative character in comparison to earlier structuralist views, such accounts have been challenged on the grounds that they downplay inter-communal or colonial violence at the turn of the twentieth century. After all, nationalism and imperialism were dominant political paradigms at a time when communities in port-cities (and elsewhere) devised ethnicity- or religion-based strategies to impose their power over other groups and the state.[4]

İzmir constitutes a case study that has preoccupied many adherents of these different approaches. This chapter, being the outcome of a much broader interest in the cultural representations and political conflicts within the Greek-Orthodox communities of the Ottoman Empire, addresses the issue of acculturation of ethnically identical groups from different geographical origins.[5] These communities became objects and subjects of proliferating cultural and social networks, in a process of temporary migration first to İzmir and then from there to Athens, where opportunities of education and social mobility promised 'a better future'.[6] With respect to this process, I argue that the very concept of 'community' needs to be redefined, since its demographic composition continually fluctuated as a result of migration. At the same time, I claim that the community administration functioned as a major tool of acculturation, despite its pledge to multiple loyalties. From the point of view of the wider Mediterranean, it is precisely such inter-regional networks as the ones established by the Greek-Orthodox communities across the Aegean and across two different state systems (the Ottoman Empire and the Hellenic state) and the demographic fluctuations shaping them that tended to create a common space and employ a discourse cutting across nationalism and imperialism.

İzmir, a Crossroads of Cultures and Products

Already at the turn of the seventeenth century, İzmir had become an important center for many European merchants who soon established their own communities there, thus enhancing the city's multi-communal character with the already existing Muslim, Greek-Orthodox, Armenian and Jewish communities. Daniel Goffman has suggested that in the seventeenth century İzmir was formed in the midst of turmoil, as the European search for goods and markets converged a commercial network at the port: 'The town quickly became a cosmopolitan city acting like a magnet upon commercially sensitive communities and establishing itself as a rival to Istanbul for the people and products of its expanding hinterland'.[7]

The second half of the eighteenth century marked an era of expansion for the city, due to favorable conditions in international trade.[8] The significance of this period's transformation in export trade lies in the fact that it mainly concerned the agricultural products of Western Asia Minor. In other words, İzmir was developed from a transfer point of products from the East into a center of export for local products. This increased the volume of agricultural production in the region four- or fivefold. British and, later on, other European commercial agencies commissioned local merchants to cooperate with overwhelmingly non-Muslim intermediaries who proved indispensable for their purposes. This interaction initiated a reorganization of the internal hierarchy of local communities. The Greek-Orthodox, for instance, who were involved in agricultural production as well as in trade, secured greater influence and, hence, to a certain extent replaced the Jews who in the seventeenth and eighteenth century had more intimate relations with the Ottoman government. The Armenians retained their position while profiting in certain cases at the expense of the Jews.[9]

The boom of commercial activity resulted in an unprecedented development of the city at the end of the nineteenth century, as its population increased at least twofold over that in the previous century. The fact that locally-based groups controlled this activity meant that the port-city itself controlled the whole hinterland of Western Asia Minor. Thus, in İzmir one could find different kinds of financial and commercial institutions – such as banks, insurance houses, commercial firms and buildings for storage and processing. These institutions formed the core of the network and the site of collection and transference.[10] As a result of this boom, the old organization of the city into ethno-religious neighborhoods gave place to a new arrangement. The new criterion tended to be social status rather than ethnic affiliation, transforming the traditional city into a modern one. This enhanced the contacts among different communities, contacts which had already been promoted by commercial and social interaction in the bazaars and places of recreation.[11] The Greek-Orthodox merchants took advantage particularly of their local networks and their mobility within and beyond the empire and managed to take on as their clientele prominent European merchant families, İzmir residents themselves. This meant that, in addition to spreading commodities, 'they became the intermediaries of also a certain kind of bourgeois culture that united in outlook people who were in a similar position in other major commercial centers of the southern Mediterranean and the Near East'.[12]

The western coasts of Asia Minor had attracted Greek-Orthodox migrants from the Aegean islands and the Peloponnesus as a result of wars, natural disasters or opportunities for a better life since the end of the seventeenth century.[13] These groups could be fairly easily distinguished from the mainly Turkish-speaking and predominantly rural indigenous population. The immigration accelerated in the 1770s due to the favorable circumstances that the Treaty of Küçük Kaynarca (1774) entailed for all Christian subjects of the sultan. But immigration assumed a more systematic character in the aftermath of the 1830s, despite the distrust of Ottoman authorities toward Greeks after the 1821 Greek War of Independence. But the Greek-Orthodox still took advantage of the policy of free trade in the wake of the Anglo–Ottoman Trade Agreement in 1838. In a way, the Greek-Orthodox community increased its economic power, thus compensating for the loss in social and political influence. Therefore, in this period they enhanced their position in commercial networks without having to (but also without being able to) press for political representation.[14] In this atmosphere of liberal economy and imperial rivalry, they could be granted the status of *protégé* or even become subjects of a foreign power, frequently switching from one nationality to another depending on the circumstances and thus creating a space of social activity in which the imperial authorities could hardly intervene. At the same time, several of these non-Muslim elite groups who were involved in the local power networks extending from the region to the capital, which allowed them to monopolize state contracts, were not favorably disposed towards the nineteenth-century reforms in the Ottoman Empire.[15] While many among the newly arrived Greek-Orthodox entrepreneurs took advantage of the liberal economy that prevailed in the second half of the nineteenth century, indigenous families with older ties to the region resisted this transformation. Moreover, as it has been argued for the whole of Western Asia Minor during that period, local non-Muslim commercial elites did not simply act as intermediaries for European interests, but actually antagonized them and rather relied on their privileged position within the local networks.[16]

Urban Elites from Empire to Nation-State

In this context, it is important to trace the experiences and motives that led different elite groups to make an attempt at establishing political hegemony in a period when there were many different political projects regarding the imperial territories. Such elites made alliances either with local state authorities or a foreign government, depending on their own interests. This was also the case of the Greek-Orthodox community in İzmir. The growth of the commercial elites due to the expansion of trade and their political involvement was an important factor in the context of the rise of the nation-state in the region.

As mentioned above, the commercial elites have been described as a 'bourgeois class'.[17] However, historians who have studied the formation of British society have treated this class as a cultural construct and have tried to investigate the relation between 'experience' and 'consciousness'. They have argued that political discourse is not directly related to economic and social developments and that the political representations of the bourgeois

class are inconsistent and contentious.[18] As a result, the formation of bourgeois classes such as the one of the Greeks in İzmir can be addressed by
looking at urban activity, associations and foundations, as well as at the
cultural aspects of bourgeois life that reveal the diverse sources of experience in the formation of class consciousness.[19] Thus, instead of focusing on
the economic conditions of social transformation, I argue that it is exactly
the cultural aspects of bourgeois life that provide a privileged field for the
study of the acculturation process of the Greek community in İzmir. Two
factors further privileged İzmir as a port-city that demographically grew in
the second half of the nineteenth century: the absence of a more widespread urbanization in the region, and the presence of a mixed population,
resulting in a multi-ethnic division of labor.

From the 1850s onwards, both the Hellenic state and Istanbul elites had
undertaken the project of hellenizing the Greek-Orthodox populations in
Macedonia and Asia Minor. Through this activity, urban communities
managed to incorporate rural populations of the surrounding areas. İzmir
played a major role in this process. It contributed both to the proliferation
of networks initiated from outside and to the creation and enhancement of
regional ones. Most significant among these were educational and commercial networks. Besides foreign merchandise, the port also transported
educational material and the skills of teaching personnel who helped increase the impact of the city on the life of the surrounding populations.
Many children from the hinterland and neighboring towns would be sent
to boarding schools in the city. When they graduated, they would return to
their village or hometown to work as teachers.[20] This resulted in a growing
number of people who perceived themselves as Smyrniots.

In the urban centers of the empire, and in İzmir par excellence, a nexus
of associations, charitable foundations, educational institutions, and, most
importantly, the community administration itself prepared the ground for
the process of hellenization during this period. Furthermore, the profess-
sional contribution of individuals can be traced both through the services
they offered to the community and through their involvement in the debates taking place within these institutions that provided an arena for political antagonism and carried many characteristics of a public sphere.
Moreover, as Anagnostopoulou has argued, in the urban centers of Western Asia Minor we can follow the activities of numerous skilled professionals whom she describes as a 'Hellenic bourgeois class'. Taking advantage of the favorable regulations initiated by the Tanzimat,[21] most of these
individuals concluded their studies at the University of Athens and then
returned to their hometowns where they exercised their profession as

teachers, lawyers and medical doctors.[22] I find the term 'Hellenic bourgeois class' far-fetched and consider the term 'new urban elites' more accurate in order to describe these individuals who were recognized as such
by their community particularly because of their expertise and authority in
their professions. Moreover, their professional authority was related to the
fact that they were graduates of the only Hellenic university, a fact that
was highly appreciated in the Greek-Orthodox communities of the empire.
Therefore, they cannot simply be considered products of their own communal ties. In a way, they brought their community into a dialogue with
different loci, both in geographical and cultural terms.

However, concepts such as 'community' and 'acculturation', though
significant for our understanding of collective experience, should be
employed with caution. Taking into consideration the post-colonial critique on the experience of migration and the margins of the nation can
further enrich the discussion of the flexible nature of community. Homi
Bhabha describes the emergence of the later phase of the modern nation
as a phenomenon combining mass migration within the West and colonial
expansion in the East. Under these circumstances, the nation replaces
community and kin, which have been uprooted, and 'turns that loss into
the language of metaphor which [...] transforms the meaning of home
and belonging [...] across those distances and cultural differences that
span the imagined community of the nation-people'.[23] Thus, the trauma
of migration transforms 'lost communities' into national ideologies, as
the nation becomes 'an obscure and ubiquitous form of living the locality
of culture; a form of living that is more complex than "community"'.[24]

I find this approach particularly relevant to our endeavor here. The conceptual pair described by Bhabha as the key notions for the cultural experience of the nation are locality and temporality.[25] However, when
writing on Smyrniot Greeks, I consider it absolutely legitimate to use concepts such as society, country, patrie, state, ideology, hegemony, citizen,
subject, and civility, despite Bhabha's own assertion that these are obscure
notions. It is true that the consolidation of these terms in social practice
presupposes institutions and mechanisms as markers and indicators of
modernity. However, even if the period under consideration seems to be
only on the verge of modernity and such institutions are just finding their
way in, I shall use these terms, being aware of the slippery methodological
ground. The key term which lies at the core of my analysis, i.e. community, needs to be discussed in the light of this approach.

In most accounts on the Greek-Orthodox communities of the Ottoman
Empire, the concept is taken for granted, not to mention in most traditional

historiography trying to trace the origin of the communities to antiquity or Byzantium and thus to create a historicist narrative of national continuity. In recent historiographical debates, the somewhat late development of these communities in the eighteenth and nineteenth centuries and their regional differences are adequately described. However, these developments are presented within the framework of the formation of nationalist ideology, which implies the advent of modernization and progress in conservative, religious-inspired populations. Thus, diverse conflicts are explained as clashes between the new and the old, the traditional and the modern.[26] What this approach ignores is that, although we deal with the period of the formation of the imagined community of the nation and the dissolution of local communities and kin, communities and kin do not evaporate as people migrate from the countryside to the city. Instead, they are transformed into networks of solidarity based on common origin, which also take the shape of interest groups. Thus, what we call community is actually an aggregation of several communities which gradually moved to the city –groups bound by ethnicity, locality, profession and kinship.[27] If we only consider how easy it was for someone to become a Smyrniot, we will have a measure of the community's complexity. The 1910 regulation of the Smyrniot community grants the right to vote to any Greek-Orthodox who has settled in the city for at least two years. Thus, institutionally, there was no way of distinguishing between native Smyrniots and newcomers. However, in everyday life, in local politics, and in cultural representation, the divisions within the community were evident. The groups formed earlier and the new migrants, the ones from Cappadocia and the ones from the islands, the guild members and the professionals, the ones whose names ended with 'oglou' and those that ended with 'idis', the ones who could speak Turkish and those who could not, the ones who were Ottoman subjects and those who were not (these did not always overlap). Thus, creating a line of distinction that cut through these groups is not helpful. There still is a need, however, to take into account all these distinctions for the simple reason that all these groups had a different perception of what a Smyrniot was, regardless of the fact that everybody was given the right to vote. This discrepancy is reflected very well in the developments within the community administration.

Already from the end of the eighteenth century onwards, when immigration into the city increased, a major division developed between those who were involved in international networks and commerce and those who were mainly engaged in local economic activities. The gradual domination of powerful mercantile groups in social and economic life duly led to challenging the traditional way of administration. The first instance of the conflict between the 'old world' (indigenous elites and the clergy), and those wealthy individuals who did not have access to the community administration broke out in 1785 and resulted in arrangements described in an agreement known as 'Compromise' (Συνυποσχετικόν). However, in the course of the nineteenth century tensions were not eliminated. On the contrary, due to the ongoing social differentiation among the Greek Smyrniots, more groups represented by various professional guilds began to claim positions in the community administration.[28]

Indeed, after the foundation of the Hellenic state social and political conflicts followed a different course and evolved around two poles: on the one hand, the traditional scheme of community administration within the Ottoman context, and, on the other hand, the development of an autonomous ethno-religious community with independent mechanisms of representation.[29] This development resulted in a series of crises regarding the status of the indigenous Elders Council (Δημογεροντία), whose authority was now challenged by the new Hellenic urban elites. The latter, not allowed to participate in the community administration under Ottoman law, forged institutions of their own. The controversy concluded with a clear victory of the newcomers, who through the establishment of a Central Committee (Κεντρική Επιτροπή) in 1878 managed to restrict the authority of the Elders Council.

The changes in the political context after the Greek–Ottoman War of 1897 further encouraged such distinctions, as Ottoman authorities imposed severe restrictions on nationality. Hellenic subjects lost the beneficiary clauses of the pre-existing treaties between the two countries, especially those of the Kanlıca Convention of 1855, which had given Greece the same privileges that Western European states enjoyed. The Ottoman authorities also attempted to eliminate exemption from taxation by forcing Hellenic subjects to either chose Ottoman nationality or leave the country.[30] Two figures who would lead the pro-Ottoman camp at the turn of the century played a key role in this conflict: Sokratis Solomonidis, the editor of the leading Greek Smyrniot newspaper, Amalthia, and for decades the foremost figure in the Elders Council; and the lawyer Emmanouil Emmanouilidis who would later develop close relations with the local branch of the Committee of Union and Progress and become a deputy in the Ottoman Parliament. These individuals, together with Pavlos Carolidis, also a parliamentary deputy, and Aristidis Pasha Georgantzoglou, a member of the Ottoman meclis-i ayan (a legislative body similar to a senate) and a minister, were in close contact with each other; not only because of their common place of origin, Cappadocia, but also through family bonds. A series of accusations of intrigue and personal interests directed against these individuals and their circles point to an articulate network beyond family and social ties among those originating from Cappadocia. This network resulted from the reproduction of community administration networks through charitable foundations that this group of Cappadocians controlled in an attempt to dominate the whole system of community representation. In this sense, perhaps it is more expedient to talk of a quasi-bureaucracy, acquired through the practice of the above-mentioned skills and knowledge necessary for running community affairs. One could go even further and suggest that this quasi-bureaucracy, for one reason or another, had not profited from the city's expanding commercial activity which contributed to the formation of new commercial elites. Therefore, in order to counterbalance the social impact of these elites, this quasi-bureaucracy wished to dominate the only field available, namely community administration. This does not mean, as I already have pointed out, a clear distinction between political parties or even population groups. It is indicative, however, that a few years later, during the Ottoman boycott of Greek commercial products between 1909 and 1912, a part of the community remained unaffected, as their involvement in the community administration had rendered them immune. The solidarity between Hellenic and Ottoman subjects during the boycott somewhat reduced the impact of this commercial war. Especially with the arrival of the new Metropolitan Chrysostomos in 1912, the community's quasi-bureaucracy experienced a period of prosperity, with many new buildings being constructed.

Mechanisms of Migration and Acculturation
Towards the end of the nineteenth century, young people from different regions in Asia Minor could rely on social and cultural networks for financial support to study either in İzmir, in Athens, or at the school for teachers on the island of Patmos near the southwestern coast of Asia Minor. The Association of People from Asia Minor (Anatoli) was established in 1891 out of Mikrasiates, another Asia-Minor-based Hellenic association in Athens and Pireaus.[31] As Maria Sideri argues, this sub-group of Mikrasiates wished to set up a connection between their place of origin and what they considered their 'national center' (i.e., Athens) where they had created a new life. Membership to the association was determined by three elements. First, members came from Asia Minor, not from the Hellenic Kingdom, but they had many cultural features in common with the Hellenic Greeks. The association allowed them to consolidate their social

relations in the new environment. Secondly, most of the members were professors or students at the University of Athens, or professionals such as lawyers and medical doctors. Apart from the academic interests of its members, the new association's activities were related to the general educational purposes of the hundreds of local associations founded by the Greek-Orthodox in all Ottoman territories during this period. Thirdly, the main task was to provide support to their brethren outside the Hellenic state, as a concrete aspect of the 'Great Idea'. Moreover, as Sideri points out, 'the foundation of this association coincided with a new orientation of Greek nationalism which abandoned irredentist policies and focused on improving the living conditions of the "unredeemed" populations. Moreover, for Anatoli, the term "brothers" did not only refer to an 'imagined community', but rather to a group of people with real kinship relations'.[32]

The major concern that instigated this initiative was the perceived loss of Greek language among populations in Asia Minor, notably in Cappadocia and other regions where the Orthodox population was Turkish- or even Armenian-speaking.[33] The issue of Turkish-speaking Greeks has been recently tackled in Greek historiography in an innovative approach that demonstrates the engagement of different criteria for Greek ethnicity. Both in Macedonia as well as in Asia Minor, Orthodox populations who did not speak Greek were considered to have lost their Greek tongue due to interaction with other ethnic elements or due to foreign suppression. However, they presumably retained their Greek consciousness and, therefore, deserved to be included in the national body.[34] Anatoli undertook the task of providing scholarships to young people from different regions of Asia Minor and sent them to Athens or elsewhere to study. After graduation, these students would be appointed by their respective communities to serve 'national interests' in their locality. As Magda Kitromilidis has pointed out, 'the ideology dictating these views believed that Hellenic civilization should not be wiped out from its ancient Asia Minor cradle, but survive through individual commitment to the progress of Greece'.[35] However, two comments are necessary in order to understand the nature and degree of this commitment to Hellenic civilization. First, the range of professions supported by Anatoli was broader than that of teachers. Students of medicine or law who did not have the means to continue their studies applied to the society for support.[36] Secondly, I would argue that, although devotion to Greece and Hellenic culture was an incentive that attracted many young people and their patrons, this involvement also seemed to have been the only means to safeguard geographical and social mobility. In this respect, the role of the individual was crucial in spreading a particular ideology. Whether the protégés of Anatoli had a sense of a broader imagined community to which they belonged, Hellenic or Greek-Orthodox, is sometimes difficult to assess. But apparently personal interests motivated them. They sought better education, well-paid jobs, and social recognition. Most likely, such networks between different regions provided particular individuals with opportunities unknown up to that point. Yet, the outcome was contingent on individual strategies and the negotiations they entailed. Moreover, as it has been pointed out, scholars and writers from Asia Minor formulated their own version of Hellenic history, a version that not only incorporated the lands of Cappadocia or the Pontus (the Black Sea region) into the mainstream narrative about national continuity, but also attributed to their communities key positions as true cradles of national culture.[37]

Margaritis Evangelidis (1850–1932), the head of the association, provides a good example in his speech in 1900, on the occasion of the ninth anniversary of the foundation of Anatoli. He pointed out the importance of Athens in world history, claiming that its contribution to all fields of the social sciences, from philosophy to politics, would not be possible without the heritage of the Ionian centers in Asia Minor. Evangelidis concluded his speech by exclaiming: 'Athens... remember who contributed the foundations of your historical grandeur. Remember our own perpetual zeal and don't procrastinate in reciprocating'.[38] In 1844, in an important speech during the debate on the first constitution of the Hellenic Kingdom, Prime Minister Ioannis Kolettis (1773–1847), who dominated political life during that period, coined the term 'great idea' (*megali idea*) of the Hellenic race. He argued that in the past Greece had enlightened the West and that its rebirth had now destined it to offer its light to the East. In a sense, one could argue that at the turn of the twentieth century scholars from Asia Minor wished to reverse the above statement by claiming that Asia Minor, i.e. the East, had in the past generously spread its culture to the continental Greek city-states, i.e. the West, and that it was high time for Athens, the capital of the Hellenic state, to pay back the benevolence.

Both Evangelidis and Konstantinos Lameras, the secretary of the association, received numerous petitions from instructors asking for jobs and from distinguished community members who had taken on the protection of young people. The correspondence that arrived in Athens from İzmir, now kept in the Archive of the Association Anatoli–İzmir Branch (AAA–IB) housed at the Hearth of Smyrniots in Athens offers much information about such individuals and their particular involvement. The famous Greek-Orthodox medical doctor Mihail Tsakiroglou, one of the few

Smyrniots who had studied in the imperial Medical School (*Tıbbiye*) in Istanbul, expressed in his letter his joy about having been accepted as a member.[39] A great deal of the correspondence is composed of recommendations by members of the Smyrniot society whose involvement is an indicator of their social prestige. For instance, Vassilios, the Greek-Orthodox Metropolitan of İzmir,[40] in a recommendation letter that he sent to Pavlos Carolidis, professor of History at the University of Athens,[41] as well as to the board of the association, introduced Mihail Konstantiou Kantartzopoulo from Aksaray, Cappadocia, as a Turkish-speaker and 'worthy of protection'. The young Cappadocian probably traveled to Athens to study. The Metropolitan also mentioned that 'last week, four more Cappadocians and one person from Edirne (Adrianople) departed for there [Athens] in order to be enlightened, and when they arrived they received the desired [welcome]. I wish the same for the others as well, most of whom live in darkness'.[42] The practice of sending youngsters to Athens 'in order to be enlightened', especially under the protection of the above-mentioned association and of Carolidis himself, seems to have been widespread. In another instance, Vassilios addressed Evangelidis regarding two youngsters, Athanasios Iomeoglou from Vourdourion (Burdur) near Sparti (Isparta) and Leonida Papastefanou. Interestingly, he claimed that the second individual was a victim of conversion (without mentioning to what confession) and was sent away to be saved.[43] During the second half of the nineteenth century the Orthodox communities of Istanbul and Asia Minor viewed the presence of Catholic and Protestant missionaries as very threatening, and one could assume that Papastefanou was converted by one of them.[44] Clearly, the Orthodox Metropolitan of İzmir, although originating from Macedonia, owed the key role he played in the network of the Mikrasiates to his position.

Most of the requests concerned funding for education. Efthalia Oulkeroglu, a young lady from Sparti who had only managed to graduate from the third grade of the Central Girl's School of Agia Fotini in İzmir,[45] requested the association's assistance to become admitted to the Arsakion Girl's Boarding School in Athens.[46] Another field of activity was religious education. The religious brotherhood Efsevia[47] had reached an agreement with Anatoli, the latter financing young gentlemen to study at the Rizarios Religious Boarding School in Athens, by paying the annual fee of 600 Drachma, a significant amount at the time. The association had already sponsored Hatzi Anesti from Sinopi (Sinop) for that purpose. It is also suggested that another gentleman from Palia Fokaia (Old Foça) would study to become a teacher and later on return to his birthplace where he would be ordained as a priest to serve his community.[48] This is a typical example of the petitions sent by the community that pledged to support the education of youngsters and to ensure that graduates respected the conditions of returning and working in their birthplaces.

Soon after the association established its own religious school on the island of Patmos, Efsevia petitioned Evangelidis, asking for young gentlemen to be sponsored as students there as well.[49] If the religious schools faced difficulties, as was the case in 1900 when the proper imperial decree had not been issued, the alternative for Efsevia was to arrange to host the students temporarily at the Evangelical School the most important and widely known Greek-Orthodox high school in İzmir.[50] In another instance, Ioannis Kavasilas, a member of Efsevia, recommended a poor Smyrniot youngster who wished to study at the Rizarios School in Athens to become either a teacher or a preacher.[51] These letters emphasize both the services of the students upon their return to their homelands and the gratitude they would all bear toward their benefactors.[52] Another letter by Emmanouil Lountzopoulos, who claimed to be one of Evangelidis' friends, informs us that, according to an article published in *Amalthia*, Anatoli would sponsor eight Turkish-speaking Greeks from Asia Minor, enabling them to study at the teachers' school in Athens. Lountzopoulos also points out that there were many who wished to study theology, but did not have the resources, as the local rich people did not support them.[53] This is clearly a sign of the resentment harbored against local elites who, despite their prosperity, did not seem eager to support such theological initiatives. But perhaps more importantly, it is also clear that the target group was not the Smyrniot youngsters who would have no problems in mastering the Greek language in İzmir.

There were also cases in which students were funded by someone in İzmir but still remained under the association's observation, which would then report on their progress. This was the case with the student G. Mavrokaliviti, *protégé* of Melektidis.[54] In another example, Loukas Pavlidis described the efforts of the student Nikolaos Georgiadis who had some savings to pay for the first few years of his studies, but who relied on the association to finance their conclusion.[55] In another petition, the Educational Brotherhood of Agioi Anargyroi (Εκπαιδευτική Αδελφότητα, Άγιοι Ανάργυροι) requested that Georgios Skandalis, an excellent student, receive the protection of the associaton, since he wanted to study at the Polytechnic School in Athens. The Brotherhood acknowledged its inability to cover these expenses because its limited resources supported the poor in İzmir and its suburbs. Moreover, the Brotherhood claimed that its *ad hoc* operations covered a narrower scope than that of the Anatoli who were responsible for the whole of Asia Minor.[56] Consequently, two sorts of circles are described here: a larger one with Athens at its center, and many others with their centers in small towns, attempting to replicate the larger one and to proliferate its activity.

In his own letter, Ioannis Hatzi Nikolaou expressed his gratitude to Evangelidis for having supported his nephew Kosmas Spanidis for three years in Athens, as well as for his nephew's consequent appointment, first as a school headmaster in Kasaba near İzmir and then in an even better position in Cairo.[57] Clearly, these networks between Asia Minor and Athens extended far beyond that region. In another case, the Metropolitan provided a letter to a Greek-Orthodox called Georgios Tzouros who had arrived from Egypt and therefore was not strictly speaking a Mikrasiatis, asking the association to give him protection or a job.[58] A similar petition spoke on behalf of Dimitrios Iasas from the island of Mytilini (near the northwestern coast of Asia Minor) who worked on the cartography of Asia Minor.[59] The association's geographical scope becomes obvious in the letter of a poor unemployed teacher, Dimitrios Glyptis, who stated that he would accept any job in Epirus, Macedonia, or even Cyprus.[60] İzmir, however, held a far stronger appeal for anyone who was bound to return from Athens. A friend of Kosmas Spanidis, N. Ioannidis, also originally from Sparti, eventually chose İzmir where he was employed at the Evangelical School with a monthly salary of 240 *mescid*, despite offers he had from schools in Philadelphia (Alaşehir), Koula and Kasaba.[61] Kleoniki Apostolidou, a qualified kindergarten teacher and graduate of the Pallas School in Athens, had worked for twelve years in Vryoulla (Urla), İzmir, Denizli, and Levisi (Kayaköy). She petitioned the society for an appropriate job in İzmir or any other big town, except Istanbul.[62] There indeed was one vital reason why someone would choose to be employed in İzmir rather than in Istanbul: living costs were cheaper. Apostolidou escaped from Istanbul, leaving the position there precisely because of the high living costs.[63] Aikaterina Syropina, a graduate of the Central Girls School of Agia Fotini in İzmir, had been working in the small village of Mousalia near Aydın, but she still applied for a position in İzmir, because she believed that she deserved a place in a 'more developed community'.[64] In a second letter, she almost begged, pointing out that she had to support a whole family on her own. In certain letters, the names of important figures of the community are provided as references. In this last case it was Miltiadis Seizanis, the editor of the second most important Smyrniot newspaper *Armonia,* a rival to Sokratis Solomonidis' *Amalthia.*[65] Indeed, in his recommendation letter addressed to Evangelidis, Seizanis expressed his gratitude for the eventual appointment of the young teacher in

Trapezounta (Trabzon) and even asked for the necessary travel expenses on her behalf.[66] In a second letter sent a few days later, Seizanis asked for money once again, but this time the amount of FF 400 to 500 requested initially had been reduced to FF 100.[67] It seems that requests for money could not be easily met and that perhaps they were occasionally exaggerated.

In any case, it seems to have been easier to find teaching positions through the support of Anatoli rather than through the support of local networks. Georgios Kokolas, a graduate of the Evangelical School, had studied law in France; however, he preferred teaching French to practicing law. Indeed, he ended up teaching at the famous Zosimaia School in Jannina. When he was ousted because of his status as Hellenic citizen, the association sent him to İzmir to teach at a school. Later, the French teacher lost his employment again and asked for another job.[68] Dimitrios Hamoudopoulos, a member of an important family of İzmir,[69] complained in his letter that all positions teaching ancient Greek at the Evangelical School were filled. The young language teacher also mentioned a project aiming to establish a commercial school. Hamoudopoulos expected that the head of the board of trustees, Pavlos Jovanof, at the same time president of the colony of Hellenic subjects of İzmir, would support his candidacy for this position.[70] This kind of correspondence became more intensive during the summer, as jobs for the following year were negotiated.

There were also those who wanted to go as far away from İzmir as possible. The above-mentioned Dimitris Hamoudopoulos was pleased to learn about two available positions in Büyükdere and Kaisaria. He actually preferred the second option which, being far from İzmir, offered 'fertile potential for national work [...] for a young scientist'.[71] Eventually, however, under the pressure of his parents, he had to accept the first choice. Interestingly, he describes the conflicts which at that time also preoccupied the leadership of the community interested in the administration of the Evangelical School. Hamoudopoulos declared that the teachers were disillusioned by such conflicts and that he himself would be pleased to go as far away as possible. Fate was benevolent to the young scientist. His comments apparently reached the head of the association and he was eventually appointed to the religious school at Patmos, where he felt he would have every chance to promote his 'national endeavor'[72] and presumably bring honor to his alma mater, the University of Athens.

This systematic exposure of young people to official Hellenic education accounts for the process of acculturation that took place on the western shores of the Aegean at the end of the nineteenth century. When a teachers' association was established in İzmir, its members asked Anatoli as well as the teacher's association in Athens for their directives in order to formulate their own aims accordingly.[73] Curricula of the schools in Athens drew a similar interest in Asia Minor. For instance, Sokratis Oulkeroglu, an employee of the Crystal Warehouse of Vassilios Papadopoulos, requested the curriculum of the Rizarios School in Athens, so that his brother could receive similar private lessons in Sparti.[74] Oulkeroglou had already been sending 160 Drachma every three months to his sister who studied at Arsakion. This amount would cover all expenses and also provide some pocket money to her.[75] It is worth mentioning that Anatoli routinely sent money to students besides keeping abreast of their progress, even in those cases in which the association did not cover the entire expenses. Efthalia Oulkeroglou eventually graduated and the society was asked to complete all relevant formalities.[76]

Constantinos Psaltoff, the well-known lawyer,[77] who for years had been one of the trustees of the Omirion Girls School,[78] the second most important girl school in İzmir after the Central Girls' School of Agia Fotini, wrote to Evangelidis about Ioanni Sarikaki, the son of the vice-headmistress at Omirion. Ioannis wanted to study medicine. Psaltoff urged the head of Anatoli to suggest to Ioanni Pezmazoglou, the famous Costantinopolitan banker and owner of the Bank d'Athènes, to accept him as one of the five fellows that the Greek banker supported every year.[79] Psaltoff described the family of the student: The father, a lawyer practicing on the island of Syros (close to continental Greece) and in Egypt, was from Urla, and the mother, the sister of the Headmaster Zolota, from Chios. The family had many children and could not support all of them to study. This application was supported by the board of trustees and by the president Dionysio Markopoulo personally.[80]

Over time educational institutions such as the Greek girls' schools became more self-confident and assertive and addressed the association with more comprehensive proposals. The above-mentioned Omirion Girl's School, where Costantinos Psaltoff held a prominent role, adressed the association with the request that 'the Association of People from Asia Minor, either through their own funding or through other resources such as those of rich Mikrasiates, provide five fellowships for poor girls from the interior, to be nominated by their communities or the Metropolitans in each region, either through the said association or the board of Omirion'.[81] In addition, the board of Omirion decided to reduce the accommodation expenses and fees to only 20 *liras* for the whole year and to also include the summer season for those students who wished to remain there. The petition concluded by pointing out that 'the interior of Anatolia and Asia Minor in general including the islands, were in economic decline'.[82] Therefore, all those participating in the board firmly believed that it was not reasonable to ask the contribution of communities that could not even support their own needs.[83]

School boards also petitioned Anatoli for educational material and, most importantly maps, which constituted another means of cultural affiliation with Hellenic identity. The administration of the Omirion School sent a letter asking for Zafiropoulos maps, the standard material used in Greek schools everywhere at the time.[84] Actually, the curriculum of this institution for girls also mirrored the prevailing idea about Greek women on the other side of the Aegean, as Constantinos Psaltoff declared in a speech at the school. He pointed out that '[we] admire moderate and liberal Christian commands in favor of women as well as the scientific principles related to them, but we are not going to see their fine dresses being dirtied in the mud of the market; we are not going to see them take over manly jobs and fight in the electoral arena'.[85]

The association continued to provide different bookshops with guidelines and even books considered dangerous by the Ottoman government.[86] The material they sent occasionally became a source of embarrassment. Papamihalakis, the owner of a bookshop in İzmir, for instance, protested that the local inspector, most probably attached to the Office of Education, confiscated everything that had on it the seal of the association.[87] The Central Girls' School asked the association's assistance to obtain through the Hellenic Consulate a famous series of publications called *Maraslios Library*, divided into parts so that it would not raise any suspicion.[88] Eventually the association undertook the task of binding the volumes before sending them.[89] At the same time, the association collected statistics about the locals of different regions, particularly about areas populated by turcophone Greek-Orthodox, such as Ankara, Philadelphia, Kaisaria, and Sinasos (Mustafa Pasha).[90] The association thus received reports about the number of Orthodox schools and their needs, as well as the numbers of missionary schools in different regions.[91]

Local communities also addressed the association either to inquire about scholarships or to send them teachers. Before doing so, however, they first sent their own agents to İzmir. This was the case of H. K. Iliadis who was sent by his community in Sparti to find an experienced kindergarten teacher with some knowledge of Turkish.[92] They announced the available position and finally recruited an applicant who accepted to work for a smaller salary. The other teachers were not at all happy about this. This was the case also of Savvas Avramidis who abandoned Urla to search for a better job in

İzmir; he found out that for each job opening there were more than two applicants. He then seems to have settled for a position at Kastelorizo (Meis), which was definitely much less competitive than Urla.[93]

Concluding Remarks: Negotiating Acculturation

The association soon turned itself into an unauthorized ministry of education, very much like the Hellenic Philological Society of Constantinople that took upon itself the task to promote Hellenic education in Asia Minor while disseminating a certain version of national ideology.[94] In this respect, İzmir played a key role, as it was not only the place of origin of several ambitious young men and women who wished to complete their studies in Athens, but also a destination for those originally from villages in the interior, in many cases turcophone Greek-Orthodox, who wished to study in İzmir. The capital of Ionia, as it was described in contemporary accounts, was located exactly in the center of such networks, and its cultural and social vivacity contributed much to their transformation. The difference, of course, stems from the fact that, while the Hellenic Philological Society that addressed almost the same population drew its resources and inspiration from the Greek-Orthodox elites of the Ottoman capital, Anatoli could draw the same from the capital of the Hellenic state. This accounts for a great deal of the 'national mission' or 'national salvation' discourse that one comes across in several of the relevant correspondence. Certainly, not all members of the association had received a Hellenic education or were militant supporters of a Hellenic version of collective identity. Such a sweeping conclusion would lack the important particularities of locality and temporality which, as I have argued, were (and still are) pertinent to patterns of mobility. However, bearing in mind the rifts developing within the Smyrniot Greek-Orthodox community, it seems that Anatoli contributed immensely to the hellenization of a significant number of young people who migrated from different regions of Asia Minor to İzmir and then to Athens, often having committed themselves to return and work in their community of origin. These young candidates of acculturation, however, should not be considered only passive instruments in a larger process. It happens so that many among them used the opportunity for social as well as geographical mobility. Eventually, they successfully negotiated both their commitment and their professional strategies in ways that put personal, familial, and local well-being above their 'national mission'.

Global Networks, Regional Hegemony, and Seaport Modernization on the Lower Danube

Constantin Iordachi

In August of 1854, in the midst of the Crimean war (1854–56), a French expeditionary army led by Saint-Arnaud, accompanied by 700 regular Ottoman cavalry and 2,500 irregular bands of *başıbozuk*s (bashi-bazouks), launched a military expedition in Dobrudja to fill in the vacuum left by the retreating Russian troops. The campaign proved ill-fated: although the allied troops did not engage in any military battles, a cholera epidemic resulted in heavy human casualties.[1] The 'death march' of the French troops would be responsible for the stigmatization of Dobrudja as an 'unhealthy' province in the Western press and the public memory. But the French expedition also pulled the province into the modern world. In 1855, a technical mission led by the engineers Lalanne and Michel built the first modern road between Constanţa and Raşova. On this occasion, the French *L'Illustration* published a long report about Dobrudja. While presenting the province as an uncivilized part of the Orient, *L'Illustration* praised the civilizing role of the French expeditionary troop, regarded as a proof of France's *mission civilisatrice*. The press coverage led to the 'discovery' of the region by Western Europeans, attracting investments in its infrastructure.[2] Due to Dobrudja's strategic geopolitical position, all great powers and many neighboring countries established consulates in the province (France, England, Russia, Austria,

Sardinia, Prussia, United States, and also Greece) and engaged in fierce economic competition, resulting in attempts at regional hegemony.

Underscoring the growing importance of the Lower Danube and the wider Black Sea region to the international trade in the modern period, the current article reviews institutional responses to geopolitical rivalry in the region, ranging from plans of unilateral domination to pan-European cooperative arrangements. Connected with these, I identify several competing, but also overlapping, projects of economic modernization on the Lower Danube, implemented during the nineteenth and twentieth centuries by the Ottoman authorities (up to 1878), by the great European Powers (mostly between 1856 and 1914), by the Soviet Union (mainly in the 1950s), and by Romania (between 1878 and 1939 and again, with vigor, in the 1980s).

In order to illustrate these attempts at institutionalizing international networks as effective means of regional hegemony and successful integration into the world market, this essay will give an overview over the nineteenth- and twentieth-century development of three important ports situated in the historical province of Dobrudja –namely the Danubian ports of Sulina and Tulcea, and the Black Sea port of Constanţa (*Köstence* in Turkish), inhabited by a cosmopolitan multi-ethnic and multireligious population and dominating the trade of the larger Lower Danube region. The three cities provide a rich and instructive historical comparison on several accounts. Although they all existed in different forms in pre-Ottoman and Ottoman times, their development as port-cities was linked with three distinct modernization projects: Tulcea with Ottoman economy, Sulina with European economy, and Constanţa with the Romanian nation-state. The changing administrative functions of the three cities in the modern period highlight these different strategies of modernization, largely corresponding to major political changes and patterns of international trade: Until 1878, Tulcea was Dobrudja's main administrative and economic center under Ottoman rule, linked to the imperial capital of Istanbul and functioning as its main commercial outpost. Constanţa would become the most important Dobrudjan city under the post-1878 Romanian rule, directly linked to the national capital, Bucharest. After 1856, Sulina developed as a main debauchee of European trade on the Lower Danube, turning into a *porto franco*. Linked to leading Central European cities, such as Vienna and Budapest, Sulina served as a main commercial gate between Central Europe and Asia Minor.

From a theoretical point of view, this article is in line with ongoing efforts to reform area studies by identifying new, more dynamic, models of global scholarship centered on maritime interactions and networks, and to highlight the importance of certain under-researched regions such as the

Lower Danube, as nodal points of interaction and convergence.[3] More specifically, I argue that the profound economic and political transformations that the Lower Danube region underwent in the modern period are transnational in nature and require a relational approach. Port-cities dominated economic and demographic growth in the early modern and modern period,[4] their construction being part of the structural transformations that enabled British global hegemony.[5] The history of the Dobrudjan port-cities is a case in point, their development being closely interwoven with the history of British economic penetration in the region of the Lower Danube, especially after the 1838 Anglo–Ottoman Trade Agreement under which European goods were bought and sold freely on the Ottoman market with low customs tariffs. If until the nineteenth century trade with Europe was of secondary importance for Dobrudjan cities, the penetration of Ottoman economy by foreign (mainly British) capital led to the development of transnational commercial and trade relations. Although the three cities I study existed since ancient or medieval times, in the modern period they developed into port-cities involved in 'core-periphery' economic relations.

The article regards port-cities as genuine 'human laboratories' reflecting great social transformations engendered by the encounter with the expanding capitalist world.[6] As spatial representations and mediators of core-periphery relationship, port-cities are barometers of global changes in patterns of trade, organically linked with nationalism, imperialism and colonialism. The history of the three cities is relevant in this respect. On the one hand, Dobrudjan port-cities served as intermediary links between Central Europe and the Middle East, facilitating the transit of commodities and people and, thus, taking part in the regional as well as global flow of capital and exchange of ideas. On the other hand, the encounter with the outside world brought changes in the administrative organization and urban structure of Dobrudjan port-cities, in the life style of their inhabitants, and in the relationship between port-cities and their hinterland.

The article also highlights the role that well-connected 'proxy' regions play in stimulating development in adjacent zones, as gateways to the larger international trade, in this case the Eastern Mediterranean in relation to the Lower Danube. The history of the Lower Danube and the Black Sea ports has been intimately linked to the historical development of the Mediterranean. Ever since antiquity the shores of the Black Sea have functioned as a corridor of transit between the demographic reservoir of the northern steppes and the Balkans and Asia Minor.[7] Leading Mediterranean city states established commercial outposts on the Black Sea shores.[8] From a geopolitical perspective, military control of the sea and its straits, the Bosphorus and the Dardanelles, provided a strategic tool to the domination of the Eastern Mediterranean Basin. These multiple links expanded in the modern period: up to World War II, the three leading countries in shipping on the maritime Danube were the non-riparian Greece, England and Italy, the first and the third testifying to the strong Mediterranean presence on the Lower Danube. Connected to the wider Black Sea and Mediterranean worlds, Dobrudjan port-cities shared a number of similarities with other Mediterranean ports, among which the most important were their 'openness' and 'porosity', their absorption of large migration influxes and the resulting cosmopolitan and multi-ethnic character of their population, made up mostly of Jews, Greeks and Armenians.[9] The three cities also emulated Mediterranean models of urban planning and architectural development, resulting in the reorganization of their urban space.[10]

The interdependence between the Black Sea ports and the leading Mediterranean ports calls for comparative interdisciplinary studies under a common theoretical framework. A pioneering effort in this respect belongs to the Romanian historian Gheorghe Brătianu (1898–1953) who authored a seminal history of the Black Sea up to the Ottoman conquest, highlighting multiple links with Mediterranean ports.[11] He also studied the history of Genoa's and Venice's economic connections with the agrarian hinterland of the Black Sea, and the socio-political impact of these cities' commercial outposts on the region. Yet, with few but notable exceptions, this field of research has not been followed up. Although the Black Sea area gained a growing economic and geopolitical importance in the nineteenth century, the urban development and commercial role of its port-cities and their connection with the Mediterranean and the rest of the world have remained largely under-researched.[12]

The first part of this article provides a short overview of the history of Dobrudja and delineates the main features of the Ottoman project of modernization on the Lower Danube. The second part focuses on the European political and commercial involvement in the region of the Lower Danube, centered mainly on the activity of the European Commission of the Danube, which was regarded as an innovative experiment in international law. The third part presents Romania's plans of seaport modernization after the annexation of Dobrujda in 1878, underscoring its steady efforts to nationalize the river for protectionist economic gains. The last part provides a brief overview over seaport modernization on the Lower Danube during the short twentieth century, focusing mostly on the Romanian and Soviet strategies of modernization. Based on this theoretically-minded empirical case study, the article tackles issues such as the impact of globalization and internationalization on port-cities and their impact on regional networks of communication.

An Imperial Borderland: Dobrudja under Ottoman Rule

Throughout its history, the province of Dobrudja has held a strategic geopolitical position, which accounts for the multiple commercial and political interests competing over its domination. Dobrudja was part of the area of ancient Greek colonization, conquered by the Roman Empire, lost to the Slavs (602–972), and later re-conquered and included in the Byzantine province of Paristrion. Due to its position, Dobrudja also served as a corridor of transit for migratory peoples from the Eurasian steppes to the Balkans from the fifth century onwards, such as the Huns, Avars, Bulgars, Pecenegs, Uz, Cumans, and so forth.

Following its occupation by the Ottoman Empire in the fifteenth century, Dobrudja served as an imperial military and commercial corridor of transit. The province fulfilled multiple functions, defending access to Istanbul, controlling the principalities of Wallachia and Moldova, and allowing communications with Crimean Tartars on the military line of Istanbul–Isaccea–Babadağ. In economic terms, Dobrudja was a pastoral region, dominated by cattle and sheep breeding, agriculture coming second.

As elsewhere in the empire, the Ottoman rule set into motion important demographic changes. The province was declared an important frontier area as it became subject to an intense military colonization of Turkish and Tartar populations from the Southern Crimea and Asia Minor, transforming it into an Islamic area. As a frontier zone of the Ottoman economy, Dobrudja attracted innumerable immigrants from the neighboring provinces, who tried to escape military service or feudal obligations. During the eighteenth and nineteenth centuries, the province was demographically linked to a larger territory, absorbing numerous Romanian and Bulgarian peasants from the Wallachian plains, the Balkan Mountains and Southern Bessarabia as well as Cossacks from the Dniepr Delta, Lipovans from Central Russia, and German colonists from Southern Russia. Because of its large pastures and its mild Mediterranean climate, the province during winter and early spring became the meeting point of Romanian, Bulgarian and Greek shepherds from Transylvania, the Balkan Mountains, and Salonica, who practiced a kind of long distance seasonal migration specific to the pastoral life in the Balkans.

Consequently, Dobrudja acquired a highly mixed ethnic composition: Slavic fishermen populated the Danube Delta; Italian, Jewish, Greek and Armenian merchants inhabited the cities; Romanians the eastern bank; Bulgarians dominated the north, the Turks and the Tartars the center and south. Therefore, the Romanian historian Nicolae Iorga identified, at the time of annexation by Romania in 1878, 'three Dobrudjas', three parallel strips of land along the north–south axis of the province: the coast of the Black Sea as a commercial outpost; the central part of the province as a boulevard of military communications between Istanbul and Southern Bessarabia; and, finally, the agricultural bank of the Danube, inhabited mostly by Romanians and in permanent contact with the neighboring Wallachian counties.

Despite providing fiscal and political advantages to Muslims, the Ottoman state did not engage in cultural homogenization, proving rather tolerant to ethnic and cultural diversity. Thus the *millet* system provided for confessional autonomy of major ethnic groups, while the *Tanzimat* reforms inaugurated in 1839 favored the emergence of a category of local Christian notables, many of them of Romanian ethnic origin, who penetrated the administration of the province. The Ottoman social system also prevented the consolidation of a local Muslim hereditary aristocracy; in Dobrudja, the position of large land-owners was further undermined by the complete collapse of the Ottoman administration and the massive Muslim emigration caused by the 1877–78 Turco–Russian War. In addition, ethnic groups in Dobrudja were predominantly rural but still very heterogeneous with a low level of nationalist mobilization. Among them, only Bulgarians and Romanians developed significant national movements, starting mainly in the third quarter of the nineteenth century.

An Imperial Center: The Port-City of Tulcea

Prior to the integration of the Lower Danube into the capitalist world economy, the port-city of Tulcea functioned as Dobrudja's main Ottoman administrative and commercial center in the region. From Tulcea, Ottoman authorities kept domestic trade under strict control during the seventeenth and eighteenth century when international trade on the Danube was virtually closed to European countries.

Due to its central administrative and commercial role, Tulcea acquired during that time a highly heterogeneous population, made up of Turks, Tartars, Romanians, Bulgarians, Russians, Jews, Greeks and Armenians. Socially, inhabitants were divided into two main categories, the ruling elites and ordinary city-dwellers, the latter including Muslims as well as non-Muslims. Obviously, as a regional center, Tulcea was inhabited by Ottoman military and administrative elites such as bureaucrats, military garrisons, the military chief of the frontier area, or other officials responsible for the maintenance of law and order. Numerous notables such as leaders of religious orders, representatives of craftsmen, and wealthy merchants acted as intermediaries between the rulers and urban population. Ordinary city-dwellers consisted mostly of craftsmen working in the local shipyard or in professional guilds, of tradesmen, and port workers, the latter being either regular inhabitants or seasonal migrants.

While Tulcea remained Dobrudja's main administrative center throughout the Ottoman rule until 1878, the economic importance of the city declined after the Crimean War, at a time when Dobrudja was gradually integrated into the European world economy. This outcome was due to a combination of internal and external factors. On the one hand, the European
commercial penetration into the Ottoman economy in the second half of the
nineteenth century required different nodes of economic activity, generating
a shift in the local economy towards new and better-located port-cities. On
the other hand, Ottoman authorities implemented their own modernization
project in the region, encouraging the development of agriculture, the expansion of urbanization and of regional communications centered on Constanţa,
in order to transform Dobrudja into an agrarian hinterland for the imperial
capital, Istanbul. This comprehensive project of modernization undertaken
in the Ottoman Empire during the *Tanzimat* was carried out with Ottoman as
well as with European capital, mostly British and French.

Dobrudja, a Pilot Project of Ottoman Modernization
The Crimean War (1854–56) had a strong impact on Ottoman developmental
policy in Dobrudja. The manifest Western geopolitical and economic interest
in the region stimulated Ottoman administration to transform the province into
a nodal point of communication with Central Europe and the Mediterranean
world, by building transportation networks and encouraging new human
settlements. In order to facilitate the implementation of their ambitious modernization projects, Ottoman authorities replaced the ordinary state council
with a new 'Council of Public Works', made up, besides Turkish officials, of
four French engineers, two Russians and an Englishman. Keen on expanding
British economic control over the Lower Danube, British consular representatives in Dobrudja pointed out that a single British member in the council could
scarcely assure 'adequate protection' for their interests. They demanded the
nomination of an additional British member so that 'all the public works of
any importance are in English hands and are carried on with English capital'.[13]
    The main creator of the Ottoman plans of modernization of the Lower
Danube was the British engineer John Trevor Barkley. Before 1855, Barkley
had served as one of the directors of the coalmines near Heraclia for the
English government.[14] After successfully collaborating with the allied forces
during the Crimean War, Barkley became the engineer-in-chief of 'The Black
Sea to Danube Railway Company', representing a group of British investors
interested in developing the Lower Danube region. In September of 1857, the
company obtained from Sultan Abdülmecid the concession to build a railway
across Dobrudja, from the Black Sea port of Constanţa to the Danubian

harbor of Cernavodă. Abdülmecid granted the concession for 99 years, but the contract stipulated that the Ottoman authorities retained the right to 'supervise' the railway. Although this stipulation was not new from a legal perspective, it was nevertheless proof of the great economic and political importance of the province for the Ottomans.[15] Nevertheless, in order to exploit the benefits of the new line to their fullest extent, the British company also obtained the right to expand and exploit the Constanţa harbor, effectively gaining control of export and import commerce on the Lower Danube.

The 40-mile-long railway was built entirely with English capital and technology. On 9 October 1858, the London-based newspaper *The Times* informed its readers that work on the railway had broken ground and that the first nine miles would be completed before the cold season, since the difficulties were 'trifling' and labor 'of the better kind' was 'plentiful', originating mainly from the neighboring Wallachia, 'while the starving Tartar population which has been settled at Mecidiye, close to the projected line, will supply the rest'.[16] The railway opened on 16 October 1860, being the first line opened in the Ottoman Empire, before major railroads were built between İzmir and Aydın (1866), İzmir and Turgutlu (1866), and Istanbul and İzmit (1873),[17] a fact that testifies to the economic and geopolitical importance of Dobrudja. During a pompous inauguration ceremony attended by the high official Ethem Pasha, the train traveled from Constanţa to Cernavodă, where it was welcomed by a large crowd, 'wearing the distinctive features and costumes of the different races, Turks, Greeks, Albanians, Bulgarians, and several varieties of Tartars'.[18] According to the correspondent of *The Times*, in Cernavodă 'there were also naval, military, consular, or other uniforms of almost every nation of Europe' making viewers believe that 'the Crimean War has broken anew'.[19] The completion of the railway stimulated the work on the harbor 'with additional vigor', in the hope that 'in a short time vessels of a large size will be able to receive their cargoes, which will be shot into them directly from the railway carriages, in perfect security'.[20]

In addition to economic investments, Ottoman authorities made sustained efforts to repopulate the province. Dobrudja served as a constant military battlefield during the Russian–Turkish wars (1768–1878), the province being occupied by the Russian army in 1771–74, 1790–91, 1809–10, as well as in 1829 and 1853. This situation provoked anarchy in the administration and great fluctuations in the population. Between 1770 and 1784, some 200,000 Crimean Tartars took refuge in Dobrudja.[21] However, as a consequence of the particularly devastating 1828–29 war, the total population of the province decreased to 40,000 inhabitants, to increase to 100,000 by 1850.[22] After the Crimean War, Ottoman authorities settled in Dobrudja over 100,000 Tartars from the Crimea and Circassians from Kuban and the Caucasus, who were assigned military tasks within a privileged legal category of border warriors. Ottoman authorities also paid attention to the urbanization of the province. In 1860, Sultan Abdülmecid traveled to the province and founded the city of Mecidiye called after himself in the south.[23]

The Ottoman project of modernization was nevertheless hindered by recurrent military confrontations in the region, resulting in insecurity and instability in the administration. Ultimately, the Ottoman rule in the province came to an end in 1878, as a result of yet another Russian–Ottoman war and the ensuing reorganization of the region's *status quo* by the Berlin Congress.

The Danube as a Vital European Artery

In the post-Ottoman period, plans of modernization in Lower Danube region were continued and even amplified through the collective effort of the great powers. To understand this development, one needs to refer to the growing commercial and military importance of the Danube for European affairs.

The Danube is Europe's second-longest river, after the Volga, with circa 1,800 miles from beginning to end. If in the Middle Ages the river was overwhelmingly dominated by the Ottoman Empire, which monopolized navigation on its lower part,[24] starting with the last quarter of the eighteenth century the Danube had become a major artery of connection between Central Europe and the Middle East and acquired an important economic and strategic value, as an integral part of the broader 'Eastern Question'. This was mostly due to the gradual decline of Ottoman domination, marked by the opening of navigation to great powers, such as Russia (1774) and the Habsburg Empire (1791). In addition, through the annexation of Bessarabia in 1812, Russia became a riparian country on the Danube, thus breaking the Ottoman commercial monopoly over the river and the Black Sea. Its protectionist trade policies disrupted Ottoman commercial networks on the coastal zones of the Black Sea, posing a direct challenge to Ottoman domination.

The Russian-Ottoman Treaty of Adrianople (1829) meant another step toward the opening of the Danube by forcing the Ottoman Empire to lift its de facto monopoly over the grain trade of Moldova and Wallachia. As a result, the two autonomous principalities could take part in international trade, a fact that soon resulted into an unprecedented volume of grain export to the West. Thus, in 1837 there were 98,380 quarters of wheat exported via the Danube at Galați; in 1838 there were 171,913, and in 1839 there were 148,117, at a significantly higher price than in 1837.[25] England was particularly interested in this new source of grain supply. At a time when the Irish Famine and the repeal of the Corn Laws increased the demand for cereals,

English companies discovered, in the words of Barkley, 'this rich store, and at the same time laid the foundations of Romania's prosperity and importance'.[26] Consequently, the number of English ships engaged in trade on the Danube increased from seven in 1843 to 128 in 1849; soon, two-thirds of the English trade in the Black Sea region was conducted on the Danube.[27]

The growing number of references to the Danube in the international press is indicative of the significance the river acquired in international trade. In *The Times*, the first references to the river appeared at the end of the eighteenth century, mostly in connection with the military clashes between Russia and the Ottoman Empire.[28] In the first quarter of the nineteenth century, numerous articles were published on the navigation of the river,[29] and on the wheat trade of Moldova and Wallachia, named at the time 'the Danubian principalities'.[30]

The opening of the Lower Danube to commercial navigation increased the importance of the river as a European commercial artery. In direct connection to improvements in communication and seaport facilities in Dobrudja, regularizing the upper course of the river also became important in order to facilitate naval transportation on the commercial route Vienna–Budapest–Galaţi–Brăila and with the Black Sea. The correspondent of *The Times* in the Lower Danube understood that the Danubian principalities and European Turkey 'are of high importance in a commercial point of view for the raising and exportation of grains', mostly to England,[31] and suggested a comprehensive and concerted policy of the Western and Central European powers in the region, in order to shelter their common interests against Russian domination. In 1839, traveling from the Iron Gates to Galaţi, the correspondent expressed 'a sentiment of wonder in considering at once the magnitude and extent of the Danube and the neglect with which the question of its actual commercial opportunities has until very lately been regarded'.[32] He highlighted the extraordinary advantages of the river for the 'inland commerce from the very center of Europe', connecting it with almost all other parts of the continent with the Upper and Lower Danube.[33]

The correspondent of *The Times* also argued that 'a new order of things must shortly of necessity take place upon the Danube'.[34] In his view, Austria and England should have opposed the unilateral Russian domination and unite in a community of commercial interests on a free-tariff basis: 'Austria should openly join with England in disregard of the quasi-protection of Russia over this portion of Europe and thus to enter upon the compact under the most liberal and comprehensive designs'. He pleaded for 'a commercial unity of interest' between the two countries that would endow Austria as a commercial power, 'increasing her ascendancy in Europe', by detaching it 'from the grasping scheme of Prussia' and, instead, uniting it with other riparian countries 'in an unrestricted foreign commerce'. The author pointed out the integrative role played by the Danube river, connecting land-locked regions such as southern and eastern Germany, Austria, Hungary, Transylvania and part of the Balkans with the Eastern Mediterranean by Trieste, and 'with the wide commerce of the world' by way of the Black Sea, 'hence preserving the integrity of Europe'.[35]

Indeed, as it is apparent in this article, the growing economic role of the Danube generated a stiff commercial rivalry among great powers for the control of the river. England and Austria assigned an important role to their Danubian trade and, therefore, favored unrestricted navigation on the Danube. In contrast, although it did not impede the free trade on the Danube, Russia was nevertheless directly interested in channeling the grain trade of the West toward its Black Sea port of Odessa and, therefore, deliberately neglected the proper maintenance of the navigation conditions in the Delta. By the 1850s, this had resulted in the three channels of the river becoming almost non-navigable. In reaction, European powers made plans of neutralizing the waterway of the Danube as a way of guaranteeing free and quality navigation, and of preventing its domination by a single power.[36]

The European Commission of the Danube and Sulina
The opportunity for a common European policy on the Danube was provided by the defeat of Russia in the Crimean War. The Paris Congress that followed the end of the war in 1856 detached Southern Bessarabia from Russia and returned it to Moldova. Having thus removed Russia from the river, the great powers could implement their plan of granting an international status to the Danube and assuring liberty of transit.

To this end, Article XV of the Paris Congress stipulated that 'the navigation of the Danube cannot be subjected to any impediment or charge not expressly provided for by the stipulations contained in the following Articles'. Most importantly, the article charged the newly instituted European Commission of the Danube, composed of the Ottoman Empire, Russia, Great Britain, Austria, France, Prussia, and Sardinia (and thus dominated by representatives of non-riparian great powers), with the jurisdiction over the Lower Danube, between the Black Sea and the Moldovan Danubian harbor of Galaţi. The Commission had the task 'to clear the mouths of the Danube, as well as the neighboring parts of the sea from sand'[37] and to improve the quality of navigation. Although it initially had a limited mandate for two years, the efficiency of the European Commission in clearing up the Danube convinced the powers to extend its mandate until 1871, and then again until 1883. Another conference of the great powers held in London in 1883 extended the mandate of the commission for an additional twenty-one years and stipulated that it would be automatically extended every three years if not explicitly denounced by one of its members.[38]

While formally the center of the European Commission was at Galați, its personnel, technical sub-commissions and bulk of commercial activities were located at Sulina. The port-city of Sulina was chosen by the commission as its main center because it was ideally located at the mouth of the Danube, because it offered good conditions for navigation, and because it did not have its own trade activity monopolizing the harbor. A report on the condition of the three canals of the Danube (Sulina, Saint George and Kilia) concluded that 'although it is the most insignificant of the three great branches of the Danube', Sulina nevertheless 'seems able naturally to maintain somewhat a better bar than either of the two outlets'.[39]

The internationalization of the Danube and the major improvement in naval conditions resulted in a rapid growth of commercial activity. According to the statistics of the commission, 3,015 ships exited the river in 1862, transporting a total of 450,014 tons of goods; 3,099 ships exited in 1863, carrying 519,332 tons of merchandise; 3,448 ships exited in 1864, with 585,894 tons. In 1866, the fleet of riparian states had an important share in the total trade activity, such as Turkey with 437 ships and 36,785 tons of carried goods; Russia with 103 ships and 20,910 tons; and the United Principalities with 53 ships and 6,096 tons. Apart from the riparian states, the most important fleets belonged to Greece, with 1,053 ships and 136,922 tons of goods; England with 243 ships transporting 82,679 tons; Italy with 205 ships transporting 50,035; Austria with 204 ships and 60,932 tons; Norway with 37 ship and 12,196 tons; and France with 40 ships and 5,104 tons, followed by Sweden, Prussia, Serbia, and Denmark.[40]

In the same year, 361 ships carrying 133,934 tons transited the port-city of Sulina, indicative of the city's importance for the Danubian trade. Under the direct jurisdiction of the Commission, Sulina obtained in 1870 the status of *porto franco*, meaning that all merchandise exported was exempt from taxes. This policy resulted in an impressive growth of the amount of goods exported, from 3,761,167 tons in the period between 1871 and 1875 to 15,806,932 tons in the period between 1906 and 1910, thus multiplying more than fourfold in 35 years.[41]

The European Commission in Sulina acted as a genuine 'state-within-a-state', having its own jurisdiction, police force, and navigation regulations.[42] It collected its own taxes and possessed land and numerous buildings. The commission functioned as a social institution as well. It built hospitals, supported local social institutions, and improved sanitary conditions in the region, effectively changing the face of the city. Because of its strong international status, the commission also mediated local conflicts and was involved in the delimitation of the border between Moldova and the Ottoman Empire on the Kilia branch under the 1856 Treaty of Paris. It also received complaints concerning the legal status of local inhabitants and intervened on their behalf through diplomatic channels, as was the case with the fishing rights of the Old Believers of the village on the right side of the Kilia, granted to the Ottoman Empire under the 1856 Treaty of Paris; they appealed to the commission between 1860 and 1862 to preserve their rights.[43]

In many ways, the city of Sulina was thus the creation of the European Commission of the Danube, its destiny being closely related to the existence of the commission during the period between 1856 and 1939. Thus benefiting from strong European involvement, Sulina evolved from a small fishing village to a prosperous and highly cosmopolitan town, inhabited by more than twenty-two ethno-religious groups, comprising permanent inhabitants, the personnel of the European Commission, harbor workers and transit merchants. Due to the extraordinary amount of transited goods, wages were higher in Sulina than in the neighboring port-cities, and opportunities of employment attracted many seasonal workers from all over the Balkans. The official language of the commission was French, while the spoken language of the urban population was mainly Greek, as the Greek community was Sulina's largest ethnic group, with 2,056 members in 1904.

However, unlike Tulcea and Constanța, the city of Sulina did not develop at the same pace with its harbor. That was because Sulina was not a merchant city *per se*, since it did not have a well developed local economy. Its harbor was rather a point of collection and further dispersion of European goods transported on the Danube. The remarkable prosperity of the city of Sulina was therefore dependent on its privileged legal status under the jurisdiction of the European Commission. With the loss of this status in 1939, the city declined.

Romania as a Buffer State on the Lower Danube

With the end of Ottoman rule in Dobrudja and its 1878 annexation by Romania, a new political actor emerged in the region of the Lower Danube. Initially, Romania acquired Dobrudja on behalf of the Great Powers, in its role as a buffer state among rival great powers. During that time, Romanian authorities nevertheless developed their own project of modernization, putting forward claims to the nationalization of the Lower Danube.[44]

In 1878, as part of the general political reorganization of Southeastern Europe, the Berlin Congress devoted special attention to the international status of the Danube, regarding its neutrality as a milestone of the new political make-up of the region. The main concerns of the congress had to do with devising a package of measures to compensate for Russia's reacquisition of Southern Bessarabia and, thus, to preserve the neutrality of the river. It was to this end that the Treaty of Berlin granted Dobrudja and the Danube Delta to Romania and accepted the country as a member of the European Commission of the Danube.

The congress chose Romania for two paramount reasons: First, due to its geographical position, the emerging newly-independent state was ideally positioned to serve as a buffer state between the great powers in the region and to prevent a unilateral domination of the river. Second, as a 'weak state', Romania could neither oppose the internationalization of the Danube nor attempt to nationalize the river. The Treaty of Berlin could thus safely maintain and even enlarge the prerogatives of the European Commission of the Danube. According to the Treaty of Berlin, in spite of the fact that the commission by that time operated solely in Romanian territory, it worked 'in complete independence of territorial authorities'. Significantly, this extraterritorial status could not apply to the Russian sector of the river, where local legislation had priority over international stipulations.[45]

Regardless of the juridical controversies over the extraterritorial jurisdiction of the European Commission of the Danube, the Treaty of Berlin granted Romania Dobrudja and the Danube Delta and, by doing so, strategic control over maritime Danube. Romania became the center of 'the Danubian question' and a factor in the 'European equilibrium' in Eastern Europe. Romanian political elites were eager to speculate on the important role Romania acquired in the maintenance of political equilibrium in Eastern Europe. While some politicians opposed the annexation of Dobrudja in view of the potential geopolitical complications and its multi-ethnic population, the majority of Romanian politicians pointed out the intrinsic relationship between Romania's possession of Dobrudja and the country's new political role in Europe. Prime Minister Brătianu summarized the pro-annexation arguments during the 1878 parliamentary debates about the Treaty of Berlin: 'Dobrudja was imposed on us by Europe. You all refused it, we protested and did not want to accept it but [..] Europe gave us Dobrudja since it saw that we are a strong nation, distinguished and full of vigor, with our own national character, different from all the nations in the Orient.'[46] Indeed, Brătianu argued that Europe supported the annexation because it was in its interest to have Danube in the hands of people who could assure its liberty.

Along the same lines, the Minister of Foreign Affairs, Mihail Kogălniceanu, connected the annexation of the province to Romania's European identity and civilizing vocation: Dobrudja was 'a land given [to us] by Europe and [one] which sets us in contact with Western Europe'.[47] In his view Romania's control over Dobrudja and the Danube Delta was conceived as the country's main asset in becoming a Western (anti-Russian) military bastion, a guarantor of political stability in Eastern Europe and an essential link in the commercial transit between the 'Occident' and the 'Orient'.

The Port-City of Constanţa

After 1878, Romanian political elites implemented in Dobrudja a nationalist modernizing project, meant to incorporate the province into the expanding national economy and to elevate Romania's integration into the Western economy. In doing so, Romanian political leaders were influenced by the protectionist arguments put forward by the 'father' of the national economy, Frederick Liszt, who emphasized the role of the sea in fostering economic development.[48] The most important promoter of the program of Romania's commercial expansion on the sea was the liberal economist Petre S. Aurelian. The creator of the economic policy of the Liberal Party and also Prime Minister between December of 1896 and April of 1897, Aurelian pointed out the organic link between the evolution of industry and the development of a comprehensive system of naval transportation: 'the manufacturing industry is essential for the development of the navigation, the more the manufactures are developing, the more the commercial navigation is growing'.[49]

Maritime transportation was all the more important for Romania, since the economy of the country depended heavily on the export of grain, wood, oil and other raw materials to the West. Aurelian pleaded therefore for a national program of major investments in Dobrudja in order to link the province with Romania through a system of railways and naval communication, and to build a major seaport at Constanţa which would serve as a commercial debauchee for Romania's exports. Ion Brătianu, the leader of the Liberal Party, was an enthusiastic supporter of Aurelian's economic program. Brătianu suggestively expressed the strategy of the Liberal Party regarding Dobrudja's modernization: 'Constanţa is the lung of Romania, the mouth through which the country is breathing. Constanţa will also become the fortress for Romania's defense; through it we will set contact with the whole world, and we will secure the most important communication route for our trade'.[50]

The economic incorporation of Dobrudja into Romania was an important part of the liberal campaign for sheltered industrialization and coincided with the increased role that the Romanian state played in the development of the national economy. The province benefited from exceptional material investments, mostly concentrated in communications. In this respect, Romanian authorities continued the developmental strategy envisioned by John Trevor Barkley, a fact that highlights the continuity between the Ottoman and Romanian efforts of regional modernization and their collaboration with international capital. After 1878, Barkley understood that the expansion of the railway network in the Balkans would lead to new commercial routes 'superseding the Danube as a means of export and import', while increasing the importance of seaports as commercial outlets for international trade.[51] He recommended that Romanian authorities build one or several railway bridges over the Danube toward the seaport of Constanţa to save the roundabout trip to the Danube Delta. 'When this gap is filled up, the produce of Romania, and subsequently of Transylvania, will be conveyed by railway, summer and winter, without break, from the depots of the interior to steamers in the Black Sea, as the present circuitous and, irregular water carriage will be gradually abandoned'.[52]

Indeed, because of the lack of regular naval transportation and bridges over the Danube, in 1878 the province was almost completely isolated from Romania. This situation was especially grave in the winter during which navigation used to be suspended for long periods due to the freezing river. In October 1882, the Romanian state bought the Constanţa–Cernavodă railway from the 'The Black Sea to Danube Railway Company' for FF 16 million (gold); invested an additional 35 million in a major bridge at Cernavodă; and completed the railway connection between Cernavodă and Feteşti in order to link the line Constanţa–Cernavodă to the national railway system, via Feteşti–Bucharest. Designed by Angel Saligny and inaugurated in 1895, after ten years of intense work, the 'grandiose' 1,662 meters iron bridge named 'King Carol' was the longest bridge in Europe and the second-longest in the world at that time. The public viewed the bridge as a symbol of Romania's technological achievements and of Dobrudja's union with 'the mother-country'.[53] It had a pivotal role in the commercial transit between the capital and the sea, shortening the traveling time by about seven hours. The bridge was the 'shortest link' between Asia Minor and Western Europe: Constanţa became the terminal station of the Orient Express, the place where Western travelers embarked for Asia Minor.[54]

Most important, in October 1896 the Romanian state began the construction of a major harbor for redirecting national exports from land to the Black Sea. Unlike the Danubian ports of Galaţi and Sulina, the new Black Sea harbor was not placed under the supervision of the European Commission of the Danube and, hence, regarded as a symbol of Romania's economic independence. Soon, the Constanţa harbor became a major instrument of the Romanian national economy and turned into 'the lung of the country': The total volume of Romania's sea exports grew from 89,400 try': The total volume of Romania's sea exports grew from 89,400 tons in 1889 to 1.5 million tons in 1913, amounting to one-third of Romania's exports.[55] The port acquired an important role in the connection between Central Europe and the Middle East and provided a strategic commercial route between Constanţa and Rotterdam, by way of adjacent canals.

The urban development of Constanţa was a symbol of Dobrudja's modernization. Benefiting from substantial real estate investments such as those of the leading Parisian banker Alléon, attracted there by Mihail Kogălniceanu, the city grew from 5,000 inhabitants in 1878 to a modern city of 31,000 in 1912. Shaped by numerous French architects, the architecture of Constanţa was dominated by neoclassic, romantic, eclectic and art nouveau styles. These cosmopolitan influences provoked the reaction of the Romanian national school of architecture and resulted in a sharp competition over building a casino in Constanţa. The construction was ultimately entrusted to the French architect Daniel Renard, who designed an impressive art nouveau building, which subsequently became one of the icons of the city.

Urbanization made important progress in the entire province, the increase in urban population being generally provided by ethnic Romanian colonists. Under Ottoman rule, Dobrudja had fourteen cities, largely dominated by merchant colonies of Greeks, Armenians and Jews. After 1878, the state-sponsored urbanization altered this ethnic composition. In 1912, Dobrudja had an urban population of 94,915, accounting for a quarter of its total population. Together with the administrative centers of Tulcea and Constanţa (22,262 and 31,576 inhabitants respectively), there were also six other towns over 5,000 inhabitants. Privileged by the new political order, Romanians monopolized the state administration and added to the number of city inhabitants. In 1909, urban Romanians acquired majority in seven cities, representing 98 per cent in Cuzgun, 92 per cent in Ostrov, 66 per cent in Măcin, 68 per cent in Cernavodă, 61 per cent in Hîrşova, 51 per cent in Isaccea, and 50.6 per cent in Mahmudia. In another six cities, Romanians held a relative majority, with a proportion of 37 per cent of the population in Mecidiye, 34 per cent in Constanţa, 33 per cent in Babadağ, 28 per cent in Mangalia, 27 per cent in Kilia, and 26.8 per cent in Tulcea. The Romanian urban element was in minority only in Sulina, at 17 per cent.[56] The rising Romanian urban bourgeoisie also succeeded in nationalizing the commercial activity in the province, while the economic role of former Ottoman urban elites was systematically decreased. Thus, if in 1878 'the few Romanian merchants in Dobrudja could be counted on the fingers of a single hand', in 1909, of the 7,664 registered Dobrudjan merchants, 4,815 or 62 per cent were Romanians and 2,849 or 38 per cent 'foreigners' (Greeks, Jews and Armenians).[57]

Uneven Development in Dobrudja

This success was highly praised by the Romanian elites who used economic progress as a legitimizing factor for their rule. In 1903, twenty-five years after Dobrudja's annexation, the geographer M. D. Ionescu enthusiastically assessed that 'in the economic domain Dobrudja has advanced with gigantic steps'.[58] Based on statistical comparisons with other provinces of Romania and with different European countries, Ionescu documented Dobrudja's miraculous transformation, from a 'pile of ruins' to a prosperous province.

In fact, Dobrudja exhibited a specific case of 'the development of the underdevelopment'.[59] Its economic structure was tailored almost exclusively as an appendage to metropolitan needs, at the expense of local patterns of economic development. The location of the cities and the allocation of massive investments in the province followed the strategic communication route between Bucharest and Constanţa. As a result, the development in the province was regionally uneven. Advantaged by its strategic location, the county of Constanţa benefited from a national program of economic expansion: The bridge over the Danube, the railway, the major national harbor and the regional capital were all there. Consequently, Constanţa experienced an unprecedented level of economic prosperity: According to official financial censuses, in 1890 Constanţa occupied the last place among the 32 counties of Romania in regard to wealth, but it soon advanced to number 28 in 1891, to number 22 in 1895/96, to number 14 in 1905/6, and to 13 in 1907.[60] In the same vein, between 1890 and 1906, the number of tax payers in the county increased, and the county advanced fourteen steps in national ranking from the 30th place in 1890/1 to the 16th in 1905/6.[61] In contrast, disadvantaged by its many lakes, swamps and the vast Danube Delta and its more eccentric geographical location, the county of Tulcea was linked to the Romanian national railway system only in 1938. Consequently, Tulcea developed at a relatively slow pace, its transportation network remaining largely dependent on the Danube harbors of Sulina and Tulcea and its economy dominated by agriculture and fishing.[62] Therefore, the national ranking of Tulcea's economic wealth stagnated, moving from the 24th place in 1890 to the 26th in 1895/6, and again to the 24th in 1905/6.[63]

Similarly, the number of tax payers in Tulcea increased, and the county advanced only five places in national ranking from the 29th to the 24th place. The same conclusion is highlighted by the level of urbanization and population growth in the two counties. Between 1800 and 1900, Constanţa developed at a demographic rate of 122.76 per cent, compared to only 45.26 per cent in Tulcea.[64] Thus, if in 1880 Tulcea was superior in population by 24,124 inhabitants, Constanţa exceeded it by 4,747 inhabitants in

1900 and by 28,629 in 1912. This pattern of local development was best expressed by the shift of the regional nucleus from the former Ottoman administrative center of Tulcea to the new Romanian center of Constanța. This demographic evolution affected the proportions of Romanian population and their share of landed property. Constanța had a higher proportion of ethnic Romanians, while Tulcea had a greater concentration of Bulgarians (29,633, as compared to 12,342 in Constanța) and Russians and Lipovans (29,016 in Tulcea, as compared to 2,103 in Constanța).[65] Official statistics reveal that, by 1905, landed property was overwhelmingly concentrated in the hands of Romanians in Constanța (77 per cent), but dominated by Bulgarians in Tulcea (38.3 per cent as compared to 34.3 per cent of land owned by Romanians). This situation alarmed many Romanian nationalists who claimed that due to inefficient state policy 'we are now in a worse situation than under the Ottoman rule'.[66] The concerted campaign of Dobrudja's prefects resulted in an intensive colonization campaign of the Romanian state especially in the late 1910s. Thus, massive state investments in Dobrudjan port-cities accompanied a campaign of ethnic and cultural homogenization that stigmatized cosmopolitanism as a sign of decadence, a relic of the backward Ottoman imperial legacy.

From the 'Concert of Europe' to Military Confrontation: The Lower Danube during the Short Twentieth Century

On the eve of and during World War I, Dobrudja was yet again a military battlefield. In 1913, during the Second Balkan War, invoking geopolitical imperatives, Romania annexed Southern Dobrudja from Bulgaria, made up of the counties of Durostor and Caliacra. This event opened a pandora's box of regional conflicts, triggering Bulgaria's retaliation during World War I. In response, in 1916 Dobrudja was invaded and ultimately occupied by the allied forces of the Central Powers, made up of German, Austro-Hungarian and Bulgarian military contingents. Military confrontations in 1916 and 1917 resulted in massive material loss, destroying the bridge over the Danube and ruining Constanța's harbor, the very symbols of Romanian rule in the province, and reversing the demographic effects of Romania's policy of ethnic colonization. Following Romania's defeat, despite Bulgaria's desire to annex the region and thus replace Romania as an 'arbiter' of the Lower Danube, Dobrudja was organized as a condominium under German and Austro-Hungarian influence.

After the war, Romania restored the province, while the Treaty of Versailles reconfirmed the international status of the Danube. The conditions of navigation were spelled out by a new 'Danube Convention', signed in

1921 by 12 European riparian and non-riparian states. The convention decided to continue the existence of the European Commission of the Danube, in charge of 'maritime' Lower Danube, from Brăila to the sea. However, unlike in the pre-war period, when the commission was ruled by the great powers in concert, in the inter-war period the European Commission was made up only of the victorious European powers, namely Great Britain, Italy and France, and by the riparian country of Romania. In addition, the convention established a new 'International Commission of the Danube' composed of all riparian states as well as the non-riparian great powers of the European Commission with jurisdiction over the 'fluvial' Upper Danube (from Brăila in Romania to Ulm in Germany).

Two main developments characterized geopolitical relations in interwar Danubian affairs. First, the collapse of the Austro-Hungarian monarchy, the Ottoman Empire and Tsarist Russia led to the disintegration of former imperial markets and commercial networks. Taking advantage of the new regional context and consolidated by great territorial gains, riparian nation-states assumed a stronger political role in the region of the Lower Danube, challenging the great powers' domination and pursuing plans of nationalizing the river. Romania was in the forefront exploiting the rivalry and dissent among the great powers: the government started an open diplomatic offensive for the abolition of the European Commission of the Danube. Due to its insistence, two agreements signed in 1929 and 1933 limited the commission's jurisdiction over the Navigation Court in Galaţi and the Kilia mouth of the Danube and granted Romania the leadership of the Sulina port.[67] These agreements strengthened Romania's position, but the government continued to request the commission's abolition. In 1936, Nicolae Titulescu, Romania's Minister of Foreign Affairs, characterized the Danube Commission as a 'legal anachronism' perpetuating 'a regime of servitude and foreign control'.[68] Titulescu blamed the commission's technical incompetence and financial weakness and argued that its existence hindered Romania's national sovereignty.

Secondly, with the radical change in the balance of power in favor of revisionist powers in the second half of the 1930s, Germany and Soviet Russia (the two former great powers excluded under the new Danubian Convention) began a diplomatic campaign to reassert their influence in the region. This offensive was led by Germany, eager to recover its status as an influential player in Danubian affairs. After long diplomatic negotiations, in March of 1939 England, France and Italy admitted Germany as a full member to the Danubian Commission while also limiting the commission's sanctions and granting Romania full control over Sulina.

Full membership did not alleviate German resentments. In order to alter the stipulations of the Versailles system over the Danube radically, in September 1940 Germany convened at Vienna a conference of riparian states that suppressed the International Commission of the Danube, thus excluded Britain and France from the fluvial Danube. During World War II, the Danube turned into a 'German river' forcefully serving the Nazi war effort. However, while the Danube Commission became *de facto* inactive, domination of Germany was not institutionalized in a new international organization.

Soviet Hegemony on the post-1945 Balkans

The geopolitical status of the Lower Danube radically changed yet again after World War II, when the Danube became a 'Soviet river', reflecting the strong Soviet domination of the Balkans. As pointed out above, in order to keep the Danube Delta from Russian influence, in 1856 the great powers had neutralized the Lower Danube, while in 1878 the Berlin Congress had granted Dobrudja to Romania. 67 years later, the Soviet military victory dealt a decisive blow to British and French interests in this region (expressed in the inter-war European Commission of the Danube) and reinstated Soviet Russia as the new center of power.[69] The Soviet Union became yet again a riparian country through the 1940 annexation of Bessarabia, temporarily lost to Romania between 1942 and 1944. Between July and August of 1944, as part of the Soviet military offensive Dobrudja became an area of military operations. Given the strategic importance of the province, after the war the USSR stationed there the biggest Red Army contingent in Romania, with Constanţa serving as the headquarters of the Soviet Command for the entire southeastern flank of the Red Army.[70]

In order to sanctify its domination over the Danube, in 1948 the Soviet Union convened an international conference on the river's status, attended by delegates from the riparian countries of Czechoslovakia, Hungary, Yugoslavia, Romania, Bulgaria, as well as the United States, Great Britain, and France. On 18 August 1948, the riparian participants, by that time all placed within the Soviet sphere of influence, signed the Convention regarding the 'Regime of Navigation on the Danube' as a new international legal body. They also decided to establish a new Danubian commission, based in Budapest and composed only of riparian states.[71] Having been excluded, the other victorious allied powers (Great Britain, France and the United States), refused to sign the convention, thus bringing to a formal end the international mechanism that had functioned since 1856.[72]

The Soviet domination of Lower Danube was yet another episode in the great powers' struggle to dominate the region, allowing the USSR to be actively present in the Eastern Mediterranean basin and, thus, to counter-balance NATO's military presence in Greece and Turkey. However, while previous plans of hegemony simply attempted to secure commercial routes with the Mediterranean for securing supremacy in world trade, the Soviets attempted to seal off the area by disconnecting it from the world economy and integrating it more firmly with the Soviet Euro-Asian space.

As a strategic geopolitical bridgehead to the Balkans and the Eastern Me-diterranean, Dobrudja was the main building block of Soviet domination over the Lower Danube. Consequently, the province served yet again as a pilot project of modernization, this time communist-style. Soviet advisers were dispatched to the region in order to assist the Romanian government in reor-ganizing the region economically and militarily, in accord with Soviet inter-ests. Due mainly to Soviet pressure, in 1957 Dobrudja became the first fully collectivized region in Romania, preceding by five years collectivization in the rest of the country.[73] The economic development of the province was dec-lared an official priority and benefited from substantial state investments. The regime's propaganda presented Dobrudja as a case of socio-economic meta-morphosis from 'the country's most backward region' into a region with the highest standard of living for the rural population and advertised it as a model of development for the entire country. In 1959, the Soviet leader Khrushchev visited the province to inspect the results of Soviet-style modernization.

In terms of economic reorganization in Dobrudja, the Danube–Black Sea Canal was considered crucial. It was to shorten access to the Black Sea by 400 kilometers, following an old idea first explored by Ottoman authorities in 1855.[74] Council for Mutual Economic Assistance (CMEA) decided its construction on 25 January 1945, under Soviet command that promised technical and financial support. The attentive Soviet supervision of the canal works (the most substantial economic investment in CMEA countries at the time) as well as the building of military facilities throughout Dobrudja (a Soviet submarine base was designed for the town of Mangalia) and the modernization of Constanţa's port, fed the Romanians' suspicion that the project was part of an economic and military Soviet strategy to improve its access to the Danube and strengthen its grip on the Balkans. Rumors also circulated, claiming that upon completion of the canal, the Soviets would annex the Danube Delta and let Romanians reach the Black Sea only via the canal.[75] After four years of toil, work on the canal was halted in 1953, after Stalin's death, due to insurmountable technical and financial problems. With the failure of Soviet-type modernization, the theme of Dobrudja's economic advancement faded away in official propaganda, the province assuming yet again its semi-peripheral place both in public discourse and economy.

Dobrudja's Socialist Modernization in the 1980s

The project of Dobrudja's modernization was resumed in the 1980s, when Romania embarked on a program of economic autarchy in order to consolidate its political autonomy from Moscow. Under the rule of Nicolae Ceauşescu (1965–1989), Dobrudja was to be a pilot project again in communist modernization. In order to reaffirm Romania's strong grip of the province, Dobrudja housed numerous large-scale economic projects, such as new industrial units and port facilities in Constanţa, Midia, Năvodari and Mangalia, the Cernavodă nuclear power plant, and the completion of the previously abandoned Danube–Black Sea Canal. Completed in 1984 at a huge cost evaluated at about two billion dollars, the canal provides a shortcut to the sea through Dobrudja's mainland, from Cernavodă to the modernized port of Constanţa, allowing ships to avoid the lengthy trip through the Danube Delta. Encouraged by this achievement and highly praised by the official propaganda of the regime as 'a milestone in Balkan history', Ceauşescu launched a grandiose plan for a second canal in order to link Bucharest with the Danube, thus transforming the capital into a major port-city. The canal project encompassed four docks and two major ports in Bucharest and Olteniţa. By 1989, when the regime collapsed, about 70 per cent of the project had been completed.[76] The regime had also invested in mechanized agriculture and organized an intensive 'rational economic exploitation' of the Danube Delta resources, with dramatic environmental consequences.

The communist regime's project of modernization was multifaceted. On the one hand, it seemed that Romania's dream of nationalizing the Lower Danube finally succeeded, placing it under a largely autarchic national economy. In addition, decades of state-sponsored industrialization and intensive labor colonization had radically altered the province's multi-ethnic composition. Today, with over 90 per cent of the population being ethnic Romanians, Dobrudja's 'ethnic Babylon' is but a fading memory. Yet, on the other hand, the extension of the network of ports in Dobrudja and their prospective link to the capital Bucharest is indicative of the regime's efforts to create new commercial outlets for the national economy as a means of securing the country's position in international trade, and thus bypassing Soviet restrictions.

While reconfirming previous trends, the evolution of Dobrudja's port-cities also diverged from other communist projects of economic modernization and social engineering that failed. Benefiting from successive investments in its infrastructure, the port-city of Constanţa grew as Romania's second largest city and the most important Black Sea port. Since 1967, the port area has gradually been extended to about 3,900 hectares, allowing the transit of 62.2 million tons of goods in 1988 and over 100 million in 2006, outgrowing the other major Black Sea ports of Odessa, Ilyichevst and Novorossisk.[77] In contrast, despite communist plans to reinvigorate Tulcea and Sulina by developing tourism, building large naval yards, and declaring the latter a free economic zone in 1977, the two cities continued their downturn. According to recent press reports, with the collapse of communist modernization, Sulina 'has died out' with less than 5,000 inhabitants, barely half of its nineteenth-century population, and over 40 per cent of the active labor force unemployed. It displays the image of a city 'frozen in time'.[78] The city's architecture still speaks of its cosmopolitan past, having as main landmarks the former palace of the European Commission, the Orthodox Cathedral of St. Nicholas, the Catholic Church, the Old Believers' Orthodox Church, and the cemetery formerly administered by the European Commission, where Muslims, Eastern Orthodox, Orthodox Old-Believers, Roman-Catholics and Protestants, of such diverse ethnic backgrounds as Romanian, English, French, Italian, Greek, Hungarian, Jewish and Turkish rest together.

Conclusion

This essay has provided a broad overview over the Lower Danube's geopolitical status in the modern period. I have argued that during the nineteenth and twentieth centuries the Danube became a great transportation artery, linking Central Europe with the Black Sea and the Mediterranean world and thus effectively linking 'East' and 'West'. Especially important was the province of Dobrudja, which, due to its strategic position on the mouth of the Danube, was regarded by the landlocked countries of Central Europe and the Balkans as their main access route to world markets. For this reason, the great European powers attempted to establish political and military control over the region, as a means of sheltering their commercial and geopolitical interests.

This article has focused in detail on the development of three main port-cities of Tulcea, Sulina and Constanţa during a particularly formative period when the Lower Danube was integrated into the world economy: long-term regional institutions and legal mechanisms were set up as the port-cities passed from Ottoman imperial rule to nation-state. The three cities were subject to various modernization projects, promoted by Ottoman authorities, by the great European powers, and by the Romanian nation-state. The first comprehensive plan of modernization in the region of the Lower Danube was carried out by the Ottomans, together with active financial and technological assistance from the great powers, most notably England, but also France and Austria. Eager to become integrated into the European modern system of states and to participate in the European concert with equal rights, Ottoman authorities understood that their main geopolitical asset was the strategic position of the empire at the crossroad of international trade linking the Lower Danube and Black Sea region, on the one hand, with Anatolia, the Middle East and India, on the other hand. Therefore, after the Crimean War, in response to changes in global trade patterns, Ottoman authorities launched a pilot project of modernization in the region of the Lower Danube, investing in railroad communications and developing the port-city of Constanţa. Ottoman plans of economic investment in Dobrudja are significant, since they refute later allegations that the main source of under-development in the Balkans in the modern period is an 'Ottoman legacy'.

The gradual weakening of the Ottoman rule in the Balkans generated an intense geopolitical rivalry between the great powers over the Lower Danube. After successive failed attempts to gain unilateral domination, the great powers internationalized the river and devised a system of collective control over the Lower Danube's commercial route, which can be regarded as a form of 'collective imperialism'. Trade with Europe led to the rise of two cities, Sulina and Constanţa, and the decline of Tulcea. That was because Tulcea was linked to the Ottoman economy and, therefore, suffered a gradual decline with the disintegration of the Ottoman market in the region. Sulina was developed by the European Commission of the Danube, mandated by the great powers, and transformed into the main commercial gate of the trade between Western Europe, the Balkans and the Eastern Mediterranean. Through Sulina, the agrarian economy of the Principalities of Moldova and Wallachia and the Ottoman Lower Danube became an appendix to European capitalism, whose primary function was to provide raw material to core regions.

The third strategy of modernization belonged to Romania and was to have the strongest long-term impact, due to its annexation of Dobrudja. Continuing the approach of the Ottomans, the Romanian project of modernization centered on the Black Sea port of Constanţa. My analysis documents the shift in the regional economic balance from Tulcea to Constanţa, as well as the connection of the latter with the wider regional and world economy. I argue that Constanţa was developed by Romania as a means for the country's integration into the world economy. It served as an alternative commercial gate, escaping the control exercised by the great powers over Sulina.

In the post-1945 period, Soviet Russia re-emerged as a dominant power on the Lower Danube, implementing its own version of Danubian economic modernization and institutional design enabling its hegemony over the region. Significantly, while Western powers were interested in internationalizing the Danube and guaranteeing free trade and developments in infrastructure for sheltering their regional economic domination, Soviet hegemony rested not only on the socio-political Sovietization of the region, but also on de-linking the area from the 'capitalist system' of international trade.

The case study of Dobrudja highlights the fact that port-cities as commercial gates to the wider world were the preferred medium of creating and sustaining international networks in the modern period. For large commercial metropolises, port-cities were necessary interfaces of international exchange, their construction and modernization being part and parcel of strategies to dominate regional patterns of trade. For peripheral regions, port modernization was one effective way of integration into the capitalist world economy and of taking part in the global exchange of goods. In reviewing the plans of port-cities modernization at the Lower Danube, one can nevertheless detect a dual tension: between attempts at hegemony against the great powers' collaboration; and between the cosmopolitanism and diversity so specific to port-cities against concepts of state sovereignty and strategies of nationalization and cultural homogenization, inherent in the institutional logic of the nation-state. Surely, as building blocks of the Westphalian international system of states and 'key agencies of the process of formation and expansion of the Eurocentric capitalist system',[79] newly-formed riparian nation-states benefited greatly from the new opportunities of economic development and international trade opened up at the Lower Danube by the great powers' presence. From this perspective, it was in the vital economic interest of the new nation-states to collaborate with the great powers within the European Commission, benefiting from its laborious activities to improving conditions of navigation. However, riparian states' efforts at state-building and national economic development also contradicted the great powers' interests as the initiators and guarantors of the Lower Danube's international regime.

In an incipient form, these tensions were evident in the Ottoman state's relation to the great powers, as a militarily weakened and unequal economic partner; they became paramount with the emergence and consolidation of modern nation-states in the region, as Romania and Bulgaria have all attempted to appropriate parts of the Lower Danube, transforming it into 'national waters'. The post-communist period adds new dimensions to these tensions, bringing forward new regional actors, such as the Ukraine,[80] as well as novel institutional designs: On the one hand, the newly-built Rhine–Main–Danube Canal increases the importance of the Danube and the Black Sea in Europe's new integrated economic structures, effectively linking Europe's two largest rivers, the Rhine and the Danube. On the other hand, with new opportunities to develop the Danubian basin into 'Europe's newest, prospective zone of expansion',[81] new regional and continental interests emerge, resulting in innovative institutional arrangements, such as the Black Sea Economic Cooperation.[82]

Competition as Rivalry:
İzmir during the Great Depression

Eyüp Özveren and Erkan Gürpınar

The stock exchange crash of 1929 in the USA triggered the most important economic crisis of the twentieth century, which came to be known
as the Great Depression. The Great Depression was significant not only
for its economic magnitude, but also for the profound impact it had on
the economic theorizing that culminated in the Keynesian Revolution,
which paved the way towards the so-called Golden Age of capitalism,
with the welfare state in developed countries and the developmental state
in less-developed countries. Both the welfare state and the developmental state, in spite of their fundamental differences, require the existence
of an effective nation-state in the first place. Before the age of the nation-state, however, İzmir, as a port-city, had had its share of the so-
called Great Depression of the nineteenth century (1873–96) and, hence,
already had some experience in dealing with an economic crisis. Nevertheless, the Great Depression was still a major litmus test for the newly
founded and economically inexperienced Turkish Republic in its very
first decade. The national government had to prove its ability to come to
terms with this economic recession and to steer the economy towards a
new path of development.

According to the statistics of 1929, the share of İzmir's hinterland in the country's total exports was more than half.[1] Other statistics for the region indicate that in 1927 per capita exports were 20 *liras* more than the per capita imports. This is a clear indication that on the eve of the Great Depression İzmir's exports outweighed its imports, in compliance with the standard definition of a peripheral port-city, and that there existed considerable room for capital accumulation that could potentially trigger further economic development, both regional and national.[2]

This study is based on the premise that the Great Depression provided the ultimate endpoint for the economic processes seen as constitutive of nineteenth-century Ottoman port-cities, even though the corresponding political processes were interrupted much earlier with the dismemberment of the empire in the wake of World War I.[3] İzmir, along with Alexandria, Beirut, Salonica, and Trabzon, was one of several major port-cities of the Eastern Mediterranean. As such, it set an example as far as second-generation port-cities (such as Mersin, Alexandretta, Saida, Jaffa, and Port-Said) were concerned. By the time of the Great Depression, it had already attained a state of maturity that was to be tested by the dire circumstances of economic hardship. As the commodity structure of İzmir's trade came under pressure, competition amidst crisis took the form of intensified rivalry. İzmir was caught up in a competition with other port-cities that occupied a similar economic role in the international division of labor, as well as with Istanbul, the major port of entry for Turkey's imports, but also with Ankara, the seat of the new nation-state where the government undertook a more comprehensive and active developmental policy initiative.

To the historian and lay reader, the distinction between 'competition' and 'rivalry' maintained in our title might well beg for an explanation. Within the tradition of economic thought, this distinction occupies a central yet overlooked place. Whereas classical political economists building their approach upon the works of Richard Cantillon (1680–1734) and Adam Smith (1723–90) understand 'competition' as the behavior of two or more rival parties (usually businessmen) serving consumers for the sake of profit, the more dominant neoclassical economists who have been trained in the tradition of Antoine Augustin Cournot (1801–77) and Léon Walras (1834–1910) understand competition as a final state, a situation of ultimate equilibrium. It is only with a new generation of Austrian economists such as Friedrich Hayek (1899–1992), Israel Kirzner (born 1930) and Ludwig Lachmann (1906–90) that the notion of competition has become identified again as a process in the former sense of classical political economy, and not as a situation. Accordingly, competition has become redefined as a 'discovery procedure' in which economic agents actively engage in rivalry in the old sense of the term, based on their differences of knowledge concerning the actual state of things.[4] To put it differently, far from remaining passive recipients of the effects of a market situation in the neoclassical sense, economic parties with differences in knowledge, interpretation and creativity actively seek to improve their relative positions amidst a state of intensifying competition. The contention of this work is that İzmir during the Great Depression of 1929 can best be understood by using this paradigmatic formulation that bridges classical political economy with Austrian economics. We will see below how İzmir actively responded to the increasing competition coming from both rival ports and Ankara as the seat of national government by exploring new policies. Instead of standing passively in the face of uncertain times, İzmir strove hard to reverse its fortunes. In the end, this effort might not have amounted to much. However, the fact that such a conscious effort was made deserves consideration and must have had long-lasting consequences on the formation of İzmir's urban identity.

This work attempts to discuss the intensification of İzmir's rivalry with an eye to information networks in the wake of the Great Depression. The evidence for İzmir's business community's rising awareness about the city's role and place in the nexus of this multifold competition (with other port-cities, with Istanbul as a port of entry for imports, and with Ankara for shaping economic policy) can be found in its highly developed local press. Moreover, business shaped the viewpoint of the urban community at large and bestowed upon it a sense of 'us' versus the 'others'. As a result, İzmir could take certain positions as if it were a single agency. At a time when economic prospects were dim and competition intensified, acquisition of information attained new importance. This was an era when information was of vital economic value for shaping the commodity structure of trade. Leading merchants readily responded to demand conditions in distant markets by virtue of what they heard or read before their rivals and the producers in the countryside. Shifts in the investment preferences of merchants gave important signals for the ultimate relocation of resources in agriculture and thereby transformed the commodity structure of trade. İzmir relied on a multitude of channels through which such information could be gathered. First of all, there was the press, attentive to ongoing changes elsewhere. Secondly, there were regular correspondents of the Chamber of Commerce whose reports were published regularly in the chamber's bulletin. Finally, there were informal channels of communication that worked through émigré networks, such as the one in Trieste. Unfortunately, this last channel of information still remains the least accessible source for researchers.

Making our primary sources explicit at this stage is important because the objective of this study is twofold. As apparent from the title, we wish to establish how the Great Depression affected İzmir's economic prospects and historical trajectory as a port-city. To this effect, we will present the evidence found in primary sources from that tumultuous era. However, we are equally interested in how these apparent facts were actually filtered through these sources which reflect not only certain impressions, but also the prevailing level of consciousness among citizens. We should remind ourselves that until the 1950s, İzmir had access to Istanbul's 'national' newspapers with a regular one-day delay. As of the 1950s, regular flights on Mondays and Thursdays connected İzmir to Istanbul, and İzmir started to enjoy the privilege of same-day access to the national press on those two days. Even so, on five days of the week İzmir continued to function with a news lag.[5] In other words, by the time press news reached İzmir, it had already lost its newsworthy quality. In general, up-to-date news was quite scarce in İzmir and hence extremely valuable for the business community for its day-to-day transactions and decisions.[6] A business community functions by relying on its ability to obtain information as quickly as possible at the least cost, in order to build a comparative advantage over its rivals, since some always get the news before others. Hence, İzmir's desperate struggle to find second-best solutions in order to compensate for this deficiency in accessing information is a manifest reflection of its collective business interest.[7]

Our first source is the archive of an influential daily newspaper, Yeni Asır (The New Century).[8] To this day, it continues to be an important daily newspaper of wide circulation not only in the city, but also in its hinterland, and is noted for its local and regional diffusion and influence. At a time when İzmir was faced with a vacuum of information, Yeni Asır, known for its pro-business stance and liberal commitments, fulfilled an important function. It was virtually unrivalled in İzmir and its environs throughout the Depression years, offering a major platform to the residents of İzmir, irrespective of their political convictions, for the interpretation of the Great Depression and the discussion of policy proposals.[9]

Our second primary source is the periodical publication of İzmir's Chamber of Commerce.[10] As early as 1923, the chamber considered publishing a monthly journal; but because of poor funds and staff, it had to put the idea on hold for several years.[11] Starting in January 1926, however, the chamber published a regular journal containing statistics of economic significance and economic news and reports in Turkish and French.[12] The objective of the publication was proclaimed in the first issue: Announcing to the public the decisions of the chamber; providing public information on the economic affairs of Turkey and other countries compiled by the chamber's Divisions of Intelligence and Information; printing trade tables concerning İzmir and other cities and towns in its vicinity; diffusing official rules and regulations; introducing Turkish and foreign merchants to one another; spreading the chamber's point of view on economic matters; informing foreigners about İzmir's export items; publishing the views of experts and businessmen; and, last but not least, serving the national economy as well as the world economy.[13] In this journal, we find information on İzmir's trade, commercial and industrial activities, reports covering the situation in the city's hinterland, as well as communiqués from ports on the receiving end of export circuits (such as Marseilles, Hamburg and Trieste) and from diverse rival exporting-countries (such as Bulgaria, Romania, Greece, the French colonies in North Africa, and even Iran).[14] In short, İzmir's business community had learned well from nineteenth-century foreign predecessors and proved itself well prepared for the task of information management.[15] Since for a port-city like İzmir commerce was a matter of life and death, we will first and foremost turn to the official organization of merchants and its publication that closely followed the heartbeat of the commercial community in the throes of the Great Depression. It is as if they were documenting a story with themselves as the main characters, a story that unfolded day by day in front of their eyes and the end of which they themselves did not yet know.

The structure of the rest of this chapter will be as follows: We will first briefly survey the historical trends that brought İzmir to the eve of the Great Depression. We will then dwell on how the Great Depression helped intensify rivalry among cities and countries with similar economic roles in the international division of labor, and on the effects of this process on the city's and the region's economy as well as on the business community. Finally, we will focus on İzmir's relationship with the new nation-state's developmental economic policies in order to reach a set of conclusions.

A Brief Survey of Historical Trends

İzmir was one of the most important port-cities of the Eastern Mediterranean and the major port-city of Anatolia; as such, it by far surpassed its rivals such as Trabzon, Samsun, Ayvalık, Mersin, and Alexandretta. Originally, İzmir had developed as a major port of trade of the Ottoman Empire. During the so-called 'seventeenth-century crisis', İzmir advanced its position considerably so as to become both the leading port of the Anatolian peninsula and a major city of the nexus of links between the Ottoman Empire and Europe.[16] In the nineteenth century, İzmir developed from a traditional yet overgrown port-of-trade into a port-city proper by enforcing its regional monopoly over both its Anatolian hinterland and the Aegean islands. In other words, the structure of its trade favored exports over imports under normal circumstances, thereby allowing rapid local capital accumulation.[17] This paved the way not only for the city's development as a cosmopolitan *bürgerliche* entity, but also for further economic development both within the city and its environs. This process ushered in a major transformation of property relations and economic activities in the hinterland, with major distributional effects and social consequences.

Pre-war statistics indicate that İzmir was the most important port of the Ottoman Empire after Istanbul.[18] Because İzmir was not directly involved in the First World War, unlike some other parts of the Ottoman Empire, the city's economy was not adversely affected. On the contrary, İzmir adapted itself to the war conditions and accumulated further wealth. Meanwhile, thanks to the Frederick Liszt inspired *Milli İktisat* (National Economy) orientation of the Ottoman governments, Muslim and/or Turkish merchants benefited from the insular effects of the war and considerably advanced their position *vis-à-vis* their Christian counterparts.[19] In any case, following the war İzmir appeared to be an island of prosperity amidst the ruins of the Eastern Mediterranean.[20] When Greece occupied it after the war, it was the Greek merchants who improved their lot at the expense of their Turkish rivals. After the Turkish War of Independence, the Ankara government favorably approached the city and the liberal economic policy it represented. The fact that the Turkish Economy (*Turkish Economic Congress*) was summoned in İzmir as early as in the spring of 1923, at a time when the Lausanne Peace Treaty talks were not yet finalized and the new Republic not yet proclaimed, demonstrates the importance given to the city.[21] In retrospect, this congress became identified with the city and came to be called İzmir Economic Congress. In light of this fact, it is no surprise that İzmir regained its economic strength and importance after a period of reconstruction. İzmir was able to recover its former economic status by dissociating itself from the Aegean islands and re-orienting itself

towards its Anatolian hinterland, as well as by substituting Jews and im-
migrant Turks for the expatriated Greeks. The same economic machine
that had formerly characterized the port-city could now be run again by a
different ethno-religious set of functionaries.[22] Nevertheless, loss of
access to the Aegean islands as a market for re-exports and the Turkish–
Greek Population Exchange Treaty had one important consequence. The
former factor reduced the size of the potential market for imports, thereby discouraging merchants from investing in import trade where economies of scale were no longer obtained.[23] In addition, to avoid expat-
riation and to benefit from the exceptional clauses of the treaty pertain-
ing to Istanbul, some Greek merchants shifted their business from İzmir
to Istanbul. During this process, these businesses started to concentrate
more on import trade. In the post-war period, it became clear that İzmir
had thus lost part of its import trade to Istanbul. To put it differently,
İzmir and Istanbul had become rival ports of entry for the potential
imports of İzmir and its hinterland. Therefore, the seeds of rivalry between these two cities were already planted long before the Great Depression. This rivalry would only intensify once the Great Depression set
in and jeopardize the export prospects of İzmir's merchants who then
felt that they should reclaim their import trade.[24] However, when they
did so in the wake of the Great Depression, they saw a strange coalition
of interests emerge against them, the Ankara government together with
the relatively strong business interests identified with Istanbul.

The above factor set aside, had it not been for the Great Depression,
this period of reconstruction and recovery for İzmir might perhaps have
ultimately led to another phase of major economic growth along outward-looking, export-oriented lines. No one can know for certain, and
we can at best speculate about this historical alternative. However, the
harsh realities of the Great Depression forced a turn of the tide. With the
international markets on the verge of collapse, worldwide instinctive
reactions to the worsening economic conditions took the shape of unilat-
erally restrictive trade policies. Such policies strongly affected İzmir and
its export-oriented hinterland especially after 1930. İzmir was caught in
a spiral of competition with other port-cities of the Eastern Mediterranean amidst gravely worsening international trade prospects. As the
traditional export-based commodity structure of İzmir's trade came
under increasing pressure, competition amidst crisis took the form of an
intensified rivalry with several different adversaries simultaneously.

As if İzmir's difficulties with the world at large were not enough, the
final blow came from a different direction. Disillusioned by the economic

conditions of the Great Depression, the Republican government in Ankara reversed its economic policy. Whereas during the early years of the
Turkish Republic, the new regime had given priority to jump-starting the
economic engine inherited from the Ottoman Empire by focusing its
attention on İzmir as the major outlet of the Anatolia, as of the 1930s the
new nation-state adopted a more comprehensive developmental policy
initiative. This meant a major shift from an outward-looking development
strategy to an inward-looking, import-substituting industrialization policy. This implied the marginalization of İzmir from the viewpoint of
national economic policy. This unfavorable shift in economic orientation
was all the more difficult for İzmir to understand and to accept, as the
city's business notables and intelligentsia had long identified themselves
with liberal economic policies. The combined effect of these two new
rivalries, one originating from the outside world and the other from Ankara, was to undermine İzmir's privileged position. As a result of these
two distinct yet complementary effects, İzmir was no longer a typical
port-city by the end of the 1930s. However, İzmir was not alone in this
misfortune. Other port-cities suffered from the same fate because of the
changing world-economic circumstances and the impetus this process
provided to the implementation of nation-state formation.

İzmir and the Intensification of Rivalry

The daily *Yeni Asır* announced one of the successive waves of the financial
crash under the title 'Crisis in the New York Stock Exchange' in the lower
right corner of its front page. This was accompanied by the picture of a
wide boulevard where the shadowy figures of anonymous people seemed
to crumble under the weight of tall buildings exemplifying the best of
modern architecture.[25] The newspaper referred to New York's Bank Street
as the site of the world's noisiest stock exchange. Probably, not too many
readers had as of yet prefigured the strong effect that this event would have
on their lives. The chain of events followed this course: The crash and the
concomitant recession first hit the developed countries hard; these countries
reacted by raising their trade barriers, which in turn greatly reduced the
volume of international transactions throughout the world. The restrictions
on international trade affected peripheral countries, but especially their
enclaves or regions where international trade was of vital importance. For
Turkey, Aegean Anatolia was a very important region and İzmir its major
port of export. The region held a significant place in the national economy
at a time when the Çukurova plains in Southwest Anatolia, served by the
port-city of Mersin, came only as a distant second.[26]

İzmir served as the gateway for the region's exports of primarily agricultural products. Main regional exports consisted of tobacco, cotton, raisins, figs, opium, carpets, barley; licorice, valonia oak, olives and olive oil accounted for 92 per cent of the region's total exports.[27] Among the main purchasers of İzmir's exports were Germany, the United Kingdom, Italy, Holland, Belgium and the USA. These exports reached Europe by two passageways, one through Trieste, and the other through Hamburg. Numerous Greek merchants expatriated from İzmir had moved to these two ports where they continued to trade with the help of their local Turkish or Jewish business partners.[28] During the inter-war period these two European ports of import came into fierce competition for diverting the Mediterranean exports exclusively to their own harbors. As the rivalry between Trieste and Hamburg intensified, so did the difference of quality and prices in their ports and services. Trieste had many more advantages in this competition because of its Mediterranean location and, hence, proximity to export outlets. Therefore, it attracted the bulk of the Eastern Mediterranean exports.[29] Even so, Hamburg successfully encroached upon Trieste's monopoly because it provided easier access to the potentially expandable consumer markets of the wealthier Northern Europe.[30]

Whereas occasional news concerning the Great Depression appeared in the press as early as in 1930, news on the regional effects of the Great Depression came to dominate the media only in the following year. This was because İzmir and its hinterland perceived the hazardous effects of the crisis especially after 1930. This paved the way for the discussion of the economic difficulties that plagued the region within the dual context of the Great Depression and the intensified rivalry with other port-cities and countries. In terms of news content, the press raised some issues in relation to the external events that influenced the local economy adversely. Usually, there were no detailed policy suggestions to overcome such problems. Policy proposals remained limited in scope and few in number, and the press sought to show the gravity of effects rather than addressing the root causes. Yet, the same press opened the floor to an in-depth discussion of the Great Depression and welcomed advocates of contesting views to express their opinions. Whenever this was the case, we can observe that the quality of the debate reflects a level of sophistication rarely encountered among popular economists in Turkey even today.[31] The sides to the debate adopted theoretical positions ranging from a pragmatic liberalism to cooperativism, from historical economics to Marxism, without succumbing to the attraction of an outright ideological confrontation in public.

The main effect of the Great Depression was that the core countries' demand for exports originating from the periphery decreased. According to those hard-core liberals who were not ready for radical changes in policy, nothing could be done except to wait and see, as long as the crisis lasted. Core countries put into effect trade restrictions by way of tariffs and quotas (as in the cases of Italy and the USA) and sought to rely on their own internal resources.[32] Especially when such restrictions were imposed on agricultural imports, İzmir and its hinterland were hit all the worse. As if this were not enough, the devaluation of the British currency in 1931 placed a further burden on the agricultural producers who already had made contracts based on the Pound Sterling.[33]

Among the external factors deeply affecting the region's economy and stirring a reaction in İzmir's press, Russian and Japanese dumping policies were of importance. Russian dumping in June 1931 influenced the prospects of İzmir's two leading export goods: tobacco and raisins. Although the volume of Russian tobacco production was not sufficient to substitute for that of Turkish tobacco, it was nevertheless influential in cutting down the price in Hamburg's tobacco market. The same story held true as far as Russian raisin dumping was concerned.[34] The crisis in tobacco production continued well into 1932. Bulgarian tobacco started to replace Turkish tobacco in the German market. The statistics of the first five months of 1932 indicate that, under the assumption that the same trends would prevail throughout the rest of the year, tobacco revenues were expected to fall by approximately two-thirds.[35] In a similar way, in September 1931, Japanese cuts in cotton prices also affected the export prospects of Turkish cotton.[36] The press covered these economic events widely, precisely because they concerned a wide segment of the readership.

The above examples also suggest that the problems went beyond the effects of the Great Depression. If anything, the Depression helped reveal underlying structural problems by aggravating them. These structural factors were responsible for weakening the competitiveness of İzmir and its hinterland in international markets. The journal of the Chamber of Commerce delved into these deeper causes much more than the press, but all our sources give several illuminating examples concerning the loss of competitiveness. For instance, while Turkish tobacco exports to Germany decreased between 1930 and 1931, Bulgarian exports continued to rise. We also know that, first, there were no climatic differences between the two countries for that particular harvest; thus, differences in output cannot be attributed to weather conditions. Secondly, the rising Bulgarian exports were a function of the rising Bulgar-

ian output.[37] Given that the Great Depression was of worldwide significance, it remains to be explained as to why output could decrease in one
case and increase in the other. A similar observation can be made about
the region's fruit exports to Egypt: since the Ottoman times, Egypt had
remained a loyal customer of traditional Turkish fruits. However, this
picture started to change beginning with 1932, as Italian and Greek fruits
replaced Turkish fruits in the Egyptian market.[38]

The local press and the Chamber of Commerce emphasized two main
reasons responsible for this general failure. The first reason was that
İzmir and its hinterland were caught unprepared by the intensified rivalry of the crisis-ridden international economic environment. Regional
suppliers had little or no knowledge of marketing tactics and strategies;
as a matter of fact, they remained ignorant of the significance of marketing until the very last minute. Resident merchants of İzmir came to
realize the importance of making their products known only late,
whereas their rivals had been participating for quite some time in exhibi-
tions and fairs held in Europe. However, the problem was not confined
to marketing alone. The region's export items were usually neither standardized nor particularly noted for their quality. Perhaps they had compensated for these defects by their price competitiveness before, but with
the collapsing agricultural prices worldwide, this advantage no longer
existed. It was noted that Greek raisins had become more popular in
European markets because of intense advertisement and even propaganda.[39] Even American wheat penetrated the Italian market because of
its lower cost of production that more than compensated for its high
transportation cost.[40] Therefore, as one apt writer appealing to the public
at large, but understandably much more to the merchants and producers,
put it, it was high time to stop blaming the Great Depression and start
finding new and cheap ways of producing export goods.[41]

İzmir versus Ankara's New National Economic Policy

Because İzmir was at the center point of international trade between core
countries and its peripheral hinterland, it can reasonably be argued that
this economic position led the urban bourgeoisie and their associates in
the hinterland to endorse liberal economic policies in general. When the
Republican government decided to change its policy towards an inward-
looking import-substitution strategy revolving around the principle of
étatisme, President Atatürk, well aware of the city's liberal economic
outlook, confronted this difference of opinion in a most outright manner
during his visit to İzmir in 1931. In his speech to the local congress of the

Republican People's Party, he expressed his favorable views on *étatisme*. His choice of İzmir for this purpose is telling in itself. A few days later, when he addressed İzmir's Chamber of Commerce, he further elaborated on the junior partnership expected from the private sector within the context of the policy that would also promote cooperativism among the producers in the countryside.[42] Be that as it may, any trade restrictions, tax increases, or state intervention in the economic life caused immediate dissatisfaction on the part of the local community of merchants. Obviously, during the Great Depression economic prospects were dim and competition was all the more intensified. Furthermore, as we have seen, the region's export power declined from one day to the next and, as we have already discussed above, there were different reasons behind this failure. However, some liberal-minded notables of the business community preferred to put the blame on the new nation-state's supposedly 'wrong' policies. Furthermore, in line with these discontented voices, the local press also insisted that some of these policies were rather discriminatory as far as the region's economic prospects were concerned. Whether these complaints have any basis in fact is not the point. Far more worthy is that these views reflected a sense of 'us', i.e. the urban community versus the 'others' and that such views were actually articulated in the press at a time when Europe and the neighboring countries were plagued by repressive regimes and Turkey was under one-party rule.

The bulk of the complaints raised by the leading figures of İzmir's public life concerned taxes. According to the Chamber of Commerce, both direct and indirect taxes were already so high that they had a negative impact on investment decisions. It was argued that the government's only concern behind this tax policy was to raise revenues. However, those who complained insisted that the result of this obsession was to discourage and misdirect private investment and to reduce trade which in turn decreased future tax revenues.[43] According to the local press, this was in fact the manifestation of a broader problem: lack of qualified civil servants and economic institutions needed to coordinate economic activity and develop strategic plans in order to alleviate the hardships involved in such a crisis.[44] In any case, large-scale government interventionism made higher taxes inevitable, and these overburdened the business sector, thereby undermining the competitiveness of the region.[45]

Another group of complaints was related to the discriminatory effects of the new nation-state's policies. Lack of response on part of the central government was manifest in instances such as the voicing of demands for infrastructural improvement, a must for the fulfillment of port-city functions. In fact, the Chamber of Commerce had already voiced discontent about port services and facilities several times, but so far nothing had been done. The port was already decrepit, and its layout was unsuitable in the light of modern engineering and management principles. This assessment is actually supported by a special economic report presented to the National Assembly in 1930 but initiated in 1929 before the Great Depression broke out. The report notes that although İzmir had the second-most important port facility in Turkey, it left much to be desired, especially in comparison with rival ports such as Pireaus and Salonica which were continuously expanded under the auspices of the Greek state. The report contended that the upgrading of İzmir's port would require between six and seven million Turkish *lira*s. Finally, it recommended the establishment of free zones in order to recapture the *entrepôt* function of İzmir that had been lost to the Aegean islands, if not to Pireaus.[46] The overall approach of this report matched the liberal outlook of İzmir's influential business establishment. However, the report was set aside once Şakir Bey (Kesebir), the liberal-minded minister of economy who had undersigned it, was forced to leave his cabinet post because of allegations of inappropriate conduct. Shortly after this incident, the government opted for a more comprehensive reform program to overcome economic difficulties; hence, the report was ignored as far as basic policy priorities were concerned.

Still falling under the same group of complaints, one interesting problem was heatedly debated in the local press in 1932. The contention was that different tax rates had discriminatory effects on the region. According to this argument, Istanbul was taxed differently and more favorably than İzmir. The tax rates for grain transportation were the same between Konya and Afyon and between Konya and Istanbul. Therefore, grain coming from Konya to İzmir was taxed twice (first for the Konya–Afyon route and then for the Afyon–İzmir trip). Hence, rather than coming directly from Konya, İzmir's wheat supply was actually transshipped from Istanbul. According to the local press, this policy reflected the grudge of the national railways company against the private local railway company *Kasaba Şimendifer İdaresi* (Kasaba Railways Company). In order to prevent the local company from making money, the government adhered to this otherwise illogical policy. Most ironically, the critics insisted that 60 per cent of the revenues of this private local company did in fact find its way into the treasury anyway.[47]

Facing such problems, some critical writers went so far as to claim that the ongoing economic crisis in the region as well as in the country was not part and parcel of the worldwide Great Depression, but rather the result of internal factors such as 'wrong' economic policies and structural misfortunes.[48] Accordingly, Turkey and the region were already in crisis well before the Great Depression. Therefore, in order to cope with the additional hardships originating from the Great Depression, the writers argued, one first had to come to terms with problems of a domestic nature.

Conclusion

In the dispute concerning the impact of the Great Depression on İzmir, some gave importance to external factors, whereas others pointed out the importance of internal factors in explaining the city's decline. Some argued that behind economic difficulties lay the 'incorrect' economic policies of the new and relatively inexperienced nation-state. High interest rates, an enormous tax burden, lack of strategic planning and regionally discriminating policies were, in their view, some examples of such 'wrong' policies. If pushed to its logical extreme, according to this view, Ankara appeared as the ultimate obstacle to İzmir's economic development. A more widespread segment of the local community dissented from this extremism and appealed for moderation by emphasizing the harsh conditions of the Great Depression. In their eyes, the local crisis was derivative of the worldwide crisis. In retrospect, we can suggest that the reason for İzmir's decline was a combination of both internal and external factors, the former gaining further strength under the determining influence of the latter. Furthermore, it seems that the essential collaboration between the state and the merchants at a time of exceptionally difficult economic conditions was not forthcoming beyond signs of goodwill. The new nation-state had lost its patience with liberal economic policies that relied on jump-starting the economic machine centered on İzmir and, consequently, had lost its interest in the problems of the city and the region. The government may have thought that time was ripe for a substantially different economic policy that would leave little room for İzmir's traditional transnational aspirations. At the same time, the urban business community in particular grew more and more skeptical of the state and, in principle, did not want the state's active participation in economic life. Whatever the real reason, as of 1931 there was one obvious fact: The months of August, the beginning of the export season, no longer heralded the signs of optimism, enthusiasm, and prosperity.

Some of the critics from the local press and the Chamber of Commerce may have been short-sighted. Others may have missed the point of changing times. Be that as it may, they reflected the interests of involved and concerned residents of İzmir. In the face of their port-city's changing prospects, members of the business community of İzmir tried their best to come up with policy suggestions that could affect, if not the course, then at least the rate of change[49]. In retrospect, we can conclude that they failed to change the course of history and to preserve İzmir as a port-city. As far as affecting the rate of change is concerned, they fared no better. This does not mean that their efforts amounted to nothing. By voicing their discontent and actively defending their interests in a constructive manner, İzmir's business community managed to win for itself a significant partnership in the new industrial economic policy. This meant that they could preserve their fortunes in a new economic context and gain crucial time to adjust to the new economic circumstances. Eventually, several notable families (such as the Eczacıbaşı family) accumulated enough wealth and know-how to move their businesses to Istanbul and became industrial tycoons by the 1960s.[50] While they made considerable gains in this way, İzmir certainly lost them. From the viewpoint of the greater part of İzmir's remaining business community, participation in the industrial economic policy was the second-best policy of survival, with modest gains until the early 1950s when foreign trade was once again liberalized. It was only then that these businessmen could re-order their priorities and benefit from being intermediaries between the city's commercialized and semi-industrialized hinterland and overseas trading partners. In other words, by virtue of this strategy, İzmir's businessmen gained time and through readjustment saved themselves either individually or as a whole.

The other side of the coin deserves equal, if not greater, attention as far as the objective of this work is concerned. Whatever the reasons behind the economic difficulties of the port-city and the region, İzmir was obviously falling from strength amidst increased rivalry from a multitude of parties, foreign or otherwise. A significant share of the foreign markets was already lost. Major traditional export items of the region were no longer in demand, as they had been before. In fact, statistics are a witness to this demise of international trade in the region. As of 1930, the region had already lost almost a third of its export power in terms of value and a fifth in weight within one year. It comes as no surprise that within the same year, its share in Turkey's exports dropped significantly in both value and volume.[51] In light of these circumstances, İzmir had come to the verge of irretrievably losing its quintessential port-city characteristics. As times changed, so would port-cities. With or without internal causes, this final outcome would have inevitably taken place, and İzmir was no exception.

The Deep Structures of Mediterranean Modernity

Edmund Burke III

Despite the well acknowledged deep structural historical unity of the Mediterranean, two important facts (and their attendant interconnected historical narratives) have until now prevented any effort to think the history of the modern Mediterranean as a whole. One is Islam. The second is colonialism. However, while colonialism has ended (independent states now exist around the rim of the Mediterranean), Islam has not. The result is that the history of the Mediterranean continues to operate at two speeds, and the colonial past continues to shape the ways in which we understand the modern histories of the eastern and southern Mediterranean, of Turkey, the Balkans and the Arab Mediterranean, placing them apart from the history of the western and northern Mediterranean. As we will see in this brief epilogue, there are important underlying structural similarities in the ways in which the societies of the Mediterranean came to modernity, as well as in" the characteristic conflicts to which this process gave rise. In this fashion we seek to provide a larger context for understanding the commercial cities in the Eastern Mediterranean in this book. For not just its eastern part, but the entire Mediterranean was challenged by the forces of modernity, and the remarkable florescence of cosmopolitan cultures around the Eastern Mediterranean in the nineteenth century was undermined by deeply etched fault lines.

A cultural fracture zone whose modern history contains deep structural continuities at the political and cultural levels, even as it displays equally obvious discontinuities, the Mediterranean is the region where Europe, Asia and Africa come together. A cultural and economic crossroads as well as a political and cultural barrier between Europe and the regions outside it, the Mediterranean in the modern era has shared a common fate. Starting in the mid-sixteenth century, it became increasingly peripheral to the new economic center of gravity in northwestern Europe. Increasingly semi-peripheral with respect to the capitalist world system and characterized by weak state structures, delayed or muffled class formation, agrarian backwardness and the persistence of pastoralism, the Mediterranean's path to modernity foreshadows the historical experience of the Third World. The Mediterranean is therefore an excellent platform from which to examine world history, as well as a site to begin the process of unraveling civilizational narratives. Finally, the Mediterranean is a place from which to assess the costs and consequences of the transformation of Europe. This is true because the changes that affected the Arab and Muslim portions affected the entire region, producing some broadly similar consequences, as well as some divergent ones.

We will now briefly look at each of these changes. In Spain, Italy, France, and to a smaller degree Greece after 1830, the liberal reform policies were the primary engine of change. The mechanisms of political change operated in much the same fashion. At the level of the state we can summarize these changes as efforts by the elites to introduce reform measures inspired by the French Enlightenment, the purpose of which was to greatly expand the ability of the state to organize and control its citizens so as to govern more efficiently. Removing the church's control over land was central to this reform package. Conceptually, we can apply this logic to the Ottoman Empire, where the 1828 seizure of the *waqf* (pious foundations) and the 1858 introduction of private land property with the *tapu senedi* (title deed) can be seen as broadly parallel developments. These changes gradually were adopted throughout the Mediterranean region, sometimes, but especially in the Maghrib, under the auspices of colonialism. It also meant replacing older military and governmental elites rooted in patron-client relations with newer ones for whom efficiency, discipline and *laissez-faire* were the key watchwords. Under its *aegis*, the nineteenth-century state with its bureaucracy sought to increase control over society, modern armies were established, and modern schools and methods of communications developed.

In the Ottoman provinces this process was known as the *Tanzimat* movement. It inevitably led to a collision between reform-minded state bureaucrats and local elites, eager to defend their traditional rights and liberties. The *Tanzimat* also stimulated conflict with peasants and artisans, for whom the encroachment of the state was experienced primarily in the form of military conscription and increased taxation. Egypt and Tunisia had their own quasi-autonomous state building programs; though both were juridically part of the Ottoman Empire, they possessed autonomous capabilities for change. The reform impulse was weaker in precolonial Morocco, despite the accomplishments of Hasan I (r. 1876–94).

Here we must emphasize the relatively recent origin of the political boundaries of the region. In 1800, the Habsburg Empire in both its Spanish and Austrian incarnations, as well as the Ottoman Empire remained heteroclite and poorly integrated assemblages, the boundaries of whose domains were porous and subject to change without notice. The Kingdom of the Two Sicilies is only the most obvious of these cases.

The rise of the modern nation state with its homogenous narrative still lay in the future. The decline of old political units and the emergence of new ones drastically affected the context of elite politics everywhere in the region. As modern states emerged along the north coast of the Mediterranean, they developed new, more efficient and intrusive fiscal systems. These brought them into collision with old agrarian elites and established religious elites.

Within this history, the Ottoman case, along with Egypt and Tunisia, differs only in degree. Its would-be state builders were no less jealous of their power and no less eager to demolish entrenched interests, and by the latter third of the nineteenth century they had some solid achievements to their credit, a point that is strongly underscored by the contributions to this book.

The incorporation of the Mediterranean into the world economy stimulated a second and in some ways more far-reaching type of change, which cumulatively affected even relatively isolated regions with weak states. Its effects, however, were differentially greater upon those regions and societies which stood astride major world communications links such as the Marseilles area, northern Italy, Istanbul, Egypt and the littoral of the Arab East. Economic incorporation led to the rise of a new urban middle class whose fortunes were linked to northern European elites, and to the emergence of an urban-based class of landowners engaged in commercial agriculture for export. It also resulted in the decline of artisans and peasants unable to adapt to the changing economic tides.

To the fiscal and other pressures of the centralizing state were added others based on incorporation into the capitalist world market.

The nineteenth-century commercial cities of the Eastern Mediterranean provide an important window onto these processes. Communications technology such as steamships, railroads, telegraph, printing and newspapers, enhanced their connections to foreign markets as well as to provincial cities and towns, giving them new political leverage locally while also enhancing quasi-colonial ties with European states. Powerfully linked to political and economic elites based in northwestern Europe as well as to emergent national elites, the urban elites of the commercial cities constantly threatened to escape the control of the states in which they were embedded. At the same time their fragile cosmopolitanism and urbanity made them models of the modern to those less favorably placed socially and geographically. Cities like Istanbul, İzmir, Salonica, Beirut, Cairo and Alexandria were thus theaters of social struggle between emergent working classes and local and provincial elites. Within their confines, a host of different political and social trends, anarchism, mason networks, and nationalism of many stripes, competed for influence. New legal arrangements primarily derived from the French code law shepherded both elites and popular classes from communal conceptions of society toward more individualistic relations. In the process, old Mediterranean patriarchal norms found themselves precociously challenged by emergent notions of female personal autonomy and rights. As the city spilled over into the countryside via new political and economic relations, displaced rural migrants in turn invaded the city. By the eve of World War I, Eastern Mediterranean port-cities found themselves the sites of struggle between increasingly volatile religious and linguistic nationalisms, as well as movements of social protest and cultural identity. The war, in this respect, provided a drastic simplification of the manifold tensions that divided these cities. These trends can be found across the entire region.

Where the experience of the Middle East diverges from that of Europe and joins that of the rest of the Third World is in the colonial context of its modernization of politics. The establishment of European hegemony challenged basic cultural values even as it distorted the impact of change in significant ways and set in motion deeply rooted responses throughout the region. One place to evaluate the impact of Western dominance upon Middle Eastern societies is in their influence on internal processes of political change, where collaboration with imperialism worked to undermine the legitimacy of local elites even as it strengthened their power. In this ambiguous context, the national struggle tended to take precedence over the class struggle. Thus, European dominance shored up the precarious power of old elites who successfully capitalized upon their position to maintain control of the nationalist movement and insured that when new classes made their long deferred emergence on the political scene after World War II, their impact would be muffled. This era is only now drawing to a close.

It is precisely here that we can note the presence of 'colonial' patterns in the economic trajectories of the various 'souths' of the European Mediterranean, in Andalusia, parts of the Languedoc, Corsica, the Mezzogiorno, and Sicily. The transformation of the systems of landholding and their dominance by liberal elites linked to northern Europe is one element of this pattern. A second is the dominance of the regional economies of the various Mediterranean 'souths' by financial groups and institutions headquartered in the north. Until recently, many would have added a third element to this comparison: the late development of industry. But after the recent work of a disparate group of European economic historians, this assertion no longer seems to play out when we examine the actual histories of industrialization. The basic new story is one that emphasizes the existence of a southern European road to industrialization, one that does not conform to the northern (British) model of textile-led development. Scholars such as Jordi Nadal, Gérard Chastagnaret, Olivier Raveux and Luigi de Rosa have identified a distinctive path to industrialization common to Barcelona, Marseilles, and Naples, respectively.[1] Already by the 1830s (and not the 1870s, as some would have it), they note the role of local entrepreneurs in developing the metallurgy, food processing and vegetable oil industries. What happened in the last third of the nineteenth century was the colonization of these enterprises by 'northern' capital, as well as their insertion into colonial circuits of exchange, for example, of West African ground nuts. Whether nineteenth-century Egyptian, Lebanese and Ottoman entrepreneurs conformed to these patterns has so far not been examined. However, several of the essays in this volume provide evidence of how these trends operated in particular cities. In general they appear to have participated in the industrialization of their respective economies, often in partnership or under the tutelage of foreign (especially French) interests. Although the semi-colonial pattern remains clear, we must also recall that the worldview and aspirations of the reform-minded elites of pre-colonial Egypt, Tunisia and the Ottoman Empire were broadly shared with the Euro-Mediterranean elite in other ways. Albert Hourani's *Ara-*

bic Thought in the Liberal Age is in many respects a group biography of this cosmopolitan ruling group.[2] These individuals were often educated in Europe, spoke English and French among themselves, and often sat on the boards of directors of the same enterprises. Quintessential liberals, their nationalist vision readily accommodated European difference. The emergence of more deeply rooted populist and radical nationalisms, starting with Mustafa Kemal Atatürk in Turkey in the inter-war period, sounded the death knell for this class.

The onset of modernity in its diverse manifestations from 1750 provoked a series of bitter struggles along the cultural fault lines of the Mediterranean region. If we look at the patterns of struggle over the forms of modernity in the Mediterranean in the *longue durée*, we can observe that all groups were split and that the lines of cleavage were continually reshaped even as they persisted. Elites, the church, workers and peasants all were affected. In particular, the struggles centered around three major arenas: the place of religion in the state, gender (especially sexuality and the public role of women), and the land question. It is crucial is to understand that these struggles and the cleavages they provoked and laid bare, beyond their complex local characteristics, derive from common sources.

As modernity came to the region in the nineteenth century, the place of religion, previously a central element of ethnic identity everywhere, became a focal point of struggle. Religious complexity was and continues to be an important organizing feature throughout the region, regardless of confessional adherence. Religion indeed has provided the framework for the grinding of cultural tectonic plates up to the present; Braudel was not wrong in his assessment.[3] The place of religion as a marker of identity in the nineteenth century was further strengthened by colonialism. Indeed, despite the claims of linguistic nationalisms to have supplanted religion as the core of identity, religion remains central to the underpinning of even these national projects. By the end of our period, Eastern Mediterranean commercial cities proved unable to resist the drift toward polarization along religious lines. In this respect, the fate of Salonica is emblematic of the broader situation.[4]

We should note that the nineteenth-century reform project, especially in its French variant, similarly stigmatized religion as backward and marked it for elimination. But it was not only Latin Europe that was ravaged by the struggle between clerical and anti-clerical interests in the nineteenth century. Although this is usually not recognized, the same cultural confrontation also forms a leitmotif in the deep structural history of modern Turkey. The bureaucrats of the *Tanzimat*, no less than the liberal bureaucrats of nineteenth-century Spain, France and Italy, saw in the clergy the enemy of all reform and thus they gave it no quarter. At opposite ends of the Mediterranean popular anticlerical passions spilled over in attacks against Spanish convents and Turkish Sufi lodges. Like the return of the repressed, Islamist groups now terrify the power holders all around the rim of the Muslim Mediterranean in the name of populist virtue and justice. As I have suggested elsewhere, the torments of contemporary Algeria must be seen in the context of a Jacobin French colonial state that all too efficiently demolished the central institutions of Algerian Islam.[5]

Everywhere in the nineteenth-century Mediterranean, the reform project was appropriated by certain groups to be used against others. Those possessing privileged ties to the state or to European business interests were often in a position to profit disproportionately, while urban artisans and rural agriculturalists found themselves squeezed from all sides. After the establishment of European political control, groups willing to serve as intermediaries gained substantially, while overt opponents suffered from various forms of political and economic discrimination. The complex sequence of changes thus set in motion intersected with one another, generating powerful cross currents which eroded old established interests and remolded new ones. Social protest and resistance found fertile ground in the circumstances thus created. Commercial cities therefore existed in the nooks and crannies of the emerging new order. While they displayed astonishing resilience in the face of dramatic changes over the course of the long nineteenth century, in the end they proved unable to withstand the convulsive collapse of the old order in World War I.

Contributors

Isa Blumi, Assistant Professor of History, Georgia State University in Atlanta, Georgia, USA, and visiting Professor of History, American University of Sharjah, United Arab Emirates.

Edmund Burke III, Professor of History, Director of the Center for World History, University of California, Santa Cruz, USA.

Johann Büssow, PhD student, Institute for Islamic Studies, Freie Universität Berlin, Germany.

Erkan Gürpinar, PhD Student, Department of Economics, Middle East Technical University, Ankara, Turkey.

Vilma Hastaoglou-Martinidis, Professor, School of Architecture, Aristotle University of Thessaloniki, Greece.

Constantin Iordachi, Assistant Professor of History, Central European University, Budapest, Hungary.

Vangelis Kechriotis, Assistant Professor of History, Boğaziçi University, Istanbul, Turkey.

Çağlar Keyder, Professor of Sociology, Boğaziçi University, Istanbul, Turkey and State University of New York, Binghamton, USA.

Carla Keyvanian, Assistant Professor of Architectural and Urban History, Rome Program of the Iowa State School of Architecture, USA.

Biray Kolluoğlu, Associate Professor of Sociology, Boğaziçi University, Istanbul, Turkey.

Eyüp Özveren, Professor of Economics, Middle East Technical University, Ankara, Turkey.

Christina Pallini, Assistant Professor, School of Architecture, Milan Polytechnic University, Italy.

Faruk Tabak (d. 2009), Assistant Professor of Sociology, Walsh School of Foreign Service, Georgetown University, Washington DC, USA.

Meltem Toksöz, Associate Professor of History, Boğaziçi University, Istanbul, Turkey.

Notes

**Mapping Out the Eastern Mediterranean: Toward a Cartography of
Cities of Commerce (Biray Kolluoğlu and Meltem Toksöz), pp. 1–13**
We wish to thank many people for their immeasurable assistance to the making of this
volume. First of all, thanks are due to Georges Khalil and Christine Hoffmann of the
Wissenschaftskolleg zu Berlin, for helping us to organize the workshop in Beirut. Jens
Hanssen was also very instrumental in planning and convening the workshop which we
have conceptualized during our work at the Wissenschaftskolleg. Furthermore, we
greatly benefited from numerous discussions we had with Gudrun Kramer and Ulrike
Freitag. Many thanks also to Emre Yalçın, Şengül Terim, Jayne Ansell, Cengiz Kırlı,
Zafer Yenal, and Nina Ergin for their assistance and support in the various stages of
conceptualizing, writing and editing.

[1] Predgrad Matvejevic, *Mediterranean: A Cultural Landscape* (Berkeley, 1999), p.12.
[2] Çağlar Keyder, Eyüp Özveren, Donald Quataert (eds), 'Port-cities of the Eastern Mediterranean, 1800–1914', *Review* xvi/4 (1993); Reşat Kasaba, *The Ottoman Empire and
the World Economy: The Nineteenth Century* (Albany, 1988); Ravi Palat, *Pacific–Asia
and the Future of the World-System: Contributions in Economics and Economic History)* (Westport,1993).
[3] André Raymond, *Cairo* (Cambridge, Mass., 2002); Robert Ilbert, *Alexandrie 1830–
1930: Histoire d'une communauté citadine* (Cairo, 1996).
[4] Daniel Goffman et. al., *The Ottoman City betwesen East and West: Aleppo, İzmir and
Istanbul* (Cambridge, 1999); Leila Fawaz, *Merchants and Migrants in Nineteenth-
Century Beirut* (Cambridge, 1983); Jens Hanssen, *Fin de Siècle Beirut: The Making of
an Ottoman Provincial Capital* (Oxford, 2005); Mark Mazower, *Salonica: City of
Ghosts, Christians, Muslims and Jews, 1430–1950* (New York, 2005).
[5] This similarity is most clear in 'Introduction: Toward a New Urban Paradigm', in Jens
Hanssen, Thomas Philipp, Stefan Weber (eds), *The Empire in the City: Arab Provincial
Capitals in the Late Ottoman Empire* (Beirut, 2002).
[6] Nelly Hanna, *Money, Land and Trade: An Economic History of the Muslim Mediterranean
(*The Islamic Mediterranean) (London, 2002); Leila Fawaz, C. A. Bayly (eds), *Modernity
and Culture from the Mediterranean to the Indian Ocean, 1890–1920* (New York, 2002).
[7] See John Friedmann, 'The world city hypothesis', *Development and Change* xvii/1
(1986), pp.69–83; John Friedmann, G. Wolff, 'World city formation: An agenda for

research and action', *International Journal of Urban and Regional Research* xi/3 (1982), pp.309–44; Paul Knox, Peter J. Taylor (eds), *World Cities in a World System* (Cambridge, 1995); Saskia Sassen, *The Global City: New York, London, Tokyo* (Princeton, 1991). Fredrick Cooper attempts to provide an African spatial framework to globalization in his 'What is the concept of globalization good for? An African historian's perspective', *African Affairs* 100 (2001), pp.189–213.

8   Giovanni Arrighi, 'The Global Market', *Journal of World-System Research* 5 (1999), pp.217–51.

9   See Ulf Hannerz, 'Cosmopolitans and locals in world culture', in Mike Featherstone (ed), *Global Culture* (London, 1990), pp.239, 248. See Ackbar Abbas, 'Cosmopolitan de-scriptions: Shanghai and Hong Kong', *Public Culture* xii/3 (2000), p.711. In other words, cosmopolitanism is potentially vulnerable to being equated with Western universalism. That is why critiques of Eurocentrism argue that cosmopolitanism is 'a practice yet to come, something awaiting realization'. Sheldon Pollock et. al., 'Cosmopolitanisms', *Public Culture* xii/3 (2000), pp.577–89.

10   See Abbas, 'Cosmopolitan de-scriptions', p.711. See also Pollock et. al., 'Cosmopolitanisms', p.577.

11   Matvejevic, *Mediterranean*, p.14.

12   For the significance of the *hans* in the operation of a city of commerce see: Wolfgang Müller-Wiener, 'Der Bazar von İzmir: Studien zur Geschichte und Gestalt des Wirtschaftszentrums einer ägäischen Handelsmetropole', *Mitteilungen der Fränkischen Geographischen Gesellschaft* 27–28 (1980–81), p.432.

13   For a documentation of the proliferation of spaces of leisure and socialization in İzmir, see John Kingsley Birge, 'General Information', *A Survey of Some Social Conditions in Smyrna, Asia Minor* (typescript, May 1921), pp.1–14.

14   For the significance of clock towers in modernizing cities of commerce, particularly in the case of İzmir, see Biray Kolluoğlu Kırlı, 'Cityscapes and Modernity: Smyrna Morphing into İzmir,' in Çağlar Keyder and Anna Frangoudaki (eds), *Ways to Modernity in Greece and Turkey: Encounters with Europe, 1850–1950* (London, 2007), pp.217–35. For the significance of the clock-tower in Beirut, see Jens Hanssen, '"Your Beirut is on my Desk": Ottomanizing Beirut under Sultan Abdülhamit II', in Peter Rowe and Hashim Sarkis (eds), *Projecting Beirut: Episodes in the Construction and Reconstruction of a Modern City* (Munich, 1998), p.56.

15   For community schools (*cemaat mektebi* in the Ottoman context), see Ilias Anagnostakis and Evangelia Balta (eds) *La Decouverte de la Cappadoce au Dix-Neuvieme Siecle* (Istanbul, 1994); and Rashid Khalidi, 'Society and Ideology in Late Ottoman Syria: Class, Education, Profession and Confession', in J. Spagnolo (ed.), *Problems of the Middle East in Historical Perspective: Essays in Honour of Albert Hourani* (Oxford, 1992).

16   For the residential layout of these cosmopolitan communities, see Fawaz, *Merchants and Migrants*. For Istanbul, see Zeynep Çelik, *The Remaking of Istanbul: Portrait of an Ottoman City in the Nineteenth Century* (Los Angeles, 1986).

17   For further evaluation of this argument through the case of İzmir in the nineteenth century, see Biray Kırlı, *From Ottoman Empire to Turkish Nation State: Reconfiguring Spaces and Geo-bodies* (PhD Dissertation, Binghamton University, 2002).

18   For the latter, see Sheldon Pollock, 'Cosmopolitan and Vernacular in History', *Public Culture* xii/3 (2000), p.602.

19   For the various aspects and mechanisms of port construction, see Sibel Zandi-Sayek, 'Struggles over the shore: Building the quay of İzmir, 1867–1875', *City and Society* xii/1 (2000), pp.55–78.

20   For a regional perspective to such changes in landholding patterns in the Ottoman Empire, see Meltem Toksöz, *The Çukurova: From Nomadic Life to Commercial Agriculture , 1800–1908* (PhD Dissertation Binghamton University, 2000). For a recent attempt at conceptualizing property changes in the Middle East, see Roger Owen (ed), *New Perspectives on Property and Land in the Middle East* (Cambridge, Mass., 2001).

[21] For a historical treatment of the family networks linking rural and urban landscapes in the Mediterranean, see Meltem Toksöz, 'A migrant-merchant family from Mersin: The Mavromatis', in Vangelis Kechriotis et al. (ed), *Economy and Society on Both Shores of the Aegean* (Istanbul, forthcoming 2010); Beshara Doumani, 'Adjudicating family: The Islamic court and disputes between kin in greater Syria, 1700–1860', in Beshara Doumani (ed), *Family History in the Middle East: Household, Property and Gender* (Albany, 2003), pp.173–200; Margaret L. Meriwether, *The Kin who Count: Family and Society in Ottoman Aleppo, 1770–1840* (Austin, 1999).

[22] Reşat Kasaba, 'A Time and Place for the Nonstate: Social Change in the Ottoman Empire during the "Long Nineteenth Century"', in Joel S. Migdal, Atul Kohli and Vivienne Shue (eds), *State Power and Social Forces: Domination and Transformation in the Third World* (New York, 1994), and Reşat Kasaba et. al., 'Eastern Mediterranean port-cities and their bourgeoisies', *Review* x/1 (1986), pp.121–35. Aspects of networks that help the city of commerce carve such autonomous niches across the Mediterranean are studied by a variety of scholars. See, for example Robin Ostle, 'Alexandria: A Mediterranean cosmopolitan center of cultural production', in Fawaz and Bayly (eds), *Modernity and Culture*; Robert Ilbert, 'International Waters', in Robert Ilbert and Ilios Yannakakis with Jacques Hassoun (eds), *Alexandria 1860–1960: The Brief Life of a Cosmopolitan Community* (Alexandria, 1997), p.12.

[23] Meltem Toksöz, 'Ottoman Mersin: The Making of an Eastern Mediterranean Port-Town', *New Perspectives on Turkey* (31) (2004), pp.71–91.

[24] Çağlar Keyder, 'Peripheral Port-Cities and Politics on the Eve of the Great War', *New Perspectives on Turkey* (20) (1999), pp.13–37.

[25] In successfully moving beyond nationalist historiographies and tying Arab nations of today back to their Ottoman past, scholars working on the Arab provinces inadvertently brought the issue of state power and centralism back to the agenda. See Ussama Makdisi, 'Rethinking Ottoman Imperialism: Modernity, Violence and the Cultural Logic of Ottoman Reform', in Jens Hanssen, T. Philipp, S. Weber (eds), *The Empire in the City: Arab Provincial Capitals in the Late Ottoman Empire* (Beirut, 2002). For valuable contributions that ally the elite and the non-elite in the same dynamic processes, see Timothy Mitchell, *Colonising Egypt* (Berkeley and Los Angeles, 1991); Roger Owen, 'Imperialism, globalization and internationalism: Some reflections on their twin impacts on the Arab Middle East in the beginnings of the twentieth and twenty-first centuries', *Occasional Papers, Center for Contemporary Arab Studies, Georgetown University* (Washington DC, 2004). Available from: http://www12.georgetown.edu/sfs/ccas/ccas/www/files/OccPaper_Owen_2004.pdf.

[26] Italo Calvino, *Invisible Cities* (New York, London, 1978), p.44.

Port-cities in the Belle Epoque (Çağlar Keyder), pp. 14–22

[1] For British hegemony in world history, see Giovanni Arrighi, *The Long Twentieth Century: Money, Power, and the Origins of Our Times* (London, 1995).

[2] See, for example Daniel Lerner, *The Passing of Traditional Society* (New York, 1958).

[3] Hobsbawm's account of the bourgeois city captures this triumphal stance very well: E.J. Hobsbawm, *The Age of Capital, 1848–1875* (New York, 1975).

[4] This is, of course, similar to Manuel Castells' description of the workings of globalization in its second incarnation in late twentieth century. See Manuel Castells, *The Rise of the Network Society* (Oxford, 1996).

[5] See Gülnihal Bozkurt, *Batı Hukukunun Türkiye'de Benimsenmesi: Osmanlı Devleti'nden Türkiye Cumhuriyeti'ne Resepsiyon* (Ankara, 1996); and Nathan J. Brown, *The Rule of Law in the Arab World: Courts in Egypt and the Gulf* (Cambridge, 1997).

[6] F. F. Conlon, 'Ethnicity in a colonial port city, 1665–1830', in D.K. Basu (ed), *The Rise and Growth of the Colonial Port Cities in Asia* (Lanham, 1985), pp. 49–53.

[7] Arguably, state-directed modernization-from above was the shared project of all peripheral societies in the twentieth century. The concept derives from Barrington Moore, Jr., *Social Origins of Dictatorship and Democracy: Lord and Peasant in the Making of the Modern World* (Boston, 1966).

[8] The increase in trade volume was not as impressive in the Ottoman Empire, except in Egypt. See Charles Issawi, *The Economic History of Turkey, 1800–1914* (Chicago: The University of Chicago Press, 1980), and Şevket Pamuk, *The Ottoman Empire and European Capitalism, 1820–1913: Trade, Investment, and Production* (Cambridge: Cambridge University Press, 1987). For an explanation see Çağlar Keyder, 'The agrarian background and the origins of the Turkish bourgeoisie', in S. E. Ibrahim, Ç. Keyder, and A. Öncü eds. *Developmentalism and Beyond: Society and Politics in Egypt and Turkey* (Cairo: AUC Press, 1994).

[9] On Salonica, see, M. Anastassiadou, *Salonique, 1830–1912: Une ville ottomane à l'age des Reformes* (Leiden, 1998).

[10] Max Weber, *The City* (Glencoe, 1958); Henri Pirenne, *Medieval Cities: Their Origins and the Revival of Trade* (Princeton, 1952).

[11] On 1838, see Issawi, *Economic History*; and Ç. Keyder and D. Quataert (eds), *The Impact of the 1838 Trade Convention on Anatolia*, Special Issue of *New Perspectives on Turkey* 7 (1992).

[12] See the papers in, Faruk Birtek and Thalia Dragonas (eds), *Citizenship and the Nation-State in Greece and Turkey* (London, 2005).

[13] See the essays on İzmir, Salonica, Trabzon and Beirut in, Çağlar Keyder, E. Özveren and D. Quataert (eds), *Port-Cities in the Eastern Mediterranean*, Special Issue of *Review* 16 (1993).

[14] Benedict Anderson captures the emergence of nationalist thought out of a background of colonial mentality. See his *Imagined Communities: Reflections on the Origins and Spread of Nationalism* (London, 1993).

[15] Mark Mazower, *Salonica, City of Ghosts: Christians, Muslims and Jews, 1430–1950* (New York, 2005).

[16] S.T. Rosenthal, *The Politics of Dependency: Urban Reform in Istanbul* (Westport, 1980).

[17] On İzmir, see, Biray Kolluoğlu Kırlı, 'Cityscapes and modernity: Smyrna morphing into İzmir', in Anna Frangoudaki and Çağlar Keyder (eds), *Ways to Modernity in Greece and Turkey: Encounters with Europe, 1850–1950* (London, 2007).

[18] Çağlar Keyder, 'The Consequences of "The Exchange of Populations" for Turkey', in Renee Hirschon (ed), *Crossing the Aegean: The Exchange of Populations between Greece and Turkey* (Oxford, 2004).

[19] See Amin Malouf's nostalgic account in fiction, *Les Echelles du Levant* (Paris, 1996).

[20] However, this connection has not been made. For world cities, see Saskia Sassen, *Cities in a World Economy* (Thousand Oaks, 2000).

[21] For a good discussion of the positions, see Mark Purcell, 'Citizenship and the right to the global city: Reimagining the capitalist world order', *International Journal of Urban and Regional Research* xxvii/3 (2003).

Economic and Ecological Change in the Eastern Mediterranean (Faruk Tabak), pp. 23–37

[1] Alfred Crosby, *Ecological Imperialism: The Biological Expansion of Europe, 900–1900* (New York, 1986), pp.65–66; Janet Abu Lughod, *Before European Hegemony: The World System AD 1250–1350* (New York, 1989), chapter 7; Michael W. Dols, *The Black Death in the Middle East* (Princeton, 1977); Frederic Lane, *Venice: A Maritime Republic* (Baltimore, 1973), pp.196–201.

[2] Maguelonne Toussaint-Samat, *History of Food* (Cambridge, Mass., 1992), p.554; J. H. Galloway, 'The Mediterranean sugar industry', *Geographical Review* lxvii/2 (1977), p.189.

[3] Donald Harreld, 'Atlantic sugar and Antwerp's trade with Germany', *Journal of Early Modern History* xii/1–2 (2003), pp.162–63; William McNeill, *Venice: The Hinge of Europe* (Chicago, 1974), p.76.

[4] Emmanuel LeRoy Ladurie, *Les paysans de Languedoc* (Paris, 1966), vol. 1, pp.69–73.

[5] Maurice Aymard, *Venise, Raguse et le commerce du blé pendant la seconde moitié du XVIe siècle* (Paris, 1966); Zeki Arıkan, 'Osmanlı imparatorluğu'nda ihracı yasak mallar (*memnu meta*)', in *Prof. Dr. Bekir Kütükoğlu'na Armağan* (Istanbul, 1991).

[6] Halil İnalcık, 'Ottoman state and economy', in Halil İnalcık with Donald Quataert (eds), *A Social and Economic History of the Ottoman Empire* (New York, 1996).

[7] This is masterfully documented in, Wolf-Dieter Hütteroth, 'The influence of social structure on land division and settlement in Inner Anatolia', in Peter Benedict et al. (eds), *Turkey: Geographic and Social Perspectives* (Leiden, 1974), pp.19–47; Norman Lewis, *Nomads and Settlers in Syria and Transjordan, 1800–1980* (New York, 1987).

[8] On the extending dominion of the 'trio of Mediterranean crops' during the seventeenth and eighteenth centuries, see Faruk Tabak, 'The Waning of the Mediterranean, c. 1560–1860', in Eyüp Özveren et al. (ed), *The Mediterranean World: The Idea, the Past and the Present* (Istanbul, 2006), pp.61–83.

[9] On Venetian news and speculations on the Mediterranean grain markets, see Pierre Sardella, *Nouvelles et spéculations: Venise au début du XVIe siècle* (Paris, 1948), pp.19–20.

[10] Fernand Braudel, *The Mediterranean and the Mediterranean World in the Age of Philip II* (New York, 1972), vol. 1, pp.543–606.

[11] Peter Earle, 'The commercial development of Ancona, 1479–1551', *Economic History Review* xxii/1 (1969), pp.38–39.

[12] R.J. Barendse, *The Arabian Seas* (Armonk, 2002), pp. 341–44.

[13] Ömer Şen, *Osmanlı Panayırları (18. –19. yüzyıl)* (Istanbul, 1996).

[14] Fernand Braudel, *Civilization and Capitalism, 15th–18th Century, vol. 2: The Wheels of Commerce* (New York, 1982), p.189.

[15] Fernand Braudel, *Civilization and Capitalism, 15th–18th century, vol, 1: The Structures of Everyday Life* (New York, 1981), pp.126–29.

[16] Emmanuel Le Roy Ladurie, *Histoire humaine et comparée du climat: Canicules et glaciers XIIIe–XVIIIe siècle* (Paris, 2004), pp.91–181.

[17] On timber and famine in the Mediterranean in the sixteenth century, see J.R. McNeill, 'Woods and warfare in world history', *Environmental History* ix/3 (2000).

[18] See H.H. Lamb, *Climatic History and the Future* (Princeton, 1977). See also Ramzi Touchan et al., 'Reconstructions of spring/summer precipitation for the Eastern Mediterranean from tree-ring widths and its connection to large-scale atmospheric circulation', *Climate Dynamics* 25 (2000), pp.88–90; and R. D'Arrigo and Heidi Cullen, 'A 350–year reconstruction of Turkish precipitation', *Dendrochronologia* 19 (2001), pp.169–77.

[19] 'The Middle Ages, in the Mediterranean as elsewhere, were more fortunate: the waterways were more abundant and became once more the source of good-river valley soil [...] It was in about the sixteenth century that the balance swung back the other way. Erosion began once more, the rivers cut channels through the ancient flats (sometimes forty meters deep) and carried off into the sea all the sand and mud accumulated there.' Fernand Braudel, *Memory and the Mediterranean* (New York, 2001), p.11.

[20] Cevdet Çulpan, *Türk Taş Köprüleri: Ortaçağdan Osmanlı Devri Sonuna Kadar* (Ankara, 2001).

[21] Xavier de Planhol, *De la plain pamphyliennes aux lacs pisidiens: Nomadisme et vie paysanne* (Paris, 1958); Mübeccel Kıray, 'Social Change in Çukurova: A Comparison of Four Villages', in Peter Benedict et al. (eds), *Turkey: Geographic and Social Perspectives*; Francis Beaufort, *Karamanya* (Antalya, 2002), pp.55, 58.

[22] See Emmanuel Le Roy Ladurie, *Peasants of Languedoc* (Illinois, 1972).

[23] Haim Gerber, *Social Origins of the Modern Middle East* (Boulder, Co., 1987), p.86.

[24] Bruce McGowan, *Economic Life in Ottoman Europe: Taxation, Trade and the Struggle for Land, 1600–1800* (Cambridge, 1981). On changes in the fortunes of Edirne in the seventeenth and the early part of the eighteenth centuries, see Rıfat Osman, *Edirne Sarayı* (Ankara, 1st ed. 1957, reprint 1989), pp.31–39.

[25] Braudel, *The Mediterranean and the Mediterranean World*, pp.41–43.

[26] W.W. Rostow, *The World Economy: History and Prospect* (Austin, 1978), p.147.

[27] Ironically, the advent of quinine, or the Jesuit bark, into the Mediterranean precisely at the time when malaria was becoming widespread in the latter half of the sixteenth century failed to offer a lasting remedy to the affliction, because how the ailment spread continued to remain a mystery. Saul Jarcho, *Quinine's Predecessor: Francesco Tortini and the Early History of Cinchona* (Baltimore, 1993); also Faruk Tabak, *The Waning of the Mediterranean, 1550–1870: A Geographic Approach* (Baltimore, 2008), chapter 4.

**Maps and Wars: Charting the Mediterranean in the
Sixteenth Century (Carla Keyvanian), pp. 38–60**
I wish to thank Heghnar Zeitlian Watenpaugh with whom I taught a seminar at MIT during which some of these questions were discussed at the beginning, and Robin A. Greeley
for an illuminating conversation at the end. Thanks are also due to the Biblioteca Vaticana
and the Gabinetto delle Stampe Nazionale in Rome for permission to reproduce prints,
and to the helpful staff of the Map Division of the New York Public Library.

¹ For a comment on approaches that intertwine the study of art and science and their
relation to cartography, see the concluding essay by Thomas DaCosta Kauffmann in
Pamela H.Smith and Paula Findlen (eds), *Merchants and Marvels: Commerce, Science
and Art in Early Modern Europe* (New York, 2002).

² A posthumous collection of essays of a leading figure in the field is J. B. Harley, *The
New Nature of Maps: Essays in the History of Cartography* (Baltimore, 2001). Denis
Wood, *The Power of Maps* (New York, London, 1992) is a classic.

³ See Mark Monmonier, *How to Lie with Maps* (Chicago, London, 1996) with bibliography;
by the same author: *Rhumb Lines and Map Wars: A Social History of the Mercator Projection* (Chicago, 2004). Pioneering work that remains important is J. B. Harley, 'Maps,
knowledge and power', in D. Cosgrove, and S. Daniels (eds), *The Iconography of Landscape: Essays on the Symbolic Representation, Design and Use of Past Environments*
(Cambridge, New York, 1988); and, by the same author: 'Silences and secrets: The hidden
agenda of cartography in early modern Europe', *Imago Mundi* 40 (1988), pp.57–76; the
same essay is published in William K. Storey, (ed), *Scientific Aspects of European Expansion* (Aldershot, Brookfield, 1996), and in Harley, *The New Nature of Maps*, pp.83–107.

⁴ Florence, the birthplace of the Renaissance, was a prime center for geographical knowledge
as well. See David Woodward, *Maps as Prints in the Italian Renaissance: Makers, Dis-
tributors and Consumers* (London, 1996), p.3. On the printing industry in Rome and Venice,
see 'I centri incisori di Roma e Venezia', in Fabia B. Salvadori, *Carte, piante e stampe
storiche delle raccolte Lafreriane della Biblioteca Nazionale di Firenze* (Rome, 1980).

⁵ On Leonardo's plan, see Mario Docci, 'I rilievi di Leonardo da Vinci per la redazione
della nuova pianta di Imola', in S. Benedetti and G. Miarelli Mariani (eds), *Saggi in onore
di Guglielmo de Angelis d'Ossat*, special issue of *Quaderni dell'Istituto di Storia
dell'Architettura* 1/10 (1983–87), pp.181–86. The fundamental article on orthogonal or
ichnographic plans, as they were also called, remains: John Pinto, 'Origins and Development of the Ichnographic City Plan', *Journal of the Society of Architectural Historians* 35
(1976), pp.35–50. Most recently, see David Friedman with Paul Schlapobersky, 'Leonardo Bufalini's orthogonal *Roma* (1551)', in E. Naginski (ed), *Concerto Barocco*, special issue of *Thresholds* 28 (2005), pp.10–16, and bibliography on p.16, n.1.

⁶ John Marino, 'Administrative mapping in the Italian states', in J. R. Akerman and D.
Buisseret (eds), *Monarchs, Ministers and Maps: The Emergence of Cartography as a Tool
of Government in Early Modern Europe* (Chicago, 1992), pp.5–25, suggests that the widespread use of geometric maps started in the third quarter of the sixteenth century. But compare to Woodward, *Maps as Prints*, p. 101, who argues for earlier beginnings, closer to the
start of the century. A collection of essays, each focusing on a country is James R. Akerman (ed), *Cartography and Statecraft: Studies in Governmental Mapmaking in Modern
Europe and its Colonies*, monographic issue of *Cartographica* lii/35 (1998).

⁷ A useful overview of the development of city views is still P.D.A. Harvey, *The History of
Topographical Maps: Symbols, Pictures and Surveys* (London, 1980); see also, by the
same author, 'Local and regional cartography in Medieval Europe', in J.B. Harley and D.
Woodward (eds), *Cartography in Prehistoric, Ancient and Medieval Europe and the
Mediterranean: The History of Cartography*, vol. I (Chicago, London, 1987). For a theo-
retical approach to the relationship between landscape painting and cartography that fo-
cuses on how images of places affect viewers, see Edward S. Casey, *Representing Place:
Landscape Paintings and Maps* (Minneapolis, London, 2002).

⁸ On bird's-eye views, see the fundamental Juergen Schulz, 'Jacopo de' Barbari's view of
Venice: Map making, city views, and moralized geography before the year 1500', *Art Bul-*

letin lx/3 (1978), pp.425–74. A more recent essay with a broader scope is Lucia Nuti, 'The perspective plan in the sixteenth century: The invention of a representational language', *Art Bulletin* 77 (1994). On city views in general, see Naomi Miller, *Mapping the City: The Language and Culture of Cartography in the Renaissance* (London, New York, 2003).

[9] The fundamental work is Elizabeth L. Eisenstein, *The Printing Press as an Agent of Change: Communications and Cultural Transformations in Early-Modern Europe*, 2 vols. (Cambridge, New York, 1979); and the abridged version: *The Printing Revolution in Early Modern Europe* (Cambridge, New York, 1983).

[10] On the evolution of printed images in general, their production and distribution, see: David Landau and Peter Parshall, *The Renaissance Print, 1470–1550* (New Haven, London, 1994). The book focuses on high-quality prints authored by important artists, but there is also a brief discussion of printed maps on pp.240–44. See also Michael Bury, *The Print in Italy, 1550–1620* (London, 2001), which lists techniques and materials of printing, as well as the main producers and cities involved in the trade. On the technical aspects of maps, see David Woodward (ed), *Five Centuries of Map Printing: The Kenneth Nebenzahl Jr. Lectures in the History of Cartography at the Newberry Library* (Chicago, 1975).

[11] The accuracy of portolans improved little until modern times; see Tony Campbell, 'Portolan charts from the late thirteenth century to 1500', in Woodward Harley, *Cartography in Prehistoric, Ancient and Medieval Europe*, p.371, and n.5 for a bibliography. The entire essay is a substantial introduction to portolans. A richly illustrated and extensive work on portolans is Michel Mollat du Jourdin and Monique de la Roncière, *Sea Charts of the Early Explorers: 13th to 17th Century* (New York, 1984), translated from the French: *Les portulans: Cartes marines du XIIIe au XVIIe siècle* (Freiburg, 1984). Focusing on Ottoman production of nautical charts, but also discussing portolans in general is Svat Soucek, *Piri Reis and Turkish Mapmaking after Columbus: The Khalili Portolan Atlas* (London, 1996).

[12] Corradino Astengo, *La cartografia nautica mediterranea dei secoli XVI e XVII* (Genoa, 2000), pp.12–15.

[13] Inexpensive printed versions of portolans were produced in Rome, but did not meet with commercial success. Astengo, *La cartografia nautica*, pp.15–24.

[14] A collection of essays published over the years, recently collected in a volume that attempts to chart the cultural and technical consequences of the geographical discoveries on cartography is W.G.L Randles, *Geography, Cartography and Nautical Science in the Renaissance: The Impact of the Great Discoveries* (Aldershot, 2000). For an approach that relies more specifically on the evidence provided by maps, see Thomas Suàrez, *Shedding the Veil: Mapping the European Discovery of America and the World, Based on Selected Works from the Sidney R. Knafel Collection of Early Maps, Atlases, and Globes, 1434–1865* (Singapore, Rever Edge, 1992).

[15] See Salvadori, *Carte, piante e stampe*; and Almagià, Roberto, *Monumenta Cartographica Vaticana: Carte geografiche a stampa di particolare pregio o rarità dei secoli XVI e XVII esistenti nella Biblioteca Apostolica Vaticana*, vol. II (Vatican, 1948).

[16] An exception is David Woodward who pointed out that eight out of thirty-six dated plates (that is to say, almost a fourth) issued in Venice in 1566, a peak production year, were related to the Turkish wars. Of the remaining, nineteen were maps of various countries, while two were maps of Europe and one was a world map. David Woodward, 'Foreword', in Albert Ganado, *Valletta: Città Nuova, A Map History (1566–1600)* (San Gwann, 2003), pp.xii–xiii. According to another calculation, about one third of printed maps of this period are city views, a large part of which depict wars and sieges. The author of this estimate bases it on one of the largest existing collections, that of the Bibliothèque Nationale, but does not specifically refer to the Ottoman wars. Marcel Destombes, *Les Cartes de Lafreri et assimilées 1532–1586 du Département des Estampes de la Bibliothèque Nationale*, Extrait de *Nouvelles de L'estampe* 5 (1970), p.1.

[17] Enrico Stumpo, *La Gazzetta de l'anno 1588* (Florence, 1988) reports the content of the *avvisi* published in 1588, as well as an introductory essay.

[18] David Woodward, 'Foreword' to Albert Ganado and Maurice Agius-Vadalà, *A Study in Depth of 143 Maps Representing the Great Siege of Malta of 1565*, 2 vols. (San Gwann,

1994), p.xiii. The same author provides an estimate for the production of a print by Paolo Forlani, who engraved 100 square centimeters a day, whereby a small, medium-density map took three days to produce. David Woodward, 'Paolo Forlani: Compiler, Engraver, Printer, or Publisher?', *Imago Mundi* 44 (1992), pp.45–64. A map by Niccolò Nelli, one of the earliest of the siege, is estimated to have been distributed around the middle of June 1565 (the Turkish armada had arrived in Malta on 18 May). See Ganado and Agius-Vadalà, *A Study in Depth*, I, pp.3–10, and pp. 4–5 for estimation.

[19] See Ganado and Agius-Vadalà, *A Study in Depth*, I, p.xvii; and Ganado, *Valletta*, p.xvii.

[20] Woodward, 'Foreword' to *A Study in Depth*, I, p.xiii.

[21] On this map, see Roberto Almagià, *Monumenta Cartographica*, p.105, n.48. Salvadori, *Carte, piante e stampe*, p.25, n.67, adds a list of the sources in which the map is cataloged. On Antonio Lafreri (or Antoine Lafréry), see 'I centri incisori di Roma e Venezia' in the same volume; Woodward, *Maps as Prints*, chapter two; and most recently Peter Parshall, 'Antonio Lafreri's *Speculum Romanae Magnificentiae*', *Print Quarterly* xxiii/1 (2006), pp.3–28, with bibliography on p.3, n.2.

[22] A short introductory essay on the *isolarii*, with a contribution by Elizabeth Clutton, is P.D.A. Harvey: 'Local and regional cartography,' pp.482–84. The essay focuses on Buondelmonti's *Liber Insularum Arcipelagi*, the earliest known *isolario*, compiled about 1420.

[23] Ganado and Agius-Vadalà, *A Study in Depth*, I, p.xviii.

[24] Ganado and Agius-Vadalà, *A Study in Depth*, I, n.23, pp.79–85. The authors attribute the map to the Palombi print shop in Rome and estimate its publication date to be October 1565. See also: Roberto Almagià, *Monumenta Italiae Cartographica*, 33a (XI).

[25] Orlandi's birthplace is unknown, but he flourished between 1590 and 1640. He was first active in Rome, at least until 1613, then in Naples. His cartographic production is thought to be limited to 1600–04, and 1602 was a peak year. Thirty-nine maps, including the one showing the harbor of Malta, have been so far recorded with Orlandi's imprint of that year. In the cartouche of this print, Orlandi added his name and date above Lafreri's. On this map, see: Ganado and Agius-Vadalà, *A Study in Depth*, I, n.51a, pp.243–45, also for the estimated date of the original edition; and p.243, n.2 for a bibliography on Orlandi.

[26] Ganado and Agius-Vadalà, *A Study in Depth*, I, n.50, pp.237–40. On Cassar, see: n.103, pp.434–38.

[27] For a brief biography of Jean de Valette, which emphasizes his role in the 1565 siege, see: Ganado and Agius-Vadalà, *A Study in Depth*, II, p.9. News of the thanksgiving ceremonies is in vol. I, pp.xv–xvi, for which the author does not provide bibliographic references.

[28] A brief biography is in: Ganado and Agius-Vadalà, *A Study in Depth*, II, p.11.

[29] See Valeria Bella and Piero Bella, *Cartografia Rara: Antiche carte geografiche, topografiche e storiche dalla collezione Franco Novacco* (Milan, 1986), p.146. See also Salvadori, *Carte, piante e stampe*, p.77, n.233.

[30] Almagià, *Monumenta Cartographica Vaticana*, p.3, reports the participation of Cornelisz Anthonisz.

[31] The print, which is emblazoned with Salamanca's initials, is reproduced in Bella, *Cartografia Rara*, p.12.

[32] Salvadori, *Carte, piante e stampe*, pp.xi–xii; Almagià, *Monumenta Cartographica*, pp.115–20; Parshall, 'Antonio Lafreri's *Speculum*,' pp.4–9.

[33] South is indicated with 'Mezo Giorno' in the Musi print and 'Mezo Di' in the Algiers view; both words mean 'midday' in Italian.

[34] The meaning of the whole inscription is: 'Gentlemen, please note that the position of Algiers, with respect to Italy and Spain, is in the site marked "A" and therefore this image is truthful in every part and proportion and has been illustrated in this view of the city'.

[35] See the facsimile edition: *Civitates Orbis Terrarum: Beschreibung und Contrafactur der vornembster Stät der Welt, von Georg Braun und Franciscus Hogenberg*, 6 vols, (Plochingen, 1966), vol. II, p.58.

[36] See Salvadori, *Carte, piante e stampe*, p.78, n.235; and Egon Klemp, *Africa on Maps Dating from the Twelfth to the Eighteenth Century* (Leipzig, 1968), p.37.

[37] *Civitates Orbis Terrarum*, vol. 2, p.59.

[38] The first bastion is dedicated to '*La religione di S.to Joanni*', the Order of St. John, the official title of the Knights of Malta. The next, counter-clockwise, is dedicated to '*Andrea Deoria*', and the following two respectively to 'S.or Vicere', the Viceroy of Sicily, Don Garcia de Toledo, and 'S.or Andrea Gonzaga', the Duke of Mantua.

[39] The peak of Duchetti's activity was between 1581 and 1585, the year of his death. See Parshall, 'Antonio Lafreri's *Speculum*', esp. pp.22–24.

[40] On the partnership, and the collaborators of the shop, see Woodward, *Maps as Prints*, p.44; and A. Bertolotti, *Artisti francesi in Roma nei secoli XV, XVI e XVII* (Mantua 1886, reprinted Bologna, 1975).

[41] Either Duchetti or Orlandi stripped the original plate of the legend, which might have become obsolete, but whose existence is testified by the presence of letters marking the main features of the image.

[42] The dispatch was addressed to the Grand Master of the Knights of Rhodes, from his secretary. The *avviso* is reported in: Salvadori, *Carte, piante e stampe*, p.78, n.236.

[43] Salvadori, *Carte, piante e stampe*, pp.48–49. See also Bella, *Cartografia Rara*, p.64.

[44] On this map, see Giuseppe Fumagalli, 'La più antica pianta di Tripoli', Accademie e Biblioteche d'Italia 6 (1932–33), pp.28–40, who agrees with previous authors that the print was originally produced in Venice. See also Salvadori, Carte, piante e stampe, p.78; and Bella, Cartografia Rara, p.145.

[45] The figures indicating length are preceded by the abbreviation 'ca.' for *canne*, a Roman unit of measurement roughly equivalent to 2.2 meters. If the print was indeed originally produced in Venice, the measurements must have been added once the map was reissued in Rome.

[46] The coat of arms of the Florentines (five balls in the round, visible also in the flags of the land army) were particularly easy to recognize. For a list of the other coats of arms, see Fumagalli, 'La più antica pianta', p.32.

[47] Fumagalli, 'La più antica pianta', p.34.

[48] Fumagalli, 'La più antica pianta', p.34, reports that the print is included in Lafreri's stockpile. Further specimens exist with Claudio Duchetti's imprint, who reissued Lafreri plates.

[49] See, for example Numa Broc, *La Geografia del Rinascimento* (Modena, 1989), p.25. Translated from the French as *La géographie de la Renaissance* (Paris, 1986).

[50] Jerry Brotton, *Trading Territories: Mapping the Early Modern World* (London, 1997), analyzes different cases but reaches similar conclusions. See his introductory comments on pp.17–45.

[51] Brotton, *Trading Territories*, p.34, and the chapter on 'Disorienting the East: The geography of the Ottoman empire', pp.87–118.

[52] See Destombes, *Les Cartes de Lafreri*, p.23; and, for subsequent editions of the print, Salvadori, *Carte, piante e stampe storiche*, p.102, n.306.

**Geographic Theatres, Port Landscapes and Architecture in the
Eastern Mediterranean: Salonica, Alexandria, İzmir (Cristina Pallini), pp. 61–77**
This paper presents ten years of research on Alexandria and Salonica, benefiting much from the valuable help of my supervisor, Prof. Antonio Acuto. A part of it has been used in my PhD thesis, entitled *Architecture and City Reconstruction in the Eastern Mediterranean: Alexandria and Thessaloniki* (Venice School of Architecture IUAV, 2001). This study's portion on İzmir has been made possible by a fellowship granted by the Alexander S. Onassis Public Benefit Foundation.

[1] For a general overview of railway and port developments in the Eastern Mediterranean during the nineteenth century, see Vilma Hastaoglou-Martinidis' contribution to this book. See also Vilma Hastaoglou-Martinidis, 'The advent of transport and aspects of urban modernization in the Levant during the nineteenth century', in R. Roth and M.N. Polino (eds), *The City and the Railway in Europe* (Aldershot, 2003).

[2] In most Ottoman cities, a community was recognized as a self-governing group of individuals of the same religion, represented by their religious authorities. A colony consisted of a group of individuals from the same place of origin and represented by the consulate. While membership to a religious community expressed identity, citizenship

of a nation implied protection. Around 1915, E. M. Forster remarked that in Alexandria the 'modern commercial communities' tended to 'regard religion as an expression of nationality rather than a dogma'. See Edward Morgan Forster, *Alexandria: A History and a Guide* (Gloucester, 1968), p.227. More recently the French historian Robert Ilbert seems to suggest a case-by-case approach to the composite social fabrics characterizing Ottoman port cities. See Robert Ilbert, *Alexandrie 1830–1930* (Cairo, 1996).

3 Robert Ilbert (ed), *Alexandrie entre deux mondes. ROMM* 46 (1987).

4 Michael Reimer, *Colonial Bridgehead: Government and Society in Alexandria* (Cairo, 1997).

5 Michael Haag, *Alexandria: City of Memory* (New Haven and London, 2004).

6 Robert Ilbert, and Ilios Yannakakis (eds), *Alexandrie 1860–1960: Un modèle éphémère de convivialité: Communautés et identité cosmopolite* (Paris, 1992).

7 Marie-Carmen Smyrnelis (ed), *Smyrne, la ville oubliée? 1830–1930* (Paris, 2006).

8 Enis Batur (ed), *Three Ages of İzmir: Palimpsest of Cultures* (Istanbul, 1993).

9 Center for Asia Minor Studies, *Smyrna: Metropolis of the Asia Minor Greeks* (Alimos, 2002).

10 Kostis Moskof, *Thessaloniki 1700–1912: A Cross-Section of the Bazaar-City* (Athens, 1974) [in Greek].

11 Gilles Veinstein (ed), *Salonique 1850–1918: La 'ville des Juifs' et le réveil des Balkans* (Paris, 1993).

12 Paul Risal, *La ville convoitée: Salonique* (Paris, 1924).

13 Mark Mazower, *Salonica, City of Ghosts: Christian, Muslim and Jews, 1430–1950* (New York, 2004).

14 This idea is clearly expressed by Marie-Carmen Smyrnelis in her PhD dissertation. See: Marie-Carmen Smyrnelis, *Une société hors de soi: Identités et relations sociales à Smyrne aux XVIII et XIX siècles* (Ecole des Hautes Etudes en Sciences Sociales, Paris 2000), p.27.

15 Forster, *Alexandria*, p.xv.

16 Isthmian ports are ports located along routes connecting two seas at meeting points with other routes extending far inland such as the Via Egnatia between the Adriatic and Black Seas, the overland passage trough Egypt linking the Mediterranean and the Red Sea, or the route though the Anatolian plateau connecting the Mediterranean with the Persian Gulf.

17 Kalamaria today is one of the municipalities east of Salonica; although the name originally indicated all the eastern suburbs.

18 *Dönme*s are Jews who embraced Islam in the mid-seventeenth century, as followers of Sabbetai Zevi, a rabbi from İzmir.

19 'Next to the business district at Salonica lies the new city of Kalamaria, a separated residential district of villas each in its large garden, specifically Levantine, similar to the Island of the Princes at Istanbul.' See Jovan Cvijić, *La Péninsule Balkanique* (Paris, 1918), p.200.

20 The Kalamaria gate, now Sintrivaniou Square, was a central point of departure for several roads: Chortazidon Street, Hospital Street, Boulevard des Campagnes leading to Karaburnaki, and Boulevard de l'Armée, today extending into Konstantinopouleos Street.

21 After 1839, the Ottoman government undertook a vast program of institutional, economic and social reforms in an attempt to revive the empire and to strengthen its multi-cultural nature. Adopting solutions of proven success in European countries, such reforms included administrative centralization, modernization of the state apparatus, westernization of society, and secularization of justice and education. See Paul Dumont, 'La période des Tanzîmat (1839–1878)', in R. Mantran (ed), *Histoire de l'Empire ottoman* (Paris, 1989). Vassilis Colonas and Alexandra Yerolympos, who gave me much valuable help, were among the first scholars to research on architecture and urban planning in Ottoman Salonica. Among their many works, see Vassilis Colonas, *Greek Architects in the Ottoman Empire* (Athens, 2005); and Alexandra Yerolympos, *Between East and West: Thessaloniki and Northern Greek Cities in the late 19th Century* (1997; Salonica, 2004) [in Greek].

22 This complex included the Anti-Rabies Institute, a sanatorium and the mysterious Pasha's garden, a kind of architectural folly now in ruins.

23 The remaining part of Hospital Street is today called G. Lambraki Street.

24 This name was coined by contemporaries.

25 E. M. Forster used this powerful expression to describe the eastern suburbs of Alexandria.

[26] The landscape of Chatby in 1920 is well described in a novel by the Italian author Fausta Cialente, whose entire plot is set between Chatby and Sidi Gaber, the sea and the Mahmoudieh canal. See Fausta Cialente, *Cortile a Cleopatra* (Milan, 1962).

[27] See D. A. Zivas, S. Rautopoulos, M. Sakka, and I. Kossenas, *Preliminary Study for the Foundation of a Greek University in Alexandria*, NTUA, Athens, July 1993.

[28] The Greek community complex also included the Benachi Soup Kitchen; the Manna Home for abandoned children, now the seat of the Consulate of Cyprus; the Soter football ground; and the Greek Club.

[29] Forster, *Alexandria*, pp.178–79.

[30] See, Labib Gabr, Ali, 'L'architecture contemporaine', *L'Art Vivant* (1930, special issue on Egypt), pp.563–66.

[31] An institution, begun in the early 1920s and ratified by Mussolini in 1928, to reflect the nationalist attitude innate in Fascist philosophy and the new political concept applied to emigration: Emigrants were supposed to form a compact political force, subject to the authority of Rome, in order to further the interests of the mother country.

[32] This was to include the nursery, the primary and boarding schools, high schools, a library, extensive sports facilities, a conservatory and a theater for 2,000 people. The latter two were never built. See Giuseppe Galassi, 'Le nuove scuole italiane', *Il Giornale d'Oriente* (February–March 1933, special issue on the visit to Egypt by King Vittorio Emanuele III), p.15.

[33] During World War II the Greek Hospital admitted thousands of soldiers wounded in the Battles of Krete, Tobruk, and the Western Desert. After the Nazis occupied Greece in April of 1941, a part of the hospital was run by the Greek Army.

[34] See 'Verso il compimento di un fervido voto della Colonia', *Messaggero Egiziano*, 12 October 1920, pp.1–2.

[35] See: Jean-Pierre Épron, *Comprendre l'éclectisme* (Paris, 1997).

[36] On ancient Salonica, see *Thessaloniki, Queen of Philip: Studies on Ancient Thessaloniki* (Salonica, 1985); and Nicholas Hammond, *A History of Macedonia* (Oxford, 1972–1988). On recent archaeological work in Alexandria, see Jean-Yves Empereur, *Alexandrie redécouverte* (Paris, 1998); and also Evaristo Breccia, *Alexandrea ad Ægyptum* (Bergamo, 1914); and Anthony de Cosson, *Mareotis* (London, 1935). On ancient İzmir, see Cecil J. Cadoux, *Ancient Smyrna: A History of the City from the Earliest Times to 324 AD* (Oxford, 1938).

[37] Antigonus (381–301 BC), Lysimachus (355–282 BC), Cassander (*circa* 350–298 BC) and Ptolemy (367–282 BC) were Alexander's generals, also known as the *Diadokhi* (successors). After his death in 323 BC, the generals fought to divide the conquered territories. Antigonus took Syria, Asia Minor and Mesopotamia; Lysimachus took Thrace and its surroundings and extended his power over Asia Minor after defeating Antigonus at Ipsos (301 BC). Cassander took control over Macedonia. Ptolemy reigned over Egypt in Alexandria.

[38] Alexandria was linked to the Nile by the Canopic mouth, which silted up in the twelfth century. Lake Maryut, fed by the river flood, navigable and much larger than it is today, formed another link.

[39] Whether the first town plan for ancient Salonica regarded the area uphill of the Via Egnatia, or extended from the Via Egnatia towards the sea shore is still an open question. See M.Vickers, 'Towards a Reconstruction of the Town Planning of Roman Thessaloniki', in *Thessaloniki: Queen of Philip*, pp.466–76. See also the chapter on the historical evolution of the cşty in *Aristotelous, Redesign for the Civic Axis of Thessaloniki*, Organization for the Cultural Capital of Europe Thessaloniki, 1997.

[40] The Heptastadium was a dyke (seven stadia, or 1,295 meters, long) built by the Ptolemies to join the mainland to the island of Pharos.

[41] Eugenio Turri, *Il paesaggio come teatro: Dal territorio vissuto al territorio rappresentato* (Venice, 1998).

[42] See *Description de l'Égypte: Planches* (1809–1822; Paris, 1988).

[43] See Halford Lancaster Hoskins, *British Routes to India* (1928; New York, 1966); and Lionel Wiener, *L'Égypte et ses chemins de fer* (Bruxelles, 1932).

[44] See Yakup Bektaş, 'Distant ties: Germany, the Ottoman Empire and Construction of the Baghdad Railway', *Technology and Culture* xlv/4 (2004), pp.872–74.

[45] The German railway engineer Wilhelm von Pressel, technical advisor to the Ottoman court, was a key figure in events that led to the building of the Baghdad Railway. See Wilhelm von Pressel, *Les Chemins de fer en Turquie d'Asie* (Zurich, 1902). See also Earle Edward Mead, *Turkey, the Great Powers and the Bagdad Railway* (New York, 1924).

[46] İzmir was far better served by rail than Anatolia as a whole. The İzmir–Aydın line, which opened in 1866, and the İzmir–Kasaba line, which opened in 1867, were linked to the Baghdad system in the late 1880s.

[47] On the first railway projects to restore importance of the Via Egnatia and the Vardar Valley route, see Ami Boué, *Sur l'établissement de bonnes routes et surtout de chemins de fer dans la Turquie d'Europe* (Vienna, 1852). For an overview of railway construction in Macedonia, see Basil Gounaris, *Railways over Macedonia, 1870–1912* (New York, 1993).

[48] Girardin Saint-Marc, 'Del destino delle città: Costantinopoli, Alessandria, Venezia e Corinto', *Annali universali di statistica, economia pubblica, storia e viaggi* 67 (January–March 1841), pp.72–82.

[49] Considered to be the founder of modern Egypt, Mehmet Ali (Kavala, Macedonia, 1769–Cairo, 1849) held power from 1805 to 1849. In addition to his extensive political and military actions, his administrative, economic and cultural activities left a mark on the country's history. Among other things, he undertook a vast program of public works, shaping the present territory. His far-sighted hydraulic policy set the whole country in motion, restoring agriculture and promoting industry as well as Egypt's international role. In this period, the Nile and Alexandria became two complementary constructional priorities. The Nile was to become the single means of water control to the whole territory. Alexandria, rebuilt and linked to the Nile by the Mahmoudieh Canal, was to become both a garrison town and a bridgehead for Europe. In 1841, when England and Austria forced Mehmet Ali to give up territories won through his military victories, to abrogate his monopoly of agricultural products and introduce free trade, Alexandria definitively entered into the orbit of the Western World. The number of Europeans moving there rose daily, bringing about a sharp increase in building activity.

[50] Henry Charles Woods, 'Trieste, Salonica and Smyrna', *The Fortnightly Review* (May 1921), pp.815–25.

[51] The terms of the Treaty of Lausanne (1923) required compulsory exchanges between Turkish nationals of the Greek Orthodox religion living in Turkey and Greek nationals of Muslim religion living in Greece.

[52] Kostantinos Karatheodoris was the guiding spirit behind this ambitious project. In planning İzmir University he followed the example set by the best British universities. His idea was to promote not only sound scientific and technical education, but also positive contact among many ethnic and religious cultures of the Eastern Mediterranean. He attached great importance to establishing a modern university library, modeled on the best European and American libraries.

[53] The creation of the newly independent Balkan states had produced a first wave of refugees who settled in Salonica around 1890. After annexation by Greece in 1912, migratory movements became more intense: Greeks arrived from Turkey, Bulgaria, Serbia and Caucasus; some Jewish entrepreneurs left when they felt uncertain of the city's future; Slavic-Macedonians moved to Bulgaria; and Turks left the Balkans to resettle in Turkey. In 1915, a large contingent of French and British soldiers landed at Salonica which then became the center of Entente military operations on the Macedonian front. İzmir also suffered from similar instability in the latter part of the nineteenth century. The arrival of Muslim refugees from Russia and from the Balkans increased migratory pressure to such an extent that, in May of 1914, proposals were made for an international agreement on population exchange. World War I and the allied naval bloc induced some Greeks to leave, while others moved to İzmir from inland regions of Anatolia. Some Jews left the city during the period of Greek administration, while Greeks, Armenians and Europeans departed after the fire. See Evangelia Achladi, 'De la guerre à l'administration Grecque: La fin de Smyrne cosmopolite', in Smyrnelis: Smyrne.

[54] See Pierre Lavedan, 'Un problème d'Urbanisme: La reconstruction de Salonique', *Gazette des Beaux-Arts* (1922), pp.231–48.

[55] See Lavedan, 'Un problème d'Urbanisme'.

[56] Biray Kolluoğlu has emphasized the importance of reconstructing İzmir as part of the nation-building process. See Biray Kolluoğlu Kırlı, 'The Play of Memory, Counter-Memory: Building İzmir on Smyrna's Ashes', *New Perspectives on Turkey* 26 (2002), pp.1–28.

[57] Hébrard was the head of an international town planning commission formed by Greek, French and British experts. For a full account of the reconstruction plan for Salonica, see Alexandra Yerolympos, Alexandra, *The Reconstruction of Thessaloniki after the Fire of 1917* (1985; Salonica, 1995) [in Greek].

[58] On the İzmir reconstruction plan, see A.F., 'Le plan d'aménagement de la ville de Smyrne', *L'Architecture* XL/4 (1927), pp.117–26; Cânâ Bilsel, 'Ideology and Urbanism During the Early Republican Period: Two Master Plans for İzmir and Scenarios of Modernization', *METU Journal of the Faculty of Architecture*, xvi/1–2 (1997), pp.13–30; and Cânâ Bilsel, 'Une ville renaît des cendres: La creation de Smyrne la républicaine', in Smyrnelis: *Smyrne*.

[59] Hébrard was the first to excavate in Salonica. Before the fire occurred, he had discovered that the triumphal arch on the Via Egnatia (296–97 AD) and the imposing rotunda (300 AD) formed a single architectural whole, an appendage to the imperial palace (305 AD) extending parallel to the Hippodrome towards the sea. See Ernest Hébrard, 'Les Travaux du Service Archéologique de l'Armée d'Orient à l'Arc de Triomphe de Galère et à l'église Saint-Georges de Salonique', *Bulletin de Correspondance Hellénique* XLIV (1920), pp.5–40.

[60] A number of streets at right angles to the seafront and leading to the upper town had been remodelled during the last decades of Ottoman rule. One of these was Sabri Pasha street (today Venizelos Street), connecting Eleftherias Square along the quays with the Government House (Konak) across from the market area. Another was Boulevard Hamidié, today Ethnikis Amynis Street, already mentioned when simulating a survey in Salonica from the eastern walls to Kalamaria. In any case, Ernest Hébrard visited and extensively photographed Salonica and other cities of the region. See Haris Yiakoumis, Alexandra Yerolympos and Christian Pedelahore de Loddis, *Ernest Hébrard 1875–1933* (Athens, 2001).

[61] The French planner Gaston Bardet (1907–1989) considered Hébrard's plan one of the most representative products of the French school of formal urbanism, the only one concerned with 'composition on the grand scale' but, still according to him, neglectful of the question of social organization so vital to the life of a settlement. See Gardot Bardet, *Le Nouvel Urbanisme* (Paris, 1948), p.29.

[62] It was eventually uncovered in the 1960s, when digging to build the foundations of the town hall and the law courts.

[63] In addition to the Talmud Torà complex and the Alliance Israélite Universelle schools, the fire had destroyed the old synagogues founded by the Jews who began to immigrate to Salonica from Spain and Central Europe towards the end of the fifteenth century. These synagogues were named after the places from which their founders had emigrated.

[64] Vardari Square is the point where the western section of the Via Egnatia, coming from the Adriatic Sea and joining the Vardar route, meets the eastern section coming from Istanbul.

[65] Compare René Danger, 'La topographie dans l'urbanisme', *L'Architecture* xlii/3 (1929), pp. 65–74.

[66] This project and its alternative (further port facilities extending to the southwest) were conceived during the years of Greek administration. In order to further İzmir's commercial prosperity if the city remained under Greek control, ideas were put forward to consider Greece's Asiatic territories as a free trade area, or at least to establish İzmir itself or part of it as a bonded zone. See Woods, 'Trieste, Salonica and Smyrna', pp.822–24.

[67] See Paraskevas Savvaidis, and Anthimos Badelas, City and University: A History of the University Campus at Thessaloniki (Salonica, 2000) [in Greek]; and Alexandra Yerolympos, and Athina Vitopoulou, 'The Planning of the University Campus of Thessaloniki: The Significance of a Long-Term Plan', in Thessaloniki 6 (2002), pp.273–91 [in Greek].

[68] Many scholars claim that the area of the Culture Park was increased six-fold. In my opinion this is not the case; considering Danger's plan as published in *L'Architecture*, it is clear that the original area of his university park was exactly the same as the Culture Park eventually implemented.

[69] Kolluoğlu Kırlı, 'The Play of Memory', p.11.

[70] See Sibel Bozdoğan, Modernism and Nation Building: Turkish Architectural Culture in the Early Republic (Seattle and London 2001), pp.131–32.

The Cartography of Harbor Construction in Eastern Mediterranean Cities: Technical and Urban Modernization in the Late Nineteenth Century (Vilma Hastaoglou-Martinidis), pp. 78–99

[1] Donald Quataert, 'The age of reforms, 1812–1914', in Halil İnalcık with Donald Quataert (eds.), An Economic and Social History of the Ottoman Empire, 1300–1914 (Cambridge, 1994), p.804.

[2] Public Record Office, Foreign Office, Consular Commercial Reports, London (hereafter FO, CCR). Smyrna 1863.

[3] C. Birault, 'Le port d'Alexandrie: Historique et travaux en cours d'exécution', Le Génie Civile xlvi/6 (10 December 1904), pp.82–83.

[4] Reşat Kasaba, 'İzmir', Review xvi/4 (1993), p.392.

[5] Among the descriptions are those by Tavernier (1631), Tournefort (1708), Lucas (1717), and Chandler (1764). On the gradual occupation of the landfill by the bazaar see Filippos Falbos, 'Bedestans and khans in Smyrna', Annals of Asia Minor 9 (1961), pp.136–41; for Graves' plan see Emin Canpolat, İzmir: Kuruluşundan Bugüne Kadar (Istanbul, 1953); and Doğan Kuban, Türkiye'de Kentsel Koruma (Istanbul, 2001), pp.107–8.

[6] The city absorbed the main volume of Asia Minor's imports and exports, and its multi-ethnic population grew to some 200,000 inhabitants in 1885 (Kasaba, 'İzmir'). For a detailed account on the economic and social take-off of cosmopolitan Smyrna see Elena Frangakis-Syrett, The Commerce of Smyrna in the Eighteenth Century (1700–1830) (Athens, 1992); and idem, 'Le développement d'un port méditerranéen d'importance internationale: Smyrne (1700–1914),' in M. C. Smyrnelis (ed.), Smyrne, la ville oublieé? 1830–1930 (Paris, 2006).

[7] Luigi Storari, Guida di Smirne (Torino, 1857), pp.28–29.

[8] Zeynep Çelik, The Remaking of Istanbul: Portrait of an Ottoman City in the Nineteenth Century (Berkeley, 1993), p.74; and Ekmel Derya, 'İstanbul limanının kuruluşu', in Proceedings of the First Town Planning Conference (Ankara, 1982).

[9] May Davie, Beyrouth et ses faubourgs (1840–1940) (Beirut, 1996), pp.19–23; and Eyüp Özveren, 'Beirut', Review xvi/4 (1993).

[10] Guides-Joanne: De Paris à Constantinople (Paris, 1912), p.585; Noël Verney, and George Dambmann, Les puissances étrangères dans le Levant, en Syrie et en Palestine (Paris, 1900), p.334.

[11] Nikos Svoronos, The commerce of Salonica in the Eighteenth Century (Athens, 1996), p.384 [in Greek].

[12] Liza Micheli, Pireaus: From Porto Leone to the Manchester of the Orient (Athens, 1988), pp.28–58 [in Greek].

[13] On railway building in the Levant see: Vilma Hastaoglou-Martinidis, 'The advent of transport and aspects of urban modernisation in the Levant during the nineteenth century', in R. Roth and M. N. Polino (eds.), The City and the Railway in Europe (London, 2003).

[14] The project was granted in 1869 to the company of the Belgian banker baron Maurice de Hirsch, with Austrian, British, French and Belgian capital. The company of the Chemins de Fer de la Turquie d'Europe constructed many tracts of the Balkan railroad network after 1871. The text of the concession is published in Vahdettin Engin, Rumeli Demiryollari (Istanbul, 1993), pp.93–95.

[15] Archives du Ministère des Affaires Etrangères, Correspondence Consulaire Commerciale (hereafter AMAE, CCC), France. Smyrne, vol. 51, 14–1–1868.

[16] Public Record Office, Foreign Office, Consular Reports, London (hereafter FO, CR). Constantinople, 1879.

[17] Verney and Dambmann, Les puissances étrangères dans le Levant, p.334.

[18] FO, CR, Alexandria 1878.

[19] The École des Ponts et Chaussées is the first formal School of Engineering in history. It was established in 1775, after reorganizing the mid-1700s school of engineering created by King

Louis XV. During the nineteenth century, its graduates carried out an impressive number of public works in almost every part of the world without any significant concurrence.

[20] Information held in the French Archives Nationales, engineers, individual files F/14.

[21] Linant de Bellefonds started his Egyptian career in 1818 and associated his name with almost all great public works undertaken in Egypt between 1818 and 1883. For a detailed description of his connection with the Saint-Simonists and his activity in Egypt see Alleaume, Ghislaine, 'Linant de Bellefonds (1799–1883) et les Saint-Simonisme en Egypte', in M. Morsy (ed.), *Les Saint-Simoniens et l'Orient* (Aix-en-Provence, 1990), pp.113–32.

[22] B.Malaval and Gaston Jondet, *Le port d'Alexandrie* (Cairo, 1912), pp.117–19.

[23] On the activity of Dussaud Frères firm, see *Dictionnaire de Bibliographie Française* (Paris, 1968), vol. xii, p.866.

[24] Vilma Hastaoglou-Martinidis, 'Les villes-ports du bassin oriental de la Méditerranée à la fin du XIX siècle: Travaux portuaires et transformations urbaines', in C. Vallat (ed.), *Petites et grandes villes du bassin Mediterranéen* (Rome, 1988), pp.51–52.

[25] Werner Müller-Wiener, *Die Häfen von Byzantion-Konstantinopoli-Istanbul* (Tübingen, 1994), p.124.

[26] Jacques Thobie, *Intérêts et impérialisme français dans l'Empire Ottoman* (Paris, 1977), p.174.

[27] AMAE, CCR, Beyrouth, t.9 1868–1888, 10 February 1868.

[28] The project provided for a 1000-meter-long sea front, an 800-meter-long jetty and a 350-meter-long mole, forming a spacious wharf of 23 hectares. See Jacques Monicault, *Le port de Beyrouth et l'economie des pays du Levant sous le mandat français* (Paris, 1936), p.24.

[29] Hastaoglou-Martinidis, 'The advent of transport'.

[30] Demosthenes Pippas, 'Harbour works in Greece', *Technical Annals* 185 (1939), p.362.

[31] Vasias Tsakopoulos, *Pireaus 1835–1870* (Athens, 1984), pp.149–63 [in Greek].

[32] Angelos Guinis, *Le port du Pirée* (Athens, 1907).

[33] Archives du Monde de Travail, France (hereafter AQ). Société de construction des Batignoles 89, 2707, Ports étrangers.

[34] Société de construction des Batignoles 89 AQ 1750, Port de Varna.

[35] Nikos Mitsis, *Scio, the Port of the City* (Scio, 1988), pp.43–51 [in Greek].

[36] Société de construction des Batignoles 89 AQ 2272, Port de Patras.

[37] Société de construction des Batignoles 89 AQ 1691, Port de Jaffa.

[38] Donald Quataert, 'Workers, peasants and economic change in the Ottoman Empire, 1730–1912', in H. Batu and J. L. Bacqué-Gammont (eds.), *L'Empire Ottoman, la République de Turquie at la France* (Istanbul, 1986).

[39] FO, CR, Smyrna, 1871 and 1877–81.

[40] Charles Issawi, *The Economic History of Turkey 1800–1914* (Chicago, 1980), p.167.

[41] AMAE, CCC, Smyrne, vol. 51.

[42] *Neologos*, 23 October 1890.

[43] Fouad Debbas, *Beirut, Our Memory* (Beirut, 1986), p.38.

[44] *The Levant Times and Shipping Gazette*, 11 June 1870.

[45] Following the stand of the Defense Minister, General Arabi Pasha, against the Franco-British condominium that took control of the economy in 1876, the British fleet bombarded the city, hitting both Qaitbay Fort and the Mohamed Ali or Consuls Square, in the heart of the European quarter.

[46] Alessandro Breccia, *Il porto di Alessandria di Egitto: Studio di Geografica Commerciale* (Cairo, 1927), pp.25–26.

[47] Birault, 'Le port d'Alexandrie', pp.85–86; Malaval and Jondet, *Le port d'Alexandrie*, p.17; Breccia, *Il porto di Alessandria di Egitto*, pp.21–22.

[48] Démetrios Géorgiadès, *Smyrne et l'Asie Mineure, au point de vue économique et commercial* (Paris, 1885), pp.154–56. The duration of the concession was successively extended by thirty, forty and fifty years, redeemable on 31 Dec. 1952; see Louis Godard, 'Les ports maritimes de la Turquie: Ports existent et ports projetés', *Le Génie Civil* lv/19 (1909), p.349.

[49] Vital Cuinet, *La Turquie d'Asie* (Paris, 1984), vol. 3, p.447.

[50] The net profit amounted to 600,000 francs in 1883, and the annual income form the plots, the docks and the warehouses (6,697,114 franc in real value) was estimated to 130,410

franc. See Thobie *Intérêts et impérialisme français*, pp.134–35. For the urban development, see Cuinet, *La Turquie d'Asie*, pp.447–49; Georgiadès, *Smyrne et l'Asie Mineure*, p.145; François Rougon, *Smyrne: Situation commerciale et économique* (Paris, 1892), p.448; and *Murray's Handbook for Travelers: The Mediterranean, Part I* (London, 1890), pp.88–89.

[51] On the subject of *karşılık* see Pierre Oberling, 'The quays of İzmir', in H. Batu and J.L. Jacqué-Gammont (eds.), *L'Empire Ottoman, la République de la Turquie et la France* (Istanbul, 1986), pp.322–24. Vitali's plan is held at the Prime Minister's Archives in Istanbul.

[52] See, for instance, the following guidebooks: *Murray's Handbook for Travelers: The Mediterranean*, pp.88–89; and *Murray's Handbook for Travelers: Asia Minor, Transcaucasia, Persia, etc.* (London: 1895), p.73; *Meyers Reisebücher: Griechenland und Kleinasien* (Leipzig, 1901), p.286; and *Guides-Joanne: De Paris à Constantinople*, pp.404–5.

[53] The law of expropriation was enacted in 1856 by the Ottoman government (see below).

[54] Çelik, *The Remaking of Istanbul*, p.75.

[55] Godard, 'Les ports maritimes de la Turquie', p.359.

[56] Issawi, *The Economic History of Turkey*, p.167.

[57] The remedy adopted was to cover the bed along the docks with a sand layer with a thickness of at least two meters. See Godard, 'Les ports maritimes de la Turquie', p.359.

[58] For a detailed account of the repair works, see: Société de Constructions des Batignoles, 89 AQ 1709, Dossier d' A. Guérard sur les travaux de réfection des quais, 1896–1900.

[59] In Galata, new warehouses and offices occupied a surface area of 7,000 square meters, while in Eminönü they amounted to 13,436 square meters. See Çelik, *The Remaking of Istanbul*, p.76.

[60] Issawi, *The Economic History of Turkey*, p.168.

[61] Anonymous, 'Travaux du port de Haydar Pacha', *Le Génie Civil* xlv/15 (1904), pp. 264–65.

[62] I. Skalleridou, *Le Phare de l'Orient: Almanach de 1902* (Istanbul, 1901), pp.272–76 [in Greek].

[63] FO, DCR, Beirut, No 720, 1890, p.7 and No 908, 1891 p.2.

[64] Verney and Dambmann, *Les puissances étrangères dans le Levant*, p.347.

[65] *Baedeker Handbook for Travelers: Palestine and Syria* (Leipzig, 1912), pp.279–81.

[66] FO, CR, Salonica 1869.

[67] The plan is kept at the Prime Minister's Archives in Istanbul.

[68] FO, CR, Salonica 1870. For the intramural city, the Governor Sabri Pasha ordered the construction of a large hospital; the streets were gradually widened; and a very large plot of land was laid out as a garden and opened for the recreation of the inhabitants.

[69] FO, CR, Salonica 1882.

[70] Louis Barret, *Note sur l'aménagement des ports de commerce* (Paris, 1875), pp.85–86.

[71] Société de Constructions des Batignoles, 89 AQ 2276 Port de Salonique.

[72] For a detailed presentation of the enterprise, see Vilma Hastaoglou-Martinidis, 'The harbour of Thessaloniki, 1896–1920', in A. Jarvis and K. Smith (eds), *Albert Dock: Trade and Technology* (Liverpool, 1999).

[73] Maria Synarelli, *Roads and Ports in Greece, 1830–1880* (Athens, 1989), p.180 [in Greek].

[74] See Guinis, *Le port du Pirée*, pp.7–8. The cost of the dry docks built by the contractor-engineers L. Petitmermer and C. Respini rose to 5 million drachmas.

[75] Çelik, *The Remaking of Istanbul*, p. 44.

[76] Çelik, *The Remaking of Istanbul*, p.70.

[77] Davie, *Beyrouth et ses faubourgs*, pp.35–37.

[78] Robert Ilbert, *Alexandrie 1830–1930* (Cairo, 1996), p.325.

[79] M. F. Awad, 'Le modèle européen: L'evolution urbaine de 1807 à 1958', in Robert Ilbert (ed.), *Alexandrie entre deux mondes* (Aix-en-Provence, 1987), pp.96–98.

[80] Mübahat Kütükoğlu, 'İzmir rıhtımı inşaatı ve işletme imtiyazı', *Tarih Dergisi* xxxii/3 (1979), pp.540–45.

[81] Ilbert, *Alexandrie 1830–1930*, pp.172–73.

[82] FO, CR Beirut, 1871.

[83] FO, CR, Alexandria 1876–77.

[84] Among the construction activities of this office in Istanbul one should mention the building of the Deutsche Orient Bank, three office buildings for the telephone company,

and the English School in Nişantaşı, all in 1912. In Alexandria, the office constructed the warehouses for the Egyptian Bonded Warehouse Co. (1906), the Wadrian Terminal (1910), and the extension of the docks and the jetty (1911). In Cairo, they built the Museum of Egyptian Antiquities (1903), the Oasis Hotel (1910) and the Hindou Palace (1911) in Heliopolis. See: *Le Béton armé*, vols. 56 (1903) to 187 (1913), passim.

Mental Maps: The Mediterranean Worlds of Two Palestinian Newspapers in the Late Ottoman Period (Johann Büssow), pp. 100–115

1   *Filastin*, 2 July 1911, p.1.
2   For a detailed discussion of the political impact of the Palestinian press after 1908, see Michelle U. Campos, 'A "Shared Homeland" and Its Boundaries: Empire, Citizenship and the Origins of Sectarianism in Late Ottoman Palestine, 1908–13' (PhD Dissertation, Stanford University, 2003), pp.237–79.
3   For conceptual thoughts on the study of networks, see Jürgen Osterhammel and Niels Petersson, *Geschichte der Globalisierung* (Munich, 2003), pp.20–24.
4   Population estimates by foreign travelers are listed in Ruth Kark, *Jaffa: A City in Evolution, 1799–1917* (Jerusalem, 1990), pp.146–52. The Ottoman Atlas from 1907 gives the number of 34,000. M. Nasrullah et al., *Osmanlı Atlası* (1907), p.114.
5   Charles Issawi, 'The Trade of Jaffa, 1825–1914', in Hisham Nashabe (ed), *Studia Palaestina: Studies In Honour of Constantine K. Zurayk* (Beirut, 1988), pp.42–51.
6   See, for instance, *Filastin*'s and *ha-Herut*'s regular reports on visitors coming and going between the two cities, or the diaries of the Arab Orthodox intellectual and educator Khalil al-Sakakini who was in close contact with intellectual circles in Jaffa. Khalil al-Sakakini, *Yawmiyyat Khalil al-Sakakini*, vol. 1, ed. Akram Musallam (Ramallah, 2003).
7   Population estimates by foreign travelers are listed in Ruth Kark, *Jerusalem and Its Environs: Quarters, Neighborhoods, Villages, 1800–1948* (Jerusalem, 2001), p.28. The Ottoman Atlas from 1907 gives the number of 51,000. Nasrullah et al., *Osmanlı Atlası*, p.114.
8   For the history of the foundation of the independent district of Jerusalem in 1872, see Butrus Abu Manneh, 'The rise of the sanjak of Jerusalem in the late nineteenth century', in Ilan Pappe (ed), *The Israel/Palestine Question* (London, New York, 1999), pp.41–51. For a broader perspective on the new type of Ottoman provincial capitals that emerged after 1864, see Jens Hanssen, Thomas Philipp, Stefan Weber (eds), *The Empire in the City: Arab Provincial Capitals in the Late Ottoman Empire* (Beirut, 2002).
9   The Palestinian politician and intellectual 'Umar Salih al Barghouthi in his memoirs vividly recalls the fascination he felt during his first visit to Jaffa. 'Umar Salih al-Barghouthi, *al-Marahil* (Beirut, 2001), p.108. The Jewish journalist and educator David Yellin writes in an article before World War I that Jaffa's Jews took pride in being more modern than their brethren in Jerusalem who were still in need of 'enlightenment'. Kark, *Jaffa*, p.190. In 1908, Eliezer Ben Yehuda wrote in *ha-Tsvi*: 'It should be hoped that Jerusalem will learn from its smaller and younger sister'. *ha-Tsvi*, 6 November 1912. In many articles in *Filastin* one finds similar remarks, for instance, in a passage comparing the situation of the Christian communities in 'progressive' Jaffa with that of Christians in the more conservative cities of Gaza and Hebron. *Filastin*, 5 May 1913, p.1.
10 For an interesting contemporary discussion of the Islamic definition of the Holy Land (*al-ard al-muqaddasa*), see Rashid Rida, 'Tafsir al-qur'an al-hakim', *al-Manar* 17 (1914), p.16.
11 Some cases in point are Nasrullah et al., *Osmanlı Atlası*, p.113; the French language article 'Lettre à son Excellence Djevdet Bey, Gouverneur de la Palestine', *Filastin*, 26 August 1911, p.1; or the terminology used in the papers of the British Consulate. See also note 45.
12 Campos, 'A "Shared Homeland"', p.240.
13 Rashid Khalidi, *Palestinian Identity: The Construction of Modern National Consciousness* (New York, 1997), p.120.
14 According to *ha-Herut*, one of the 'Isa family's main sources of income was the rent received from Jewish tenants of their property in the market area of *Suq Bustrus*, among them the Anglo Palestine Company. *ha-Herut*, 16 December 1912, p.2.

[15] In 1912 a relative, Hana Niqula al-'Isa, was appointed as one of two headmen (*mukhtars*) of the Arab Orthodox community in Jaffa. *Filastin*, 15 September 1912, p.3. Another relative, Nadim al-'Isa was a merchant with trade connections to the orange market in Liverpool. *Filastin*, 22 October 1913, p.3. For the sake of clarity, the term 'Greek-Orthodox' in this article is used to designate only the Greek-Orthodox Church, its clergy, and its institutions. Its Arab-speaking members as well as their institutions are referred to by the terms 'Arab Greek-Orthodox' or 'Arab Orthodox'.

[16] Ya'kov Yehoshua, *Tarikh al-sihafa al-'arabiyya fi Filastin fil-'ahd al-uthmani (1909–1918)* (Jerusalem, 1974), p.117, citing from an article by 'Umar Salih al-Barghuti in *Mir'at al-Sharq*, 19 January 1928. Unfortunately, Yehoshua does not mention the Egyptian company's name.

[17] *Filastin*, 8 November 1911, p.3; 26 August 1911, p.3; 27 March 1912, p.2; and Ami Ayalon, *The Press in the Arab Middle East* (New York, 1995), p.197.

[18] The paper was probably named after Abu Sa'id al-Asma'i (d. 828), an early Arabic philologist. B. Lewin, 'al-Asma'i', in *Encyclopaedia of Islam*, vol. 1, pp.717–719.

[19] For further information on the movement, see Derek Hopwood, 'The Resurrection of Our Christian Brethren (Ignatev): Russia and Orthodox Arab Nationalism in Jerusalem,' in Moshe Ma'oz (ed), *Studies on Palestine During the Ottoman Period* (Jerusalem, 1975), pp.394–407, and Campos, 'A "Shared Homeland"', pp.78–90.

[20] *Filastin*, 15 November 1913, p.2.

[21] See David Tidhar, *Entsiqlopedia le-halutse ha-yishuv u-vonav* (Encyclopedia of the Yishuv and Its Founders) (Tel Aviv, 1947–69), vol. 4, p.1054.

[22] Abigail Jacobson, 'The Sephardi Jewish community in pre-World War I Jerusalem: Debates in the Hebrew press', *Jerusalem Quarterly File* 14 (2001), pp.23–35; M.D. Gaon, 'ha-Herut: Daf historiya le-qorot ha-'itonut ha-'ivrit be-Erets Yisrael lifne milhemet ha-'olam', in David Yudelovitch (ed), *Qovets ma'amarim le-divre yeme ha-'itonut be-Erets Yisra'el*, (Tel Aviv, 1936), vol. 2, pp.140–41.

[23] Avraham Elmaliah was probably a very fitting choice for this new orientation, as he had already worked with Eliezer Ben Yehuda, one of the most prominent Ashkenazi Hebrew journalists. Nevertheless, Haim Ben Atar remained a prominent member of the newspaper's editorial team and in 1912 became editor-in-chief again. See Gaon, 'ha-Herut', p.177.

[24] Gaon, 'ha-Herut', p.139.

[25] Gaon, 'ha-Herut', p.140.

[26] Gaon, 'ha-Herut', p.182.

[27] Gaon, 'ha-Herut', p.177. For a summary of A. Danon's work, see Esther Benbassa, 'Modernization of Eastern Sephardi communities', in Harvey E. Goldberg (ed), *Sephardi and Middle Eastern Jewries: History and Culture in the Modern Era* (Bloomington, 1996), p.93.

[28] This, however, is difficult to ascertain, as in both papers many reports from other towns are either anonymous or signed with the author's initials only.

[29] A case in point is the *Lloyd Ottoman*, a telegraphic news bulletin sponsored by the German government trying to foster pro-German sentiments in the Ottoman Empire. German Consulate, Jerusalem, Israel State Archives (ISA), A XXXX, 4, Grunwald to Schmidt, 21 September 1909.

[30] The practice of street-vending newspapers and news bulletins is mentioned in the papers of the German Consulate, Jerusalem: ISA, AXXX, 4/P 457/67, Brode to Wangenheim, Jaffa, 9 April 1915.

[31] In general, the circulation of Arab newspapers was still quite modest at this time. According to Ayalon, the Lebanese *Lisan al-Hal* was the largest Arabic newspaper in the Ottoman Empire and in 1914 sold 3,500 copies daily. Ayalon, *The Press in the Arab World*, pp.67–68.

[32] According to Gaon, *ha-Herut*'s forerunner *El Liberal* is said to have had a circulation of 1,500 in the year 1909. Gaon: 'ha-Herut', pp.140, 177.

[33] The numbers given for the larger papers are: *ha-Tsvi*: 1,200; *ha-Po'el ha-Tsa'ir*: 1,000; *ha-Margammal* [sic]: 1,000; *ha-Herut* 800. German Consulate, Jerusalem, ISA, AXXX, 4/P 457/67, 'Verzeichnis in Jerusalem erscheinender Zeitungen und Zeitschriften'. The German Embassy in Istanbul undertook a survey in answer to a request of 21 April 1909. For a

recent survey of literacy and reading practices in Palestine during the late Ottoman period see Ami Ayalon, *Reading Palestine: Printing and Literacy, 1900–1948* (Austin, 2004).

34 The average annual subscription for an Arabic or Hebrew newspaper cost between 30 and 70 *kuruş*. Considering the fact that, according to Barghouthi, at that time a rural school teacher received a monthly salary of 150 *kuruş*, and an average urban day laborer eight *kuruş* per day at best, it is evident that workers and employees could afford newspapers only occasionally. Bargouthi: *Marahil*, p.83. See also Campos, 'A "Shared Homeland"', p.241.

35 In the absence of reliable figures on the literacy rate during the period under review, we have to content ourselves with approximations. These approximate numbers lie, according to the sources consulted, between a low 2 per cent (the estimate by 'Isa and Yusuf al-'Isa in the quote above) and 5 per cent for the whole population, the percentage among men being higher than among women. The first official statistics on literacy in Palestine dates from the Mandate Period. See E. Mills, *Census of Palestine*, 2 vols, (London, 1932). For a summary see Khalidi, *Palestinian Identity*, p.225, n.33.

36 *Filastin*, 11 June 1913, p.3.

37 Since its foundation during the *Tanzimat* reforms, the gendarmerie had provided communication with remote villages in the empire and still does so in modern Turkey. There is unfortunately even less information available on gender distribution among *Filastin*'s readership. That at least the editors were conscious about women's issues is shown by a number of articles. I have come across only one article written by a Palestinian woman, signed 'Muhiba al-'Isa, student at the Teachers' Seminar in Bayt Jala', probably a relative of 'Isa and Yusuf al-'Isa. *Filastin*, 3 March 1913, p.1.

38 *Filastin*, 2 July 1911, p.1. A survey of the *circa* 300 local personalities mentioned in *Filastin* between 1911 and 1914 shows that about 60 per cent of them were Muslim, 30 per cent Christians, 5 per cent Ottoman Jews, and the remaining 5 per cent recent Jewish immigrants and other foreigners. Johann Büssow, 'Die osmanische Elite Palästinas im Spiegel der Zeitung Filastin, 1911–1914' (M.A. thesis, Freie Universität Berlin, 2002), p.54.

39 For instance, Eliya Zaka', the editor of the Arabic newspaper *al-Nafir*. *ha-Herut*, 18 September 1911, p.1.

40 *Filastin*, 18 December 1912, p.2. The controversy was triggered by Zionist land sales in the vicinity of Jaffa.

41 ISA, 67/peh 457:482.

42 *Filastin*, 4 September 1912, p.1.

43 The correspondent's name was Hana Yasmina. *Filastin*, 9 September 1911, p.3.

44 *Filastin*, 2 August 1913, p.3.

45 In a leading article, Yusuf al-'Isa wrote that his 'homeland' (*watan*) extended 'from the borders of Egypt to the *Balqa* [the district of Nablus] and from the mountains of Moab [on the Eastern shore of the Dead Sea] to the Mediterranean'. *Filastin*, 31 January 1912, p.1. One year later the well-known Palestinian intellectual Raghib al-Khalidi wrote in an article entitled 'Reform in Palestine' (*al-islah fi Filastin*) that his 'homeland' was the district of Jerusalem. *Filastin*, 25 January 1913, p.1.

46 Letter to the editor by Bulus Shahada in *Filastin*, 9 July 1911, p.3.

47 In 1913, the performance in Jaffa of the celebrated actor George Abyad together with three Egyptian theater troupes became a first-order social event, with guests from among the notable families of Jerusalem, Nablus and Gaza. *Filastin*, 16 July 1913, p.1. Film screenings were such a common phenomenon in Jaffa of 1911 that Yusuf al-'Isa could even use them as a political metaphor, criticizing the reform projects announced by the new provincial council (*al-majlis al-'umumi/meclis-i umumi*) as being of the same ephemeral nature as 'cinematographic pictures'. *Filastin*, 6 December 1911, p.1. In *ha-Herut* one finds an advertisement for the film screenings of the brothers Paté from Paris in the Feingold Hall (*Ulam Feingold*) in Jerusalem. *ha-Herut*, 15 September 1912, p.1.

48 For Shakib Arslan's two visits, see *Filastin*, 6 November 1912, p.3, and 16 April 1913, p.3. Shortly after Arslan's second visit, *Filastin* printed a leading article by Arslan, which later on was translated in Ottoman Turkish newspapers. *Filastin*, 23 April 1913,

p.1, and 4 June 1913, p.2. Jurji Zaydan's visit to Jaffa and Jerusalem was covered in several articles during August of 1912. See *Filastin*, 7 August 1912, p.3, for a panegyric poem by 'Isa al-'Isa on the famous Egyptian *homme des lettres*.

[49] Yusuf al-'Isa was so appalled by the political activities of the Arabist reformers in Syria that he even refused to cover the 1913 Arab Congress in Paris in his newspaper. Campos, 'A "Shared Homeland"', p.365.

[50] The Arabic original reads 'madinat al-'ilm wal-tijara wal-haraka al-da'ima'. *Filastin*, 12 April 1913, p.1.

[51] *Filastin*, 11 October 1913, p.1. Apparently, Beirut's governor could only convene a commission (*lajna*), as he could not allow foreigners to be full-fledged members of the municipal council, a practice that had existed before but had been made illegal by an Ottoman law of the same year.

[52] This may be part of one of several long-standing traditions of local identification, as Dana Sajdi's work on the world-views of eighteenth-century Arabic chronicles suggest. Dana Sajdi, 'Peripheral Visions: The Worlds and Worldviews of Commoner Chronicles in the 18th Century Ottoman Levant' (PhD Dissertation, Columbia University, 2002), p.333.

[53] Issawi, 'The Trade of Jaffa', p.45; *Filastin*, 22 October 1913, p.3.

[54] *Filastin*'s second title reads *La Palestine*. Yusuf al-'Isa often cited French authors such as La Fontaine or Victor Hugo in his articles, two authors who were studied and emulated also by two of the Arabic intellectuals he admired most, Jurji Zaidan and Ruhi al-Khalidi. Politically, Yusuf al-'Isa also showed clear pro-French sympathies, as he identified with the French population in Alsace and criticized German politics of land acquisition in Agadir, Morocco. *Filastin*, 2 July 1911, p.2, , 12 October 1911, p.1.

[55] Especially active was the correspondent Mikha'il Buyuk in Santiago de Chile, who regularly reported on political and communal events in Chile. For an example see *Filastin*, 2 July 1911, p.3. For some time during 1911, the paper even had a regular column with letters of an anonymous Palestinian who wrote to his friend in the American diaspora (*rasa'il min muqim ila muhajir*).

[56] For an analysis of al-Karmil's anti-Zionist articles, see Khalidi, *Palestinian Identity*, pp.124–26.

[57] A good example of such a career is the physician and journalist Shimon Moyal who frequently wrote in *ha-Herut*. He was born in Jaffa to a Jewish family from Morocco. While studying medicine in Beirut he married Esther Azhari, a journalist and women's rights activist. They moved to Cairo where they started writing for different newspapers and eventually returned to Jaffa to pursue a joint career as journalists and Zionist activists. For a short vita of Shimon Moyal, see Abigail Jacobson, 'Alternative voices in late Ottoman Palestine: A historical note', *Jerusalem Quarterly File* 21 (2004), pp.42–44. Similar trajectories can be found in other Sephardic families, such as the Chelouche from Jaffa or the Amzalaks from Jerusalem. See David Tidhar, *Entsiqlopedia le-halutse ha-yishuv u-vonav* (*Encyclopedia of the Yishuv and Its Founders*) (Tel Aviv, 1947–1969), vol. 4, p.1789; Ruth Kark, Joseph Glass, *Sephardi Entrepreneurs in Eretz Israel: The Amzalak Family, 1816–1918* (Jerusalem, 1991), p.160.

[58] See for instance the rather detailed report on the elections to Istanbul's regional council (*meclis-i umumi*) in *ha-Herut*, 28 October 1910, p.1.

[59] *ha-Herut*, 25 December 1912, p.3.

[60] For case studies concerning this topic, see Thomas Philipp, Birgit Schaebler (eds), *The Syrian Land, Infrastructures and Communication: Processes of Integration and Separation in Bilad al-Sham from the 18th Century to the Mandatory Period* (Stuttgart, 1998).

[61] For the most comprehensive historical account on Gaza to date, see 'Abd al-Karim Rafiq, 'Ghazza: Dirasa 'umraniyya wa-ijtima'iyya wa-iqtisadiyya min khilal al-watha'iq al-shar'iyya 1273–1277/1857–1861', in 'Abd al-Karim Rafiq, *Buhuth fil-tarikh al-iqtisadiyya wal-ijtima'iyya fi Bilad al-Sham fil-'asr al-hadith* (Damascus, 2000), pp.4–95.

[62] On the loss of power of local strongmen in Palestine, see Alexander Schölch, *Palestine in Transition (1856–1882): Studies in Social, Economic and Political Development* (Washington DC, 1993), part 3. For a view from inside this development, see the mem-

oirs of the son of the last feudal landlord of a village in the vicinity of Jerusalem: al-Barghouthi, *Marahil*, chapter 1.

[63] I borrow this expression from Dana Sajdi, 'Peripheral Visions', p.333. What is striking in contrast to the eighteenth-century chroniclers she examines is the almost complete omission of the empire's religious capital, Mecca.

Adding New Scales of History to the Eastern Mediterranean: Illicit Trade and the Albanian (Isa Blumi), pp. 116–138

[1] For further details, see Isa Blumi, 'Beyond the margins of the empire: Searching the limitations of Ottoman rule in Yemen and Albania', *MIT Electronic Journal of Middle Eastern Studies* (2003), pp.10–18.

[2] Isa Blumi, *Rethinking the Late Ottoman Empire: A Comparative Social and Political History of Albania and Yemen, 1878–1918* (Istanbul, 2003), pp.134–74.

[3] For an invaluable study of this neglected family's history, see Hamdi Bushati, *Bushatllinjtë: pajisur me shënime, ilustrime dhe një Suplement nga Nexhmi Bushati* (Shkodër, 2003).

[4] Details of the exploits of this family dynasty are found in: Archivio della Sacra Congregazione della Propaganda Fide (ASCPF), Rome, SC Servia 3, fos. 19: letter, 1788, 194: letter, 1796.

[5] For a comprehensive study on the role of Albanians in the creation of an independent Greece, see Koli Xoxi, *Lufta e popullit grek për pavarësi: kontributi shqiptar* (Tiranë, 1991).

[6] For a thoughtful analysis of the historiography on Ali Pasha Tepelen, see Katherine Fleming, *The Muslim Bonaparte: Diplomacy and Orientalism in Ali Pasha's Greece* (Princeton, N.J., 1999).

[7] Iskandar Aziz, *al-Batal al-a'zam Muhammad Ali al-kabir* (Cairo, 1976), pp.23–42.

[8] For a still worthwhile commentary on this process, see Donald C. Blaisdell, *European Financial Control in the Ottoman Empire* (New York, 1929), pp.4–14.

[9] See Isa Blumi, 'Contesting the edges of the Ottoman Empire: Rethinking ethnic and sectarian boundaries in the Malësore, 1878–1912', *International Journal of Middle East Studies* xxxv/2 (2003), pp.237–56.

[10] See the letter sent to the British Consul Green by leaders of the areas in question in: Public Records Office at Kew Gardens (PRO), Foreign Office (FO) 195/1303, dated 2 May 1880.

[11] See Haus-, Hof- und Staatsarchiv (henceforth HHStA), PA XVII/35, Montenegro, Gusinje Frage, No. 57141/11, Edhem Pasha's report to von Haymade, dated Istanbul, 9 January 1880, documents 185r to 190v.

[12] See the letters and reports from the archbishop's office in İşkodra on this process of selective mass expulsion. Albanian National Archives/Arkivi Qendror Shtetëror (henceforth AQSH), F.132.D.19.f.1–11, dated between 1880 and 1883.

[13] For numerous reports on the expulsion of Muslim Albanians from Montenegro later on in the 1880s, see Başbakanlık Osmanlı Arşivi (henceforth BOA), Yıldız Tasnifi Perakende Evrak Mabeyn Cetvelleri (henceforth Y.PRK.MYD) 4/92, 28 Receb 1303 [3 May 1886], and Y.PRK.MYD, 5/29, 20 Şevval 1303 [23 July 1886].

[14] Adrian Papajani, 'Veprimtaria Ekonomike e Firmave Tregtare Çoba dhe Bianki', *Arkivi Shqiptar* 2 (2001), pp.19–28.

[15] BOA, Y.PRK.MYD 1/60, 8 Zilkade 1297 [12 October 1880].

[16] BOA, Hariciye Nezareti Siyasi (henceforth HR.SYS) 129/45, report no. 7 from the *vilayet* of Shkodër to the Ministry of the Interior, dated 27 Zilevvel 1307 [17 December 1889].

[17] Archivio Storico del Ministero degli Affair e Esteri (henceforth ASMAE), Serie A Affairi Politici (1881–1891) Busta 1, F. 1889, no. 145/82, Consul a MAE, dated Scutari, 15 April 1889.

[18] From the consul's report we learn that Montenegrin authorities arrested four Kelmendi traders traveling between Ottoman and Montenegrin towns and put them on trial for 'illegal entry and smuggling'. While these traders had broken formal laws, it was also clear to the consul that the accused merchants regularly crossed the border in question without official harassment. The conflict arose from a sudden policy change. ASMAE Serie A Affairi Politici (1881–1891) Busta 1 F. 1890, no. 258/193, Consul a MAE, dated Scutari, 24 July 1890.

[19] BOA, Y.PRK.MYD 1/63, 13 Zilkade 1297 [16 November 1880]. That being said, there were times when Ottoman troops were required to assure that these people were given safe passage out of Montenegro after it was no longer feasible for them to resist Slav expansion into the Ulqin region. Safe passage often meant being shipped to Anatolia. BOA, Y.PRK.MYD 1/59, dated 7 Zilkade 1297 [10 November 1880].

[20] Sadly, this logic worked perfectly for the Great Powers while promoting the 'dignified resettlement' of Muslims found outside the new frontiers they created in the Balkans, resulting in the 'justified' expulsion of hundreds of thousands of Muslims and Catholics who lived in 'Orthodox' states. AQSH, F.143.D.1054.f.1, letter written to Derviş Paşa, military commander in Shkodër, detailing the flight of Muslims and Catholics from Podgoritza, 12 May 1879.

[21] See BOA, Yıldız Tasnifi Sadaret Resmi Maruzat Evraki (henceforth YA.RES) 41/13, order from legislature, 24 Rebiyülahir 1305 [9 January 1888].

[22] BOA, Meclis-i Vükelâ Mazbataklarıı (henceforth MV) 96/24, 22 Cemaziyelevvel 1316 [8 October 1898]. On the plight of the Albanians of Ulqin who settled in Ragusa (Dubrovnik) and Venice, see: BBA, MV 45/19, 12 Zilkâde 1306 [10 July 1889].

[23] Particularly in Tuz the practice caused great tension. BOA, MV 32/24, 28 Şaban 1305 [10 May 1888]. The tensions got so bad that the authorities started to move many refugees to Draç further south. BOA, MV 43/37, 19 Ramazan 1306 [19 September 1889]. As for Slav Muslims from Herzegovina, they were sent to Kocana in Kosova. BBA, MV 69/70, 27 Ramazan 1309 [25 April 1892].

[24] It is said among the Mirdita that arbitrarily removing stones marking individual property is a crime that follows you to the grave: 'Guri i kufinit nuk të lanë me zanë vend në vorr; nuk të duron vorri mbrenda po ta keshë ba ketë gjynah'. (Removing the stone [marking the] border [is such a crime that it] does not allow you to find a place in a grave; even the earth cannot accept you for committing such a sin.) Kolë Shtjefni, *Mirdita: Doke dhe Zakone* (Tiranë, 1998), pp.164–67.

[25] BOA, Y.PRK.MŞ 5/9, 7 Safer 1311 [20 August 1893].

[26] Similar patterns of thought were charted in the British Empire. See Uday Singh Mehta, Liberalism and Empire: A Study in Nineteenth-century British Liberal Thought (Chicago, 1999).

[27] See Antonio Baldacci, *Itinerari albanesi (1892–1902)* (Rome, 1917), pp.23–31.

[28] For an explanation of how this principle was to be applied in Africa and Australia respectively, consult PRO FO 84/1813, E. Hertslet, 'Memorandum on the formalities necessary for the effective annexation of territory', 18 October 1884, 246–266 and PRO FO 84/1814, Anderson Memo, 27 October 1884, f. 67–69.

[29] BOA, MV 81/42, 4 Rebiyülevvel 1312 [5 September 1894].

[30] BOA, Y.PRK.MYD 6/92, 9 C. 1305 [25 December 1887].

[31] It was not only the Ottoman state that collated the potential wealth of their territories in the *Salname*; rival imperial states collected economic data as well. For an example of how the French consul surveyed the Mirdita forests and then lobbied Paris to send investors to exploit the Catholic territories, see: Archives du Ministère des Affaires Étrangeres (AMAE), Nantes, MAE Embassy Constantinople, Consular Report no. 4, Le Rée à Comte de Montebello, dated Scutari, 3 April 1889.

[32] See Pal Pjetër Doçi, *Imzot Prend Doci, Abati i Mirditës: Jeta dhe Vepra* (Tiranë, 1997).

[33] See ASMAE, Ambass 220, summary of contract between Simini and the Skurai community, signed A. Brict (chief engineer of the *vilayet* of Işkodra) and A. Dagna, dated Scutari, 8 November 1908.

[34] By 1910, Bid Doda Pasha was on a first-name basis with Italian foreign ministry officials. A collection of his letters discussing his haggling with Italian and Austrian companies suggests that he was clearly in control of his region's resources. ASMAE Ambass 220, no. 4848, Bid Doda Pasha to Llima, 3 November 1910.

[35] Locals considered trees as so valuable that they refused to exploit their resources for the construction of amenities such as aqueducts that a priest proposed to improve their fields' annual yield. According to a British traveler to the region of Shala in Malësia e

Madhe, community debates around the cutting of 100 trees to construct a school were strained and traumatic, as they pitted local notions of security (trees provided food for livestock and shelter for people) against an investment in the future education of unborn children. Kujtim Ymeri, *Majat e Shalës: Një Kronikë e Disa Udhëtimeve midis Fiseve Malësore te Shqipërisë* (Tiranë, 2004), p.138.

[36] BOA, YA.RES 20/19, dated Vienna, 16 Cemaziyelahir 1300 [24 April 1883]. Prenk Bid Doda would soon be the center of many debates over his role as appointed *mutassarıf* of Lebanon to replace the deceased Vasa Pasha, another Northern Albanian Catholic who successfully instigated reforms in the province.

[37] It is clear that Doda Pasha similarly supported the construction of access roads into the forests to harvest the lumber (*kereste*) he controlled. BBA, Dahiliye Nezâreti (DH MUI) 92–1/22, copy of telegraph, 27 Rebiyülevvel 1328 [8 April 1910].

[38] The Roshfol Company was actively seeking to build a railroad from Draç to harvest the forests in the region. BOA, YA.RES 108/27, 16 Rebiyülahir 1318 [14 July 1900], and Yıldız Tasnifi Mütenevvi Mâruzât Evrakı (henceforth Y.MTV) 215/34, War Ministry report no. 195, 4 Safer 1319 [23 May 1901].

[39] See the initial letter reporting on Carbonne's activities in the Draç region where he and two other investors were apparently making headway in obtaining the requested concession. ASMAE, Ambass. 107, dated Durazzo, 15 December 1900. By late 1901, these negotiations had advanced to a stage at which the extent of the concession was under discussion. ASMAE, Ambass. 107, no. 401/15, Consul to Ambassador in Istanbul, dated Scutari, 5 October 1901.

[40] For details on the clash between Carbonne and Ziya and Celal, see BOA, Y.MTV 221/52, Ministry of Mines and Forest report, dated Istanbul, 9 Recep 1319 [22 October 1901].

[41] An army commission was ordered to inspect the feasibility of a railroad to connect the source with the coastline. BOA, Y.MTV 212/9, Commission Approval Report no. 513, dated 9 Zilhicce 1318 [30 March 1901].

Educating the Nation: Migration and Acculturation on the Two Shores of the Aegean at the Turn of the Twentieth Century (Vangelis Kechriotis), pp. 139–156

[1] Fundamental in this respect is the critical account by Reşat Kasaba, 'Was there a comprador bourgeoisie in mid-nineteenth century Western Anatolia?' *Review* xi, 2 (1988), pp.215–30. Kasaba was also involved in the 'Research Working Group on the Ottoman Empire and the World Economy', coordinated by Ç. Keyder and I. Wallerstein, which eventually published the special issue *Port-Cities of the Eastern Mediterranean, 1800–1914 Review* xvi, 4 (1993)].

[2] In this respect, the debate had already been initiated in Steven Rosenthal, 'Foreigners and municipality reform in Istanbul', *International Journal of Middle Eastern Studies* xi/2 (1980), pp.245–77. For a more recent account, see: Nora Lafi, 'Introduction: Municipalités méditerranéennes–pratique du comparatisme, lecture des changements institutionnels et analyse historique de l'évolution des pouvoirs urbains du XVIIIe au XXe siècle', in Nora Lafi (ed), *Municipalités méditerranéennes: Les réformes urbaines ottomanes au miroir d'une histoire comparée (Moyen-Orient, Maghreb, Europe méridionale)* (Berlin, 2005), pp.11–36.

[3] François Georgeon and Paul Dumont (ed), *Villes Ottomanes à la fin de l'Empire* (Paris, 1992), and *Vivre dans l'Empire Ottoman: Sociabilités et relations intercommunautaires (XVIIIe–XXe siècles)* (Paris, 1997) have set the state of the art until today.

[4] See, for instance, Çağlar Keyder, 'Peripheral port-cities and politics on the eve of the Great War', New Perspectives on Turkey 20 (1998); Katerina Trimi-Kirou, 'Quel cosmopolitisme à l'ère des nationalismes? Le cas d'Alexandrie', *Cahiers de la Méditerranée*, 67 (2003); Hervé Georgelin, *La fin du Smyrne: Du cosmopolitisme aux nationalismes* (Paris, 2005).

[5] Anthropologists first used the term 'acculturation' in the 1930s to describe 'phenomena which result when groups of individuals having different cultures come into continuous first hand contact with subsequent changes in the original culture patterns of either or both groups'. See R. Redfield, R. Linton, and M. Herskowits, 'Memorandum for the study of acculturation', *American Anthropologist* 38 (1936), p.149. In 1954, the Social Science Research Council revised the concept of acculturation, underlining the terms 'change' and

'adaptation'. See SSRC, 'Acculturation: An exploratory formulation', *American Anthropologist* 56 (1954), p.974. The traditional definition presupposes the transition from a tradition-oriented state to an elite-acultured stage. See L. Spindler and G Spindler, 'Male and female adaptations in culture change: Menomini', in R. Hunt (ed), *Personalities and Cultures* (New York, 1967), pp.56–78. Contemporary social research claims that acculturation is not a linear process and, indeed, assimilation, which is used interchangeably with acculturation, might take several generations. Recently, acculturation has been employed in debates related to racial, ethnic or cultural identities. Without going into the vast literature regarding those issues, I wish to investigate acculturation from an individual level of analysis and understand the relationship between acculturation, identity and the effects of social change, without labeling a group as a distinct cultural unit. For a comprehensive account, see: Joseph E. Trimble, 'Introduction: Social change and acculturation', in Kevin M. Chun, Pamela Balls Organista and Gerardo Marin (eds), *Acculturation: Advances in Theory, Measurement, and Applied Research* (Washington D.C., 2003), pp.3–13.

[6] I would like to thank Malte Fuhrmann, with whom I have shared many of the considerations here during the preparation of the workshop 'The Late Ottoman Port-Cities and Their Inhabitants: Subjectivity, Urbanity, and Conflicting Orders' that took place in the frame of the Seventh Mediterranean Meeting at the European University Institute in Florence, 23–25 March 2007.

[7] Daniel Goffman, *İzmir and the Levantine World, 1550–1650* (Seattle, 1990), pp.145–46.

[8] Reşat Kasaba, 'İzmir', *Port-Cities of the Eastern Mediterranean, 1800–1914*, Review xvi/4 (1993), pp.387–410, esp. 395.

[9] Kasaba, 'İzmir', pp.397–98.

[10] Kasaba, 'İzmir', pp.400–1.

[11] Marie-Carmen Smyrnelis, 'Smyrne au XIX siècle, organization et utilisation de l'éspace urbain', Πρακτικά συνεδρίου: Η πόλη στους νεότερους χρόνους (Conference: The City in Modern Times), EMNE- MNIMON (2000), pp.377–78.

[12] Kasaba, 'İzmir', p.398.

[13] Vassilios Sfyroeras, 'Μεταναστεύσεις και εποικισμοί κυκλαδιτών εις Σμύρνην κατά την τουρκοκρατία' (Migrations and Settlements by Inhabitants of the Cyclades in İzmir during the Ottoman Period), Mikrasiatika Chronika (1963), pp.164–99.

[14] Kasaba, 'İzmir', p.402

[15] See also Elena Frangakis-Syrett, 'Implementation of the 1838 Anglo-Turkish Convention on İzmir's trade: European and minority merchants', New Perspectives on Turkey 7 (1992), pp.91–112.

[16] Kasaba, 'Was there a comprador bourgeoisie?'.

[17] Scholars more preoccupied with proving that this 'bourgeoisie' was not of a 'compradore' character have focused solely on its economic and social aspects Reşat Kasaba, Çağlar Keyder, and Faruk Tabak, 'Eastern Mediterranean port-cities and their bourgeoisies: Merchants, political projects and nation-states', Anniversary issue: The Work of the Fernand Braudel Center, Review x/1 (1986), pp.121–36

[18] The basic argument underpinning this cultural approach is the historical and evolutionary character of 'class', rather than a category fixed in time when approached only through economic and social parameters. See, for instance, Patrick Joyce, *The Self and the Social in Nineteenth-Century England* (Cambridge, 1994). His work has shown how the differences between British workers and bourgeois elites have become less distinct from the point of view of culture.

[19] See, for instance, Jürgen Kocka and Allan Mitchell (eds), *Bourgeois Society in Nineteenth-Century Europe* (New York, 1993). This publication contains the papers delivered at the Bielefeld conference in 1989. This conference constitutes a landmark, since it provided a dialogue between debates on bourgeois culture and its dominance in England, France and Germany. The diversity of views led Kocka to talk about not one, but many 'bourgeois classes', depending on the different formations of 'bourgeois' experience. See also, Jürgen Kocka, 'The middle classes in Europe', *Journal of Modern History*, 67 (1995), pp.783–806.

[20] Pachalis Kitromilides, 'Greek irredentism in Asia Minor and Cyprus', *Middle Eastern Studies* xxvi/1, 1990, pp.3–17; Haris Exertzoglou, 'Shifting boundaries, language, community and the non-Greek-speaking Greeks', *Historein* vol. 1 (1999), pp.75–92.

[21] The term Tanzimat-i Hayriye (Beneficial Reforms) was first used in 1838, in an imperial order by Sultan Mahmut II, whose main concern was to reorganize central power and regenerate the empire. The reforms were inaugurated in 1839, with the Gülhane Hatt-ı Hümayun (Noble Edict of the Rose Garden). The edict established guarantees for the life, honor and property of the sultan's subjects and equality before the law regardless of religion. Further reforms culminated in 1856, after the end of the Crimean War, with the Islahat Fermanı (Reform Edict), which enhanced the promises made in 1839.

[22] Sia Anagnostopoulou, Μικρά Ασία 19os αι–1919 Οι Ελληνορθόδοξες κοινότητες. Από το Μιλλέτ των Ρωμιών στο Ελληνικό Έθνος (Asia Minor, 1900s to 1919: The Greek-Orthodox Communities: From the Rum millet to the Hellenic nation) (Athens, 1998), pp.307–8.

[23] Homi K. Bhabha, 'DissemiNation: Time, narrative and the margins of the modern nation', in H. K. Bhabha (ed), *Nation and Narration* (London, New York, 1990), p.292. Following Hobsbawm's project of writing the history of the modern Western nation from the perspective of the nation's margin and the migrants' exile, Bhabha states his intention to avoid the 'historical certainty and settled nature of the term nationalism and to instead deal with the Western nation'.

[24] The nation is also 'more symbolic than "society", more connotative than "country", less patriotic than *patrie,* more rhetorical than the reason of state, more mythological than ideology, less homogeneous than hegemony, less centered than the citizen, more collective than "the subject", more psychic than civility, more hybrid in the articulation of cultural differences and identifications–gender, race or class–than can be represented in any hierarchical or binary structuring of social antagonism'. Bhabha, *Nation and Narration,* p.293.

[25] Moreover, Bhabha defines the 'cultural construction of nationness' as a form of both 'social and textual affiliation', underlying thus the significance of both the social production of relations and their textual representation. His aim is to investigate the discursive choices and strategies of cultural identification which are implied under the notion of 'people' or 'nation'. In the study of these political entities, which are simultaneously sources of cultural identity, he is focusing on the temporal dimension, demonstrating the divergence in the forms of representation that these entities might entail. Moreover, the displacement of the relevant terminology demonstrates, according to Bhabha, the function of the nation as 'the measure of the liminality of cultural modernity'. Bhabha , *Nation and Narration,* p.294.

[26] See especially Anagnostopoulou, *Asia Minor.*

[27] Pioneering in this respect is Gerasimos Augustinos, *The Greeks of Asia Minor* (Kent, 1992). See also, Erini Renieri, 'Household formation in nineteenth-century Central Anatolia: The case-study of a Turkish-speaking Orthodox Christian community', *International Journal of Middle Eastern Studies* 34 (2002), pp 495–517.

[28] Anagnostopoulou, *Asia Minor,* p.338.

[29] Anagnostopoulou, *Asia Minor,* pp.340–41.

[30] Vangelis Kechriotis, *The Greeks of İzmir at the End of the Empire: A Non-Muslim Ottoman Community between Autonomy and Patriotism* (PhD Dissertation, Leiden University, 2005).

[31] *Mikra Asia* is the Greek term for Asia Minor.

[32] Maria Sideri, 'Οι σύλλογοι ως φορείς της ελληνικής εθνικιστικής ιδεολογίας στα τέλη του 19ου και τις αρχές του 20ου αιώνα. Το παράδειγμα του Συλλόγου Μικρασιατών 'Η Ανατολή' και η συγκρότηση της ελληνικής εθνικής ταυτότητας στις κοινότητες της Μικράς Ασίας' (The associations as vehicles of Greek nationalist ideology at the end of the nineteenth and the beginning of the twentieth century: The example of the association of Mikrasiates 'Anatoli' and the making of Hellenic national identity among the community of Asia Minor) (PhD Dissertation, University of the Aegean, Lesvos, 2003), p.317.

[33] Nikos Milioris, 'Ο Σύλλογος των Μικρασιατών η 'Ανατολή'' (The association of Mikrasiates Anatoli), *Mikrasiatika Hronika* IB (1965), pp.337–67.

[34] Exertzoglou, 'Shifting boundaries'.

[35] Magda M. Kitromilidou, 'Οι Έλληνες της Βιθυνίας και το εθνικό κέντρο, 1898–1903, Ανέκδοτες μαρτυρίες από το αρχείο του συλλόγου 'Ανατολή'' (The Greeks of Vithynia

and the National Center, 1898–1903: Unpublished testimonies from the archive of the association 'Anatoli'), *Deltio Kentrou Mikrasiatikon Spoudon* 8 (1990–91), pp.87–106.

[36] This becomes evident from the correspondence of the association, which has survived in a very well organized archive in the 'Hearth of Smyrniots' in Athens and bears the name 'Archive of the Association Anatoli' (AAA).

[37] Ilias Anagnostakis and Evangelia Balta, *La découverte de la Cappadoce au dix-neuvième siècle* (Istanbul, 1994), pp.17–74.

[38] *Του Μεγαλείου των Αθηνών Θεμελιωταί οι Μικρασιάται, Λόγος Πανηγυρικός απαγγελθείς κατά την ενάτην επέτειον του συλλόγου των μικρασιατών Ανατολής υπό του προέδρου αυτού Μαργαρίτου Ευαγγελίδου* (Mikrasiates as the founders of the grandeur of Athens: Speech on the occasion of the celebration of the ninth anniversary of the Association of People from Asia Minor [Anatoli], delivered by its president Margaritis Evangelidis) (Athens, 1900).

[39] AAA-İzmir, 8 January, 1896.

[40] Vassilios (1834–1910) was of modest social background. He was born in Zagoritsani, near Kastoria (Kasriye) in Macedonia. In 1870, after serving as a Metropolitan in Aghialos for five years, Vassilios was invited to take over the direction of the Theological School of Chalki (Heybeliada). During the conflict between the Patriarchate and the Bulgarian Exarchate, his opponents accused him of being pro-Bulgarian. In 1876, he returned to Aghialos where he stayed until 1884. Then, he was appointed Metropolitan in İzmir. See Adamantios Diamantopoulos, 'Βασίλειος Μητροπολίτης Σμύρνης (1834–1910)' (Vassilios, Metropolitan of Smyrna [1834–1910]), *Mikrasiatika Chronika* 2 (1939), pp.151–66.

[41] Carolidis (1849–1930) was born in Andronikio (Endürlük), near Kayseri, in Cappadocia. He spent his school years in İzmir, studying at the Evangelical School from which he graduated in 1867. He then moved to Athens and studied History at the university there. He completed his studies in Tübingen, where he graduated in 1872. He then taught for two years in Istanbul and between 1875 and 1886 he taught History and Latin at his *alma mater*, the Evangelical School. Finally, in 1886, he was appointed professor of History at the University of Athens. Between 1909 and 1912, he was deputy in the Ottoman parliament. *Amalthia*, 'Βιογραφικά Παύλου Καρολίδου' (Biographical notes on Pavlos Carolidis), 10 November 1908.

[42] Vassilios, Metropolitan of İzmir, to Carolidis, 10 June 1900, Carolidis archive, ELIA (Hellenic Literary and Historical Archive).

[43] AAA-İzmir, 29 February, 1896.

[44] Pavlina Nasioutzik, *Αμερικάνικα Οράματα στη Σμύρνη τον 19° αι. Η συνάντηση της αγγλοσαξωνικής σκέψης με την ελληνική* (American visions in Smyrna in the nineteenth century: the Anglo-Saxon meets Greek thought) (Athens, 2002).

[45] The first girls' school had been established in the Greek-Orthodox hospital after 1830 and, later on, was relocated to the courtyard of the Metropolitan Church of Agia Fotini, from where it took its name, Central Girls' School of Agia Fotini (Κεντρικόν Παρθεναγωγείον της Αγίας Φωτεινής). However, since it was not a boarding school, the Central Girls' School could not accommodate girls from the surrounding regions. These found refuge in the missionary schools. Therefore, in 1881 the Association for the Promotion of Education (Φιλεκπαιδευτική Εταιρεία) founded the first Girls' Boarding School which in 1886 was renamed Omirion (Ομήρειον Παρθεναγωγείον). Both of them were ultimately recognized as equivalent to the most famous Girls' School in Greece, namely Arsakion (Αρσάκειον).

[46] AAA-İzmir, 2 July 1900.

[47] The religious association Efsevia was founded by Vassilios in 1892. One of the main issues that such associations wished to resolve was the 'moral degradation' of the clergy. In February 1905, Vassileios announced in a circular that Efsevia had been assigned the payroll of diocese priests. Therefore, the tychera ('voluntary' contributions on the occasion of baptisms, weddings and so forth) would be abolished henceforth. Moreover, special care was given to the mission of ensuring higher education for young priests in Is-

tanbul or Kiev, who upon their return would preach in the churches. Efsevia also established Sunday schools in many neighborhoods. Christos Solomonidis, Ο Σμύρνης Χρυσόστομος (Chrysostomos of Smyrna) (Athens,1993), p.89.

[48] AAA-İzmir, 10 August 1900.

[49] AAA-İzmir, 22 September 1900.

[50] AAA-İzmir, 18 October 1900.

[51] AAA-İzmir, 24 August 1904.

[52] AAA-İzmir, 17 August 1904.

[53] AAA-İzmir, 24 October 1900.

[54] AAA-İzmir, 16 September 1904.

[55] AAA-İzmir, 1 October 1904.

[56] AAA-İzmir, 28 August 1904.

[57] AAA-İzmir, 21 August 1901.

[58] AAA-İzmir, 18 March 1900.

[59] AAA-İzmir, 22 April 1900.

[60] AAA-İzmir, 26 September 1902.

[61] A job at the Evangelical School was the most prestigious choice that an instructor could opt for. The salaries were also obviously higher than in smaller towns. An interesting aspect of the efforts of the young instructor was that he also tried to bring along his sister who was still studying in Sparti. AAA-İzmir, 28 August 1901.

[62] AAA-İzmir, 27 August 1903.

[63] AAA-İzmir, 5 July 1904.

[64] AAA-İzmir, 9 July 1904.

[65] AAA-İzmir, 11 August 1904.

[66] AAA-İzmir, 16 August 1904.

[67] AAA-İzmir, 23 August 1904.

[68] AAA-İzmir, 13 July 1904.

[69] He was most probably the nephew of Minas Chamoudopoulos, a well-known journalist, secretary of the Patriarchate, and member of the first Ottoman parliament.

[70] AAA-İzmir, 16 June 1904.

[71] AAA-İzmir, 23 July 1904.

[72] AAA-İzmir, 31 July 1904.

[73] AAA-İzmir, 14 November 1900.

[74] AAA-İzmir, 15 October 1901. This particular request was not met, however.

[75] AAA-İzmir, 15 January 1902.

[76] AAA-İzmir, 13 September 1902. An interesting element of these letters is that, despite the fact that there were no grammatical mistakes; syntax is of a very low quality. This might lead to the conclusion that Oulkeroglu was a turcophone and dictated his letters to someone who was directly translating, without making any mistakes in orthography.

[77] He was the brother of Apostolos Psaltoff, a well-known medical doctor. Both brothers had studied in Athens and probably are typical examples of Hellenic acculturation in their respective fields. See Vangelis Kechriotis, 'Between professional duty and national fulfillment: The Smyrniot medical doctor Apostolos Psaltoff (1862–1923)', in Meropi Anastassiadou (ed), *Médecins et ingénieurs ottomans à l'age des nationalismes* (Paris, 2003), pp.331–48.

[78] The purpose of *Omirion* was to offer a 'Christian and Hellenic education'. Yet, it also promoted the instruction of the foreign languages more widely used in the city, namely French and English. It was obvious that there was an urgent need to prevent Greek girls from attending missionary schools, either Catholic or Protestant, where their Greek upbringing was considered in great peril.

[79] AAA-İzmir, 20 August 1904.

[80] AAA-İzmir, 20 August 1904.

[81] AAA-İzmir, 3 May 1905.

[82] Interestingly, in the text the two terms that refer to the same geography are used next to each other.

83 AAA-İzmir, 3 May 1905.
84 AAA-İzmir, 26 November 1900.
85 Λόγος εκφωνηθείς εν τω Ομήρειω τη 12 Μαΐου 1896 υπό Κ. Ν.Ψαλτώφ, εν Σμύρνη, (Speech delivered at Omirion, on May 12, 1896, by C.N.Psaltoff), İzmir, 1896, p.16.
86 AAA-İzmir, 27 September 1903.
87 AAA-İzmir, 25 June 1903.
88 AAA-İzmir, 1 July 1904.
89 AAA-İzmir, 16 August 1904.
90 AAA-İzmir, 8 April, 20 April, 21 May, 7 June, 2 July 1904. The name of the author of the letters is not clear. Probably it was Melakopidis.
91 AAA-İzmir, A. S. Anastasiadis, 22 April 1905.
92 AAA-İzmir, 1 September 1904.
93 AAA-İzmir, 1 September 1904.
94 Haris Exertzoglou, Εθνική ταυτότητα στην Κωνσταντινούπολη τον 19° αιώνα. Ο Ελληνικός Φιλολογικός Σύλλογος Κωνσταντινούπολης 1861–1912 (National identity in Constantinople in the nineteenth century: The Greek Philological Association of Constantinople, 1861–1912) (Athens, 1996). [Turkish: Osmanlı'da Cemiyetler ve Rum Cemaati: Dersaadet Rum Cemiyet-i Edebiyesi (Istanbul, 2004)].

Global Networks, Regional Hegemony, and
Seaport Modernization on the Lower Danube (Constantin Iordachi), pp. 157–182

1 Winfried Baumgart, The Crimean War, 1853–1856 (London, Sydney, Auckland), pp.111–12.
2 For the growing political and commercial interest in the Lower Danube after the Crimean War, see mainly Major J. Stokes, 'Notes on the Lower Danube', Proceedings of the Royal Geographic Society of London iii/4 (1858), pp.206–8; Major J. Stokes, 'Notes on the Lower Danube', Journal of the Royal Geographic Society of London xxx/4 (1860), pp.162–71; Edward Suess, 'The Danube', The Geographic Journal 37 (1911), pp.642–45.
3 See, in this respect, the scholarly initiative of the Duke University entitled 'Oceans Connect: Culture, Capital, and Commodity Flows across Basins', having four main components: the Indian Ocean, the Black and Caspian 'Eurasian Seas', the Mediterranean and the Atlantic Ocean. For a brief presentation of this initiative and its scholarly implications, see Martin Lewis and Karen W. Wigen, 'A maritime response to the crisis in area studies', Geographical Review 89 (1999), pp.161–68. For the history of port-cities as an example of transnational history, see Michael Miller, 'Comparative and Cross-National History: Approaches, Differences, Problems', in Deborah Cohen, Maura O'Connor (eds), Comparison and History. Europe in Cross-National Perspective (New York, 2004), pp.115–32.
4 Richard Lawton and Robert Lee (eds), Population and Society in Western European Port-Cities, c. 1650–1939 (Liverpool, 2002).
5 On these structural transformations, see: Giovanni Arrighi, Iftikhar Ahmand and Miin-wen Shih, 'Western Hegemonies in World-Historical Perspective', in Giovanni Arrighi and Beverly J. Silver with Iftikhar Ahmad (eds), Chaos and Governance in the Modern World System (Minneapolis, 1999), pp.217–70.
6 On this point, see Çağlar Keyder, Y. Eyüp Özveren and Donald Quataert, 'Port cities in the Ottoman Empire: Some theoretical and historical perspectives', Special Issue: Port Cities of the Eastern Mediterranean, 1800–1914, Review xvi/4 (1993), pp.519–58.
7 Neal Ascherson, Black Sea (New York, 1995).
8 Michel Balard, La mer Noire et la Romanie génoise, XIIIe–XVe siècles (London, 1989).
9 On cosmopolitanism in Mediterranean port-cities, see Henk Driessen, 'Mediterranean port cities: Cosmopolitanism reconsidered', History and Anthropology 16 (2005), pp.129–41. Based on a comparison between İzmir, Alexandria and Trieste, Driessen argues that 'there is an ecological dimension to the Mediterranean cosmopolitics' and that 'the port city is one of its probable niches'.
10 For a comparative overview over the industrial history of ports during the last two hundred years, with an emphasis on the chronology of construction and their urban im-

pact, see: Henk Van Dijk and Magda Avelar Pinheiro, 'The changing face of European ports as a result of their evolving use since the nineteenth century', *Portuguese Journal of Social Science* ii/2 (2003), pp.89–103.

[11] Gheorghe Brătianu, *La mer Noire, des origines à la conquête ottomane* (Monachii, 1969). See also his *Recherches sur le commerce génois dans la mer Noire au XIIIe siècle* (Paris, 1929).

[12] More recently, the area was subject to comprehensive research. See Charles King, *The Black Sea: A History* (Oxford, 2004).

[13] 'Turkey (From our own correspondent)', *The Times*, 5 Jun 1860, p.10.

[14] 'Turkey (News) (From our own correspondent)', *The Times*, 26 February 1855, p. 9. On John Trevor Barkley's vision on the development of the Lower Danube and his political view, see the series of articles he published in *The Times*, among which I mention selectively: 'The value of the Danube as an outlet of European commerce (Letters to the editor)', *The Times*, 24 June 1878, p.4,; 'The Varna Railway and the Berlin Treaty (Letters to the editor)', *The Times*, 10 July 1879, p. 9; 'Romania: A Chapter of modern history (Letters to the editor)', *The Times*, 25 April 1878, p.4; 'Why the Berlin Treaty and the Anglo–Turkish convention should be acceptable to Russia (Letters to the editor)', *The Times*, 31 July 1878, p.11.

[15] See 'Approval for the construction of a railway from the Black Sea to the Danube to Barklay and associates, all Englishmen, Abdul Medji' in 'Two testimonies about the beginning of the Romanian railway history: An imperial edict and a postage stamp', *The Railway Journal*, available at http://www.cfr.ro/JF/engleza/2000_6/testimonies.htm. Note the appropriation of the railway –a product of the Ottoman project of modernization executed with British capital– to the Romanian railway history.

[16] 'Turkey (News) (From our own correspondent)', *The Times*, 9 October 1858, p.8.

[17] On the history and motivation of building railways in the Ottoman Empire and Turkey, see: L.D., 'Railroads in Turkey', *Bulletin of the American Geographical Society* xlvii/12 (1915), pp.934–40; and John Kolars, Henry J. Malin, 'Population and accessibility: An analysis of Turkish railroads', *Geographical Review* lx/2 (1970), pp.229–46. It is striking that the authors of the later article fail to mention the Dobrudja railway.

[18] 'Turkey (From our own correspondent)', *The Times*, 16 October 1860, p.8.

[19] 'Turkey (From our own correspondent)', *The Times*, 16 October 1860, p.8.

[20] 'Turkey (From our own correspondent)', *The Times*, 16 October 1860, p.8.

[21] Donald Quataert, *The Ottoman Empire, 1700–1922* (Cambridge, 2000), p.115.

[22] *The Encyclopedia of Islam* (Leiden, 1965), vol.6, p.613.

[23] See Kemal Karpat, 'Ottoman urbanism: The Crimean Tatar emigration to Dobrujda and the founding of Mecidiye, 1856–1878', *International Journal of Turkish Studies* 3 (1984–85), pp.1–25.

[24] See Rifaat A. Abou-el-Haj, 'The formal closure of the Ottoman Frontier in Europe, 1699–1703', *Journal of the American Oriental Society* lxxxix/9 (1969), pp.467–75.

[25] 'The Wheat Trade in The Provinces of The Lower Danube', p.5.

[26] John Trevor Barkley, 'The value of the Danube as an outlet of European commerce (Letters to the editor)', *The Times*, 24 June 1878, p.4.

[27] Paul Gogeanu, *Dunărea în relaţiile internaţionale* (Bucharest, 1970), pp.39–40.

[28] See 'The Russians have taken a small fort from the Turks, situated on an island in the Danube', *The Times*, 30 May 1791, p.3; 'Engagements between the Turks and Russians', *The Times*, 13 August 1791, p.3; 'Army of the Danube', *The Times*, 24 May 1799, p.2.

[29] See 'From the Danube, Dec. 8.', *The Times*, 14 January 1807, p.3; 'Banks of the Danube, April 3', *The Times*, 5 May 1808, p.3; 'The steam navigation on the Danube', *The Times*, 28 December 1842, p.6; E.V. Rippinggill, 'The mouth of the Danube (Letters to the editor)', *The Times*, 23 August 1852, p.5; G. Orange, 'The Danube (Letters to the editor)', *The Times*, 26 August 1852, p.8; V. Rippinggill, 'The navigation of the Danube (Letters to the editor)', *The Times*, 16 August 1853, p.9; W. Francis Alnsworth, *et. al.*, 'The mouths of the Danube (Letters to the editor)', *The Times*, 24 August 1853, p.8; *The Times*, 2 May 1854, p.9; 'The Danube (From our special correspondent)', *The Times*, 16 July 1855, p.8; 'Vi-

enna, the Danube, and Odessa (Letters to the editor)', *The Times*, 2 November 1871, p.6; 'Between the Danube and the Black Sea', *The Times*, 11 November 1876, p.6.

[30] See 'Commerce of the Danube', *The Times*, 24 December 1839, p.5; and 'The wheat trade in the provinces of the Lower Danube (News)', *The Times*, 27 July 1840, p.5.

[31] 'The wheat trade in the provinces of the Lower Danube', p.5.

[32] 'Commerce of the Danube', p.5.

[33] 'Commerce of the Danube', p.5.

[34] 'Commerce of the Danube', p.5.

[35] 'Commerce of the Danube', p.5.

[36] See Richard C. Frucht, *Dunarea Noastra: Romania, the Great Powers, and the Danube Question, 1914–1921* (Boulder, New York, 1982). See also Dan Berindei, 'La question du Danube et la Roumanie Moderne (1829–1918)', *Revue Roumaine d'Etudes Internationales* xx/6 (1986), pp.563–72.

[37] Frucht, *Dunarea Noastra*.

[38] On the international regime of the Danube, see *Rapport de la Commission technique internationale convoquée à Paris pour l'examen des questions relatives à l'amélioration des bouches du Danube* (Paris, 1858); Great Britain Parliament, *Treaties and other documents relating to the navigation of the Danube: 1856–1875* (London, 1878); Edward Krehbiel, 'The European Commission of the Danube: An experiment in international administration', *Political Science Quarterly* xxxiii/1 (1918), pp.38–55; 'Provisions concerning the neutralization of the Black Sea and Danube River contained in the General Treaty between Great Britain, Austria, France, Prussia, Russia, Sardinia, and Turkey', *The American Journal of International Law* iii/2 (1909), pp.114–16; Otto Popper, 'The international regime of the Danube', *The Geographical Journal* 102 (1943), pp.240–53. For the activity of the Commission, see the self-congratulating work entitled *La Commission européenne du Danube et son œuvre du 1856 à 1931* (Paris, 1933).

[39] Captain R.N. Spratt, *Report on the Danube of the Danube. Plans and Sections* (London, 1857), p.9.

[40] Commission Européenne du Danube, *Statistique de la Navigation à l'embouchure du Danube pour 1866*, p.2.

[41] *La Commission européenne du Danube*, p.514.

[42] Grigore Antipa, *Dunărea și problemele ei științifice, economice și politice* (Bucharest, 1921).

[43] See the diplomatic correspondence in: Archives diplomatiques du ministère des Affaires étrangères, Nantes, Serie Turquie, Constantinople.

[44] For a detailed treatment of Romania's policies of integrating and assimilating Dobrudja, see: Constantin Iordachi, *Citizenship, Nation and State-Building: The Integration of Northern Dobrogea in Romania, 1878–1913* (Pittsburgh, 2002).

[45] Frucht, *Dunarea Noastra*, p.23.

[46] Ion C. Brătianu, *Acte si cuvîntări* (Bucharest, 1939), vol.4, p.144.

[47] Mihail Kogălniceanu, *Opere, vol. 4: Oratorie II, 1864–1878*, ed. Georgeta Penelea (Bucharest, 1977), vol. 1, p.620.

[48] Nicolas Petresco-Comnène, 'La Dobrogea et la vie économique de la Roumanie', in *La Dobrogea* (Paris, 1918), p.186.

[49] See P.S. Aurelian, *Opere economice* (Bucharest, 1967), p.199; 'Inființarea unui serviciu național de navigație', *Economia națională* 11 (1887), pp.1153–57.

[50] Brătianu continues 'we will spend 16, 20 or 25 more millions, as much as it takes to build the necessary seaport and bridge over the Danube, but this will be the best proof that we are a powerful nation and that on us depends the future of the entire Orient', *Acte si cuvîntări*, vol.7, p.276.

[51] Barkley, 'The value of the Danube', p.4.

[52] Barkley, 'The value of the Danube', p.4.

[53] M. D. Ionescu, *Dobrogea în pragul veacului al XX-lea* (Bucharest, 1904), p.540.

[54] M. D. Ionescu, *Dobrogea în pragul veacului al XX-lea* (Bucharest, 1904), p.540.

[55] Alexandru Rădulescu, Ioan Bitoleanu, *Istoria românilor dintre Dunăre și Mare: Dobrogea* (Bucharest, 1979), 295; see also Valentin Ciorbea, 'Preocupari privind

modernizarea şi transformarea portului Constanţa în port national, 1878–1900', *Revista Istorică* 11–12 (1990), pp.1005–13.

[56] Petresco-Comnène, *La Dobrogea*, p.137.

[57] Vasile Kogălniceanu, *Dobrogea, 1895–1909: Drepturi politice fără libertăti* (Bucharest, 1910), p.105.

[58] Ionescu: *Dobrogea în pragul*, p.929.

[59] Andre Gunder Frank, *The Development of Underdevelopment* (Indianapolis, 1969).

[60] Kogălniceanu, *Dobrogea, 1895–1909*, pp.101–2.

[61] Kogălniceanu, *Dobrogea, 1895–1909*, pp.101–2.

[62] Petru Zaharia and Lenuţa Gherasim, 'Situaţia economică a judetului Tulcea în anii 1878–1916', *Peuce* ix (1984), pp.401–7.

[63] Kogălniceanu, *Dobrogea, 1895–1909*, pp.101–2.

[64] Sabin Manuilă, 'La population du Dobroudja', in *La Dobroudja Roumaine* (Bucharest, 1938), p.188.

[65] Manuilă: 'La population', p.188.

[66] Luca Ionescu, *Judeţul Tulcea: Dare de seamă prezentată consiliului judeţean* (Bucharest, 1904), p.363.

[67] Carmen Atanasiu, 'Activitatea României pentru desfiinţarea Comisiei Europene a Dunării', *Analele Dobrogei* vi/1 (2000), pp.281–92.

[68] Nicolae Titulescu, *Discursuri* (Bucharest, 1967), p.547, cited in: Atanasiu: 'Activitatea României', p.285.

[69] See David T. Cattell, 'The politics of the Danube Commission under Soviet control', *American Slavic and East European Review* xix/3 (1960), pp.380–94.

[70] Adrian Rădulescu, Ion Bitoleanu, *Istoria Dobrogei* (Constanţa, 1998), p.451.

[71] Today, the commission includes eleven member states, namely Austria, Bulgaria, Croatia, Germany, Hungary, Moldova, Romania, Russia, Serbia, Slovakia, and Ukraine. See its home page at http://www.danubecom-intern.org.

[72] John C. Campbell, 'Diplomacy on the Danube', *Foreign Affairs*, xxvii/2 (1949), pp.315–27.

[73] Constantin Iordachi, '"Constanţă, prima regiune colectivizată": Colectivizare şi propagandă în Dobrogea, 1949–1962', in Dorin Dobrincu, Constantin Iordachi (eds), *Ţărănimea şi puterea: Procesul de colectivizare a agriculturii în România, 1949–1962* (Iaşi, 2005), pp.178–209.

[74] See, in this respect, the report on the issue prepared for Ottoman authorities by an appointed team of Austrian engineers: 'Projected canal between the Danube and the Black Sea', *The Times*, 30 August 1855, p.9.

[75] Nicolas Spulber, 'The Danube–Black Sea canal and the Russian control over the Danube', *Economic Geography* 30 (1954), pp.236–45.

[76] With the collapse of the communist regime, the project was abandoned due to its high costs and negative environmental impact.

[77] See the website of Constanţa port at http://www.portofconstantza.com/.

[78] Monica Iordache, 'Sulina–oraşul încremenit', *Jurnalul Naţional* (28 June 2004), available at http://www.jurnalul.ro/stire-descoperirea-romaniei/28-iunie-2004-sulina-sulina-orasul-incremenit-66181.html.

[79] Giovanni Arrighi, 'The rise of East Asia and the withering away of the interstate system', *Journal of World-Systems Research*, ii/15 *(1996), p.17.*

[80] On the Ukraine, see its project to build its own Danube–Black Sea canal on the Kilia and Bystroye branches of the Danube, with the declared aim of braking Romania's 'monopoly' on Lower Danubian navigation. Initiated in 2004, the project's implementation was slowed down by domestic and international concerns over ecological damage.

[81] Hristo Marinov, Reinhold Castenson, 'The Danube–Rhine water system as a European regional integration structure', *European Planning Studies* v/2 (1997), pp.241–55.

[82] The Black Sea Economic Cooperation was established in 1992 as a regional initiative proposed by Turkey and joined by eleven founding nations; since 1998, it has been developed into a fully fledged organization. See Roberto Aliboni, 'Globalization and the wider Black Sea area: Interaction with the European Union, Eastern Mediterranean and

the Middle East', and Marius Vahl, Sergiu Celac, 'Ready for a breakthrough: Elements for a European Union strategy towards the Black Sea region', *Journal of Southeast European and Black Sea Studies*, vi/2 (2006), pp.157–68 and 169–91, respectively.

Competition as Rivalry: İzmir during the Great Depression (Eyüp Özveren and Erkan Gürpınar), pp. 183–197

[1] *Türkiye Cumhuriyeti İzmir Ticaret ve Sanayi Odası Mecmuası/Republique Turque: Bulletin de la Chambre de Commerce et d'Industrie de Smyrne* (Bulletin of the Chamber of Commerce and Industry), March 1930, p.240.

[2] The bulletin of the Chamber of Commerce reported that, according to the statistics dated 1927, total seaborne exports of the region was 99,493,408 *lira*s, yielding a per capita value of 42 *lira*s and 53 *kuruş*. The same region's total value of imports was 33,531,718 Lira, implying a per capita value of 14 *lira*s and 33 *kuruş*. *İzmir Ticaret ve Sanayi Odası Mecmuası*, April 1929, p.101.

[3] Çağlar Keyder, Eyüp Özveren, and Donald Quataert, 'Port-cities in the Ottoman Empire: Some theoretical and historical perspectives', *Review* xvi/4 (1993), p.546.

[4] Robert B. Ekelund, Jr., and Robert F. Hébert, *A History of Economic Theory and Method* (New York, 1990), pp.571–73.

[5] Tarık Dursun K., *Gâvur İzmir, Güzel İzmir* (Istanbul, 2004), p.55.

[6] İzmir depended on the radio transmission of news for making up for this lag to a certain extent. An İzmir-born writer recollects how at a time during the Second World War, when radios were still considered a luxury, people gathered in coffee shops in order to listen to the news. He recounts how a well-to-do wholesale fruit and vegetable dealer residing in their neighborhood opened up his windows so that the public could benefit from the news broadcast of his living-room radio. See Dursun, *Gâvur İzmir*, p.149.

[7] A further consequence of this relative isolation and maintenance of a local press has been the long-term continuation of İzmir's cultural regionalism, if not outright provincialism.

[8] This newspaper was an offshoot of *Asır* (The Century) which was first published in 1895 in another Ottoman port-city, namely Salonica. *Asır* had changed its name to *Yeni Asır* after the Young Turk Revolution of 1908. After a brief period of publication in Istanbul, the newspaper finally moved to İzmir in 1924. See Turan Akkoyun, 'Atatürk dönemi İzmir basınının genel durumu', in Tuncer Baykara (ed), *Son Yüzyıllarda İzmir ve Batı Anadolu* (İzmir: 1994), p.241.

[9] Eyüp Özveren, 'Türkiye'de yaygın iktisat: Nereden nereye?', in Ahmet Haşim Köse, Fikret Şenses, Erinç Yeldan (eds), *İktisat Üzerine Yazılar II: İktisadi Kalkınma, Kriz ve İstikrar: Oktar Türel'e Armağan* (Istanbul: 2003), pp.175–89.

[10] İzmir's Chamber of Commerce, originally founded in 1885, was inspired by the semi-formal exclusivist associations of resident foreign merchants in the city. As it attained a mature form, it involved the active participation of merchants of various ethnic and religious backgrounds, thus befitting the cosmopolitanism of an Eastern Mediterranean port-city. After 1926, it gained new momentum under the leadership of Turkish merchants.

[11] Erkan Serçe, 'Osmanlı'dan cumhuriyet'e İzmir Ticaret Odası', in *Ondokuzuncu Yüzyıldan Yirmibirinci Yüzyıla İzmir Ticaret Odası Tarihi* (İzmir, 2002), p.102.

[12] R. Funda Barbaros, *1830–1930 Döneminde Sosyo-Ekonomik Çözüm Arayışları Çerçevesinde İzmir'de Sanayileşme* (İzmir, 1995), pp.61–62.

[13] 48 pages of the first issue appeared in Turkish and 28 in French. The front cover of the journal included a map of İzmir and its western Anatolian hinterland, as well as the full title, *Türkiye Cumhuriyeti İzmir Ticaret ve Sanayi Odası Mecmuası*. The pictures of the twelve most important export items, namely, tobacco, raisins, figs, cotton, valonia oak, licorice, opium, carpets, barley, horse beans, sesame, and pine nuts encircled the map. The back cover had the same layout, with the French title *Republique Turque: Bulletin de la Chambre de Commerce et d'Industrie de Smyrne*. Within the same year the number of subscribers reached some three-hundred and steadily increased afterwards. See Serçe, 'Osmanlı'dan cumhuriyet'e', pp.101–3.

[14] Eyüp Özveren, 'Büyük buhran'da bir liman kenti: İzmir 1929–1932', *İzmir Kent Kültürü Dergisi*, 6 (2003a), p.267.

NOTES

239

[15] In the eighteenth and early nineteenth century, French and English consuls serving in the Eastern Mediterranean ports were appointed by the Chamber of Commerce of Marseilles and the Levant Company respectively. They used to supply their headquarters regularly with information on trade. We might as well infer that the informants of İzmir's Chamber of Commerce who prepared these reports in the wake of the Great Depression replicated in reverse the previous function of these European consuls.

[16] Daniel Goffman, *İzmir and the Levantine World, 1550–1650* (Seattle, 1990).

[17] Reşat Kasaba, 'İzmir', *Review* xvi/4 (1993), pp.387–410.

[18] Vedat Eldem, *Osmanlı İmparatorluğu'nun İktisadi Şartları Hakkında Bir Tetkik* (Ankara, 1994), p.109.

[19] Serçe, 'Osmanlı'dan Cumhuriyet'e', pp.55–58.

[20] Doktor Nazım Bey cited in: Zafer Toprak, *Türkiye'de "Milli İktisat" (1908–1918)* (Ankara, 1982), p.411.

[21] Yahya Sezai Tezel, *Cumhuriyet Döneminin İktisadi Tarihi (1923–1950)* (Ankara, 1982), pp.135–39.

[22] See Özveren, 'Büyük buhran'da bir liman kenti'.

[23] In order to compare the current economic state of İzmir and its environs with the pre-war period, the bulletin of the Chamber of Commerce compiled statistics with which we can construct the tables below, by calculating imports and exports in terms of Ottoman and Turkish *lira*s and pounds sterling approximately.

Year	Exports in Liras	Exports in Pound Sterling	Imports in Liras	Imports in Pounds Sterling
1911	65,805,693	6,467,390	51,246,286	5,036,490
1913	67,179,281	6,602,386	53,680,988	5,275,581
1926	75,592,444	8,084,753	33,530,000	3,586,096
1927	99,493,408	10,461,978	36,000,000	3,785,489
1928	80,812,778	8,444,386	38,000,000	3,970,742

1 gold *lira* was on average equal to 9 *lira*s and 25 *kuruş*, that is, a quarter. The conversion from Gold *lira* to Ottoman *lira* for the years 1911 and 1913 was quoted by the bulletin itself. One Pound Sterling equaled 1.1 Ottoman gold *lira* for 1911 and 1913. See Şevket Pamuk, *Osmanlı İmparatorlugu'nda Paranın Tarihi* (Istanbul, 1999), p.226. The conversion rates for 1926, 1927, 1928 are taken as 9.35, 9.51, 9.57, respectively, from Tezel, *Cumhuriyet Döneminin İktisadi Tarihi*, p.172. In any case, as the bulletin concluded, therefore, the value of current exports was more than that of the pre-war period, whereas the value of current imports was less than that of the pre-war period. See *İzmir Ticaret ve Sanayi Odası Mecmuası*, March 1930, p.127.

[24] Özveren, 'Büyük buhran'da bir liman kenti', pp.268–70.

[25] *Yeni Asır*, 10 March 1930.

[26] Melike Kara, 'Cumhuriyetin ilk yıllarında Mersin limanının gelişimi', in *Tarih İçinde Mersin* (Mersin, 2005), p.133. Although Samsun and Trabzon combined appear as second and Mersin as third in some statistics, this was because of the role of Iran's significant transit trade through the latter port. İlhan Tekeli and Selim İlkin, *1929 Dünya Buhranında Türkiye'nin İktisadi Politika Arayışları* (Ankara, 1983), pp.37, 538. For the history of Mersin's place in Ottoman economy, see Meltem Toksöz, 'Ottoman Mersin: The making of an Eastern Mediterranean port-town', *New Perspectives on Turkey* 31 (2004), pp.71–91.

[27] *İzmir Ticaret ve Sanayi Odası Mecmuası*, April 1929, p.102.

[28] Tekeli and İlkin: *1929 Dünya Buhranında Türkiye'nin İktisadi Politika Arayışları*, pp.107–8.

[29] *İzmir Ticaret ve Sanayi Odası Mecmuası*, May 1929, p.144.

[30] *İzmir Ticaret ve Sanayi Odası Mecmuası*, May 1929, p.143–5.

[31] See Özveren, 'Türkiye'de yaygın iktisat'.

[32] *İzmir Ticaret ve Sanayi Odası Mecmuası*, April 1932, pp.58–63.

[33] *Yeni Asır*, 12 October 1931.

[34] *Yeni Asır*, 9 June 1931.

[35] *Yeni Asır*, 22 June 1932.

[36] *Yeni Asır*, 21 September 1931.

[37] *Yeni Asır*, 22 June 1932.

38 *Yeni Asır*, 10 August 1932.
39 *Yeni Asır*, 31 August 1931, and *İzmir Ticaret ve Sanayi Odası Mecmuası*, January–February 1932, p.50.
40 *Yeni Asır*, 24 November 1932.
41 'If our goods are not sold, then we are obliged to do as others and apply other nations' methods in our country. That is, we should acquire the means to produce neatly and at very low costs. We have to keep up with the requirements of the international markets. [...] our products are not credible as theirs. They are not standardized, the quality of our seeds has deteriorated, and we lack storage facilities. [...] our internal costs of transport are high. [...] Complaining about the global Great Depression and putting the blame on it without coming to terms with these problems would amount to fooling ourselves.' İsmail Hakkı Bey (Baltacıoğlu), *Yeni Asır*, 24 November 1932.
42 Atatürk cited in Bilsay Kuruç, *Belgelerle Türkiye İktisat Politikası, 1. Cilt: 1929–1932* (Ankara, 1988), pp.131–33.
43 *Yeni Asır*, 24 December 1930, and 30 December 1930.
44 'The world economic depression is a crisis of industry and speculation. In Turkey we have neither a crisis of industry nor of speculation. Our crisis is one of being deprived of any economic organization. [...] if only we had economic "doctors" who could first diagnose our economic ills and then cure them, we would not now be as deeply affected and preoccupied with this world economic crisis'. Muhittin Bey (Birgen), *Yeni Asır, 16* November 1930.
45 'As we repeat time and again the overburden of taxes, that is, the inability of the Turkish nation to support budgets of some 300 million *lira*s...' İsmail Hakkı Bey, *Yeni Asır*, 9 November 1930.
46 Tekeli and İlkin: *1929 Dünya Buhranı*, pp.545 and 553.
47 İsmail Hakkı Bey, *Yeni Asır*, 14 December 1931, and İsmail Hakkı Bey, *Yeni Asır*, 15 July 1932.
48 One such critic was Feyzi Bey, a merchant who wrote a series of articles. See *Yeni Asır*, 23 December 1930, and 24 December 1930.
49 It has rightly been argued that '[t]he rate of change is often of no less importance than the direction of the change itself; but while the latter frequently does not depend upon our volition, it is the rate at which we allow change to take place which well may depend upon us.' Karl Polanyi, *The Great Transformation: The Political and Economic Origins of Our Time* (Boston, 1944), pp.36–47. Whereas this now-classic argument is related to the effectiveness of government policy, we can also relate it to the actual policies of interest groups that constitute civil society.
50 Alp Yücel Kaya, 'Epilogue: "La ville te suivra"', in Marie-Carmen Smyrnelis (ed), *Smyrne, la ville oubliée? Mémoires d'un grand port ottoman, 1830–1930* (Paris, 2006), pp.225.
51 *İzmir Ticaret ve Sanayi Odası Mecmuası*, July–August, 1932, p.41.

The Deep Structures of Mediterranean Modernity (Edmund Burke III), pp. 198–204
1 For an overview, see Gérard Chastagnaret and Olivier Raveux, 'Espace et stratégies industrielles aux XVIIIe et XIXe siècles: Exploiter le laboratoire méditerranéen', *Revue d'Histoire Moderne et Contemporaine* 2–3, (2001), pp.11–24. See also Olivier Raveux, Gérard Chastagnaret and Paul Aubert, *Construire des mondes: Elites et espaces en Méditerranée, XVIe–XXe siècle* (Aix-en-Provence, 2005); Jordi Nadal, *Moler, Tejer y fundir: Estudios de historia industrial* (Barcelona, 1992); Gérard Chastagnaret (ed), *Crise espagnole et nouveau siècle en Méditerranée: Politiques publiques et mutations structurelles des économies dans l'Europe méditerranéenne, fin XIXe–début XXe siècles* (Madrid, 1998); and Luigi de Rosa, *La rivoluzione industriale in Italia* (Rome, 1985).
2 Albert Hourani, *Arabic Thought in the Liberal Age* (Oxford, 1962).
3 Fernand Braudel, *The Mediterranean and the Mediterranean World in the Age of Philip II* (Paris, 1947 and subsequent editions).
4 Mark Mazower, *Salonica: City of Ghosts* (New York, 2006).
5 Edmund Burke III, 'The terror and religion: Brittany and Algeria', in Gregory Blue, M. Bunton and R. Croizier (eds), *Colonialism and the Modern World* (New York, 2002), pp.40–50.

Index

www.ingramcontent.com/pod-product-compliance
Lightning Source LLC
Chambersburg PA
CBHW050418280326
41932CB00013BA/1904